REVELATION REVEALED

REVELATION REVEALED

Revised Edition

A Comprehensive Training and Reference Guide
to the Database Management Software, Revelation.

by Hal J. Chapel and
Richard G. Clark

Paradigm Publishing
San Francisco, California

Published by:
Paradigm Publishing
111 Pine Street, Suite 1405
San Francisco, CA 94111

ISBN 0-941019-66-7

Printed and bound in the United States of America.

This book is sold as is, without warranty of any kind, either express or
implied, respecting the contents of this book, including but not
limited to implied warranties for the book's quality, performance, or
fitness for any particular purpose. Neither Paradigm Publishing nor
its authors, dealers or distributors shall be liable to the purchaser or
any other person or entity with respect to any liability, loss, or
damage caused or alleged to be caused directly or indirectly by this
book.

90 89 88 87   8 7 6 5 4 3 2

Revelation is a trademark of COSMOS, Inc.
dBASE II and dBASE III are registered trademarks of Ashton-Tate.
80286 is a trademark of Intel Corporation.
IBM, PC-XT, and Personal Computer AT are trademarks of
International Business Machines, Inc.
Lotus and 123 are trademarks of Lotus Development Corporation.
Rainbow is a trademark of Digital Equipment corporation.
TI Professional Computer is a trademark of Texas Instruments, Inc.
R:base 5000 and R:base System V are trademarks of Microrim, Inc.
MS DOS is a trademark of Microsoft Corporation.

To my parents and my wife.

                    - H.C.

To Dian

                    - R.C.

Managing Editor
Debbie Danielpour

Cover Design
Catherine Flanders, San Francisco

Cover Photograph
Larry Keenan, San Francisco

TABLE OF CONTENTS

PART ONE:
CONCEPTUAL FRAMEWORK

CHAPTER FOUR: MISCELLANEOUS CONCEPTS   49

PART TWO: FUNCTIONAL DESCRIPTION

CHAPTER NINE: DISPLAYING DATA AND GENERATING REPORTS   **183**

CHAPTER TEN: FILE OPERATIONS   217

PART THREE: COMMAND REFERENCE

APPENDICES

ACKNOWLEDGEMENTS

The authors would like to thank the people at COSMOS for their enthusiasm throughout this project. Particular gratitude is extended to Steve Kruse for his advice and support on structuring and marketing the book. The show of support from Mike Pope and Gary Bennett also helped us stay motivated.

The following people have provided important support during this project: John Ashton (FHLB), Craig Chapel (AT&T), Richard Danielpour, Flip Gianos (Interwest Partners), Raphael Nemes, Mark Reuschenberg (Computerland), and Mehri Weil.

We also appreciate the work of Geoff Berlin, who took the time to read the manuscript and offer helpful insight.

Jack Marrinan and James Newton are especially due thanks for their abundant help during our first experiences with Revelation and for their suggestions and comments during the "Alpha" phase of the creation of this book.

PART ONE: CONCEPTUAL FRAMEWORK

INTRODUCTION

WHAT IS REVELATION?

Revelation is one of the most powerful database management programs for microcomputers. Introduced in 1984 by Cosmos, Inc., it was developed from the PICK operating system, a popular database operating environment for minicomputers. Because it has greater power and flexibility than other database management systems, Revelation is quickly becoming the database management system of choice for developers of sophisticated application software.

A Brief Overview of Personal Computer Software

More and more companies are utilizing personal computers in their information systems, and the crucial task in developing these systems is creating software which addresses a company's specific information requirements. There are several options for obtaining application-specific software. A company may purchase a generic software package developed for their particular industry or they may have custom software developed by in-house programmers or outside consultants.

Some application software, both generic and custom, is written directly in a programming language such as Pascal, C, or Basic; although generally it is easier to write application software to run on top of another program called an "application tool".

Application tools make up the bulk of personal computer software sales and include programs such as Lotus 123, DBASE III, Framework, and Rbase 5000. Application tools can be divided into several categories including electronic spreadsheets, database management systems, and project management software.

Revelation: A Database Management System and More

Revelation is generally considered a database management system (DBMS). Database management software instructs your computer on how to efficiently store, sort and display large amounts of logically related data. Typical database management applications organize and track mailing lists, company personnel records, order entry systems, and general accounting systems. Revelation is one of the most powerful DBMSs for personal computers because it handles large amounts of data, manages complex relationships between data elements, and provides a customized interface with the computer operator.

But Revelation is really more than just a database management system; it is an application development environment capable of providing complete solutions to business information problems. It contains a high level programming language, a text processor, and an applications developer which generates customized data entry and report programs.

Who is Using Revelation?

While many of Revelation's first users were programmers already familiar with PICK, today many non-programmers (and programmers without PICK experience) are also learning Revelation. For example, many of the companies that purchased a commercial application package which runs on top of Revelation want to use Revelation to customize that package. Furthermore, many large corporations are choosing Revelation as their standard microcomputer DBMS because of its compatibility with larger computer systems and its Local Area Network capabilities.

Revelation Revealed was written to meet the needs of all of these groups. The book is an excellent learning tool, offering a conceptual overview of Revelation and thorough step-by-step instructions for developing an application. It is also designed to serve as a reference guide, with a comprehensive Command Reference section, an easy-to-use index, and detailed technical appendices.

REVELATION COMPARED TO OTHER DATABASE MANAGEMENT PACKAGES

Designers of computer software must make tradeoffs between power and ease of use. Because Revelation is considerably more powerful and flexible than most other personal computer DBMSs, it is somewhat more difficult to learn and use. Yet because it has so many built-in features, Revelation will ultimately make your work easier for applications of even moderate complexity.

Deciding whether to use Revelation or one of the other DBMSs depends on whether you need (or will need in the future) its superior power and flexibility to solve your company's information needs.

If your database applications are very simple, you may not need Revelation. On the other hand, Revelation is the most appropriate database management tool for information systems with large amounts of data, lengthy text entries, complicated cross references, or sophisticated logic features.

WHO SHOULD BUY THIS BOOK?

End Users

Revelation Revealed is written primarily for end users. By end user we mean two groups: those who have a commercial application package running on top of Revelation which they want to modify, and those who purchased Revelation to develop their own application solutions.

One of the major objectives of *Revelation Revealed* is to allow the user to quickly learn enough Revelation to develop relatively sophisticated applications. Fortunately, Revelation is designed so that much of its power can be tapped without getting into complex programming or technically difficult features. Although the book covers these advanced technical features, it is organized in such a way that the new user can skip over these complicated topics until he/she is ready for them.

Programmers

As a reference tool, *Revelation Revealed* is a necessity for programmers. Because Revelation is more complex than most personal computer software, even an experienced programmer will benefit from the book's conceptual discussions. The book also contains numerous features which are not covered in the software documentation.

Additionally, the book is a good reference manual because of its detailed topic organization, command syntax explanations, functional as well as alphabetical listing of commands, and complete index.

Users Shopping for the Right Database Management System

You can waste a lot of time if you discover that the database management system you purchased is not powerful enough for your needs. Therefore, it is important to choose a DBMS which will provide the power and flexibility you need now, and may need in the future. *Revelation Revealed* provides a thorough overview of Revelation's power and features which will help the software shopper compare Revelation to other database management systems.

HOW THE BOOK IS ORGANIZED

The book is divided into three parts. Part I, CONCEPTUAL FRAMEWORK, discusses the concepts behind database management systems in general and Revelation in particular. It provides a broad framework for learning Revelation and contains a brief summary at the end of each chapter.

Part II, FUNCTIONAL OPERATIONS, contains a detailed discussion of how to use Revelation to develop an application solution. It provides, in logical sequence, the steps for creating a database, generating data entry screens and output reports, and writing advanced programs.

Part III, COMMAND REFERENCE, lists in alphabetical order all of Revelation's operating commands, programming language statements, and internal functions. It provides syntax, rules of usage, examples, and notes for each listing. It also lists the items by their functional usage, allowing you to easily locate a specific command, statement, or function.

The following is a brief overview of the chapters in *Revelation Revealed*:

I. CONCEPTUAL FRAMEWORK

Chapter One, **"Introduction to Database Management"**. A conceptual briefing on database management in general. The chapter also explains why Revelation is conceptually different from most other microcomputer database management systems.

Chapter Two, **"Revelation Overview"**. A discussion on how Revelation is more than just a typical application tool, how it is actually an operating environment providing the user tremendous power and flexibility. This chapter provides an overview of how Revelation is organized and how you will use it to develop application solutions.

Chapter Three, **"How Revelation Organizes Data"**. How Revelation organizes and stores data. Understanding these concepts will make it easier to later understand file operations and how to access data stored in a Revelation file.

Chapter Four, **"Miscellaneous Concepts"**. An explanation of several of Revelation's more complex features so that they will be easier to understand when you encounter them in later chapters.

II. FUNCTIONAL DESCRIPTION

Chapter Five, **"Getting Started"**. Detailed instructions on installing and logging onto Revelation. It also includes other background information such as a description of keyboard functions.

Chapter Six, **"Creating a Database"**. The first chapter which starts you on actually developing an application. This chapter and the following four chapters provide a detailed description of how to use Revelation to develop an application. Chapter Six explains setting up a database and defining its structure. The Revelation commands, screens, and prompts are explained in detail with numerous examples.

Chapter Seven, **"Entering Data"**. How to design a data entry screen and enter data into that screen.

Chapter Eight, **"Cross References"**. This is one of Revelation's more powerful features, but one which is often difficult to understand. Therefore numerous examples are used to explain how to establish a cross reference between two fields, and how to access the cross reference from data entry screens.

Chapter Nine, **"Displaying Data and Generating Reports"**. How to retrieve ad hoc information from a data file and how to design a report program in order to generate the standard output reports for your application. This chapter covers the ways in which your database can be sorted, selected, and otherwise manipulated.

Chapter Ten, **"File Operations"**. A discussion of housekeeping chores such as moving, deleting, copying, and joining files.

Chapter Eleven, **"Networking"**. Using Revelation on a Local Area Network. In addition to providing information on converting single-user systems to a LAN environment, this chapter discusses network requirements and warns of the pitfalls that may arise in a multi-user environment.

Chapter Twelve, **"Introduction to Programming with R/BASIC"**. An explanation of when you will need to program with Revelation's advanced programming language. The chapter explains how programs are written, compiled, and run, and gives a description of the variables and expressions used by R/BASIC.

Chapter Thirteen, **"Programming Operations"**. A functional description of R/BASIC operations such as assigning variables, conditional statements, loops, and modular programming.

Chapter Fourteen, **"Text and Line Editor"**. How to use Revelation's full page text editor and line editor to simplify data entry and program writing.

III. COMMAND REFERENCE

A listing of commands, programming statements, and internal functions first by functional usage and then by alphabetical order, giving complete syntax and rules of usage for each. This section also includes helpful notes on how to use the commands and statements effectively.

HOW TO USE THIS BOOK

Assumed Knowledge of the Reader

Every computer book must make an assumption about its readers' level of computer expertise. In writing *Revelation Revealed* we have assumed the reader has the following computer knowledge:

- a working knowledge of PC DOS or MS DOS,

- some amount of conceptual understanding of database applications,

- familiarity with some other business software such as Lotus 123, Dbase III, or Rbase 5000,

- familiarity with a word processor or text editor.

If you do not have this level of computer experience, you should still be able to learn Revelation with this book, but it may help if you can refer to other reference books on database management, structured programming and your computer's operating system.

We have also assumed that readers of *Revelation Revealed* will have a wide range of computer knowledge. Therefore, the technically advanced material is separated from the rest of the text. In many chapters, advanced subjects are grouped into sections titled **"Advanced Topics"**. In addition, you will occasionally find a paragraph labelled as an "Advanced Topic".

Using the Book as a Learning Tool

Revelation Revealed was written to be used as a learning guide as well as a reference book.

There are two approaches to learning a computer software package. The first approach is "learning by association", in which you experiment with the software and make associations between commands and their effect, without having any overall conceptual framework. After a while, all of the commands and their effects become "grooved" in your mind and you can then use your recall ability to select the correct command to accomplish a desired task.

The other approach is "conceptual understanding", in which you first develop a conceptual framework through an understanding of the design objectives of the software package. Then, as you learn the specific features of the package, you fit them into this overall framework.

The association method works well on simple packages like word processors, but the conceptual understanding method is more efficient with large sophisticated packages, like Revelation, that have many interrelated features. Therefore, a new Revelation user should devote significant time to understanding the software's conceptual framework before getting into the operational details.

The first step you should take in learning Revelation is to read Part I, CONCEPTUAL FRAMEWORK. Next, read through Part II, FUNCTIONAL DESCRIPTION. Don't worry if some features are not fully understood as you read them; they should become clear the first time you use them in an actual application. Unless you are an experienced programmer, it is probably best to skip over the sections titled "Advanced Topics" at this point.

Now you are ready to develop a real application. Reread each topic in the FUNCTIONAL DESCRIPTION before you start that portion of your application development. Use the COMMAND REFERENCE to look up any commands.

As you become more experienced, go back and read the "Advanced Topics" sections you skipped earlier. Also read through the COMMAND REFERENCE part of the book to familiarize yourself with all of Revelation's commands, as not all of these are covered in the FUNCTIONAL DESCRIPTION chapters.

CONVENTIONS USED IN THIS BOOK

For purposes of clarity, the following conventions are used in this book.

1. **Major topics** are shown in large, capitalized type size and extend to the left of the main text area, such as:

TYPES OF DATA

2. **Subtopics** are shown in the same type, upper and lower case, but remain flush left with the margins of the main text area, such as:

Numeric

3. Examples of **commands, prompts and error messages** are shown on a separate line, indented and generally in Upper case, such as:

:RUN DOS A:INSTALL.UTL

Some long commands will carry over to a second line, but should be entered on one line on your screen.

4. When prompts, responses, or commands are included in the text of a paragraph, they will be **BOLD and/or IN UPPER CASE.**

5. The **<E>** symbol means press the enter key.

WHAT IS NOT COVERED IN THIS BOOK

Obviously, we could not include in one book everything that you may want to know about developing an application solution with Revelation. Specifically, we do not discuss the fundamentals of personal computers nor how to use their operating systems. We only briefly discuss the principles of database management and the fundamentals of structured computer programming.

We have made every attempt to make this book comprehensive and understandable, however you may find errors or hard-to-understand passages. We would genuinely appreciate any suggestions concerning recommended changes or additions. Comments can be addressed to the authors through:

Paradigm Publishing
3315 Sacramento Street #225
San Francisco, CA 94118
Attn: Hal Chapel or Richard Clark

CHAPTER ONE: INTRODUCTION TO DATABASE MANAGEMENT

The purpose of this chapter is to give the reader a quick refresher in database management concepts, explain some database terminology, and discuss relational database structures.

DEFINITION OF A DATABASE

A database is a collection of related information in one or more files. An example of a simple database file is the customer list shown in **Figure 1.1**.

CUSTOMER NUMBER	CUSTOMER NAME	PHONE NUMBER
0001	HOME FURNISHINGS, INC	347-1854
0002	ACE HARDWARE CO.	389-1284
0003	BROOKS BUILDING SUPPLY	952-6830
0004	TOM'S BUILDING MATERIALS	952-4279
0005	ALLIED HOME REPAIR	347-5873

Fig. 1.1 Sample Customer Database

The information in this example includes the customer number, customer name, and phone number. A more complex database might include customers with several phone numbers, or a link between the customer numbers in this database file and the customer numbers in a separate invoice database file.

Types of Data

Information stored in databases is either alphanumeric or numeric. Alphanumeric data, sometimes referred to as text, consists of alphabet characters, numerals, and special keyboard characters (#,$,%,>,.,etc). This kind of data is read by the computer as a series of characters and cannot be used for mathematical calculation.

Numeric data are number values which can be used in mathematical operations.

Many software packages require you to define data entries as either alphanumeric or numeric. This can be confusing with certain data such as a zip code. For example, the zip code, 02138 could be either alphanumeric (text) or numeric, but in most cases, there is no need to make it numeric since you probably won't be using this value in mathematical calculations.

Fortunately, Revelation does not require this labelling of data; alphanumeric and numeric characters are stored the same way regardless of whether you plan to use them in mathematical operations or not. This allows great flexibility in data manipulation, but requires a little more care to ensure you don't attempt to perform mathematical operations on non-numeric values.

TYPES OF DATABASE STRUCTURES

There are three broad categories of database structures: relational, hierarchical, and network. Each category uses a different kind of relationship between the elements of the database. Revelation uses an advanced relational database structure.

Relational Databases

Relational database structures are the simplest of the three categories to learn and are used in almost all microcomputer database management software. Both DBASE III and RBASE 5000 use a relational structure.

Each file of a typical relational database consists of a two dimensional matrix of information such as the one shown in **Figure 1.2.**

FIELDS

	CUSTOMER NUMBER	CUSTOMER NAME	PHONE NUMBER
	0001	HOME FURNISHINGS, INC.	347-1854
	0002	ACE HARDWARE CO.	389-1284
RECORDS	0003	BROOKS BUILDING SUPPLY	952-6830
	0004	TOM'S BUILDING MATERIALS	952-4279
	0005	ALLIED HOME REPAIR	347-5873

Fig. 1.2 Relational Database

Each row can be thought of as a single entry of related information, while each column represents information of the same type. By convention, rows are referred to as **records** and columns as **fields.** The result is a matrix of cells, each containing a single piece of data.

The second characteristic of a relational database system is that relationships can be set up between files in the system. These relationships are possible because the matrix system of storing data elements makes it easy to refer to a particular data element in a file.

Normally, each field in a relational database file is defined by a **field name, data type,** and **width.** The second field in our example database could be given the field name CUST.NAME. Its type could be defined as alphanumeric, and you could assign it a width of 30 characters. Note that the assigned width must be large enough to accommodate the largest possible entry in any of the records.

Simple relational database structures such as the one we described have certain limitations.   First, each field and therefore each record has a predetermined size, wasting storage space when fields are left empty or have an entry shorter than the field width. Second, each cell can have only one value at a time, making it cumbersome to handle a situation such as a customer with two phone numbers.

Revelation's Structure

Revelation data files have a flexible relational structure with advanced features not found in most relational databases, such as multi-valued fields and variable length fields.   In fact, records in the same Revelation file can even contain different field structures!

These advanced features separate Revelation from the other common microcomputer database management systems. As a result, it is easier to develop sophisticated applications with Revelation and the resulting programs will run much more efficiently.

In many situations, it is sufficient to consider Revelation as a simple relational database consisting of a matrix of records and fields. But to use Revelation's advanced features in developing complex applications, you will need to understand Revelation's more advanced file structure which is discussed in Chapter 3.

CHAPTER SUMMARY

1. Database Management Systems are designed to facilitate the development of applications which store, manipulate, and retrieve large amounts of related information.

2. A relational database structure is a relatively simple matrix of records and fields. This type of structure, which is used by most microcomputer DBMSs, is easy to learn and efficient for many simple database applications.

3. Revelation's file structure differs from that of a typical relational database in that it contains many of the advanced features used on large computer systems, including multi-valued fields, variable length fields, and the ability to maintain complex relationships between the data elements.

4. For simple applications, Revelation can be thought of as a relational database made up of a two dimensional matrix of records and fields; but for more complex applications, Revelation offers a powerful advanced file structure.

CHAPTER TWO:
REVELATION OVERVIEW

This chapter explains in broad conceptual terms what Revelation is, how it is organized, and how you will use it to develop application solutions. Understanding this overview will serve as a framework for helping you learn the rest of Revelation.

Revelation is used to develop customized database application solutions. With Revelation, you can develop complex data entry screens, design standard output reports, establish relationships between fields in different data files, and link an application together with menus. For very complex applications you can even use Revelation's structured high level programming language to write your own powerful application programs.

HOW REVELATION IS ORGANIZED

Revelation is organized into the following five areas which are described in detail later in this chapter.

TCL: **Terminal Control Language.** Command level from which you will perform miscellaneous system functions, such as file management operations, and run programs.

R/DESIGN: **Prompt-driven applications developer.** Creates a data file, defines its field structure, and designs data entry screens without the need for complex programming.

R/LIST: **Report generator.** Accessed through a set of seven TCL commands which perform powerful database management reporting functions.

R/BASIC: **Revelation's advanced programming language.** Combines the easy-to-use syntax of BASIC and the structured programming features of Pascal. R/BASIC allows you to write and compile programs which solve the most complex management information problems.

UTILITIES: Includes two editors for writing programs or editing text as well as other utilities for performing miscellaneous tasks such as data conversions.

HOW YOU WILL BE USING REVELATION

There are two major tasks which any database application must accomplish - get data into the the data files, and then retrieve the data for displaying reports. You will use R/DESIGN for entering data into your data files and R/LIST for producing reports.

For most users, R/DESIGN is the real guts of Revelation. With it, you will create data files and define the characteristics of the fields in those files, such characteristics as field name, display format, and how the data will be stored. Then you will design a data entry screen. It is in the design of the data entry screen that you will incorporate the bulk of Revelation's powerful database management features such as cross references, data verification checks, and default entry values.

You will use the completed data entry screen to enter information into your data file. When you display the data entry screen, it will prompt you to enter values for the fields you have specified. You will also use this data entry screen for displaying and editing data records which were previously entered.

The next thing you will want to do is produce reports from the stored information. For this you will use R/LIST and its English-language-like commands. In your output report you can specify such features as which records to use, the fields to display, and the page and column headings.

Creating data files, designing data entry screens, entering data, and producing reports are the major functions of a database application. However, you will also need to execute various Revelation commands from TCL to perform file management operations (such as moving, clearing, renaming, and deleting files) as well as other miscellaneous tasks.

R/BASIC is Revelation's programming language. For many applications, R/BASIC will only be used to accomplish fairly simple tasks such as multiplying two data fields in order to display this product in a data entry screen or report. However, for experienced developers, Revelation's real power comes from R/BASIC because, as a sophisticated, structured, programming language especially designed for database management, it provides tremendous flexibility in solving complex database tasks.

This should give you a pretty good picture how you will be using the five areas of Revelation to develop an application. In the following sections we will provide a more detailed discussion of each of these areas.

TCL

TCL **(Terminal Control Language)** is the operating level of Revelation from which you perform miscellaneous system functions. Entering commands at the TCL prompt (:) is similar to entering commands at the DOS prompt in that you can perform file operations such as creating, copying, or deleting files and you can run programs.

TCL recognizes a large number of command words which are defined in the **VOC** (vocabulary) file. One of the powerful features of Revelation is that you can create your own command words and store them in VOC.

R/DESIGN

There are certain tasks which must be accomplished in developing any database application such as defining field characteristics, specifying how data will be input, deciding how the operator will be prompted, and constructing menus. Rather than start from scratch each time you develop an application, Cosmos has produced R/DESIGN to make it easier to perform these common tasks.

An Applications Developer

You can think of R/DESIGN as an "applications developer", or a front end to Revelation's standard database management features. R/DESIGN is actually a set of routines (written in R/BASIC) which prompt you for information to help build your application. Some of the features you can build into your application with R/DESIGN include:

- Pattern and range checks of entered data (for example, your data entry screen could automatically check that an entry consists of three numeric characters between the values of 100 and 300).

- Prompts on data entry screens which will automatically input default values (for example, if you were entering numerous records with "CALIFORNIA" as the value of one of the fields, you could make that the default value which would automatically be entered unless the operator entered another value).

- The displaying of acceptable input values for the operator during data entry.

- Protected status once the data is entered.

- Automatic updating of cross referenced index files.

How R/DESIGN Creates Programs

Throughout this book we speak of using R/DESIGN to create data entry screens (or data entry programs). It is important to understand what actually occurs when you use R/DESIGN to accomplish this task.

When you create a data entry screen, R/DESIGN prompts you for information about each field which the operator is going to input to the data file. Your answers are stored as parameters in a record in a file called **RDES**.

Your data entry screen can then be displayed by running R/DESIGN's standard data entry program, named ENTER, which uses your previously stored parameters to determine the specific features of the screen. This is called an interpreted data entry screen because the ENTER program "interprets" the parameters stored in the RDES file.

Revelation also allows you to generate what is called a compiled data entry screen. This is done by generating an R/BASIC program from those same parameters you stored in the RDES file. This gives you the opportunity to modify this source code to perform features which can't be done with an interpreted screen. However, with a good understanding of R/DESIGN and the use of some ingenuity, you can do almost anything with an interpreted screen.

Therefore, we recommend that you stay away from compiled data entry screens because it is much easier to design an interpreted screen than it is to figure out how the R/BASIC source code of a data entry screen works.

If you wanted to, you could also use R/DESIGN to generate output reports. It will walk you through the construction of an R/LIST command, write an R/BASIC program from this command, compile the program, and store it. However, this doesn't save any time and isn't any easier than producing a report straight from R/LIST, therefore you generally will not be using R/DESIGN for output reports.

R/DESIGN's Routines

R/DESIGN consists of the following ten routines with which you will create your data files, design data entry screens, and construct menus:

1) **DEF:**   Defines and creates a database file.

2) **BUD:**   Builds the "dictionary" part of each file which contains the information defining the data fields in the file.

3) **PGMR:**   Names, and is the first step in developing, a data entry screen.

4) **SEL:**   Selects the data fields which the operator will input into the data entry screen.

5) **SCR.GEN:** Generates the standard data entry screen using inputs from BUD and SEL.

6) **SCR:**   Allows customization of the data entry screen.

7) **GEN:**   Generates R/BASIC source code for a compiled data entry screen.

8) **BLD.MENU:** Builds a menu.

9) **DOC:**   Generates documentation for the portions of your application developed with R/DESIGN.

10) **ENTER:** Displays the data entry screen you created and prompts for each data field on the screen.

The first two routines are used to create and define the structure of a database file. Routines 3 - 6 are used to design an interpreted data entry screen, while a compiled screen would also use routine 7. Routine 8 builds a menu to tie together several screens, programs, or other menus. If you were to use R/DESIGN for generating an output report, you would use routines 3, 4 and 7.

The following sections explain in more detail how the ten routines are used.

DEF

DEF (DEFine File) is used to name a new file and define such characteristics as file size and its location on the disk. DEF is also used to create a synonym file name to point to an existing file.

BUD

BUD (BUild Dictionary) prompts you for the names of the fields in the data file and for various parameters which define each field such as display length and format, input edit checks, input and output data conversions, etc.

PGMR

PGMR (Program name and type) defines an R/DESIGN program as either a data entry screen or a report program.

SEL

SEL (SELect) is used to select which fields of the data file will be displayed on the data entry screen.

SCR.GEN

SCR.GEN (SCReen GENerator) produces a standard data entry screen based on the parameters specified in BUD for the fields chosen with SEL. If you want to modify this standard data entry screen, you will continue to SCR.

SCR

SCR (SCReen Customization) is used for modifying the data entry screen produced by SCR.GEN and adding more sophisticated features than are available with SCR.GEN. With SCR, you can change the layout of the screen prompts (the prompts the computer operator will see when he/she runs the data entry screen), make entries optional or mandatory, automatically input default values, establish cross-reference fields, etc.

ENTER

ENTER displays the data entry screen for adding new records to your data file, or displaying and modifying previously entered data.

GEN

(GENerate R/BASIC Code) GEN takes the parameters you have specified for a data entry screen or output report and turns them into an R/BASIC program.

BLD.MENU

BLD.MENU (BuiLD MENU) builds a menu which will present the operator with a list of choices. Menu choices may call a data entry screen, produce a report, run an R/BASIC program or TCL command, or display another menu.

R/LIST

R/LIST produces reports using commands similar to the English language. The following three commands, executed from TCL, are used to perform the most important R/LIST functions.

LIST
Produces reports from the contents of a data file. The LIST command can contain various phrases which will select and sort records, total numeric fields, select fields to display, and add text headers and footers. LIST actually generates a full output report and is by far the most important R/LIST command. LIST can also be used to generate R/BASIC source code which you can modify for even more customized reports.

SELECT
Creates a list of records meeting specified conditions. These records are not displayed but are available for use by programs or commands, and may be saved for future use. This is the second most important R/LIST command.

FORM
Technically speaking, the FORM command is not part of R/LIST, but we include it here since it is also used to produce an output report. Whereas the LIST command produces a columnar report (fields are displayed in columns and each line represents one record of data), the FORM command will merge information from a data record into a template report form. Typically, FORM is used to merge a data file with a custom form; for example, a mailing list data file with a standard letter.

R/BASIC

R/BASIC is Revelation's high level structured programming language. By "structured" we mean that it uses logical programming loops, internal and external subroutines, and many pre-defined functions.

Why use R/BASIC instead of one of the other high level languages like C or PASCAL? The answer, simply stated, is that R/BASIC is a structured programming language specifically designed for database file handling containing powerful yet easy-to-use capabilities for manipulating data structures.

When to Use R/BASIC

There are three primary situations in which you will use R/BASIC. The first is when you have an application that needs some sophisticated features integrated with R/DESIGN (for example, a wrap-up program which is executed after data entry). In this case you will need to write your own programs to supplement Revelation's R/DESIGN features.

R/BASIC is also used for "symbolic" fields which calculate results based on the contents of other fields (as opposed to "data" fields whose values are input by the operator). The formula for these "symbolic" fields are written using R/BASIC and stored during BUD as part of the file's dictionary structure.

The third use of R/BASIC is in programs to perform the same kind of tasks for which you would use any high level language. This might be file management operations or any miscellaneous tasks you need to accomplish.

While teaching the fundamentals of structured programming is not included in the scope of this book, Chapters 12 and 13 and the COMMAND REFERENCE provide a thorough description of R/BASIC operations and functions. They also include a number of examples of how to accomplish various programming tasks and how to tap many of Revelation's advanced powers using R/BASIC.

For those end users who are not programmers -- don't despair. Many applications can easily be created using R/DESIGN and only some rudimentary R/BASIC programming.

UTILITIES

Revelation contains several highly useful utilities. Some are internal to the system, while others are programs which come on the Utilities Diskette.

The most useful utility is the **TEXT Editor,** which edits text much like any word processing package. It is used for writing programs and for editing text records from a file. Revelation also has a **Line Editor** which is used to edit one line of data at a time.

Additionally, there are a number of other utilities which restore corrupted files, transfer files between Revelation format and ASCII format, and perform various other file operations and data conversions.

DESIGNING AN APPLICATION SOLUTION

Before you start working on the design of your application, you should have a thorough understanding of your information needs and desired report outputs. You should make a conceptual outline or diagram of how the application will function: what information will be in which database file, how the information will be input, what relationships between data elements will be established, and what information will be pulled for reports and screen displays. Preparing a clear conceptual plan can save you from wasting time later.

As you develop the system, document your work to provide a map for yourself six months later when the system is not as fresh in your mind. Thorough documentation is also a tremendous help to anyone else who needs to figure out the structure of your application.

Finally, it is important to test the system (with test data) as thoroughly as possible before relying on its output. It is much less painful to fix errors resulting from a test than to repair the damage done from using a faulty application on real data.

CHAPTER SUMMARY

1. Revelation is more than a rigid applications tool; it is an operating environment with its own unique file structure, advanced programming language, and an easy-to-use applications developer.

2. TCL is the command or control language of Revelation from which you perform various file management operations and run programs.

3. R/DESIGN is Revelation's applications developer which is used for setting up a data file, generating data entry screens, and constructing menus. R/DESIGN consists of the following routines:

> DEF - DEFine File.
> BUD- Build Dictionary.
> PGMR - Defines program type.
> SEL - SELects the data fields which will be used
>   in a data entry screen.
> SCR.GEN - GENerates the standard data entry
>   SCReen.
> SCR - Customizes a data entry SCReen.
> ENTER - Displays the data entry screen and
>   prompts for operator inputs.
> GEN - GENerates R/BASIC source code for data
>   entry screens and report programs.
> BLD.MENU - BuiLDs a MENU.
> DOC - Generates application DOCumentation.

4. R/LIST is a report generator which uses seven commands entered at TCL to perform typical DBMS functions such as selecting, sorting, and listing records from a database file. The most important R/LIST command is LIST which is used to build an output report, either an ad hoc output or a standard report.

5. R/BASIC, Revelation's advanced structured programming language, is designed specifically for working with database management systems. It is used to write the formulas for symbolic fields, for sophisticated application programs beyond the scope of R/DESIGN, and for miscellaneous tasks you may need to accomplish.

6. Revelation has several utilities, the most important of which is the TEXT editor which functions like a word processor and is used for writing programs and editing records.

CHAPTER THREE: HOW REVELATION ORGANIZES DATA

This chapter explains how Revelation organizes and stores files and the data within files. Specifically, we will discuss the relationship between accounts, media, files, records, and data fields. Understanding these concepts will make it easier to perform file operations and learn some of Revelation's more advanced features.

ACCESSING AND STORING REVELATION FILES

Revelation operates through DOS, but substitutes some of its own operating system functions. One of these functions is the naming of files. When you create a file in Revelation, you will give it a Revelation file name. This is the name you will use whenever you refer to the file while in Revelation. However, when Revelation stores this file through DOS, it assigns the file an entirely different file name. In fact, it might not even be a single file, but consist of several DOS files.

Storage Media

Before it can access a file, Revelation needs to know on what disk drive and in which directory the file is located. When you log onto Revelation the current DOS drive and directory is the default "medium" of Revelation. Unless you tell it otherwise, this is where Revelation looks for files to use and where it stores new files.

If you want to use another medium (disk drive and directory) for storing information, then you must first identify it for Revelation using the **NAMEMEDIA** command. This TCL command names the medium or "volume" (these terms are used interchangeably by Revelation), and creates a DOS file on that medium named **ROSMEDIA.MAP**, which keeps track of the Revelation files on that medium.

For example, you might have a subdirectory on your hard disk for storing administrative applications written in Revelation. You could give it the medium name ADMIN using the NAMEMEDIA command. If you were to then go into DOS and perform a DIR of this subdirectory, you would see a file named ROSMEDIA.MAP. This file contains information which Revelation uses to access the files stored on this subdirectory.

ROS and LINK File Structures

As mentioned earlier, Revelation uses two different file management systems for storing data: **LINK** and **ROS** (Revelation Operating System). When you create a file, Revelation will prompt you for information about the file, and determine the file's management system as follows:

-    If the file is going to be a shared file on a Local Area Network, then it will be a LINK file.

- If it is not shared and is estimated to be smaller than 200k bytes, then it will be a ROS file.

- If the file is not shared but will be larger than 200k bytes, then a Revelation prompt suggests you make it a LINK file.

Both of these file structures store data in DOS files with names different than the Revelation file name. Furthermore, the ROS structure breaks up a Revelation file into several DOS files.

For example, if you created a ROS file with a Revelation name of CUSTOMERS, and then used the command DIR to get a DOS directory of that medium, you would find several files with names like ROS10001.000 and ROS10001.010. These are the DOS files into which CUSTOMERS has been broken. Fortunately, the ROSMEDIA.MAP keeps track of these DOS files for you; all you have to remember is the Revelation file names. Appendix V has additional technical information on the Revelation file management systems.

ACCOUNTS

What are Accounts?

You can think of an account as the collection of database files which relate to a specific application. For example, you may set up separate accounts for your company's administration, payroll, production control, and invoicing. Each account can have its own password to provide access security.

Accessing Accounts

When you load Revelation, you log into a specific account. You can only be in one account at a time; if you log into another account you automatically are logged off of the current account. Revelation comes already set up with one account named **SYSPROG**. In this account are located all of the Revelation system files. From SYSPROG you can create other accounts if you wish.

In general, the files in an account can only be accessed by an operator logged into that account. For example, assume you created an account named ADMIN and created three files in that account: PERSONNEL, PAYROLL, and CORRES-PONDENCE. You could only access those files while you were logged into the ADMIN account.

There are two exceptions to this rule. The first is that any file can be made a **"global"** file which makes it accessible from any account. (One of the Revelation system files, VERBS, comes as a global file). The second exception is that you can set up a **file pointer** in one account which allows you to access the data of a file in another account. File pointers are described in detail in Chapter 4.

Accessing Files in Another Medium: ATTACH.

When you initially log onto an account, Revelation "attaches" the files for that account located on the default medium. By attaching the files, Revelation internally stores where they are located and knows that they are accessible to you while you are in this account. But what if there are files for your account located in other medium? Revelation will <u>not</u> know they exist.

You must tell Revelation to look in this other medium and attach any files for your account located there. This is done with the ATTACH command, for example:

:ATTACH C:\REV\DATA

would attach the Revelation files for the current account located on the DATA subdirectory of the C drive.

(Note that the colon prior to the command means the command was entered at TCL.) You can set up Revelation to automatically attach the files in several media when you log into an account. This is covered in Chapter 5, "Getting Started".

Subdirectories and Accounts

Most users of Revelation will have a hard disk drive and could keep all of their Revelation files in one subdirectory, with different accounts to keep the applications separated. This will work, but we recommend keeping each application on a separate subdirectory so that you can backup and restore an application by performing the DOS BACKUP/RESTORE command on just that particular subdirectory.

One minor drawback to this system is that there is no way to change the default medium in Revelation -- meaning that each time you create a file you will need to specify the medium on which you want that file stored.

The Global Account

Files which will be available to all accounts must be assigned to the GLOBAL or NULL account. These words may be used interchangeably. To reassign a file to a different account, see Chapter 10. You do not need to create this special account since it is not a real account, but only a way to let Revelation know to attach this file when logging into any account.

DICTIONARY AND DATA PARTS OF FILES

Every file you create in Revelation has two parts, a **"Dictionary"** part and a **"Data"** part. Look at the structure of the data file shown in **Figure 3.1**.

DICT

DICT.ID	TYPE	FIELD.NO	DISPLAY
%FIELD.COUNTER%	F	0	
@ID	G		
@CRT	F	1	
NAME	F	2	CUSTOMER
STREET	F	3	STREET
CITY	F	4	CITY
STATE	F	5	STATE
ZIP	F	6	ZIP CODE

DATA

NAME	STREET	CITY	STATE	ZIP
JACK JONES	114 HOWARD	ATLANTA	GA	45983
TOM SMITH	45 JACKSON	RICHMOND	VA	93761
KATE RAINEY	701 PINE	TULSA	OK	74620
JANE BLACKMUN	29 FORREST	BOSTON	MA	96102

Fig. 3.1 Sample Data File

This example is a simple mailing list with five data fields, NAME, STREET, CITY, STATE, ZIP. The **data** part of the file contains the two dimensional matrix of records and fields which we normally think of as the data file.

The records in the **dictionary** of the file store parameters which define the fields of the data part. Notice that there is a record in the dictionary for each field in the data part. These dictionary records contain descriptive information about the data fields such as input/output transformation, and display format (only part of this information is shown in Figure 3.1). The place for storing the information in the dictionary of a file is automatically created when you create the file The descriptive information is stored in the dictionary with the BUD routine.

You can have two dictionary records which refer to the same data field. This is useful if you want to display the data in different formats at different times. For example, assume you have a data field containing a detailed 13 digit product code. You could create two dictionary records, one named CODE.LONG for when you want to display all thirteen digits, and the other named CODE.SHORT for when you just want to display the 5 digit version.

You don't have to have dictionary records in a file, but they are necessary if you want to access the data fields by their field names or if you want to control the input and output format of stored data.   For example, Revelation stores R/BASIC programs as records in files. Since it doesn't make sense to talk about the fields of these records, the file does not need to have any dictionary records defined.

There are three special records automatically placed in the dictionary of data files.   These are shown in **Figure 3.1.** @ID contains information about the file and is also used to refer to the identifying key of each data record in the file. This dictionary item is discussed in detail in Chapter Six. @CRT is a special field which determines the default data fields to be displayed with a LIST command (discussed in Chapter 9). Both @ID and @CRT are created automatically whenever a file is created.   %FIELD.COUNTER% is a sequential counter used to assign position numbers to your data fields during BUD (its use is explained in Chapter 6).

Having a separate dictionary as part of the file structure is a powerful feature of advanced database management systems like Revelation.   This feature allows you to modify field definitions without changing the actual data stored in the file.

The terminology surrounding Revelation's file structure can get confusing. When discussing the attributes of the fields in a data file, sometimes we will refer to a dictionary record and other times we will refer to the name of the field itself. In both cases we are referring to the definition of a data field.

DATA FILES AND SYSTEM FILES

In an earlier example, we created an account named ADMIN and put three files in it. If you listed the files attached by the ADMIN account (using the **LISTFILES** command) the result would look like **Figure 3.2**.

Revelation Filename	Volume	Native Filename	Modulo
VERBS	C:	ROS00001	04
VOC	C:	ROS10035	LNK7
LISTS	C:	ROS10036	LNK7
QFILE	C:	ROS10035	LNK7
MD	C:	ROS10035	LNK7
CORRESPONDENCE	C:	ROS10040	02
PERSONNEL	C:	ROS10041	LNK334
PAYROLL	C:	ROS10042	02

Fig. 3.2 Files in the ADMIN Account

There are four columns of information in Figure 3.2. The **Revelation Filename** is obviously the name of the Revelation files. The **Volume** is the drive and subdirectory where the file is located (if the volume is the default directory, then only the drive is displayed; e.g. if C:\REV is the default directory, only C: would be displayed). The **Native Filename** is the first part of the name of the DOS file (or files) where the information is stored. The **Modulo** has to do with the ROS or LINK file structure -- disregard this for the moment.

System Files Maintained on All Accounts

The **VERBS** file is composed primarily of compiled programs used by TCL, R/LIST, and R/DESIGN. This is a global file and therefore will show up when you use LISTFILES from any account (as will any other global files you create). Another file which you will want to make global is the **HELP** file (making a file global is covered in Chapter 5). This gives you access to Revelation's on-line help program from any account.

Revelation created the next four files when you created the ADMIN account. The **VOC** (vocabulary) file consists of all the commands and words recognized by Revelation at the TCL prompt. As you develop applications in this account, you will cause other entries to be made in the VOC file.

The **LISTS** file is used by Revelation during large sorting routines and also to store lists you create using R/LIST. (Select lists are discussed in Chapter 4).

The next two files are file pointers which are explained in Chapter 4. Finally, the last three are the data files created as part of your administrative application.

There is one more file that you will need to create on each account before you can use any of the R/DESIGN features of Revelation -- the **RDES** file which can be created from TCL using the **CREATE-FILE** command. If you don't create this file, you will get an error message the first time you try to use R/DESIGN. (See Chapter 5).

In Chapter 2, we said that the R/DESIGN routines prompted you for information which then was stored in the RDES file. The RDES file will keep a separate record for each data entry screen, report program, menu and cross reference relationship you make in this account.

System Files on the SYSPROG Account

There are three more system files which appear on the SYSPROG account. The **ERRORS** file contains many, but not all, of the error messages used by Revelation. The

SYSTEM file keeps track of the account names and passwords you have created. And the **SYSOBJ** file contains the compiled code for the R/BASIC compiler and other system programs.

HOW DATA IS STORED WITHIN FILES: DYNAMIC ARRAYS

What is a Dynamic Array?

Most of the time it will suffice for you to think of a data file as a two dimensional matrix of records and fields. However, when performing certain functions it is useful to think of each record the way Revelation actually stores them -- as a dynamic array of three kinds of elements: fields, values, and subvalues. An array is "dynamic" because its elements do not have fixed lengths; the more information you enter, the longer the array becomes.

Traditional Storage Systems

Traditional database systems for the microcomputer environment use a fixed-length method for storing data.

Name	Address	City	St
JOHN MATHEWS	241 MAPLE ST.	WOLAND	TX
BARBARA JOHNSON	18 DANA ST.	CAMBRIDGE	MA
ABDUL SMITH	1520 PARKWAY DR.	LOS ANGELES	CA

Fig. 3.3 Example data records

In **Figure 3.3**, the NAME field is up to 15 characters in length, the ADDRESS is also up to 15 characters in length, the CITY may be up to 11 characters long, and the STATE is 2 characters in length, for a total record size of 43 characters or bytes.

Even if a person has no address, the record will still occupy 43 characters on the disk. And the database processor uses this fact to find information. For example, if it wants to print the city for a given record, it simply counts in 30 bytes and reads the next 11 characters. In this kind of structure, there is an absolute location for any given field in a record.

Advantages to Revelation's Structure

The Revelation system has some significant advantages over this kind of fixed record structure. The most obvious advantage is that with Revelation, you are not required to limit the length of a field. You could enter an address as long as required (the length of displayed output is controlled separately).

This is a very useful feature because even if you expect the name to only require 25 characters, you can bet that someone will come along with a longer one. Unlike other database systems, Revelation does not require you to guess at the longest possible entry and thus waste all that unused space on smaller entries.

How Dynamic Arrays Work

Each Revelation record is stored as a dynamic array with special **delimiters** to separate the fields, values, and subvalues (a delimiter separates the elements of a character string). Different delimiters are used to distinguish the different kinds of elements (**Figure 3.4**):

DELIMITER NAME	ASCII CHARACTER	GRAPHIC SYMBOL
FIELD MARK	254	■
VALUE MARK	253	2
SUBVALUE MARK	252	n

Figure 3.4   *Dynamic array delimeters*

The record length is stored as a number at the beginning of the record. This is how Revelation knows where one record stops and the next starts.

For example, assume you have a record with three fields having the following values: "John", "235", and "Blue". It would be stored as:

013JOHN■235■BLUE

(The first three characters tell Revelation the length of the record).

If the second field had three values -- "235", "984", and "487" -- instead of one, the record would be stored as:

021JOHN■235^{2}984^{2}487■BLUE

Likewise, if the third value of the second field contained three subvalues, -- 4,8,7, -- instead of 487, the record would be stored as:

023JOHN■235^{2}984^{2}4^{n}8^{n}7■BLUE

Fortunately, R/DESIGN automatically takes care of placing information in its proper place within a dynamic array. Note, however, that R/DESIGN uses only fields and values, not subvalues.

R/BASIC provides several programming functions for directly extracting, adding, and deleting all the delimiters from a dynamic array.

ADVANCED TOPICS

TCL Commands and the VOC File

The first word in all TCL commands must exist in the VOC file. The rest of the words in a TCL command fall into one of four categories:

1) filenames
2) data record IDs.
3) record IDs from the dictionary of files (field names).
4) connectors/modifiers located in the dictionary of VOC.

The dictionary of VOC is a kind of generic dictionary; if TCL cannot find a word in the dictionary of the file specified on the command line, it will check the dictionary of VOC for that word.

For example, consider: **LIST CUSTOMERS F1**. Although F1 may not be in the dictionary of the CUSTOMERS file, Revelation will look in the DICT of VOC and use the F1 entry located there. In this case, the first field of every record will be listed.

You can create a synonym for any VOC entry using the COPY command, for example:

:COPY VOC LISTMEDIA TO: LM

Placing DOS Commands in VOC

One way to run any DOS program from within Revelation is to use the PC command from TCL. Another way is to create a VOC entry with ID = DOS command and field 1 = PCPERFORM. Since Revelation comes with the DIR command already entered in VOC, you can create the VOC entry for other DOS commands with the COPY command. For example:

:COPY VOC DIR TO: FORMAT

would create a VOC entry for the DOS FORMAT command. Note that when you use the VOC command you can attach parameters and these will be passed to DOS just as the DOS command would; e.g. **:FORMAT A:** would pass the A: parameter.

NEWAC and DICTNEWAC

NEWAC is a dictionary record in the VOC file containing a list of the VOC records which will automatically be copied into the VOC file of a new account. Similarly, **DICTNEWAC** is a dictionary record in VOC containing a list of the VOC dictionary records which will be copied to the dictionary of the new VOC file.

You may want to change NEWAC and DICTNEWAC for several reasons. For example, maybe you will be creating several new accounts where you want to limit access to certain TCL commands such as **DELETE-FILE** and **CREATE-FILE**. You could edit the NEWAC record in the DICT of VOC and delete these two entries. Then, whenever you create a new account, these records will be absent from the new VOC file.

Furthermore, you may want to place the name of R/DESIGN data entry screens in NEWAC so that when you copy these programs to a new account, the VOC entries for these programs will already be there.

CHAPTER SUMMARY

1. In Revelation, the DOS drive and path name of a disk directory is referred to as the "medium" or "volume". You must name a medium with the **NAMEMEDIA** command before you can store Revelation files on it. That will set up a DOS file named **ROSMEDIA.MAP** to keep track of the Revelation files on that medium.

2. Files which will be shared on a network, or very large files, use the **LINK** file management system while smaller files use the **ROS** file management system.

3. An **account** is a collection of files used for a particular application. You can only be logged into one account at a time. **Global** files can be accessed by all accounts. When you log onto an account, Revelation automatically **"attaches"** the files for that account located on the default medium. You must tell Revelation to attach files located on other media.

4. When you create an account, Revelation creates a **VOC** (vocabulary) file and a **LISTS** file (for storing select lists). If you want to use R/DESIGN with this account, you will need to create an **RDES** file.

5. All Revelation files consist of a **dictionary** part and a **data** part. The dictionary part contains the information which defines the fields of the data part.

6. Each record in a Revelation file is a **dynamic array** consisting of data elements separated by **delimiters.** A different delimiter is used to distinguish between fields, values, and subvalues. R/DESIGN automatically maintains these delimiters for you. Certain functions in R/BASIC can address a specific field, value, or subvalue based on its position in the dynamic array.

CHAPTER FOUR: MISCELLANEOUS CONCEPTS

The purpose of this chapter is to provide a concise summary of some of Revelation's key concepts and features. Don't worry if you are not able to fully understand some of the topics in this chapter; they will become clearer when you use them in PART II.

The concepts covered in this chapter are:

- file pointers
- record IDs
- select lists
- multi-valued fields
- associated multi-valued fields
- text and multi-lined fields
- input and output conversions
- pattern matching
- advanced topics

FILE POINTERS

File pointers are used in place of a file's actual name. There are two situations in which you use a file pointer. The first is when you have a file with a long name such as CORRESPONDENCE, and you would like to use a shorter name for simplicity. For example, you could set up a file pointer, CP, to use in place of the file name CORRESPONDENCE.

The second situation is when you want to access a file in another account -- for example, if you are in the account SALES.FORCE and would like to access the PERSONNEL file. Unfortunately the PERSONNEL file is in the ADMIN account, and you do not want to make PERSONNEL a global file because not everyone should have access to the personnel records.

The solution would be to set up a file pointer in the SALES FORCE account which points to the PERSONNEL file located in the ADMIN account.

qfile Pointers

Although the concept is straightforward, the terminology which Revelation uses for file pointers can be somewhat confusing. Revelation calls these file pointers **"qfile pointers"**. Revelation has one special qfile pointer which is named **QFILE**. This special qfile pointer is automatically created by Revelation whenever you create an account (notice that QFILE was listed as a file name in our example ADMIN account in Figure 3.2). QFILE is a special pointer because it is set to point to a file with the TCL command, SET-FILE; for example:

:SET-FILE SYSPROG RDES C

You may now use QFILE to refer to the RDES file in the SYSPROG account on the C drive. If you used the command

:LIST QFILE

you would get a listing of the records in the RDES file from the SYSPROG account.

There are two ways to set up qfile pointers. One is to set the QFILE qfile pointer with the **SET-FILE** command as explained above. The other is to use the DEF routine of R/DESIGN to name the qfile pointer and specify the file to which it will point.

QFILES File

Usually the information which defines the qfile pointer is stored in a record in the VOC file of the account. To log onto an account faster, it is better to set up a special file to hold your qfile pointers. But guess what that file must be named -- QFILES (not to be confused with the generic expression "qfile pointers", or the special pointer, QFILE!). We explain how to create this file and transfer your existing qfile pointers into it in Chapter 5.

If you log into an account without a QFILES file, Revelation must search every record in the VOC file to see which ones are qfile pointers. Because the VOC file is fairly large, this takes some time.

MD qfile Pointer

Another qfile pointer is the **MD** qfile. MD stands for **Master Dictionary** and is a holdover from the PICK operating environment. Since the VOC file is considered the master dictionary for Revelation, containing all the valid commands and words used throughout the system, the MD qfile points to the VOC file.   Unless you are planning to use some applications that were developed on a PICK system, you probably won't need to use the MD qfile pointer.

RECORD ID'S

As discussed in chapter 3, Revelation stores information as records within a file. All information used by Revelation is viewed by the system as records in a file. Therefore, even programs in DOS are seen as "records" in the file called "DOS".

Every database management system needs to have some way of identifying each record -- some unique value. Some DBMSs assign a sequential record number to each record as it is entered. Revelation uses a different system.

When you set up a data file's structure with the BUD routine, you should designate an **identification field** from the fields you have defined. This identifying field is called the record **ID** or **key** (these terms are used interchangeably by Revelation and this book).

For example, you could set up a data file, CUSTOMERS, to hold information on your company's customers. It might consist of separate fields for first name, last name, company name, street address, city, state, zip, and phone number. You might choose the "company name" field as the record ID.

Naming a Record with the ID

The record ID, or key, is essentially the name of the record and is is used to direct Revelation to locate information in the file.

When you store an R/BASIC program, for example, it will be stored in a file with a record whose ID is the name of the program. Thus, if you created a program named CHECK.BALANCE and stored it in the BASIC.PROGRAM file, it would be stored as a record whose key (or ID) field contained the value CHECK.BALANCE .

Multiple Part Keys

Sometimes the field you want to use as the record ID does not contain a unique value for each record. For example, what if you assigned Last Name as the record ID and you had two customers named Jones? Revelation would not be able to tell the records apart. One solution would be to assign a sequential number to each record and use that as the key.

Revelation also allows for **multi-part keys**. These consist of two or more fields which, when taken together, result in a unique record identification. In the above example, you could use a multi-part key consisting of the first name field and the last name field to produce unique record IDs. These individual fields are referred to as the key parts and are assigned a key part number.

Be forewarned, however -- working with a data file that uses multi-part keys can be cumbersome. We therefore recommend staying away from them if at all possible.

SELECT LISTS

A select list is a group of records which meet certain specified conditions. This subset of records from a data file can be used in an output report or for various other operations.

For example, in the CUSTOMERS file, you could form a select list of all of the customers located in California by using the R/LIST command **SELECT**:

```
:SELECT CUSTOMERS WITH STATE = CA
>
```

After creating a select list, the very next TCL command which is executed will use the select list of records instead of the whole file. This is indicated by the normal TCL prompt ":" being replaced with a select list prompt ">". If you now listed the CUSTOMERS file, you would only see the customers located in California.

```
:SELECT CUSTOMERS WITH STATE = "CA"
>LIST CUSTOMERS
```

If you want to use this same list of records again in the future, you can either recreate it each time, or you can give it a name and save it with the **SAVE-LIST** command.

It's important to realize that when you create a select list, Revelation creates a list of just the record IDs. When you save this list, you are saving a list of record IDs only. This list of IDs is stored as a record in the LISTS file with its record ID equal to the name you gave it with the SAVE-LIST command. You use the GET-LIST command to retrieve a previously saved list. Each field in that record will be one of the selected record IDs.

MULTI-VALUED FIELDS

What happens if, in our CUSTOMERS example, you have several phone numbers for a customer and you want to include all of them in your data file? One option would be to make a separate record entry for each number. Another would be to set up extra fields in the data file structure to hold these extra phone numbers (e.g. PHONE#1, PHONE#2, etc). Both of these solutions are cumbersome and waste disk space. Revelation uses a more sophisticated solution, multi-valued fields.

Multi-valued fields allow you to enter as many values for a field as you wish (limited to 99 in R/DESIGN). Thus, in the above customer example, you would simply make the phone# a multi-valued field, and enter as many values to this field as necessary.

Remember from Chapter 3 that each record in a Revelation file consists of fields, values, and subvalues (you will not use subvalues very often), separated by field markers, value markers, and subvalue markers. Fortunately, Revelation places these markers for you. All you do is define the fields, decide which will be multi-valued, and Revelation will take care of the rest.

When a multi-valued field is printed out with R/LIST, each value will print on a separate line.

Associated Multi-Values

What if you have a customer file which contains invoices for each customer, and you have set up a multi-valued field for invoice number and another multi-valued field for invoice amount. Obviously, these two multi-valued fields are associated in that each invoice number corresponds to a particular amount.

R/DESIGN recognizes the concept of associated multi-values. But it is important to understand that associated multi-values are not part of the file structure itself. The only time that the association is made is when you generate a data entry screen with R/DESIGN.

This means that your data entry screen will display these fields together and prompt you for the entire set of associated fields whenever you input or edit any one of them. That's all there is to associated multi-values; there's nothing else in Revelation to prevent you from getting these fields mis-aligned.

TEXT AND MULTI-LINED FIELDS

These two terms describe how a field will be displayed. Before talking about these terms, it is important to mention that there are two places where data is displayed: the first is in output reports generated with R/LIST, and the second is the data entry screen after the data has been entered.

In general, the parameters you enter in the BUD routine determine how data will be displayed in data entry screens and reports. You may modify how data is displayed on a data entry screen by changing the parameters with R/DESIGN's SCR routine.

Text Fields

When you define the fields of your data file with BUD, one of the parameters you set is the display width. If you made the display width 10 characters, and the actual data stored in the field is 30 characters (remember that with variable length fields you can always enter as much data into a field as you wish), then when the field is displayed *in a report*, it will be truncated to 10 characters. If you had made this field a **text** field, the entire 30 characters would be displayed on three lines of 10 characters each.

You can also make a field a text field on the data entry screen. In this case the effect will be different. When the operator is prompted for an input to this field, the TEXT Editor utility will automatically be invoked (the TEXT Editor is fully described in Chapter 14).

Multi-Lined Fields

A multi-lined field only affects data entry screens. It will allow several lines of input text to be displayed on the screen.

INPUT AND OUTPUT CONVERSIONS

What are Input and Output Conversions?

Another topic in Revelation which is conceptually straight-forward but somewhat confusing in practice is input/output conversions. They control the way data is stored on the disk and then later displayed. In general, it is more efficient for the computer to store and manipulate numeric information as whole integers than as decimal numbers.

For example, if you had a lot of accounting data which was in dollars and cents, it would help processing efficiency if all the numbers were multiplied by 100 as you entered them into the computer and divided them by 100 when you retrieved them. Thus, 593.74 would be stored as 59374 but returned to its proper value for any output reports. With proper input/output conversions, this is done automatically.

Input and output conversions are also used to convert dates to a numeric value so that dates can be compared, added, etc.

The confusion arises in actually using input/output conversions. It is important to remember that generally, if you apply an input conversion to data, you must apply a corresponding output conversion. You must also be careful when performing calculations with numeric fields -- the form in which the data is stored is the form in which it is retrieved for calculations. You should either reconvert the data or ensure the other values in the calculation have the same input conversion.

Setting Input and Output Conversions

For an application developed with R/DESIGN, there are two sets of conversions: one in the field definition you created with BUD, and another in the data entry screen. The conversions you enter in BUD will automatically become the initial values of your data entry screen. Normally, these two sets remain the same -- but they don't have to and this can sometimes cause problems.

The input conversion of BUD serves no purpose other than to be passed to your data entry screen when it is generated with SCR.GEN. The input conversion in the data entry screen converts data for storage on the disk.

The output conversion has two purposes. The output conversion entered in BUD determines the output conversion for reports. The output conversion in your data entry screen, however, determines what is displayed on the data entry screen after data is entered.

After your data entry screen has been created, you can go back to BUD and change the input conversion of a data field -- this will not affect the data entry screen. But if you change the output conversion of BUD, it will change what is displayed on reports.

Similarly, you could change the conversions in your data entry screen with SCR. Changing the input conversion would change how future entered data is stored on the disk. Changing the output conversion will change the data entry screen but will not change reports.

Prompt Terminology for Conversions

One last potentially perplexing issue is the prompt terminology for conversions. For output conversions, Revelation uses "OUTPUT CONVERSION" - easy enough. But for input conversion it uses "EDIT PATTERN". At this "EDIT PATTERN" prompt you may enter not only input conversions, but also define allowable data patterns and range checks.

R/BASIC and Conversions

When R/BASIC programs or symbolic fields perform calculations with data fields, the value used in the calculation is the value stored on the disk -- unless you apply an output conversion.

For example, if you had a field titled UNIT.COST and you entered 9.32 with an input conversion which multiplies input data by 100, it would be stored as 932. If you then created a symbolic field called DOUBLE.COST, whose value was two times the unit cost, then the value of DOUBLE.COST would be 1864 and would print out as such unless you remember to give it an output conversion.

PATTERN MATCHING

Pattern matching is primarily used in data entry screens to check for valid data entry, but you can also use this logic with R/LIST commands and in R/BASIC programs. You define the pattern with the following characters:

nA   means "n" number of alphabetic characters.

nN   means "n" number of numeric characters.

nX   means "n" number of any characters, either alphabetic or numeric.

nZ   means up to "n" number of characters

The pattern can also contain literal strings mixed in with the special characters. The whole pattern must be enclosed in double quotes and any literal strings within the pattern must be in single quotes. For example, consider the following R/BASIC statement:

IF SSN MATCHES "3N'-'2N'-'4N" THEN GOTO 100 ELSE STOP

The program would proceed to line 100 if the value of the SSN variable consisted of three numbers, a dash, two numbers,a dash, and four numbers; otherwise the program would stop. In this example:

IF X MATCHES " 'INV' 3Z" THEN GOTO 100 ELSE STOP

the program would go to line 100 if X were equal to the letters INV followed by up to three more characters of any type.

ADVANCED TOPICS

Creating qfile with the Text Editor

Another way to create a qfile is to directly create a VOC qfile entry. From TCL type

:TEXT VOC qfilename

Enter "QFILE" into field 1, the account of the file being pointed to into field 2, and the name of the file being pointed to into field 3. Remember to ATTACH the medium where the real file resides in order to let Revelation know that the new qfile pointer is there.

Comparison Expressions

There are numerous instances with R/LIST and R/BASIC where you will use comparison expressions. Most of these uses are easily understood, but a few aspects of comparisons need explaining. For example, examine the following R/BASIC statement:

IF X > 10 THEN PRINT "X IS TOO LARGE" ELSE GOTO 200

This statement checks to see if the amount of the variable X is greater than 10. If it is, it prints the phrase "X IS TOO LARGE", otherwise it goes to line 200.

What actually happens in a comparison statement is that the comparison expression ("X > 10" in the above example) evaluates to a value of "0" if the condition is false and to a value of "1" if the condition is true. The R/BASIC statement reads the "0" or "1" and carries out the appropriate action. We could have said:

IF 0 THEN PRINT "AMOUNT IS TOO LARGE" ELSE GOTO 200

and the program control would jump to line 200 because the IF statement interpreted the 0 as false and carried out the ELSE action. In fact, the compare statement interprets any value other than a "0" as true. For example:

IF 5 THEN PRINT "AMOUNT IS TOO LARGE" ELSE GOTO 200

would print "AMOUNT IS TOO LARGE" because "5" is interpreted as true.

The Equals Sign

Another interesting situation involves the equals comparison. The equals sign "=" has two meanings, depending on the syntax. It can be used to assign a value to a variable as in:

X = 5.

It can also be used as a compare operator as in:

IF X = 5 THEN GOTO 100 ELSE GOTO 200

CHAPTER SUMMARY

1. Every record in a Revelation file must have a unique **record ID (or key)**. The record ID consists of one or more of the fields of the file.

2. Revelation uses **qfile** pointers as substitute file names to point to specified files. They are used for substituting a short file name for a long one, and for accessing a file located in another account.

A special qfile pointer is named **QFILE** and the file to which it points can be specified with the SET-FILE command. You can create other qfile pointers with the DEF routine of R/DESIGN.

3. **Select lists** are a powerful Revelation tool, consisting of a list of IDs for the records which satisfy specified conditions. This list can be saved as a record in the LISTS file, and can be accessed by TCL commands or R/BASIC statements.

4. Fields in data files can be specified to be either **single** or **multi-valued**. You can enter as many values as you wish for multi-valued fields -- they will be stored in the dynamic array delimited by value markers.

5. Two or more multi-valued fields can be **"associated"** so that the first value of one field corresponds to the first value of another field, the second value corresponds to the second value of the other field, etc.

This association is not built into the file structure; it is only a feature of R/DESIGN-generated data entry screens which prompts you for an entry to all of the associated fields whenever you enter a value to any one of them. Otherwise, it is up to you to keep the associated values lined up.

6. **Multi-lined** and **text** fields pertain to how text data is input and displayed. The entire contents of a "text" field will print out in a report, no matter how many lines it takes. A text field will also automatically invoke the TEXT Editor during data entry.

Multi-lined fields allow for a specified number of lines of text to be displayed on a data entry screen.

7. **Input** and **output conversions** are used to store and display numeric, date, and time information on disk using an internal numeric system representation. This provides efficiency for handling numeric information and allows for comparisons and mathematical operations of time and date information.

8. **Pattern matching** is primarily used in data entry screens to check for valid data entry. This allows you to match an expression to either a literal string or to a specified number of character types, i.e. alphabetic or numeric.

PART TWO:
FUNCTIONAL DESCRIPTION

CHAPTER FIVE:
GETTING STARTED

This is the first chapter in Part II, "FUNCTIONAL DESCRIPTION". Each chapter in this part covers different aspects of developing an application with Revelation. If you have problems understanding any topics is Part II, first look to see if that topic is covered in Part I, CONCEPTUAL FRAMEWORK. If it is, read the applicable section. If you are having trouble with a specific command, read the description of that command in Part III, COMMAND REFERENCE.

This chapter explains how to get Revelation up and running on your computer system and gives some background information you should know before starting to develop an application. It covers the system requirements and installation procedures for a hard disk or floppy disk system. The chapter then discusses how to create and log into an account.

Also covered in this chapter are a description of the keyboard functions and the on-line HELP system.

This chapter assumes that you are familiar with using DOS commands for performing file operations. If not, you should consult your DOS manual or a DOS user's book.

Revelation only recognizes commands entered in **capital letters**--remember to set caps lock on when you start each session of Revelation.

INSTALLATION PROCEDURES

System Requirements

Revelation will run on the following personal computers. For information on other computers, check with COSMOS' technical service.

IBM PC,XT,AT or compatible
Texas Instruments PC
Tandy Professional
Apricot Personal Computer
DEC Rainbow 100+
Wang Personal Computer

The installation procedures in this chapter are written for an IBM compatible computer. You will need DOS version 2.0 or later to run Revelation. If you have a different operating system, consult your operating system documentation and Cosmos technical literature for additional information.

Although it is possible to run Revelation on a two floppy disk system, we highly recommended a hard disk as your application programs will run much faster. Because you can get a hard disk for as little as $250, it makes little sense not to have one for your Revelation applications. You will also find that Revelation applications will run considerably faster on an IBM AT -- therefore an upgrade to an Intel 80286 microprocessor computer may be worth the price. Additionally, for math intensive applications, a math co-processor chip will make a significant speed improvement -- up to 30 times faster!

Before you begin installing Revelation, you will need three blank, unformatted floppy diskettes for making a backup copy of Revelation. If you are installing Revelation on a floppy disk system, you will need a fourth blank floppy diskette.

Making Backup Copies of Revelation

Making copies of Revelation for purposes other than backup is a violation of the User License Agreement. Each copy of Revelation has a serial number which should not be altered; attempts to do so will result in errors in your copy of Revelation. Also, Revelation should only be run on a computer which has an Official Revelation Authorization Stamp from Cosmos.

Use the DOS commands to make a backup copy of the three Revelation diskettes. Label these REVELATION SYSTEM, REVELATION TUTORIAL, and REVELATION UTILI- TIES. Store your original Revelation diskettes in a safe place and use the backups for the rest of this installation.

Installing Revelation on a Hard Disk System

1. Create a subdirectory on your hard disk and name it REV.

2. Copy the Revelation System diskette into your REV Subdirectory. Do **not** copy the Tutorial or Utilities diskettes to your REV subdirectory using the DOS commands; doing so will prevent Revelation from running.

3. Load Revelation. Make sure REV is the default directory. Then enter the command:

   C>REV

   Turn on the CAPS LOCK. In the Revelation Utilities, there is a program which automatically sets caps lock on. You may want to set up a batch file for invoking Revelation which runs this program before running the REV command.

4.   At the prompt for your account enter SYSPROG. Hit
     <E> at the password prompt and you should get a
     message saying that the SYSPROG files are being
     attached and then you will get the LOGON menu.
     Select option 7, INSTALL, from this menu.

5.   The install process will ask a few questions and require
     that you place your DOS disk and Tutorial disk into a
     specific drive. At the end of the install process, follow
     the directions to get back to the TCL colon prompt (:).

6.   Install the Revelation Utilities which contains additional
     Revelation files (discussed later in this book). Put the
     Revelation Utilities diskette in the A drive and enter the
     following command from the TCL prompt:

     :RUN DOS A:INSTALL.UTL

     This will install certain Revelation files on the hard disk
     and then prompt you for moving other DOS files.
     Answer "no" to this prompt and go back to the TCL
     prompt. (You may get a message during the utilities
     installation saying that the SUBS file cannot be found.
     This file was removed from the utilities diskette in a
     recent revision, so just ignore this message).

7.   If you would like to use Revelation's on-line HELP
     program from all of your accounts (generally a good
     idea), then perform this step to make the HELP file
     global. Use the MOVE command to copy HELP from
     the SYSPROG account to the "NULL" account:

     :MOVE HELP C TO: NULL HELP C

     This creates a global copy of HELP (assumes the default
     medium is \REV); check this by listing the files on the
     default medium:

     :LISTMEDIA

You should see two HELP accounts, one in SYSPROG and one with no account. Then delete the unnecessary copy of HELP from the SYSPROG account with the DELETE-FILE command:

:DELETE-FILE HELP

8.   The Advanced Topics section at the end of this chapter contains other installation procedures you may want to perform.

Installing Revelation on a Floppy Disk System

1.   Use DOS to copy the file REV.EXE from the REVELATION SYSTEM diskette to the fourth diskette. Label this fourth diskette REV.EXE. Delete REV.EXE from the REVELATION SYSTEM diskette.

2.   Next, you will log into Revelation. Turn on the CAPS LOCK lock on your computer (Revelation needs to have commands entered in caps). Put the REV.EXE diskette in the B drive and the REVELATION SYSTEM diskette in the A drive. Then from the A> prompt enter the command:

A>B:REV

3.   At the prompt for your account enter: SYSPROG. Hit <E> at the password prompt and you should get a message saying that the SYSPROG files are being attached. You will then get the LOGON menu. Select option 7, INSTALL, from this menu.

4.   The install process will ask a few questions and require that you place your DOS disk and Tutorial disk into the B drive. At the end of the install process, follow the directions to get back to the TCL prompt.

5.   Use the B drive for the diskette which will hold your application files. But before you can use any diskette, you will have to name it with the NAMEMEDIA command (covered later in this chapter). Also, whenever you desire to run any of the utilities, place the REVELATION UTILITIES diskette in the B drive.

6.   The Advanced Topics section at the end of this chapter contains other installations procedures you may want to perform.

LOGGING ON/OFF

Logging On

Make sure you are in the DOS directory which contains your Revelation files.

Load Revelation by entering REV from the DOS prompt. Revelation will show you the copyright screen and prompt for your account name.

Until you have built your own accounts, enter SYSPROG -- which is the only account which comes with Revelation. You can create your first application account from SYSPROG.

Password Protection

After entering an account name, you will be asked for the account's password -- if one exists. When you enter the password, it will not be displayed on the screen. You have the option of setting a password when you create an account. You may also create a password with the CHANGE-PASSWORD command.

Attaching Files

When you log into an account Revelation "attaches" the files for that account in the default medium (DOS drive and directory). Revelation internally stores the names of the attached files, making these the only files it will access.

If there are files for this account located in other media, you must attach them using the ATTACH command.   For example, to attach the files in the ADMIN subdirectory of the REV directory, you would use:

:ATTACH \REV\ADMIN

Note that the ATTACH command (as well as other commands referring to media) must use the DOS terminology for drive and directory path and not the Revelation media name.

If you have qfile pointers which point to files in other media, you will have to attach those media for the qfile to work (each time you attach a medium, Revelation checks all the qfile pointers in the QFILES file or VOC file to see if they point to a file on that medium).

If you set the QFILE pointer to point to a file in another medium with the SET-FILE command, Revelation will automatically attach that file. However, the next time you log to this account, the QFILE pointer will still be set to this file -- but it will not be automatically attached and you will have to attach its medium before QFILE can be used as a pointer to the file.

In the Advanced Topics section at the end of this chapter, you can find an explanation on how to automatically attach media when you log into an account.

Rather than wait to be prompted for the account name and password, you can include them when you first load Revelation. For example, to log into the ADMIN account with a password of ABC, you could enter:

C> REV ADMIN ABC

Logon Menu

After you log into the SYSPROG account, the LOGON MENU will appear on the screen.   The options on the LOGON MENU are:

1.   ATTACH REVELATION DATA DISK
      Attaches a medium (same as the ATTACH command), will prompt you for the drive/directory.

2.   HELP Menu
      Displays the HELP MENU which provides on-line help for using the Revelation commands. (See the "Getting Help" section of this chapter.)

3.   R/DESIGN Menu
      Displays the R/DESIGN MENU for using Revelation's applications developer. (Discussed in chapter 6.)

4.   LIST of Customers [ATTACH first]
      This accesses part of Revelation's tutorial. Floppy disk systems must first attach the REVELATION TUTORIAL diskette.

5.   A/R Menu [ATTACH first]
      Also part of Revelation's tutorial. Floppy disk systems must first attach the REVELATION TUTORIAL diskette.

6.   EXIT REVELATION
      Logs you off of Revelation; same as entering from TCL, the command :OFF.

7.   INSTALL Revelation
      This runs the installation program for both floppy disk systems and hard disk systems. Do NOT attach the REVELATION TUTORIAL diskette before running the install program. Once Revelation has been installed this option will no longer appear on the Menu.

Once you are famililar with Revelation you may wish to bypass the LOGON MENU since any of the options may be executed from the TCL prompt. (The advanced topics section of this chapter explains how to prevent this menu from automatically appearing during LOGON.) If you ever want to get back to this menu from the TCL prompt just enter :MENU.

Changing Accounts

If you are in the ADMIN account and want to switch to another account named INVOICING, with a password XYZ, use the **LOGTO** command:

:LOGTO INVOICING XYZ

You will be prompted for the password if you forget to include it with the LOGTO command. Remember that you can only be logged into one account at a time. Therefore, when you logto the INVOICING account the files for the ADMIN account will no longer be attached.

Logging Off

To log off Revelation just type **:OFF** from the TCL prompt.

CREATING MEDIA AND ACCOUNTS

Naming Storage Media

Revelation uses the terms "medium" and "volume" interchangeably to mean a DOS drive/directory specification. The default medium of Revelation is the drive/directory from where you loaded Revelation. This default setting cannot be changed.

Before storing Revelation files on a medium, it must be prepared with the NAMEMEDIA command. For example, to make the DOS subdirectory ADMIN a Revelation medium with the name ADMINISTRATION, you would enter:

:NAMEMEDIA \REV\ADMIN ADMINISTRATION

The NAMEMEDIA command creates a DOS file on that medium named ROSMEDIA.MAP. This keeps track of the Revelation files on that medium.

Remember that TCL commands use the DOS syntax for media and not the Revelation media names.

ADVANCED TOPIC:
The structure of the ROSMEDIA.MAP is:

> Field 1 = media name.

> Field 2 = DOS filename assigned to the next Revelation file.

> Field 3 = Account and Revelation file names (multi-valued, with the account and file name as subvalues of each value).

> Field 4 = DOS filename (multi-valued).

> Field 5 = modulo (multi-valued).

(Fields 3, 4, and 5 are associated multi-values.)

Creating Accounts

You will probably want to keep each of your applications in a separate account. This keeps your files separated and allows a different password for each application. New accounts are established using the **CREATE-ACCOUNT** command, for example:

:CREATE-ACCOUNT ACCOUNTING

would create a new account named ACCOUNTING. You will then be prompted for the new account's password. Press <E> if you do not want a password.

When you create an account, Revelation creates four files in that account: VOC, which contains the words recognized by TCL; LISTS, which will hold any select lists you save; and two

Qfile pointers, QFILE and MD. Before using R/DESIGN in this account, you will need to create another file named **RDES**. This file is used to store the parameters which define data entry programs, menus, and cross references created with R/DESIGN. RDES is created using the following command:

:CREATE-FILE RDES

You will be prompted for the number of records and average size of each record. These are just estimates Revelation uses to determine if the file structure should be ROS or LINK. It will not be crucial if your estimates are off -- you can always change them by using the **RECREATE-FILE** command. A typical RDES file may have 20 records with 500 bytes per record.

KEYBOARD FUNCTIONS

Revelation assigns special meanings to many of the keys or key combinations on the keyboard. The special keys used in TCL and R/DESIGN are listed in this section. Other special keyboard meanings apply to the Text Editor and are listed in Chapter 14 (you may need to refer to these before you get to Chapter 14).

TCL Keyboard Functions

Arrow Keys   moves left or right without deleting text.

Ctrl Arrow Keys   moves left or right one word.

Home and End   moves to beginning or end of current line.

INS key   toggles between insert mode and overwrite mode.

DEL Key   deletes character at current cursor position.

Ctrl L   clears the screen.

Ctrl X	deletes the current line of text.
Backspace	deletes character to the left of cursor.
F1	displays HELP screen for TCL commands.
Ctrl F1	displays HELP screen for keyboard features (this list of functions).
F3	displays last TCL command entered (same as the dot processor command ".1" discussed later).
F7	deletes from the cursor position to the beginning of line.
F8	deletes from the cursor position to the end of line.

Default Menu Functions

F5	moves between menus, works with both the R/DESIGN menus and application menus you create using R/DESIGN.
Ctrl F5	returns to TCL from a menu.
F9	returns to a prior menu; or, if entered at a starting menu, will return to the TCL prompt.

R/Design Keyboard Functions

Most of the TCL keyboard functions also work in R/DESIGN, with the following changes and additions. These apply to the screens R/DESIGN uses in its routines, as well as in data entry screens generated with R/DESIGN.

Up/Down
Arrows   moves up and down one prompt.

Ctrl D   deletes entire record if entered at the CHANGE? prompt; you are prompted to enter it twice to avoid mistakes (once deleted, a record can not be recovered).

END   returns to the TCL prompt without saving
(or Ctrl E)   current changes (in some cases Ctrl E doesn't work and you must use "END").

Ctrl L   accesses cross reference function (from the TCL prompt, it clears the screen).

Ctrl T   redisplays blank screen without saving current
(or TOP)   modifications.

?F   From any prompt in a data entry screen, immediately places cursor at the CHANGE prompt.

Function Keys

F1 (or "?")   when entered at a data entry prompt, displays the description you entered for that data field.

Shift F1   displays the edit checks and allowed patterns for
(or "??")   current prompt. This allows you to see the valid entries for the current prompt.

F2 (or ")   duplicates the data you entered for the same field on the previous record. For example, this is useful if you were entering addresses in a data entry screen and have several entries in a row from California. After entering "CA" for the first entry, you can just press F2 at the State prompt on subsequent records to repeat "CA".

Multi-Valued Fields Only

These next keyboard functions can only be entered after you have selected to edit a multi-valued field in a data entry screen and are then prompted: WHICH VALUE?.

Ctrl A	adds a value.
Ctrl C	clears all values.
Ctrl D	deletes a value.
Ctrl I	inserts a value.
Ctrl T **(or TEXT)**	invokes the Text Editor (note Ctrl T has a different meaning if it is entered at any other R/DESIGN prompt).
F	scrolls multi-value display forward so other values will be shown on the screen.
B	scrolls multi-value display backward.
Ctrl-Q	From within an actual multi-value field prompt, quits the multi-value prompting and proceeds to the next prompt or to the CHANGE prompt.

Some of the routines accessed from the R/DESIGN main menu prompt you for the name of your application program. Several of the R/DESIGN keyboard functions will not work at this prompt. Most important of these is the Ctrl-E function to exit the routine. You must enter END at this prompt to leave this routine.

R/DESIGN CONVENTIONS

These conventions apply to the screens R/DESIGN uses in its routines such as BUD and PGMR, as well as in data entry screens generated with R/DESIGN.

1. Add mode and Edit mode

You will interact with R/DESIGN screens in either add mode or edit mode. The mode is determined when you enter a value for the record key prompt. If it is a new record, then you will be in Add mode, and R/DESIGN starts at the top of the entry screen and sequentially moves through the prompts on the screen. The Edit mode is used to edit a record which has already been entered. The screen will show the previously entered data and display the CHANGE prompt which is described below.

2. The CHANGE Prompt

R/DESIGN screens consist of a series of prompts with a reference number next to each one. Once all the prompts have been answered (or you are in Edit mode) you will find yourself at the "CHANGE?" prompt. Entering the number of a prompt allows you to change your entry for that prompt.

At the CHANGE prompt, entering a "+" after the number to be edited will force prompting to continue through all subsequent prompts. Thus, "3+" will cause prompting to begin at prompt 3 and continue on to all the following prompts.

Pressing Ctrl D deletes the entire record.

Entering the word 'ADD' will prompt for each blank field on the screen.

3. File Names

Revelation allows file names up to 50 characters long. This contrasts with the DOS convention that requires all file names to be no more than eight characters followed by a three character extension. Thus, CUSTOMERS.NEW would be a valid file name in Revelation but not in DOS.

Certain characters may not be used in Revelation file names. These are:

$$! \# \char`^ * ( ) - + = \{ \} [ ] : ; " ' \sim , < > ? / \backslash |$$

4. Some keyboards have a left single quote key as well as the normal right single quote key ('). Do not use this left quote key.

5. PERFORM [TCL command] (ADVANCED TOPIC)

This command may be entered from any R/DESIGN prompt. The TCL command is performed and any variables or lists are passed back to the original screen. For example, suppose you wish to view from a data entry screen all customers from the state of California. At the record ID prompt, you would enter the following command:

PERFORM SELECT CUSTOMERS WITH ST = "CA"

The SELECT will be performed and those customers who live in California will be displayed on the data entry screen one by one until the select list is exhausted (each ID from the select list will in turn be entered into the ID prompt from which you performed the PERFORM command).

6. EXECUTE [valid TCL command] (ADVANCED TOPIC)

This is essentially identical to the PERFORM command shown above except no information is passed to the current screen. Entering this command from any prompt will result in the temporary suspension of current processing and the TCL command will be executed. For example:

EXECUTE TIME

will clear the screen, display the time, and then redisplay the original screen.

7. ?M.E.N

Try entering this series of symbols at any R/DESIGN data entry screen prompt -- and see what happens!   (HINT: Mike Nourse was one of the designers of R/DESIGN.)

HELP SYSTEM

Revelation has a good on-line help system for the TCL commands. The main HELP MENU which is shown in **Figure 5.1,** can be reached in three ways: 1) by selecting the HELP option from the LOGON MENU, 2) by hitting the F1 key from the TCL prompt, or 3) by typing HELP from the TCL prompt.

REVELATION COMMANDS   10:41:12   1 JUL 1986

1. ATTACH	18. EDIT	35. SELECT
2. BASIC	19. FORM	36. SET-COLOR
3. BLIST	20. FORM-LIST	37. SET-CRT
4. CATALOG	21. GET-LIST	38. SET-FILE
5. CHANGE-PASSWORD	22. LIST	39. SET-LPT
6. CLEAR-FILE	23. LISTFILES	40. SET-OPTIONS
7. COMPILE	24. LISTMEDIA	41. SORT
8. COPY	25. LOGTO	42. SSELECT
9. COUNT	26. LOOKDICT	43. SUM
10. CREATE-ACCOUNT	27. MOVE	44. TERMINAL
11. CREATE-FILE	28. NAMEMEDIA	45. TEXT
12. DELETE	29. PORT	46. TIME
13. DELETE-ACCOUNT	30. RDESIGN	47. WHO
14. DELETE-FILE	31. RECREATE-FILE	
15. DELETE-LIST	32. RENAME FILE	
16. DETACH	33. RUN	
17. DUMP	34. SAVE-LIST	

ENTER COMMAND REFERENCE NUMBER, "?", OR "?NUMBER"

Fig. 5.1 Help Menu

The prompt at the bottom of the HELP MENU shows there are three options you can enter -- actually there are just two. One option is to enter the reference number of the command you want help with. An explanation of that command will appear, and the beginning of that command will be typed at the TCL prompt waiting for you to finish the rest of the command line.

Your second option is to enter a "?" in front of the reference number. In this case, you will still get the explanation of the command, but the command will not be printed at the TCL prompt. This second option is used when you want information on a command but do not intend to run it (if you just type "?", you will be prompted for the reference number to follow).

To get back to TCL, press <E> from the HELP menu prompt.

You can bypass the HELP MENU and go straight to the explanation of a TCL command, for example:

:HELP LIST

will give an explanation of the LIST command and then return you to the TCL prompt.

You can also get context-sensitive help (i.e. help about what you are typing or have just entered) if you press the F1 key.

DOT PROCESSOR

The dot processor allows you to display and recall the last 20 TCL commands which you entered. It also allows you to name and save a long command so that it can be recalled during another Revelation session. This feature is useful, especially when you are first learning Revelation. The dot processor is used by entering a dot followed by one of the codes below:

:.L   displays the last 20 commands which were entered from the TCL prompt. They are numbered in reverse order (#1 being the most recent command entered).

:.n   recalls and displays the nth command, where n is the number corresponding to the command you want to recall. You can then edit the command or just execute it by pressing <E>.

:.Sn name   saves the nth command under the name you assign it here. It can then be executed anytime in the future by just entering this name at the TCL prompt.

:.? or .HELP   prints this list of Dot Processor Commands.

TCL COLON PROMPT (:)

The colon prompt (:) signifies that you are at the Terminal Control Language prompt. You may enter any valid Revelation command found in the VOC file. Sometimes you may see a prompt consisting of two or more colons. This means you have interupted R/DESIGN, the debugger, or one of the editors to perform other operations from a "second" level of TCL -- and something went wrong. These recursive levels are discussed in the chapters on programming. To get back to the first level, enter the word 'RETURN' or press Ctrl-R from the multiple colon prompt.

ADVANCED TOPICS

Revelation's Logon Program

When you log into an account, Revelation performs the following steps:

1. Looks at the ROSMEDIA.MAP in the default media, finds the files in the current account, and attaches those files.

2. Looks for a file named QFILES. If found, the qfile pointers are attached. (The files to which the qfiles point will not be attached unless their medium has been attached.)

3. If it did not find a QFILES file in step 3, it goes through the entire VOC file looking for records which are qfile pointers and attaches them.

4. Looks for a record in the VOC file with the same name as the account and performs the commands in it. This can be used as a kind of AUTOEXEC.BAT file to automatically attach other media and execute start-up menus.

5. If it didn't find a record with the account name in the VOC file, it looks for a record in the VOC file named LOGON and performs the commands in it.

The system variable @FILES contains a dynamic array of all the attached files.

Creating QFILES File

Logging on will take less time if you set up a QFILES file to hold your qfile pointers.

```
:CREATE-FILE QFILES 1 1
:SELECT VOC WHEN F1 = 'QFILE'
>COPY VOC (D) TO: (QFILES
```

This will transfer all the qfile pointers in the VOC file to the QFILES file.

Suppressing the LOGON Menu

You may wish to prevent the LOGON MENU from automatically displaying after Revelation has been installed and you have become familiar with the tutorial application files that are shipped with Revelation. (The LOGON record in the VOC file also may be customized.) To remove the LOGON MENU:

```
:DELETE VOC LOGON
```

CHAPTER SIX: CREATING A DATABASE

This chapter describes in detail how you will use the first two routines of R/DESIGN. You will use **DEF** to create a datafile and **BUD** to create the dictionary records which define the data fields of that file. This chapter explains each prompt of these R/DESIGN routines and gives examples to clarify the meaning of the parameters you will be defining.

R/DESIGN MENU

To invoke the R/DESIGN menu, choose item 3 from the Revelation Logon Menu. The menu shown in **Figure 6.1** will appear. You can also invoke this menu at any time from the TCL prompt with the command R/DESIGN.

```
                    R/DESIGN MAIN menu
                    13:46:09  10 OCT 1986


NEXT ->     (1)  DEF        Define and Create a File
            (2)  BUD        Build a Dictionary for a File

            (3)  PGMR       Set up a New Program
            (4)  SEL        Select Fields to be Displayed
            (5)  SCR.GEN    Generate a Standard Screen
            (6)  SCR        Customize an Existing Entry Screen

            (7)  ENTER      Enter Data Using a Program

            (8)  DOC        Produce Application
                            Documentation
            (9)  GEN        Generate R/BASIC Code
            (10) BLD.MENU   Build Menu
            (0)  TCL        Return to REVELATION Command
                            Level


            Press ENTER key for Selection Number 1 or
                 Enter your Selection Number?
```

Fig. 6.1 R/DESIGN Main Menu

CREATING A DATABASE FILE: R/DESIGN DEF

The first selection on the R/DESIGN menu is called **DEF**. This module prompts the user for information that is used to create a file on the disk. There are two ways to invoke DEF:

1) Enter selection 1 at the R/DESIGN Main Menu.
   or
2) Enter DEF at the TCL colon prompt.

Files can also be created by using the TCL command **CREATE-FILE** (see COMMAND REFERENCE).

When DEF is invoked the screen shown in **Figure 6.2** is displayed.

```
DEF              BUILD FILE DEFINITION



        01  File Name
        02  QFILE Name
        03  Owner of File
        04  Description
```

Fig. 6.2 DEF screen

The prompts in this screen are described as follows:

01 File Name

Enter the name of the file you wish to create. Each file name in an account must be unique, so if you enter the name of an existing file, DEF displays the prompt data for that file and the cursor will move to the CHANGE? prompt to wait for you to change any of the file's parameters on this screen.

Entering a new file name will display the message "You are adding a new file" and then continue to the next prompt.

Rules for file names are explained in Chapter 5.

02 QFILE name

As discussed in Chapter 4, Qfile pointers are used either to provide a shorter name for a file or to access a file in another account. If the file name you entered above is to be a file pointer, enter the account, name, and medium of the file to which the qfile points. For example:

ADMIN,CUSTOMERS,C:\REV\DATA

will point to the CUSTOMERS file in the ADMIN account. After you enter the Qfile name, control immediately passes to the CHANGE prompt because the last prompts for the owner and description of the qfile are presumably already known and therefore not necessary.

When you file this information by pressing <E> at the CHANGE prompt, R/DESIGN creates a record in the VOC file with an ID of the qfile name given in the first prompt. (If you have a QFILES file, it places this record in that file instead.)

If you try to delete the Qfile by entering Ctrl-D or "DELETE" from the CHANGE prompt, only the Qfile pointer is deleted; the actual file to which it was pointing remains unchanged.

If the file you are creating is not a Qfile, leave this prompt blank.

03 Owner of File

Enter the name of the person, group, or division who created, controls or maintains the file. This entry is optional and is used by R/DESIGN during the DOCumentation program.

04 Description

At this prompt you may enter a complete description of the file--including information on when it was created, how it will be used, other files from which it may get data, and other files that may use its data. This field is also optional and used by R/DESIGN to create application documentation. The field is multi-lined, allowing up to fifteen lines of description.

After filing this information at the CHANGE prompt, you will be asked for additional information concerning the size of the file (multi-user versions of Revelation will also ask whether the file will be shared). Your answers determine which file management system to assign to the file -- ROS or LINK. The file management system effects the efficiency of accessing records in the file and determines whether record locking can be used (record locking pertains to files shared by users on a local area network and is discussed in Chapter 11). File management systems are discussed in detail in Appendix V.

You should know that your file will work no matter what you respond to these prompts concerning the size of your file. Your accuracy in approximating the number of records and number of characters in these records only effects the disk access efficiency of the records in these files.

Revelation uses the following guidelines for determining which file management system to use.

1.   If the file will be shared, then it will be a LINK file.

2.   If the file is not shared and the estimated size based on your responses is less than 200K bytes, then a ROS file is created.

3.   If the file is not shared and the estimated size is greater than 200k, the following message will appear:

> This is a large file. Access to this file will usually be much faster if it is a LINK file.
> Do you wish to make this a LINK file (Y/N)?

If you choose a LINK file structure you will then be asked to approximate the number of dictionary items the file will have. Once again, this answer only affects the efficiency of your file. The file size can be changed if disk access to your file is slower than you think it should be (See RECREATE-FILE in the COMMAND REFERENCE).

Revelation uses your size estimations to determine the **"modulo"** of the file. If you are looking for more efficient disk access to these files, then understanding advanced topics such as modulo and frame overflow will be of importance to you. They are discussed in Appendix V.

Any combination of files using the ROS and LINK formats may be used in an account.

You will also be asked for the drive/directory where your file will be stored. Pressing <E> will cause the default drive to be used. If the default drive is C:\REV and you want this file in the ADMIN subdirectory instead, you would enter

C:\REV\ADMIN

DEF will now create the file and place two entries in the dictionary part of the file. These dictionary records are:

1.   @ID Contains parameters used for displaying the file's record keys, and also contains owner and description information about the file.

2.   **@CRT** A group field which determines the default fields to be displayed with R/LIST commands (discussed in Chapter 9).

To delete a file using the DEF program, enter **DELETE** at the CHANGE prompt (or Ctrl-D). You will be prompted to repeat the action to verify the deletion.

DEFINING THE DATA STRUCTURE: R/DESIGN BUD

One of the most important aspects of Revelation is that it is dictionary driven. This means that all words understood by Revelation are located in some dictionary. The VOC file is considered the Master Dictionary because it contains all the valid words that are recognized by TCL.

Each Revelation data *file* also has a dictionary that defines the data *fields* of that file. Generally, each data field has a dictionary record, created with BUD, containing 15 parameters which define the characteristics of that field.

Note that two or more dictionary records can refer to the same data field (to define different output display characteristics -- see example in Chapter 3). Also, when we are discussing the characteristics of a data field, we will sometimes refer to the dictionary record of that field, and at other times we will refer to the field itself.

As with DEF, there are two ways to invoke the dictionary-builder routine, BUD. Either choose item 2 from the R/DESIGN menu, or enter BUD at the TCL prompt. The screen shown in **Figure 6.3** will be displayed.

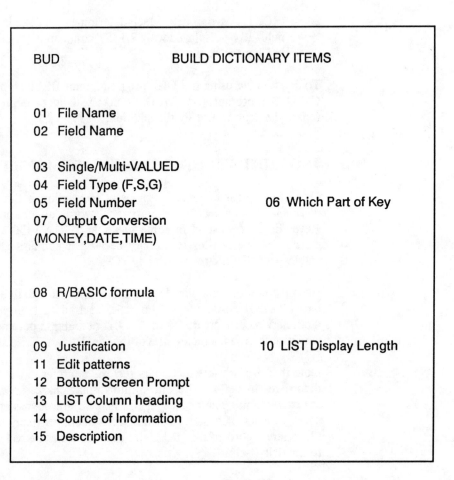

Fig. 6.3 BUD screen

This screen is used to create, view, and modify the parameters of a dictionary record. Note that a separate screen is used to define each data field, and the order in which you define the fields does not matter.

Remember that you can return to a previous prompt using the up arrow. Also, you will have a chance to change any of your entries at the CHANGE prompt -- which appears after you have answered all the prompts on the screen. The following is a description of the prompts on the BUD screen:

01 File Name

Enter the file name as it was entered in the DEF program. If a new file name is given, you will be asked if you wish to create it. A "Y" will automatically display the DEF screen, otherwise you will be prompted for another file name.

During each session of BUD, every screen will automatically display the file name that you enter on the first screen.

02 Field Name

Enter the name of the field you wish to define or modify. If you enter the name of a field which already exists, the parameters for that field will be displayed on the screen. Otherwise, you will be prompted for each of the other prompts on this screen.

Entering three question marks "???" will cause the screen to clear and display all the dictionary records already defined for this file.

A little preparation and care in naming the fields of your file can go a long way in database management. Do not hesitate to take advantage of Revelation's flexibility in naming fields. Try not to use cryptic names such as L.NM. Instead, a name such as LAST.NAME conveys much more information.

The characters "WINDOW" may not be used as the first seven characters in a field name because they have a special meaning to R/DESIGN. (See Customizing the Data Entry Screen in Chapter 7).

03 Single/Multi-valued

Indicate whether this is a single-valued or multi-valued field. Pressing <E> will default to a value of "S" for a single valued field.

Multi-valued fields use a format of "Mx.y" (e.g. M1.1, M1.2,). This format distinguishes between master and dependent fields of a set of associated multi-values.

If the field being defined is multi-valued but *not* part of an associated multi-value set, then just enter an "M" at this prompt and "M1.1" will be automatically entered.

The logic behind the use of the Mx.y format for *associated* multi-values is not easy to understand. Consider the following example of associated multi-values from the CUSTOMERS file.

05 INVOICE.NO	INVOICE.AMT	INVOICE.DATE
01> 1367	$325.25	10/01/86
02> 1375	$675.50	10/05/86
03> 1390	$ 56.00	10/20/86

INVOICE.NO, INVOICE.AMT, and INVOICE.DATE are multi-valued fields that make up an associated multi-value set. During data entry you want to ensure that the related values in the INVOICE.AMT and INVOICE.DATE fields correspond with the correct value in the INVOICE.NO field. INVOICE.NO is called the master field, and INVOICE.AMT and INVOICE.DATE are the dependent fields.

For now, we will provide an Mx.y convention to use with associated multi-values, and explain later in Chapter 7 how it is used by R/DESIGN.

For a master field, enter an "M" for M1.1. For all dependent fields, enter "M1.2". Thus, all non-associated multi-value fields, as well as all master fields of associated sets use the

M1.1 format; while all dependent multi-values, regardless of what associated set they are in, use 1.2. For the fields in the above example you would enter:

INVOICE.NO	**M1.1**
INVOICE.AMT	**M1.2**
INVOICE.DATE	**M1.2**

All you need to know for now is that the concept of associated multi-values, and the distinction between master and dependent fields, only applies to data entry screens; they do not effect output reports. How R/DESIGN uses these formats will be discussed during the design of data entry screens in Chapter 7.

04 Field Type (F,S,G)

There are three types of fields used in Revelation. **Data fields** store actual data which is input by the operator. These type of fields are given a type designation of "F".

Symbolic fields, designated by "S", do not store information in the data records; instead they use R/BASIC statements as formulas for calculating values for display. These formulas usually use one or more values from data fields. For example, you could create a symbolic field named TOTAL.COST to calculate the product of two data fields, UNIT.COST and TOTAL.UNITS. No data is stored in the data records for the TOTAL.COST field; instead this calculation is performed every time the symbolic field is displayed.

Finally, there are **group** fields which connect a group of dictionary records for display purposes. Suppose you want to list three fields from a data file, STREET, CITY, and STATE. You could specify the three field names or you could create a group field called ADDRESS which can be used to display STREET, CITY, and STATE every time the group field ADDRESS is used.

If you enter a "G" for a group field type, BUD immediately places you in prompt 13, "LIST Column Heading" and waits for you to enter the names of the fields to be included in the group. Thus the group field ADDRESS would have in prompt 13: STREET CITY STATE. The LIST command

:LIST CUSTOMERS ADDRESS

would then list the STREET, CITY, and STATE values for all customer records.

05 Field Number (FMC, field marker counter)

Remember that Revelation data records are stored as dynamic arrays. This prompt is just asking for which location in the array you want your "F" type field to be placed (group and symbolic fields do not get FMC numbers since they do not represent actual data stored in the records).

A sequential default field number is displayed at the bottom of the screen. Press <E> and the prompt will accept this number. If you bail out of the BUD screen before you get to the CHANGE prompt, (by typing "END" or Ctrl-E) the next time you come back to the screen, the next sequential field number will be one more than before -- even though you didn't save the previous dictionary record. Your file will work if you skip FMC numbers, but it will not be quite as efficient because there will be an unnecessary field marker in each record for the skipped FMC number.

You can also improve efficiency by using care in how you assign FMC numbers. Some data fields do not often have information stored in them. Your application will be more efficient if you assign these fields the highest FMC numbers in your dictionary so that they are located at the end of a record. This is because Revelation does not store the field markers for blank fields after the last actual data entered in a record. Thus a record with 5 fields may be stored as

MIKE■SMITH■■■TEXAS

If TEXAS were not entered, the record would just be stored as MIKE■SMITH.

A field number of 0 indicates that the field will be used as the record key. See next parameter.

06 Which Part of Key

Every data record must have a record key (or ID) that makes it unique from any other record. At least one of the data fields must serve as the key. This can be any "F" type field as long as this field will provide a unique value for each record.

You can also use multi-part keys. In this case, two or more fields are combined to create unique record keys. There can be as many parts to the key as you wish. This prompt on the BUD screen is used to determine if the current field is to be part of the multi-part key. If this field is not part of the key, or is a single part key, press <E> for a default value of 0.

If this field is part of a multi-part key, enter the part number in sequential order. For example, if you wanted the LAST.NAME field as the first part of the key and the FIRST.NAME as the second, you would enter:

FIELD NAME	FIELD NUMBER	KEY PART
LAST.NAME	0	1
FIRST.NAME	0	2

When referring to multi-part record keys, R/DESIGN separates the different parts with an asterisk (*). In the above example, a record key might be listed as:

GOLDSMITH*JASON

07 Output Conversion (MONEY, DATE, TIME)

Revelation can store numeric data, times, and dates with an internal format (see "Input and Output Conversions" section of Chapter 4). The output conversion determines how the internally stored information will be displayed.

All of the codes for determining output conversions are described in the OCONV internal function in the COMMAND REFERENCE. However, R/DESIGN provides you with an easy way to designate three different types of conversions without having to fully understand the OCONV function. These three conversions are:

a) for money/numeric **MD2,$** (Type MONEY at the prompt)
b) for date **D2-** (Type DATE at the prompt)
c) for time **MT** (Type TIME at the prompt)

Remember that if you use an input conversion on entered data, you will probably want to use an output conversion for displaying the data.

08 R/BASIC Formula

This entry is only used if the field type (prompt 4) is a symbolic field. Symbolic fields are used to perform calculations, extract data from other fields or files, or run R/BASIC programs. If the symbolic field is used to display calculated information, then the value it is to display must be assigned to the system variable @ANS. R/DESIGN and R/LIST use the value of this variable to display the result of calcuations of the symbolic field.

For example, if you wanted to display the total amount of a sales transaction -- the amount of money a customer owed based on the price per item and the number of items sold -- you could create a symbolic field called TOTAL with the formula:

@ANS = {ITEMS.SOLD} * {PRICE}

In this example, ITEMS.SOLD and PRICE are fields in the data file and are therefore enclosed in braces. Symbolic fields are discussed in detail later in the R/BASIC chapters.

This prompt on the BUD screen is multi-valued because each line of programming code is considered a separate value.

The TEXT editor can be invoked to facilitate writing the formula by entering the word "TEXT" at this prompt (see Chapter 14). If you find yourself accidentally in the Text Editor (as indicated by the status line at the bottom of the screen) press the shift key and the F2 function key simultaneously to exit.

09 Justification

There are four different ways to justify data for display when printing reports or displaying data on the screen.

Left Justify (L) - This will force all data to be displayed beginning at the left most point of the display space. For example, **Boston, MA_____**.

Right Justify (R) - This will force data to be displayed so that the right most character is aligned with the right most point of the display space. For example, **_____$535.00**.

Center Justify (C) - This will center the data in the display space. For example, **____Main Heading____**.

Text (T) - Text fields automatically invoke the full screen TEXT editor during data entry and allow entry of formatted text data. During display, all of the information in the field will be displayed, regardless of how many lines are required.

The justification determines how the information in a field is sorted. If the field is alphanumeric data, it should use a left justification, since we alphabetize from left to right. Similarly, numeric information should be right justified, as numeric value increases from right to left.

10 LIST Display Length

Enter the maximum number of characters that the LIST processor will display for this field (the LIST command is described in Chapter 9). This number does not limit how much data may be stored in this field; it just indicates the number of characters that will be displayed in output reports.

11 Edit Patterns

This prompt allows you to define different types of edit functions for data entered into this field in the data entry screen. These functions include pattern matching checks, range checks, and input conversions. (This topic is covered in detail in Chapter 7.) Press <E> to go to the next prompt.

If you entered an output conversion in prompt 07, an input conversion will be entered here automatically.

12 Bottom Screen Prompt

Enter the literal that you want displayed as the prompt for this field in a data entry screen. Pressing <E> defaults to the dictionary name.

When you create a data entry screen using R/DESIGN, you have the option of displaying a prompt for each data field at the lower left corner of the screen. If you choose this option, the bottom screen prompt will be taken from this entry in the dictionary.

13 LIST Column Heading

This information is used for column headings in reports. Pressing <E> defaults to the dictionary name.

For dictionary records which are group fields, enter the names of the fields to be included in the group, separated by a space. This will cause all of these fields to be displayed when the group field name is used in a LIST command.

14 Source of Information

This entry is optional and is used for documentation purposes only. It is not used as a display for any R/DESIGN reports, except when using the DOC routine of R/DESIGN to document your application.

If there are several dictionary records that will have the same Source of Information, simply enter the source in the first dictionary record, and each succeeding field will default to this entry.

15 Description

There are two purposes for this entry. The first is for documentation and therefore should include information about the dictionary record such as: how it is to be used, what action is taken by it, what are the possible responses, etc. Try to be as complete in your description as possible.

Additionally, this entry may be used to define the on-line help displayed when a person presses the F1 key at the prompt for this field in a data entry screen.

The description may be as long as you wish. The entry is multi-lined, and will display up to three lines of text on the BUD screen at one time. You can enter more than three lines and they will all be displayed when you press F1 for help in the data entry screen. You may enter "TEXT" to invoke the full screen editor while entering this description. To return to BUD, press Shift F2.

DISPLAYING DICTIONARY RECORDS

There are three easy ways of displaying the dictionary records of a file:

LIST command

Use the TCL command LIST in the following format:

:LIST DICT filename DICT.INFO

where filename is the name of the file whose dictionary you wish to display.   This will display a screen similar to the one shown in **Figure 6.4.**

```
PAGE 1                                          12:46:23  23 JULY 1986


VOC                    SM      TYPE    FMC HEADING CONV FORMULA JST LEN


%FIELD.COUNTER%                9
@ID                            F       0 CUSTOMERS                  L 10
CUST.NO                S       F       0 CUST.NO                    L 10
LAST.NAME              S       F       1 LAST.NAME                  L 15
FIRST.NAME             S       F       2 FIRST.NAME                 L 10
STREET                 M1.1    F       3 STREET                     L 25
CITY                   S       F       4 CITY                       L 15
ST                     S       F       5 ST                         L 2
PHONE                  S       F       6 PHONE                      L 12
INVOICE.NO             M1.1    F       7 INVOICE.NO                 L 10
@CRT                           G
INVOICE.AMOUNT         M1.1    S       INVOICE.AMOUN MD2 @ANS=XLATE R 10
                                                     ("INVOICE",
                                                     {INVOICE.NO}
                                                     3,"X")


12 RECORDS PROCESSED
```

Fig. 6.4   Example of :LIST DICT filename DICT.INFO

This command sorts the dictionary records by FMC number and displays the following fields: field name, single/multi-value, type, FMC, column heading, output conversion, symbolic formula, justification, and length. DICT.INFO is a group field name stored in the dictionary of the VOC file -- you can edit it with BUD just like any group field to change the parameters which it displays (enter VOC for File Name and DICT.INFO for Field Name).

LOOKDICT command

Use the TCL command LOOKDICT in the following format:

:LOOKDICT filename

This will display the screen shown in **Figure 6.5**

```
FMC   NAME              FORM, CONV     JUST FMC NAME FORM,  CONV  JUST

0     @ID                              L 10
0     CUST.NO                          L 10
1     LAST.NAME                        L 15
2     FIRST.NAME                       L 10
3     STREET                           L 25
4     CITY                             L 15
5     ST                               L 2
6     PHONE                            L 12
7     INVOICE.NO                       L 10
      @CRT             "G"
      INVOICE.AMOUNT YES    MD2        R 10




END OF LISTING.  PRESS <E> TO CONTINUE

```

Fig 6.5 LOOKDICT CUSTOMERS

This command sorts the dictionary by field type and FMC number and displays the following fields: FMC, field name, form (G = group type field, Yes = symbolic, and blank = "F" field), output conversion, justification, and display length. This command is useful for files with many dictionary records because it displays two columns of records on one screen.

BUD routine

If you enter "???" at the Field Name prompt in BUD, a list of dictionary records for the current file will be displayed on the screen in the same format of the LOOKDICT command.

DEFAULT DICTIONARY RECORDS

BUD allows you to create default dictionary records whose parameters may be used when defining new fields. This saves you from having to enter all the field parameters when you are defining a field similar to one of the default fields. Instead, you can start with the default dictionary record and simply make any necessary changes.

Default dictionary records are created with the following procedures:

1. Invoke the BUD routine.

2. Enter DEFAULT at the File Name prompt.

3. At the Field Name prompt, enter a name for this default record (this name cannot have a period included in it).

4. Enter responses to the BUD prompts as you normally would (BUD will skip over the Field Number, Source of Information, and Description prompts as these are not relevant to a default dictionary record).

Then, whenever you enter a field name in BUD whose prefix or suffix is the same as a default dictionary record, the parameters from that default record are automatically entered into your BUD screen. For example, if you set up a default dictionary record named COST and then use BUD to define fields named UNIT.COST or COST.AVG in your INVOICES file, the default parameters from the COST record will automatically be entered. You will then be prompted for the Field Number, Source of Information, and Description.

Default dictionary records can be edited and deleted just like other dictionary records and a list of the default records can be displayed by entering ??? at the BUD Field Name prompt (when DEFAULT is entered for File Name).

(**Advanced Topic**)   The parameters from default dictionary records are stored as data records in the RDES file, with their record IDs equal to the default field name appended to "DFLT*". In the example above, the key of the RDES record would be "DFLT*COST."

ADVANCED TOPICS

Creating a Dictionary Record Synonym

You may find that you want to have more than one dictionary record associated with a given data field. For example, you may want to display the field with one length for one report and with a different length for another report.

Let's assume you have one report which displays only the Customer name, address, and phone number. Another report displays these fields as well as invoice amount, previous balance, invoice date, and invoice number.

On this latter report there just isn't enough room to display all 35 characters of the CUST.NAME field that you defined for the LIST Display Length in prompt 10 of the BUD screen. Yet you don't want to change this value because on the first report you DO want all 35 characters printed. How can you manage to get what you want printed on each report?

Just create another dictionary record with a different name (e.g. CUST.NM) and give it a different LIST Display Length (e.g. 25) using the following procedure:

1)   Display the existing dictionary record (CUSTOMER) and at the CHANGE prompt enter 2 for Field Name.

2)   Enter the new Field Name, CUST.NM

3)   At the CHANGE prompt enter 10 to modify List
Display Length.

4)   Enter the new display length (in our example, 25).

5)   File the new record to disk. You will be prompted:

"DO YOU WISH TO DELETE THE ORIGINAL RECORD (Y/N)?"

An "N" will retain the original dictionary record along
with the new record, CUST.NM.

The same procedure may be used for duplicating a record from
one file to another. In this case, however, in steps 1 and 2
above, you will enter a new File Name after displaying the
original dictionary record.

CHAPTER SEVEN: ENTERING DATA

This chapter describes how to create a data entry screen using R/DESIGN.   In this chapter we describe the following R/DESIGN routines:

PGMR   names and determines the type of program.

SEL   selects the fields which will appear on the data entry screen.

SCR.GEN   generates the default data entry screen using the information from BUD and SEL.

SCR   customizes the data entry screen.

In learning how R/DESIGN works, you can easily get confused by some of the terminology such as the words "programs, screens, and prompts". First of all, we use the terms "data entry program" and "data entry screen" interchangeably. It also helps to remember how R/DESIGN creates a data entry screen. The R/DESIGN routines prompt you for information about your data entry screen and store your answers in the RDES file. Then when you enter the name of the data entry screen at the TCL prompt, R/DESIGN displays your data entry screen by running the ENTER program using your stored parameters as inputs.

The PGMR, SEL, and SCR routines use screens to prompt you for information. These screens are themselves data entry screens just like the one you are designing. When we refer to screens and prompts, sometimes we will be referring to these R/DESIGN screens and prompts, other times we will be referring to your application's data entry screen and prompts. The terms "data entry screen" and "data entry prompt" refer to your application screen, while terms like "SEL screen" or "SCR prompt" refer to the screens of the R/DESIGN routines.

If you want to interrupt R/DESIGN at any point, just enter END at any prompt and this should take you back to the TCL prompt (or the R/DESIGN menu). If this doesn't work, press Ctrl Break to invoke the debugger. Then enter END at the (!) prompt (the debugger prompt).

CREATING A DATA ENTRY PROGRAM: R/DESIGN PGMR

There are two ways to invoke PGMR:

   1) Enter selection (3) at the R/DESIGN MAIN MENU
   2) Enter PGMR at the TCL prompt.

The screen shown in **Figure 7.1** will then be displayed.

```
PGMR                                    PROGRAM SET-UP

01        Program Name
02        Type of program
03        Short Title for Heading
04        Language Used
05        Major File Used
06        Additional Files Read
07        Additional Files Written
08        In Screen Prompting
09        Description
```

Fig. 7.1 PGMR screen

The following is a description of the PGMR prompts.

01 Program Name

Enter the program name. It can be up to 50 alphanumeric characters; but must begin with an alphabetic character and may not contain any spaces.

02 Type of Program

Enter the program type. The valid types are:

ENTRY generates a data entry screen used for entering data into or updating a data file.

REPORT generates a report program which will print information from a data file.

Press <E> to enter the default value, "ENTRY".
REPORT programs will be covered in Chapter 9.

03 Short Title for Heading

Enter the title you want displayed on your data
entry screen. An input here is mandatory and
there is no default value.

04 Language Used

Enter the language Revelation will use to run this
program. Valid languages are:

INTERPRETED: Most entry programs will be
interpreted. This means that the answers you give
to the R/DESIGN prompts are stored as
parameters in a record in the RDES file. These
parameters are then used by R/DESIGN's
ENTER program to display the data entry screen
and to prompt for each field. (See Appendix VII
for a description of the RDES file.)

BASIC: Report programs are written in
R/BASIC (see Chapter 9).

(You can generate an R/BASIC data entry screen
-- this is discussed in Advanced Topics.)

Enter INTERPRETED, which is the default
value.

05 Major File Used

Enter the name of the data file you created with
BUD into which this program will enter data.

06 Additional Files Read

You will probably never use this field. Skip this
prompt by pressing <E>. Whenever your
R/DESIGN data entry screen reads or writes to
another file (e.g. a cross reference or a XLATE
function), it knows how to interact with that file
and does not need that file listed here.

ADVANCED TOPIC: If you enter a file name here and then generate R/BASIC program code, an OPEN statement will be placed in the code for this file. That is the only use for this prompt.

07 Additional Files Written
Same as 06 above.

08 In Screen Prompting
Your data entry screen will prompt for each data field that appears on the screen. Entering Y will just use the names of the fields as they appear on the screen as prompts. Entering N will cause a prompt to appear at the lower left corner of the data entry screen using the "Bottom Screen Prompt" entry in BUD. Default is N.

09 Description
Enter the description of this program. Your answer will be used by R/DESIGN when it generates application documentation for you. Your answer is multi-lined and can contain 8 lines of text.

SELECTING FIELDS FOR DATA ENTRY: R/DESIGN SEL

SEL is used to select which data fields will appear on your data entry screen. SEL can be invoked in two ways:

1) Entering selection (4) at the R/DESIGN MAIN MENU.
2) Entering SEL at the TCL prompt.

After SEL is invoked you will be prompted for the name of your data entry screen (alternatively, the program name can be included with the SEL command e.g. **:SEL CUSTOMERS.ENTRY**). If you have already used SEL with this program before, you will be asked if you want to overwrite your last selection. A No answer will take you back to the TCL prompt or the R/DESIGN menu.

A Yes wipes out the RDES parameters you previously built and starts the data entry screen all over. If you've done a lot of work creating a data entry screen and want to add some fields, use SCR to add them and you won't have to start all over.

SEL operates differently, depending on whether you are creating an entry or report program. In this chapter we are only discussing the procedures for an entry program.

SEL will display a screen similar to the example shown in **Figure 7.2**. The top half of the screen displays the data fields from your file. Notice the reference numbers to the left of the field names; these are used for selecting fields on this screen and do not correspond to the FMC numbers of BUD.

```
SEL      CUST.ENTRY (CUST.ENTRY) FILE = CUSTOMERS  PAGE 1



         01>*0 CUST.NO
         02>   NAME
         03>   COMPANY
         04>   ADDRESS






         FIELD YOU  WANT TO APPEAR ON YOUR SCREEN? (1)
           Always specify record key first
              (prompts preceded by "*")
```

Fig. 7.2 SEL screen

Enter the fields you want to display on your data entry screen using the following rules:

1.   Select a field by entering its reference number or by typing its name. The fields you select will be displayed on the screen.

2.   Enter them in the order in which you want them to appear on the screen.

3.   All the fields in a set of associated multi-values must be selected together, starting with the master field. (See Chapters 4 and 6 on associated multi-values.) If you select a dependent field which does not follow either a master field or another dependent field, you will get an error message when you try to save the selected fields at the end of the SEL process.

     Multi-values were assigned a multi-value format in BUD of Mx.y (e.g. M1.1, M1.2, M2.3, etc). SEL recognizes master fields because they have a multi-value format of Mx.1. Any field with a "y" value other than 1 is considered a dependent multi-value.

     Note that R/DESIGN makes no use of the "x"part of the multi-value format. Instead, it uses the y value and the order in which they are selected to determine which multi-values are associated. For example, the following could be selected as associated multi-values:

     INVOICE.NO   M1.1
     INVOICE.AMT M3.3
     INVOICE.DATE M5.6

     However, you can use the "x" part of the format for your own documentation to distinguish between associated sets.

4. Key fields must be entered first (the fields used as the record ID). If the key consists of more than one field, they must be entered in order (i.e. part 1, part 2, etc; see the "Record ID" section in Chapter 4). The field(s) which make up the key are marked by an asterisk.

5. If there are more than 39 fields in the data file, they will not all be displayed on the screen. You can view the rest of them by scrolling the display by entering "PG" followed by a page number (e.g. "PG2" would display the second page of fields).

6. When you are finished selecting fields, enter <E> at the selection prompt and you should see a screen something like **Figure 7.3**.

7. You will be prompted for changes. Enter the selection number of any item you wish to change, otherwise enter <E> or N for no changes. All of your entries will be saved and you will be returned to the TCL prompt or the R/DESIGN menu.

```
SEL     CUST.ENTRY (CUST.ENTRY)  FILE = CUSTOMERS  PAGE 1


        01>*0 CUST.NO
        02>   NAME
        03>   COMPANY
        04>   ADDRESS



01>CUST.NO  02> NAME   03> COMPANY  04> ADDRESS


        CHANGE (Y/N)
```

Fig. 7.3 Filled in SCR screen

THE DEFAULT DATA ENTRY SCREEN: R/DESIGN SCR.GEN

SCR.GEN is used for generating R/DESIGN's default data entry screen. It takes the parameters from BUD and SEL and combines them with a standard screen format to produce your data entry screen. For some applications this is all you will need; for others you will use SCR to add additional features to your data entry screen.

SCR.GEN can be invoked in two ways:

    1) Entering selection (5) at the R/DESIGN MAIN MENU

    2) Entering SCR.GEN at the TCL prompt

You are prompted for the program name (unless it was included with the SCR.GEN command) and a "mask" to be used in your data entry screen. A mask is a character displayed as a marker on your screen where data entries will go. Either ignore this prompt or enter a mask character (e.g. the underline character).

SCR.GEN uses the BUD parameters for the fields selected with SEL, and creates the data entry screen. SCR.GEN will then return you to either the TCL prompt or the R/DESIGN menu. You can now use your data entry screen by just entering its name at the TCL prompt.

An example of a data entry screen generated by SCR.GEN is shown in **Figure 7.4**. The fields to be input by the operator are listed down the left side. Note that the TAX.RATE field is shown to the right of the TAX.CODE field. This is because it is a symbolic field which was SELected immediately after TAX.CODE. When you enter a value for TAX.CODE the calculated value for TAX.RATE will be displayed.

When there are more that nineteen fields to be entered, the fields are displayed in two columns and any symbolic fields are shown immediately below and to the right of their related data entry field. If you consecutively selected two symbolic fields, the screen will try to display them in the same space and you will need to modify the screen using SCR.

```
  CUST.ENTRY    CUST.ENTRY                    (I-1)



  01   CUST.NO
  02   NAME
  03   ADDRESS
  04   PHONE
  05   TAX.CODE           TAX.RATE




  CUST.NO _____
```

Fig. 7.4 Data entry screen

At the bottom of the screen is the prompt for the first field, CUST.NO. As you are prompted for each input field, your answers will be displayed to the right of the field name. If an input field is multi-valued, the program will keep prompting you for more values until you type <E> or END. If you want to enter more values than can fit on one line, you will need to modify the data entry screen with SCR. Entering data into a data entry screen is covered in detail later in this chapter.

If you change some of the field parameters in BUD and want to incorporate these changes in your data entry screen, **do not** try to use SCR.GEN again! You will not be allowed to do this! Instead, use SCR to make these modifications in your data entry screen. If, however, you modify the formulae of a symbolic field using BUD, these changes will be reflected automatically in your screen. Unlike all the other parameters in your data entry screen which are stored in the file, the formulae for symbolic fields are retrieved from the dictionary of the data file during the data entry process of R/DESIGN.

ADVANCED TOPIC: SCR.GEN creates a VOC entry with the name of the data entry screen. This allows you to run the data entry screen from TCL by just entering the name of the screen.

CUSTOMIZING THE DATA ENTRY SCREEN: R/DESIGN SCR

SCR is used to customize a standard data entry screen which was generated with SCR.GEN. Though SCR.GEN should be sufficient for the requirements of many applications, the following are some of the reasons you might want to customize your data entry screen:

a) adding additional field prompts,
b) adding additional screen text,
c) repositioning screen information,
d) modifying display lengths and input pattern
    checks,

e) specifying default values,
f) referencing other data base files for data
   verification,
g) declaring a field to be required, optional, or
   protected,
h) defining cross-referenced fields.

SCR Screens

SCR uses three screens. The first, called the **SCR** screen, is the actual data entry screen generated from the SCR.GEN program, with a command line added to the bottom. From this screen you can add, delete, or insert data entry prompts; arrange the layout of the screen; or select a data entry prompt whose parameters you wish to edit.

The second screen, called the **PROMPT EDITOR**, displays and edits the 25 parameters which make up a data entry prompt.

The third screen, called the **INVERT PARAMETER ENTRY**, is used for creating cross-references and is discussed in Chapter 8.

Invoking SCR

SCR can be invoked in two ways:

1) Enter item 6 at the R/DESIGN Main Menu
2) Type SCR at the TCL colon prompt.

You will be prompted for the name of the program you wish to customize and then the SCR screen will be displayed.

The SCR Screen

Figure 7.5 shows an example of an SCR screen. There are four kinds of items on this screen which you can edit:

1. **Data entry prompts.** These are the prompts for the data fields whose values will be entered by the operator when they run the data entry program. The parameters for these prompts are edited with the prompt editor screen. Notice that each data entry prompt in **Figure 7.5** is preceded by a number. This is the reference number used by the operator during actual data entry when referring to the fields at the CHANGE prompt.

2. **Windows.** Each data entry prompt for a multi-valued field is preceded by a window which controls how the multiple values will be displayed. Although you cannot see this item on the SCR screen, it is edited with the prompt editor just like data entry prompts. This item controls how many multiple values can be entered, how they will be displayed, and also stores the "WHICH VALUE" prompt which appears when editing a multi-valued data entry.

3. **CHANGE prompt.** This is the prompt which the operator sees after answering all of the prompts on the data entry screen. The CHANGE prompt is also edited with the prompt editor by entering "CHANGE" at the SCR command line.

4. **Text.** This is any text which you want to appear on your data entry screen. This is inserted or edited with the "automatic prompting sequence" discussed later.

Use the arrow keys to select an item for editing. The currently selected item is highlighted and a "<" is displayed to the right of the item (pressing <E> will also move the selection pointer down to the next item). Each item has its own reference number which is displayed at the "MV (position)" at the bottom of the screen when the item is selected. (This includes not only the data field prompts, but windows and text.) Also, the name of the selected item is shown in the window labeled "EDITING:" at the bottom of the screen.

```
┌──────────────────────────────────────────────────────────────┐
│                                                                │
│   CUSTOMERS.ENTRY                    CUSTOMER DATA ENTRY        │
│                                                                │
│                                                                │
│   01     CUST.ID    <.....                                     │
│   02     NAME        ............................              │
│   03     COMPANY     ........................                  │
│   04     ADDRESS    01> ...................                    │
│   05     CITY        ...................                       │
│   06     STATE      ..                                         │
│   07     PHONE       ............                              │
│   08     CONTACT     ..........                                │
│                                                                │
│                                                                │
│            EDITING:  CUST.ID        MV(POSITION):2             │
│                                                                │
│   A,E,I,D(EL),R(E-NBR),S(HIFT),F,L,^,G,W,TOP,END,2N,P ?        │
│                                                                │
│                                                                │
└──────────────────────────────────────────────────────────────┘
```

Fig. 7.5 SCR screen

Three kinds of functions are performed from the SCR screen:

1) **Field and Text Maintenance** -- Items can be changed, inserted, or deleted.

2) **Global Changes and Visual Aids** -- Commands may be issued that affect the entire screen. Additionally, visual guidelines and cursor positioning are available to aid in the screen design.

3) **Update Control** -- You may file the changes, start over, delete the screen, or exit from SCR.

Command Line Options

The following is a discussion of the commands available from this screen (note that three of the commands, CHANGE, DELETE, and MASK do not show up on the command line):

Reference Pointer Commands

\<E\>   Advances the reference pointer to the next item.

^   Use the arrow keys to move the reference pointer up or down. (Shift 6, ^, does not work.)

N   Advances the reference pointer N items, where N is some integer. (The "2N" on the command line represents this option.) If N is negative, the reference pointer is backed up N items.

Field and Literal Text Maintenance Commands

A   ADDs an item to the end of the existing items on the screen. This command also places visual guidelines on the screen and invokes the automatic prompting sequence for building a screen item. This prompting sequence is explained below.

E   EDITs the item which is selected with the reference pointer and enters the automatic prompting sequence.

I   INSERTs a new item before the item currently selected and enters the automatic prompting sequence.

D   DELETEs the item currently selected and redisplays the screen. If you bail out of the automatic prompting sequence in the middle of inserting or adding an entry by pressing the Up arrow, be sure to delete the incomplete item.

P   The Prompt Editor Screen will be displayed for the selected item entry. This screen is used to customize the parameters for the data entry item. (See Prompt Editor Screen below.)

CHANGE Entering the word "CHANGE" will invoke the Prompt Editor Screen and display the parameters for the CHANGE prompt. The CHANGE prompt is automatically created for data entry screens generated by SCR.GEN. By changing the parameters for this prompt you can control what happens before and after a record is filed to disk. See the discussion of the Prompt Editor Screen below.

Global Changes and Visual Aids

?   Displays the help screen for the command line. Displays a quick explanation of the available commands. (Alternatively, you may press "F1".)

R   RENUMBERs the screen prompts. This command is used after inserting or deleting field prompts. The format for the R command is:

Rs,i

where: s = starting prompt number, and
        i = amount to increase or decrease
        (if not entered, 1 is assumed).

Example: R5   Increase by 1 all screen
                      prompt numbers from 5 on.
              R7,-2   Decrease by 2 all screen
                      prompt numbers from 7 on.

Screen prompt numbers must be sequential. For example, in **Figure 7.5**, if 08 CONTACT had been 09 CONTACT instead, an operator entering "9" at the CHANGE prompt during data entry in order to modify the CONTACT field, would get an error message "OUT OF RANGE". You should go back to SCR and enter R9,-1:

S   SHIFTs blocks of screen prompts and text up or down on the screen. This command redisplays the screen with the items positioned as specified. The format for the S command is:

Sf,i,l

where   f = the reference number (MV position) of the first screen item to be shifted,
i = number of rows to increase or decrease,
l = last screen item to be shifted.

Both i and l are optional; if left off, 1 is assumed.

Examples: S7,-2,10 Decrease screen items numbered from 7 to 10 by 2 rows.
S4   Increase all screen items starting with 4 by 1 row.

L   LOOK will redisplay the screen. This command is often used to refresh the screen after additions and insertions. It also removes the guidelines.

G   visual GUIDELINES are ruler lines printed down the center and across the bottom of the screen. The guidelines help you place an item on the screen. (Guidelines are automatically placed with the Add command.)

W   WHERE will temporarily display an asterisk (*) at the indicated row and column. This command is useful in pinpointing a position on the screen.

The format for the W command is:

Wc,r

where c = column, r = row.

Example: W13,6 Flashes an "*" at the 13th column and 6th row.

MASK   MASK will globally change or remove the input
masks for every data entry item. For example, you could
change all input masks from an underline character (_)
to a period (.). (An input mask is the character which is
displayed during data entry to mark the placement of
data in a field prompt. For example, 06 STATE ___.)

Update Control

F   FILEs the screen parameters to a record in the RDES
file, saving the current changes.

TOP   TOP or Ctrl-T will clear the screen without saving the
modifications from the current session of SCR. You will
be prompted for another R/DESIGN program name.
To avoid accidents, you will be prompted to enter TOP
twice.

END   END will clear the screen without saving the
modifications from the current session of SCR. Control
passes back to the TCL prompt or the R/DESIGN Main
Menu. To avoid accidents, you will be prompted to
enter END twice.

DELETE Deletes this data entry screen by deleting the
appropriate records from the RDES and VOC files. To
avoid accidents, you will be prompted to enter DELETE
again.

Automatic Prompting Sequence

Whenever you enter the A(dd), I(nsert), or E(edit)
commands, you invoke the automatic prompting sequence.
This is a series of prompts which define an item on the screen
(such as the dictionary name, the prompt location, and prompt
literal).

There are four responses you may enter to any prompt in this sequence, in addition to entering data.

1) Pressing <E> will leave the information unchanged.
2) "BLANK" will clear the field.
3) "GOOD" will skip the remaining prompts and return you to the command line. This saves you from having to go through the entire prompting sequence when only making modifications to one or two of them.
4) G(uidelines) will display the guidelines.

(If you type GOOD or BLANK, remember to clear out the rest of the line with the F8 key.)

The first three prompts of the automatic prompting sequence are:

1) Screen Literal,
2) Column, Row Location of Literal
3) Dictionary Name.

If no dictionary name is entered then you are returned to the SCR command line. Otherwise, you are prompted for three additional pieces of information:

4) Response Column Number,
5) Response Row Number, and
6) Format.

These prompts are described as follows:

Screen Literal
Enter the literal information as it is to appear on the screen. Lower case letters are acceptable. If the literal is for a data entry prompt, remember to use a reference number in the literal, such as "04 CITY".

Column, Row Location of Literal

Enter the coordinates in the format (column,row) where the literal is to appear on the screen. Columns are numbered from 0 on the left to 79 on the right. Rows are numbered from 0 at the top of the screen to 23 on the bottom.

Dictionary Name

If the item is a data entry prompt, enter the dictionary name of the data field. This will pass information from the dictionary record of the field to SCR. Pressing <E> will return you to the SCR command line.

If the dictionary item you enter does not yet exist, you will be asked if you want to enter BUD. This gives you the opportunity to set up the initial parameters for this field. After you file the dictionary item in BUD you must press Ctrl-E or type END to exit BUD and return to the SCR command line.

A WINDOW item must precede each data entry prompt for a multi-valued field. The WINDOW is created by pressing <E> in response to the "Screen Literal" and "Column, Row..." prompts, and then entering the dictionary name of "WINDOW.n" where "n" is the sequential number of this particular window. A set of associated multi-value prompts will have only one window. SCR.GEN automatically assigns sequential window numbers to each multi-value field or associated multi-value set it encounters during the screen generating process.

Response Column Number

Enter the column where the entered data is to appear during the data entry process.

Response Row Number

Enter the row where the entered data is to appear.

Format

Enter the format for how the data is to be displayed on the screen:

J#L

where J = the justification, and
L = the display length.

Example: L#15 will left justify data in a 15
character wide display.

These six prompts of the automatic prompting sequence determine how items will be displayed on the screen. For data entry prompts, the CHANGE prompt, and multi-value windows, there are additional parameters which can be edited using the Prompt Editor Screen described below.

The Prompt Editor Screen

The Prompt Editor Screen displays 25 pieces of information on each data entry prompt. This information comes from the dictionary record which was created with BUD, from the six prompts in the Automatic Prompting Sequence, or from information entered during a previous foray into the Prompt Editor Screen.

The Prompt Editor Screen can be invoked in two ways:

1.   After completing the automatic prompting sequence, you will be prompted: "Press Enter to Edit Prompt or (G)ood". Pressing a "G", will return you to the SCR command line. Pressing <E> will invoke the Prompt Editor Screen and display existing information about the selected item.

2.   You may enter the **P**(prompt) command from the SCR command line to directly invoke the Prompt Editor for the currently selected item, bypassing the six prompts of the Automatic Prompting Sequence (these are included in the Prompt Editor Screen anyway). The Prompt Editor can not be invoked from screen literals.

```
SCR              PROMPT EDITOR


   Program Name              Key Part
   Field Name                Field Number
03 Size of Window         21 Parameter 1
04 Text Depth             22 Parameter 2
05 Display at Row         23 Multi-value Master Flag
06 Display at Column      24 Key Field Flag
07 Display Format         25 Make Cross Reference
08 Output Conversion      26 Display Cross Reference
09 Multi-value Window
   R/BASIC formula
11 Bottom Prompt
12 Visual Mask         13 Entry Type (R,O,P,F,FP)
14 Edit Patterns
15 Null Default
16 Verifile           17 Not Verifile


18 Description

CHANGE?
```

Fig. 7.6 Prompt Editor Screen

Figure 7.6 is a sample Prompt Editor screen. The initial values for many of these parameters are taken from the dictionary records of the data fields during the SCR.GEN routine. It should also be noted that modifications made to the Prompt Editor only affect the R/DESIGN screen; they do not affect the dictionary record of the data file.

Some of the parameters displayed on this screen do not have reference numbers because they are for viewing only (they can only be modified by changing the dictionary record using BUD). The following is a description of the Prompt Editor parameters:

Program Name

The R/DESIGN program name that is being modified. This field cannot be changed.

Field Name

The dictionary item that is being modified is displayed. This field cannot be changed.

03 Size of Window

(Used only with data entry prompts for multi-valued fields). Enter the size of the multi-value window. The window size can only be changed if you are editing a WINDOW prompt. The corresponding multi-value data entry prompt will display the same window size, but you can't change it from there. The format for this entry is:

C,V

where C = the number of columns to be used, and   V = the number of total values to display.

Example: **4,8** would display 8 values at a time in 4 columns. This would require 2 rows:

01>	02>	03>	04>
05>	06>	07>	08>

SCR automatically calculates the correct spacing on each row depending on the display length entered in the Format parameter.

This entry does NOT affect how many total values you may enter, only the number of values that are displayed at one time.

If you change a WINDOW prompt's window size, the corresponding multi-value prompt(s) will not immediately reflect this change. You must first file the screen. When you invoke SCR again, you will then detect the changes made to the window size.

04 Text Depth

This prompt serves two purposes. For multi-valued fields, the depth limits the number of values that can be entered. For example, assume the operator is entering credit references into a mortgage loan data entry screen and that the loan information will be printed onto a form which only has room for three credit references. You could use Text Depth to limit the operator to three credit reference inputs.

For single-valued fields, a Text Depth entry greater than 1 makes this a multi-lined prompt and determines how many lines of the entered data will be displayed. You must adjust any the prompts displayed below this to allow room for the multi-lined entry. Finally, for text fields (Display Format = "T"), the Text Depth defines the number of lines displayed in the Text Window.

05 Display at Row

Enter the row where the data being entered is to appear. (This is different from the Column, Row Location of the Literal.)

06 Display at Column

Enter the column where the data being entered is to appear.

07 Display Format

Enter the display format for the entered data using:

J#L

where J = the justification, and
L = the display length.

Example: L#15 will left justify data in a 15 character wide display.

A justification of "T" will call the Text Editor during the data entry process (T will only be accepted if Text Depth is greater than 1).

08 Output Conversion

Enter an output conversion if it is appropriate for this prompt (see Chapter 4 for a discussion of input/output conversions). The conversion entered here just controls how the entered data will be displayed on the data entry screen; the Output Conversion defined in BUD determines how the data will be displayed on reports.

If an output conversion was specified for this field in BUD, it would be transferred to this SCR prompt (unless the BUD prompt was changed after this prompt was created in SCR).

All of the codes for determining output conversions are described for the OCONV internal function in the COMMAND REFERENCE.

09 Multi-value Window

Prompts for multi-valued data fields must have the number of their corresponding window entered in this parameter. R/DESIGN uses this number for keeping track of sets of associated multi-values. All the multi-values of a set use the same window and should have the same window number assigned.

For window prompts, this is the window number (WINDOW.n) and is already filled in.

R/BASIC Formula

Used with symbolic fields only. This field can only be changed by modifying the dictionary record using BUD.

11 Bottom Prompt

Enter the message that is to be displayed during data entry if bottom screen prompting is used (If you entered "N" at prompt 08 in PGMR, "In Screen Prompting"). If a default value is used for this field, it will be displayed along with the prompt literal you enter here.

12 Visual Mask

Enter a visual pattern that will help the user understand the format in which the data is to be entered. For example, suppose the data field calls for a date and you require a certain format. The visual mask could be MM-DD-YY. Or you could simply use underlines or periods. (The SCR.GEN process may already have placed a visual mask in all the prompts.)

13 Entry Type (R,O,P,F,FP)

R = required entry
O = optional entry
P = protected field

F = filled in by the NULL.DFLT value
FP= filled in by the NULL.DFLT value and
      protected.

Required fields will not accept an <E>, and
therefore cannot be used with the NULL.DFLT
feature.

Protected fields will not allow editing to be
performed.

"F" entry types are automatically filled in by the
NULL.DFLT field (parameter 15) and may be
edited from the CHANGE prompt. "FP" types
are filled in by the NULL.DFLT but may not be
edited.

14 Edit Patterns

This allows you to perform several edit functions
when data is entered at this data entry prompt.
The edit patterns can be pattern matches, range
checks, or input conversions. As this is a multi-
value prompt, you may enter more than one edit
pattern. Additionally, a symbolic field or
R/BASIC routine may be called to perform the
edit pattern functions; see Advanced Topics at the
end of this chapter.

A complete descriptions of Edit Patterns are given
in the "EDIT PATTERN" section later in this
chapter.

15 Null Default

Enter the value that will be entered if the
operator presses <E> at the data entry prompt.

The value of the null default will be added to the
bottom screen prompt. For example, a null
default of "St. Louis" for a CITY prompt results
in the following bottom screen prompt:

    ENTER CITY (DEFAULT=ST.LOUIS)

A prompt with a null default must not be a required entry (required entries will not allow the operator to press <E> at the data entry prompt). Also, the null default will not work with a text field.

There are eight different entries allowed in the NULL.DFLT prompt:

1. Literal text will be entered for the field value just as you enter it in this parameter.

2. **"QUOTE"** will act just as the quotation mark (") does during any data entry; it enters the same value for this field as was entered in the previous record.

3. **%D%** will default to the current system date. The display format will be whatever was entered in the Output Conversion parameter.

4. **%T%** will default to the current system time. The display format will be whatever was entered in the Output Conversion parameter.

5. **%TD%** will default to the current system time and date.

6. **%S%** will establish a sequential counter for this field. Pressing <E> will default to the next sequential number. A dictionary record is automatically created to maintain this counter. The operator can reset the counter by entering at the data entry prompt a **"="** followed by the reset number (e.g. **"=225"** would reset the counter to 225).

7. **{field name}** will use the value of the field as the null default. If the field is a symbolic field, then the value assigned to the variable "@ANS" in the symbolic field's formula will be the null default.

8. **[program name]** will call this cataloged R/BASIC program. The value assigned to the variable "@ANS" in the R/BASIC program will be the null default. Writing and cataloging programs will be discussed later in this book.

16 Verifile

Enter the name of the file that you want checked to verify that the data entered at this prompt is a record key in that file.

For example, if you were entering data into an INVOICES file and one of the entries was for the customer number, you could verify that the entered data was a valid customer number by checking it against the record keys of the CUSTOMERS file.

17 Not Verifile

Enter the name of the file that you want checked to verify that the entered data is NOT a record key in that file. This feature is useful for validating the uniqueness of data.

18 Description

Enter a description, explanation, or helpful information about this data entry prompt. Whatever you enter here will be displayed when the user presses the F1 key for help. This field is multi-lined and the Text Editor can be invoked for help in entering the description by entering TEXT. Press Shift F2 to exit the TEXT editor.

Key Part

The key part number can only be changed in the dictionary record for this prompt by using BUD.

Field Number

Field numbers can only be changed in the dictionary record by using BUD.

21 Parameter 1

Enter a value to limit the number of characters accepted by this data prompt during input.

The CHANGE prompt uses this parameter differently. It uses Parameter 1 to store the name of the next screen to be executed. This called screen must be a data entry screen created with R/DESIGN. See Linking Screens later in this chapter.

22 Parameter 2

Enter the name of the dictionary record or cataloged R/BASIC program to be called as a "wrap up" after data has been entered. Dictionary records must be enclosed in braces { } and R/BASIC programs in brackets [ ].

This parameter works as a wrap-up for data entry prompts as well as for the CHANGE prompt. In the case of the data entry prompt, the wrap-up procedure is called only if new data is entered or if the data has been modified. The CHANGE prompt wrap-up works only if the record is a new record or if a record has been modified.

There is a way to force the wrap-up procedures to execute even if no data has been entered and no modifications have occurred. With data prompts, append a colon (:) to the wrap-up call in Parameter 2, such as: {DATA.CHECK}: or

[DATA.CHECK]:. This will force the routine to
be called whenever the field is displayed. The
wrap-up for the prompt will be called even during
the initial display of the field when a record has
been retrieved and control has not yet passed to
the CHANGE prompt.

The CHANGE prompt has a similar procedure.
Appending a plus sign (+) to the wrap-up call in
Parameter 2, such as {DATA.CHECK}+ will force
the wrap-up routine to be called after pressing
<E> at the CHANGE prompt, even if there have
been no modifications to the record.

23 Multi-value Master Flag

Enter a "1" if this prompt is either a non-
associated multi-value field or the master of a set
of associated multi-values.

Enter a "0" if this prompt is either a dependent
associated multi-value or a single value.

24 Key Field Flag

This parameter indicates if this prompt is part of
the key to the file. If a prompt **is** part of the key
then enter "K". If a prompt is the **last** part of the
key then enter "KR". Thus, there could be
several prompts with a Key Field Flag of "K", but
only one prompt can have a "KR" flag.

A one-part key will have "KR" entered for this
parameter.

25 Make Cross Reference

Enter "Y" if the data element is to be indexed or
cross-referenced. A detailed discussion on cross-
references can be found in Chapter 8.

If a "Y" is entered for this parameter, then after
you have completed the Prompt Editor Screen

you will be asked if you wish to see the cross-reference parameter screen. The cross-reference parameter screen is where you will define the cross-reference.

26 Display Cross Reference (File,Field)

This parameter allows you to access and display a cross-reference list from this data entry prompt. Enter the file name and field name that was originally cross-referenced, separating them with a comma (see Chapter 8).

When you are finished entering data for the Prompt Editor Screen, press <E> at the CHANGE prompt and you will be returned to the Command Line of the main SCR screen. When you are done customizing the screen and are ready to file the record to the RDES file, enter the "F" command (don't forget this step or your changes will not be saved!).

You will then see a message about setting video characteristics. This message refers to the video characteristics of the data entry screen you just saved.

ADVANCED TOPIC: *To change the video characteristics of the screen (e.g. color, blinking, reverse video), edit the VOC record for the screen program and add the TCL command SET-COLOR with the desired parameters (see COMMAND REFERENCE and Appendix VI). This command should precede the ENTER command in the VOC record.*

All of the parameters for your data entry screen are now stored as a record in the RDES file. Typing the program's name from the TCL prompt will invoke the program and display your customized data entry screen.

ADVANCED TOPIC: *You can invoke the program from TCL because SCR.GEN created a VOC record with the program's name. This VOC record contains the TCL command "ENTER {program name}" which invokes the R/DESIGN Interpreter.*

You should now have a pretty good idea of the power of R/DESIGN to customize data entry screens. We have discussed creating and modifying data entry screens, customizing data output, performing validity checks on input data, and referencing other data files for verification.

You are now ready to enter data and discover how the data entry screen interacts with the user based on the parameters specified in SCR.

ENTERING AND EDITING DATA WITH A DATA ENTRY SCREEN

You can run your data entry screen by entering its name at the TCL prompt; for example:

:CUST.ENTRY

will display the data entry screen named CUST.ENTRY. You will be prompted for all of the fields on the screen, starting with the record ID. After you have answered all the prompts, the CHANGE prompt will be displayed. Enter the number of any prompt whose entry you wish to change or press <E> to file the record to disk. After filing the record to disk, a blank data entry screen will be displayed ready for the next record to be entered. When you are finished entering records, enter END or Ctrl E from the record ID prompt. **Figure 7.7** is an example of a filled in data entry screen.

To edit an existing record, display the data entry screen and enter the ID of the record you wish to edit. That record's data will be displayed on the screen and you will be taken directly to the CHANGE prompt. A record can also be edited with the text or line editor (discussed in Chapter 14).

```
┌────────────────────────────────────────────────────────┐
│                                                        │
│   OUT.INV              OUTSTANDING.INVOICES      (I-1)  │
│                                                        │
│                                                        │
│                                                        │
│   01      CUST.NO      00476                           │
│   02      NAME         JOHNSON ELECTRIC                │
│                                                        │
│   03      INV.NO       01> 2865       02> 2873         │
│   04      INV.AMT      01> $1,800.0002> $1,550.00      │
│                                                        │
│   TOTAL.AMT    $3,350.00                               │
│                                                        │
│                                                        │
│                                                        │
│   CHANGE? _____                                        │
│                                                        │
└────────────────────────────────────────────────────────┘
```

Fig. 7.7 Filled in data entry screen

Data entry rules and conventions

Upper and lower case

To enter lower case data requires that a %LC% be entered as an edit pattern in SCR.

Changing the ID of a record

Display the record for editing, then change the record ID value. After pressing <E> at the CHANGE prompt, you will be asked if you want to delete the original item -- answer yes.

Duplicating a record with a different ID

Display the record for editing and change the record ID value. You will be prompted if you want to delete the original item; answer no.

Browsing through records

Display the data entry screen. At the record ID prompt, generate a select list of record IDs by entering:

PERFORM SELECT filename.

(Chapter 9 has an explanation of the SELECT command). This will result in the first ID from the select list being entered into the record ID prompt on the data entry screen and the data from that record will be displayed on the screen for editing. Pressing <E> at the change prompt will display the second record from the select list and so on.

Special Entries for Data Field Prompts

Ctrl X	deletes current line.
F7	deletes from cursor to beginning of line.
F8	deletes from cursor to end of line.
END (Ctrl E)	exits data entry screen without saving current entries.
Ctrl L (\)	accesses cross reference (see Chapter 8).
Ctrl T	redisplays a blank data entry screen without saving any entered data (whether data is a new record or modified data).
F1 (?)	displays field description.
Shift F1	displays edit checks for current prompt.
F2 (")	duplicates entry from previous record (use at single value data entry prompts only).

?F	skips the rest of the prompts and goes to the CHANGE prompt.
=	changes the value of the sequential counter.

Special Entries for the WHICH VALUE Prompt of Multi-Valued Fields.

Ctrl A	adds a value.
Ctrl C	clears all values.
Ctrl I	inserts a value.
Ctrl D	deletes a value.
Ctrl T	invokes the text editor.
F	scrolls multi-value display forward.
B	scrolls multi-value display backward.
Ctrl Q	Quits multi-value prompting and proceeds to the next prompt or to the CHANGE prompt.

Special Entries for the CHANGE Prompt.

Ctrl D	deletes record.
ADD	prompts for all the blank fields.
n+	starts at prompt n and prompts for all following prompts.

EDIT PATTERNS

Input Conversions

All of the codes for determining input conversions are described in the R/BASIC function, ICONV, in the COMMAND REFERENCE. Note that all input conversions must be enclosed in parentheses.

If you entered any input conversion for this field in BUD, then the same one will be automatically entered here. Remember that the input conversion and the output conversion should be matched; otherwise the values you see on your output reports may not be what you expect. Also note that the input conversion is enclosed in parentheses while the output conversion is not.

Pattern Matching

The following pattern match forms may be entered as edit checks:

nA	requires "n" number of alphabetic characters.
nN	requires "n" number of numeric characters.
nX	requires "n" number of any characters, either alphabetic or numeric.
nZ	allows up to "n" number of any characters.
"string"	requires matching the literal string enclosed in quotation marks (single or double quotation marks may be used).
%LC%	allows lower case characters to be entered; otherwise Revelation converts all lower case to upper case.
%U%	requires that each value in a multi-valued field be unique.
"NOTEXT"	If the data field is a multi-valued field, entering NOTEXT as an Edit pattern prevents the Text Editor from being able to be called from this field's data entry prompt.

If a "0" is used with an A, N, X pattern it means that any number of that character type will be accepted (e.g. 0A would allow any number of alphabetic characters).

The pattern may contain a mixture of the above forms, for example:

3N'-'2N'-'4N

would allow an entry consisting of three numbers, a dash, two numbers, a dash, and four numbers.

This example:

'INV'3Z

would allow any entry consisting of the letters "INV" followed by up to three more characters of any type.

The EDIT PATTERN prompt of BUD is multi-valued so that you can enter several patterns; if any of the patterns is matched the entry is accepted.

Range Checks

An allowed range for numeric data can be set using a range check. The format for this edit pattern is the minimum and maximum values enclosed in parentheses, for example:

(10,35)

would allow values between 10 and 35, inclusive. If only one value is enclosed, it is taken as the maximum value. For example:

(5)

would allow values up to 5.

Combining Edit Patterns

Two edit patterns can be combined by using the underline character as a connector. If you combine two pattern match expressions, they both must be satisfied for the entry to be accepted:

0N_5Z

requires that the entry be any number of numeric characters and that it can be up to 5 characters of any type; i.e. it can be up to 5 numeric characters.

If a range check follows an input conversion, the range check uses the converted value for its comparison. For example, MD2 is an input conversion which multiplies the input data by 100. Thus:

MD2_(100,500)

would accept 4 as an entry but would reject 400.

SCR ADVANCED TOPICS

R/BASIC Entry Points into Data Entry Screens

You often must decide whether to use R/DESIGN for an application or create your own data entry screens directly from R/BASIC. The answer in 99 out of 100 cases is to use R/DESIGN. The amount of development time necessary to create your own data entry screens is just not worth the effort. Besides, using R/BASIC may not make the screens run any faster, and it will definitely make modifications more difficult.

Fortunately, there are five entry points into R/DESIGN data entry screens for employing R/BASIC code:

1) Symbolic fields,
2) Null Default
3) Parameter 2
4) Description
5) Edit Patterns

With a little imagination, you can use these entry points to perform almost any custom function as illustrated in the following examples.

1. Executing an R/BASIC Statement Before a Data Entry Field is Prompted

Suppose you want to perform a certain function, either to the screen or to the database, before a field is prompted. You could use the NULL.DFLT parameter to perform the R/BASIC code. This works because NULL.DFLT is calculated before the user is prompted for data input.

Furthermore, by inserting the R/DESIGN.COMMON variables into your code, you have access to all the information that is used by the R/DESIGN interpreter (the R/DESIGN program which interprets the parameters you have stored in the RDES file). See the discussion of these variables in Chapter Twelve and Appendix III.

2. Performing Wrap-up Routines

Another useful entry point is Parameter 2 (defined with prompt 22 of the Prompt Editor Screen), which is used to perform wrap-up routines for a given field or record. The R/BASIC code used to perform this wrap-up routine can insert the RDESIGN.COMMON variables with the statement:

$INSERT PROG,RDESIGN.COMMON

This gives access to all of the variables used by R/DESIGN, in particular the CHANGE variable, which has special significance with wrap-up routines (don't confuse this variable with the CHANGE? prompt). When R/DESIGN enters the wrap-up routine, the CHANGE variable will have one of three values:

0   Indicates that the record has not been to the CHANGE prompt yet. Therefore, the wrap-up routine for the present field is either occurring during the initial display of that field as the record is being retrieved or immediately after the field has first been prompted for a

new record. Checking the value of OLD.ITEM (another COMMON variable) will determine if it is a new record (i.e. OLD.ITEM=").

1   The field is being modified.

2   The record is in the process of being deleted. The CHANGE variable could only have this value if the wrap-up routine were being called from the CHANGE prompt itself.

The wrap-up routine can modify the value of the CHANGE variable to achieve the following effects:

0   Forces sequential prompting for each field following the current data entry prompt as if the record were first being added -- even if the record was initially in edit mode.

1   Forces prompting to go immediately to the CHANGE prompt.

ERROR   When CHANGE = "ERROR", the current field is reprompted.

STOP   When CHANGE = "STOP", current record is updated to disk, and screen data entry is terminated. This value will only have an effect if the wrap-up routine is called from the CHANGE prompt and the record has been changed, that is, OLD.ITEM <> @RECORD.

3. Accessing Fields or Programs with the Help Description

The DESCRIPTION prompt in the Prompt Editor of SCR may contain a reference to a symbolic field or a compiled R/BASIC program. To use this feature, the following syntax is used:

{field.name}   or   [program.name]

For example, assume you are entering data into a customer file. One of the fields you are entering is the name of the sales person assigned to this new customer. When you are at this prompt, you might want to see a listing of the sales force and their current work load from the SALES.STAFF file.

You can write a program in R/BASIC to display the list of sales people when a user presses F1 at this prompt. See Appendix XII for an example of this type of program.

4. Calling an R/BASIC Program for an Edit Check

You specify edit patterns at prompt 14 of the Prompt Editor screen in SCR, EDIT PATTERN. If you wish, you can run an R/BASIC program to perform the edit logic. The program can be stored as the formula of a symbolic field, in which case you enter {field name} at prompt 14, or it can be a catalogued program, in which case you enter [program name].

You can gain access to many of the variables used by R/DESIGN by inserting the following line into your R/BASIC code:

$INSERT PROG,RDESIGN.COMMON

This will place a set of common statements in your program during the compilation process.

Your R/BASIC program can use the system variable @ANS to retrieve the value entered by the operator in the data entry screen. Before returning control back to R/DESIGN, your program should re-assign a value to @ANS according to the following action table.

0   bad entry, display "Invalid Pattern Match" message and reprompt the data field.

-1   bad entry, no error message is displayed and the field is reprompted.

1   good entry, data screen proceeds to next prompt.

-2   bad entry, no error message, redisplay screen and
        reprompt (this is useful if your program called another
        screen).

2   good entry, redisplay screen.

Generated Data Entry Screens

With an interpreted data entry screen, the parameters stored
in the RDES file are used by R/DESIGN'S ENTER program.
A generated data entry screen, however, is actually an
R/BASIC program to which you have complete access to
modify. The R/DESIGN GEN routine will prompt you for the
name of the data entry screen and the file where you want to
store the R/BASIC source code. The resulting source code
makes subroutine calls to several of the R/DESIGN
subroutines. Furthermore, the generated data entry screen
still reads the parameters stored in the RDES record for the
data entry screen you designed with SCR. You can modify,
compile, and run this program just like any other R/BASIC
program.

The ENTER program is the main R/DESIGN program which
controls interpreted data entry screens; however, there are
some important R/DESIGN subroutines. The source code for
many of these programs is stored in the PROG file. These
include PROMPTER, OPERATOR, DISPLAY (used for
displaying and prompting data fields), and V44 and V62 (used
for maintaining and displaying cross references).

Null Default Sequential Counter

Defining a sequential counter for a data entry prompt creates a
dictionary record in the data file. For example, if you establish
a sequential counter for the data field INVOICE.NO, then a
dictionary item is created with the name
%INVOICE.NO*SEQ.NO%.

Verifiles

A special procedure exists for using the Verifile parameter on multi-part keys. You may concatenate information to the front of the entered data to prepare it before the verifile operation is performed. The format for this procedure is to follow the file name in the verifile parameter with the literal or dictionary reference you want concatenated.

For example, if the data entry prompt is FIRST.NAME and the verifile parameter is CUSTOMERS {LNAME} (where LNAME is a symbolic field which sets @ANS={LAST.NAME}:*), then the last name and first name will be separated by an "*" and this new string will be tested for existence in the CUSTOMERS file.

In other words, say, you've already entered the LAST.NAME of "Smith". At the next prompt you enter the FIRST.NAME of "Lonnie". This prompt has a verifile parameter of CUSTOMERS {LNAME}. {LNAME} evaluates to "Smith*", so the string "Smith*Lonnie" is checked as a record key in the CUSTOMERS file.

Linking Screens

Sometimes you may have several data entry screens that you wish to link together as one set of data entry prompts. For example, you may need to prompt for more inputs to a data file than can fit on one screen.

Each of the linked screens must refer to the same data file (and therefore, the first prompt on each screen will be for the same record ID). Then, for each screen except the last in the chain, use SCR to invoke the Prompt Editor for the CHANGE prompt and edit item 21 (Parameter 1). Enter the name of the next R/DESIGN data entry screen to be executed.

Now, when you finish entering data to a linked screen, one of two things will happen:

1)   If adding a record, pressing <E> at the CHANGE prompt will automatically take you to the next screen. After the last screen in the link you will be taken directly to a blank first screen, ready to enter another record.

2)   If editing a record, pressing <E> at the CHANGE prompt will invoke the following message:

> **Press <E> for next screen, (S) for starting screen, or number of screen?**

At the last screen, you will be asked to either press <E> to file the entire record, or to enter the number of the screen which you wish to display and modify (screen numbers are shown in the upper right hand corner; e.g. I-1/2 is Interpreted screen 1, out of 2 screens total). If you enter "FILE" at the CHANGE prompt at any of the linked screens, the record will be filed and a fresh starting screen will be displayed.

Sometimes when adding a record, you may not wish to proceed sequentially through the chain of screens; instead you may want to enter a screen number as in situation 2) above. This can be accomplished by placing a "1" flag in field 19 of the RDES record for the screen (see Appendix VII).

Suppressing Automatic Recalculation of Symbolic Fields

Whenever you edit a field in a data entry screen, R/DESIGN updates every symbolic field on the screen. If there are a lot of symbolic fields on the screen, this can be an annoying waste of time. You can modify the data entry screen so that only the symbolic fields following the edited data prompt will be updated. Do this by editing the RDES record and placing a "1" flag in field 8 (see Appendix VII).

CHAPTER EIGHT: CROSS REFERENCES

While the ability to cross reference information between record keys and other fields is one of the most powerful features of Revelation, it can also be one of the most difficult to learn. Therefore, an entire chapter is devoted to explaining how to use cross references.

This chapter discusses how to establish an index file and how to access the information maintained in this file. It also points out various types of situations where cross references can be useful.

WHAT IS A CROSS REFERENCE?

Suppose you have a data file keyed on the customer number. That means that in order to retrieve a particular customer's record in the data entry screen, you are required to enter a customer number. But what if you only know the customer's name? How can you access the record? Simple. If you could somehow design your screen so that every time you file a record, an index is automatically maintained between the customer names and customer numbers, then you would be able to call up a customer record just by entering the customer name.

Let us take a closer look at how this cross-reference file would work. Suppose you set up a data file named CUSTOMERS (**Figure 8.1**) using a data entry screen named CUST.ENTRY.

		CUSTOMERS			
CUST.NO (RECORD KEY)	F.NAME	L.NAME	ADDRESS	CITY	ST
6	KENNY	SMITH	2A PINE HILL	PORTSTOWN	CA
7	GEORGE	HARRIS	331 MARKS	HOUSTON	TX
1	JOSEPH	SMITH	123 MAIN	BAKERSVILLE	CA
2	MARILYN	HARRIS	43 MAPLE	ORLANDO	FL
4	JOSEPH	CAPONE	421 5TH	EUREKA	CA
3	MARGIE	SMITH	8765 OAK	NEW YORK	NY
5	MARILYN	POLSTER	3333 BROADWAY	PARKER	NY

Fig. 8.1 CUSTOMERS data file

The file contains the record key, CUST.NO, and five other fields. As you know, records in a file are accessed by their record keys. For example, to locate Marilyn Harris' record you would use CUST.NO "2". Notice that each record in the CUSTOMERS file must have a unique CUST.NO, but several records can have the same L.NAME value.

But now you want to access records in this file not by their customer number, but by their last name instead. You can do this if you set up an index file or cross reference file built on the customer's last name. Such a file, called XREF.CUST, is shown in **Figure 8.2**.

```
XREF.CUST
LAST.NAME              FIELD#1
(RECORD KEY)
_____

HARRIS                2²7
POLSTER               5
SMITH                 1²3²6
CAPONE                4
```

Fig. 8.2 Example index file

The key field in this file contains the L.NAME values from the CUSTOMERS file. Its other field, FIELD#1, contains the CUST.NO values corresponding to each L.NAME value. The CUST.NO values are separated by value markers (i.e. FIELD#1 is a multi-valued field).

From the CUST.ENTRY data entry screen, it would be nice to somehow force R/DESIGN to first locate a record in the XREF.CUST file which contains "HARRIS" as the key. This record contains indexed customer numbers. Since customer numbers are the keys in the CUSTOMERS file, these values can be used to locate all the customers with a last name of "HARRIS".

In essence, a cross reference or index file inverts the relationship between the record key and another field. In the example above, the CUSTOMERS file stores all customers according to their customer number, with one customer name for each record or customer number. An "index" or cross reference file lists all unique customer names with perhaps several customer numbers per name.

It is easy to understand why cross references are often called "inverts". Whatever the name -- invert, index, cross reference -- the concept is still the same: relating a record key to another field so that the record may be retrieved by that second field instead of the key.

Terminology

Before continuing, it will be helpful to use the above example to define some terminology. CUSTOMERS is the <u>data file</u> with CUST.NO as its key and L.NAME as the <u>cross referenced field</u>. XREF.CUST is the <u>index file</u> and its keys are unique values of the cross referenced field (L.NAME). FIELD#1 is the multi-valued <u>index field</u> containing the <u>inverted lists</u> of keys from the data file.

There is nothing special about any of the file or field names in this example; the index file name does not need to start with "XREF" and the index field FIELD#1 does not even need to be named at all.

USING CROSS REFERENCES IN R/DESIGN

Keep in mind that cross references are a feature of R/DESIGN data entry screens. They will be set up from prompt numbers 25 and 26 in the Prompt Editor screen of R/DESIGN's SCR routine (where you customize the design layout and input/output parameters for a data entry screen - see Chapter 7). Once you have created a cross referenced index file such as the one shown in **Figure 8.2**, it can be treated like any other file and accessed by other programs.

There are two parts to setting up cross references:

> **Building an Index File:** This process will generate an index file similar to the one shown in **Figure 8.2**. This index file can be a file you create for the sole purpose of holding the inverted lists, or it may be an existing file used for other purposes as well.

The index file will be automatically maintained by R/DESIGN; for example, the XREF.CUST file would be automatically updated every time you add or delete a record from the CUSTOMERS file using the CUST.ENTRY data entry screen.

Retrieving Cross Referenced Information: After you have built an index file you will be able to access the information in it from certain prompts in data entry screens.

BUILDING AN INDEX FILE

Invoke the SCR program either from the R/DESIGN Main Menu or by entering :SCR from the TCL prompt. Enter the name of the data entry screen containing the field you want to use as a cross reference (CUST.ENTRY in our example).

Move the reference pointer to the data field prompt that will be cross-referenced and type **"P"** to enter the Prompt Editor Screen for that field (L.NAME in our example).

From the CHANGE prompt of the Prompt Editor Screen enter **"25"** to modify the "Make Cross Reference" prompt. Enter **"Y"** in this field. This will take you back to the CHANGE prompt where you will press <E> and the following message will be displayed:

DO YOU WISH TO SEE THE CROSS REFERENCE PARAMETER SCREEN (Y/N)?

A "Y" will display the cross reference or "Invert Parameter Screen" as shown in **Figure 8.3.** This is where you enter the cross reference information.

```
V42                  INVERT PARAMETER SCREEN


      Program Name
      Field Name


   03  File Where Inverts are Maintained
   04  Field Number Where Inverts are Maintained
   05  Delimiter(s) used to Separate Words Being Inverted
   06  Smallest Word to Invert
   07  Sorting Order of Inverted Keys
   08  Delete Empty Invert
   09  File Containing Additional Display Information


   10  Dictionary names for Additional Display Info
       (???  for Listing)
```

Fig. 8.3 Invert Parameter Screen

The first eight prompts on the screen are used to create the
parameters needed to build the cross reference list. The last
two prompts determine what information is displayed when the
inverted list is retrieved.

Respond to the INVERT PARAMETER SCREEN prompts
as follows:

Program Name
SCR automatically fills in the data entry Program Name.

Field Name
SCR automatically fills in the name of the field you selected
for cross referencing.

03 File Where Inverts are Maintained
Enter the name of the index file. If this file does not yet exist you will be warned of this fact. SCR will let you continue, but don't forget to create the file later! You may enter the name of a file that is used for other purposes.

04 Field Number Where Inverts are Maintained
Enter the field number of the index file where you want the multi-value cross reference list to be located. "Field number" is the same as the FMC number in BUD.

If you created an index file just to hold your index data, then you will probably store it in field 1, as in our example. However, in the case where you are using a file that has other data, the field will probably be something other than 1. Pressing <E> defaults to field number 1.

05 Delimiter(s) used to Separate Words Being Inverted
Enter the delimiter or delimiters to separate the "words" to be cross referenced. Each unique "word" will become a record in the index file.

For example, assume there is a file which is cross-referenced on the NAME field and the record 1 of this file has a NAME value = "JOHN SMITH". If the delimiter used to separate words being inverted is a space, two records would be created in the index file -- one for "JOHN" and one for "SMITH", and both would receive a "1" as index data.

Any character can be used as a delimiter, however, there are two special delimiters:

SPACE	space
VM	value mark, ASCII CHAR(253)

Multiple delimiters must be concatenated together, for example:

SPACEVM,.

would use a space, a value mark, a comma, and a period all as delimiters.

Being able to cross reference more than one word or value allows even multi-value fields to be cross referenced.

06   Smallest Word to Invert
Enter the length of the shortest word to be cross referenced. Words shorter than this value will be skipped during the index process.

For example, perhaps you don't want middle initials cross referenced. You would make the smallest word to index equal to 2, eliminating 1 character words.

07   Sorting Order of Inverted Keys
Enter the sorting sequence to be used when updating the index file. This procedure determines where in the index field to place the new item.

Valid sequences are:

AR = Ascending order, right justified. This is useful for numeric fields. (12 comes before 112 as you move right to left.)

AL = Ascending order, left justified. This is useful for non-numeric fields. ("Abrams" comes before "Alexander" as you move left to right.)

DR = Descending order, right justified.

DL = Descending order, left justified.

This parameter often causes confusion as to what exactly is being sorted. The *records* in the index file are NOT sorted, only the indexed lists for each record are sorted. Thus, if XREF.CUST is AR sorted, it would look like the following:

XREF.CUST
LAST.NAME   FIELD#1
(RECORD KEY)

HARRIS 2^27
POLSTER   5
SMITH 1^23^26
CAPONE   4

Notice that the LAST.NAMEs are not sorted, but that the inverted lists of customer numbers are.

A null entry for the sorting order will result in new items being added on to the end of each inverted list.

08 Delete Empty Invert
Enter "Y" if a record in the index file is to be deleted when its index field is empty.

In the previous example, if customer number 5 were deleted from the CUSTOMERS file, then R/DESIGN would automatically delete the references to record key 5 from the records in XREF.CUST. But this would leave FIELD#1 of the "POLSTER" record empty. If a "Y" had been entered in the "Delete Empty Invert" parameter, then the "POLSTER" record in XREF.CUST would also be deleted. This helps keep the size of the index file to a minimum.

If the index file holds information other than the inverted lists, you would enter an "N" for this parameter . In this case you would not want to delete the record if the inverted field becomes empty because you may still want to retain the other information in the record.

09 File Containing Additional Display Information
This determines what information is to be displayed on the INDEX DISPLAY screen during cross reference retrieval (the INDEX DISPLAY screen is discussed later in this chapter).

Enter the name of the file containing the display information to accompany the inverted record keys. This is usually the data file that was initially cross referenced. In the above example you would enter "CUSTOMERS".

10 Dictionary Names for Additional Display Info
(??? for Listing)
This also determines information to be displayed on the INDEX DISPLAY screen. Enter the names of the fields from the file in prompt 09 to be displayed on the INDEX DISPLAY screen.

To see the existing dictionary records (field names) of the file entered in prompt 09, enter "???" in prompt 10.

Your response is multi-valued and may contain as many fields (dictionary records) as can be displayed in 60 columns. The display length for each field is taken from the dictionary record of that field.

When you file your changes and exit from SCR with the "F" command, a separate parameter record is created in the RDES file for each cross reference you have set up (see the Advanced Topics section of this chapter). You can now enter data in your data entry screen and the index list will be automatically maintained.

Automatic Updating of Index Files

Each time you store a record in the CUSTOMERS file, R/DESIGN goes to the XREF.CUST file and looks for a record key with the value you just entered for L.NAME. If one is found, the customer number from the CUSTOMERS file is added as an indexed value. If the last name is not found in the index file, then a new record is created and the customer number is stored as its first indexed value.

If you delete a customer record from the CUSTOMERS file, then R/DESIGN goes to the index file and deletes that customer number from the corresponding record.

RETRIEVING CROSS REFERENCED INFORMATION

Now that you understand the logic for creating and maintaining cross-references, you are ready to start using the cross-reference or index lists.

There are many ways in which you can use the information stored in an index list. The following sections demonstrate the primary ways. But before continuing, you should review the following cross reference example.

CUSTOMERS is a data file with CUST.NO as its key field and L.NAME as a cross referenced field (**Figure 8.1** shown again below). XREF.CUST is the index file and its keys are the unique customer last names (**Figure 8.2**). FIELD#1 is the multi-valued index field containing the inverted lists of customer numbers. CUST.ENTRY is the name of the R/DESIGN data entry screen which adds records to the CUSTOMERS file.

CUST.NO (RECORD KEY)	F.NAME	L.NAME	ADDRESS	CITY	ST
			CUSTOMERS		
6	KENNY	SMITH	2A PINE HILL	PORTSTOWN	CA
7	GEORGE	HARRIS	331 MARKS	HOUSTON	TX
1	JOSEPH	SMITH	123 MAIN	BAKERSVILLE	CA
2	MARILYN	HARRIS	43 MAPLE	ORLANDO	FL
4	JOSEPH	CAPONE	421 5TH	EUREKA	CA
3	MARGIE	SMITH	8765 OAK	NEW YORK	NY
5	MARILYN	POLSTER	3333 BROADWAY	PARKER	NY

Fig. 8.1 CUSTOMERS data file (shown previously)

XREF.CUST LAST.NAME (RECORD KEY)	FIELD#1
HARRIS	$2^2 7$
POLSTER	5
SMITH	$1^2 3^2 6$
CAPONE	4

Fig. 8.2 Example index file (shown previously)

How you set up the access to the cross-references depends on whether you are accessing them from the record key prompt or from some other data field prompt in a data entry screen.

Invoking Cross References From the Record Key Prompt of the Data File

One place from which you might invoke a cross reference is the record key prompt. For example, in the CUST.ENTRY data entry screen (**Figure 8.4**), you may want to modify a customer record, but don't know the record key, although you do know the customer's name.

```
CUST.ENTRY    CUSTOMER ENTRY                (I-1)



01  CUST.NO
02  F.NAME
03  L.NAME
03  ADDRESS
04  CITY
05  STATE




CUST.NO  _____
```

Fig. 8.4 Data entry screen

All you have to do is type a **backslash** (\) at the key prompt, followed by the value of the cross referenced field to be looked up (note this is the "\" character and not "/"). For example, if you didn't know the customer number for Marilyn Polster, at the prompt shown in Figure 8.4 you could enter the following:

\POLSTER

The Marilyn Polster record would be displayed as shown in **Figure 8.5**.

```
CUST.ENTRY          CUST.ENTRY                    (I-1)



01  CUST.NO         5
02  F.NAME          MARILYN
03  L.NAME          POLSTER
03  ADDRESS         3333 BROADWAY
04  CITY            PARKER
05  STATE           NY



    CHANGE? _____
```

Fig. 8.5 Filled in data entry screen

But what happens if you enter a name such as "SMITH" which has more than one inverted value? In that case the data entry screen will be replaced with the INVERT DISPLAY screen as shown in **Figure 8.6**. This screen shows all of the records that have SMITH as the customer last name and allows you to choose which customer you actually want. This screen is discussed in detail later in this chapter.

```
┌────────────────────────────────────────────────────────────────────┐
│                                                                      │
│  USING XREF FILE     XREF.CUST      INDEX DISPLAY      12:23:02 6/08/86│
│                                                                      │
│                                                                      │
│     L#      INDEX   F.NAME        L.NAME          CITY          ST    │
│                                                                      │
│                                                                      │
│     1        1      JOSEPH        SMITH           EUREKA        CA    │
│     2        3      MARGIE        SMITH           NEW YORK      NY    │
│     3        6      KENNY         SMITH           PORTSTOWN     CA    │
│                                                                      │
│                                                                      │
│                                                       PAGE 1 OF 1     │
│     LINE#, NEW-LINE, NEW WORD, (R)EFINE, (PG)#, (S)EARCH, ".", OR "END"│
│                                                                      │
│                                                                      │
└────────────────────────────────────────────────────────────────────┘
```

Fig. 8.6 INVERT DISPLAY screen

Multiple Cross References in the Same Data Entry Screen

In our previous example, L.NAME was indexed to the XREF.CUST file. But what if CITY was also indexed to a file, CUST.CITY. In other words, what happens if you have created inverted lists for both the customer name and the state? When you enter /SMITH at the record key prompt, would the cross reference logic look for "Smith" in XREF.CUST or CUST.CITY?

The answer is that R/DESIGN will look for "SMITH" in the index file of the first cross referenced field on your data entry screen. Therefore, since L.NAME is before CITY on the data entry screen, R/DESIGN will look for "Smith" in the XREF.CUST file.

To retreive a customer record from the record key prompt using a a cross referenced field which is not the first one on the data entry screen, enter a backslash (\) followed by the name of a cross-referenced field equated to a value for that field; for example, \CITY=HOUSTON. In this case, the corresponding cross reference file, CUST.CITY, will be searched for a HOUSTON record and George Harris's record would be displayed.

Invoking Cross References from Fields Other Than the Record Key

In the previous sections, you invoked a cross reference from the record key prompt of the CUST.ENTRY program. You can also invoke cross references from prompts which are not the record key prompts. For example, suppose you have a data file named INVOICES which contains the following fields:

> INVOICE.NO (record key)
> DATE
> INVOICE.AMOUNT
> CUST.NBR

Suppose that records are entered into the INVOICES file with the INV.ENTRY data entry screen, and that the values entered for CUST.NBR correspond to the values of CUST.NO in the CUSTOMERS file (which were indexed in the XREF.CUST file).

When you are entering the CUST.NBR, it would be useful if you could invoke the cross reference which has already been set up so that you could just enter the customer name. This can be accomplished by the following procedure.

Use SCR to modify the INV.ENTRY screen and select the CUST.NBR field. Invoke the Prompt Editor and choose to modify field 26, "Display Cross Reference". You will be prompted to enter the name of the data file and cross referenced field you wish to access. Since you want the cross reference that has been created for the L.NAME field of the CUSTOMERS file, enter:

CUSTOMERS,L.NAME

Notice that the file name and field name are separated by a comma.

Now, at the CUST.NBR prompt of the INV.ENTRY data entry screen, enter a backslash (\) followed by a customer name. That customer's number will be retrieved from XREF.CUST. For example, enter \POLSTER at the CUST.NBR prompt of the invoice data entry screen and a "5" will be displayed in this field. If there is more than one customer number for the name you enter, the INDEX DISPLAY screen will be displayed.

Invoking Any Cross Reference From Any Prompt

Once you have modified a data entry prompt with field 26 of the Prompt Editor, you can access any cross referenced field in any data file from that data entry prompt, as indicated by the following examples:

\POLSTER — accesses the cross referenced field you specified in field 26 of the Prompt Editor.

\CITY = NEW YORK — accesses a different cross referenced field in the same file you specified in field 26 of the Prompt Editor.

\PERSONNEL,EMP.NO=0028 — accesses the cross referenced EMP.NO field in the PERSONNEL file.

Note that these syntaxes will only function from a data entry prompt for which you have already entered a file and field name at field 26 of the cross reference prompt Editor. This initial entry is essentially the "default" cross reference for that data entry prompt.

Invoking Cross References: Multiple Values

You can enter more than one cross reference value after the backslash (\) and the index file will be searched for record keys matching all these values.

Assume that you have the CUSTOMERS data file as before, except that instead of separate fields for last name and first name, there is only one name field as shown in **Figure 8.7.**

	CUSTOMERS			
CUST.NO (RECORD KEY)	NAME	ADDRESS	CITY	ST
6	KENNY SMITH	2A PINE HILL	PORTSTOWN	CA
7	GEORGE HARRIS	331 MARKS	HOUSTON	TX
1	JOSEPH SMITH	123 MAIN	BAKERSVILLE	CA
2	MARILYN HARRIS	43 MAPLE	ORLANDO	FL
4	JOSEPH CAPONE	421 5TH	EUREKA	CA
3	MARGIE SMITH	8765 OAK	NEW YORK	NY
5	MARILYN POLSTER	3333 BROADWAY	PARKER	NY

Fig. 8.7 CUSTOMERS data file with single name field

If you index the NAME field defining "SPACE" as a delimiter in the Invert Parameter screen, the index file would look like:

XREF.CUST

LAST.NAME (RECORD KEY)	FIELD#1
HARRIS	$2^2 7$
POLSTER	5
SMITH	$1^2 3^2 6$
CAPONE	4
MARGIE	3
JOSEPH	$1^2 4$
KENNY	6
GEORGE	7
MARILYN	$2^2 5$

At the record key prompt in the CUST.ENTRY data entry screen, you could then enter the following:

\JOSEPH SMITH

The cross reference file sees this as two values separated by the SPACE delimiter (the delimiter specified when the index file was built).

The cross reference logic would first locate the record in the XREF.CUST file with a key of "JOSEPH" and determine that the index field of this record contains two customer numbers: "1" and "4". It would then locate the "SMITH" record which contains three customer numbers, " 1" and "3" and "6". R/DESIGN recognizes that only the customer number "1" is in both cross reference records and would return a "1" in the record key prompt, causing JOSEPH SMITH's record to be displayed on the data entry screen.

Notice that the cross reference logic treats multiple values as "and" conditions and only returns the record numbers which meet both conditions.

Another way to use the cross reference syntax is to index two fields to the same index file. Suppose from the CUSTOMERS file of **Figure 8.7**   you index the "ST" field as well as the "L.NAME" field to the XREF.CUST file.

The index file would look like this:

XREF.CUST

LAST.NAME (RECORD KEY)	FIELD#1
HARRIS	2^27
POLSTER	5
SMITH	1^23^26
CAPONE	4
MARGIE	3
JOSEPH	1^24
KENNY	6
GEORGE	7
MARILYN	2^25
TX	7
CA	1^24^26
NY	3^25
FL	2

Then if you entered \SMITH CA at the record key prompt of CUST.ENTRY, the cross reference logic would locate the customers who have "Smith" in their name and who are located in California.

An Alternative to the Backslash (\): Pressing Ctrl L

R/DESIGN provides an alternative method for invoking the cross reference logic. Instead of beginning the cross-reference retrieval with the backslash (\), try pressing **Ctrl L.** You will be prompted at the bottom of the screen for a value. At this point you can enter the cross reference value using the syntaxes outlined above.

THE INDEX DISPLAY SCREEN

Again, if only one record meets the criteria entered during the cross reference retrieval, it is automatically fed into the data entry screen field. If more than one record qualifies, an Index Display screen is displayed showing all the records meeting the cross referenced criteria so that you may choose among them for final retrieval. When no records qualify, a blank Index Display screen is displayed to allow for other searches.

If you entered "SMITH" at the record key prompt of CUST.ENTRY, there would be three records which qualify, and thus, an Index Display screen **(Figure 8.8)** is displayed showing all the records with "SMITH" in the customer name.

```
USING XREF FILE  XREF.CUST  INDEX DISPLAY   12:34:02  07/10/86


L#  INDEX       NAME               CITY                ST


1    1          JOSEPH SMITH       EUREKA              CA
2    3          MARGIE SMITH       NEW YORK            NY
3    6          KENNY SMITH        PORTSTOWN           CA



                                             PAGE 1 OF 1
   LINE#,  NEW-LINE,  NEW WORD,  (R)EFINE,  (PG)#,  (S)EARCH,  ".",  OR  "END"
```

Fig. 8.8 Index Display screen for "SMITH"

The fields displayed on this screen are determined by prompts 09 and 10 of the INVERT PARAMETER SCREEN of the indexed data field.

The options at the bottom of the screen help you choose which record number should be passed to the data entry screen. Most of these options are not what you literally enter -- they are only reminders of the commands available to you. They are described as follows:

LINE#
Refers to the left-most column of the screen under the heading "L#". To select MARGIE SMITH, enter "2" and customer number 3 would be passed back on the data entry screen.

NEW-LINE
Actually means to press <E> to return back to the data entry screen. No record number is passed back to the screen and you will again see the data entry screen's record key prompt.

NEW WORD
Enter another referenced name to search for, such as "HARRIS". If Harris exists as a key in the cross-reference file, any customer numbers with this name will be displayed on this Index screen for viewing and the cross reference logic will start all over.

If the new word is numeric, precede it with the word "KEYS" in order to prevent the system from thinking it is a LINE # you are trying to enter and pass back to the data entry screen.

(R)EFINE
Enter <R> to refine or narrow the current list on the Index screen. You will then be prompted:

ENTER WORDS TO REFINE CURRENT LIST

In our example, if you enter **R** and then enter "CA", only customer numbers 1 and 6 for JOSEPH SMITH and KENNY SMITH would be displayed. Of course, you could have accomplished the same result in the initial retrieval by entering \SMITH CA.

We should mention that if you entered EUREKA to narrow the list, the list would not be refined -- since the CITY data field has not previously been set up as a cross reference.

This option is particularly useful if there are several screens of records for a particular cross reference and you need to narrow the list in order to find the exact customer number, or record you need.

(PG)#
Allows user to look at different screens of information for records that exceed one screen. For example, "PG2" will display page 2 of the references.

(S)earch
This option allows you to scan through the index file to find all record keys that match a specified character string.

If you enter the <S> option, you will be prompted for the characters to search for. Suppose you are looking for a particular customer but you can't remember her exact name other than the fact that it has PO in it. In this case, you would enter the characters PO when prompted.

The cross reference file will then be searched sequentially for any key that contains "PO". If one exists, the record(s) will be displayed. In our example, the key word POLSTER would be found first and so the record for Marilyn Polster would be displayed on the INDEX DISPLAY SCREEN (if there were two POLSTER records, both would be displayed).

If this customer is not the one you are looking for, you could continue the search for the next occurrence of PO by entering a period (.) at the command line.

In our example, the next occurrence of PO is in CAPONE, so the data for Marilyn Polster would be removed and that of Joseph Capone would be displayed. Note that the character search does NOT distinguish between beginning letters and letters in the middle of a word.

When doing a search, you should not expect to see on one screen all the records matching the criteria. Remember that only one cross reference record key at a time is searched for the occurrence of the specified substring and if a match occurs, that indexed list only is displayed.

When the entire file has been searched, the message **SELECTION COMPLETED FOR "PO"** will be displayed and control will return to the command line. At any time during the search you may enter one of the other command options.

(.)
Enter a period to continue the search process. (See above.)

END
Returns to the main data entry screen and reprompts. (Same as <E>.)

MAKING A CROSS REFERENCE AFTER A DATABASE IS IN USE

It often happens that after a database has been in use and many records have already been entered, you discover an important use for establishing a cross-reference. There certainly is no problem using the Prompt Editor in the SCR program to modify the data entry screen to make a cross reference. However, only those new records entered after you establish the cross reference parameters will be cross referenced. How do you build a cross reference file from a database that already has records entered into it?

Fortunately, Revelation comes with a utility program on the Utilities disk that performs just this function. It is an R/BASIC program called **INVERT.ALL.**

The instructions in this section assume you have a hard disk. If you do not know whether the program has been copied to your disk, enter the command DIR INVERT.ALL from the TCL prompt. If the program does not exist, place the Utilities disk into the A-Drive and copy it with the following command from TCL:

```
:PC COPY A:INVERT.ALL C:
```

To use this program you must first compile its source code by using the following command:

```
:BASIC DOS INVERT.ALL
```

Once the program has been compiled you are ready to run it with the following command:

```
:RUN DOS INVERT.ALL
```

It is important that you define the cross reference parameters using the SCR Prompt Editor before you run the INVERT.ALL program. If you haven't, the program will display an error message and reprompt.

The program will prompt you for the (master) data file name as well as the field(s) you have set up for cross referencing. You may type END at any prompt to terminate execution of the program.

When the program is done, all of the previously entered records will be indexed.

Once the cross-reference file has been built, it will be maintained automatically by R/DESIGN according to the parameters you supplied in SCR.

OTHER WAYS OF USING CROSS REFERENCES

You have just begun to tap the power of cross references. Once you begin using them, you will find many uses for inverted lists. We will demonstrate a couple of examples as a way of paving the road to your further exploration.

Maintaining an Index in a File Containing Other Information

So far you have created a separate file to use as an index file. However, sometimes it is useful to maintain your inverted lists in a file that contains other data.

For example, assume that you are ready to enter the following data into the INVOICES file with the data entry screen, INV.ENTRY:

INVOICE.NO	INVOICE.AMOUNT	CUST.NBR
001	$3,080.00	4
002	$1,382.00	3
003	$2,650.00	1
004	$2,340.00	4
005	$6,928.00	5

CUSTOMERS				
CUST.NO (RECORD KEY)	NAME	ADDRESS	CITY	ST
6	KENNY SMITH	2A PINE HILL	PORTSTOWN	CA
7	GEORGE HARRIS	331 MARKS	HOUSTON	TX
1	JOSEPH SMITH	123 MAIN	BAKERSVILLE	CA
2	MARILYN HARRIS	43 MAPLE	ORLANDO	FL
4	JOSEPH CAPONE	421 5TH	EUREKA	CA
3	MARGIE SMITH	8765 OAK	NEW YORK	NY
5	MARILYN POLSTER	3333 BROADWAY	PARKER	NY

Figure 8.9   Data Stored in CUSTOMERS file

Also, you are going to cross-reference the customer numbers in the INVOICES file with the invoice numbers. You could maintain these cross references in a separate cross reference file. But it might be useful to store these inverted lists in the CUSTOMERS file (**Figure 8.9**). This would provide the added bonus that whenever you print out a listing of the CUSTOMERS file, you could also see which customers have outstanding invoices.

To accomplish this, follow the procedures outlined earlier in this chapter to cross reference the CUST.NBR field of the INV.ENTRY program. (From SCR, go to the CUST.NBR prompt and invoke the Prompt Editor. At field 25, "Make Cross Reference", enter a "Y".) After the CHANGE prompt, make the following entries in the **Invert Parameter Screen** as shown in **Figure 8.10**:

INVERT PARAMETER SCREEN

03	File Where Inverts are Maintained	CUSTOMERS
04	Field Number Where Inverts are Maintained	5
05	Delimiter used to Separate Words Being Inverted	SPACE
06	Smallest Word to Invert	0
07	Sorting Order of Inverted Keys	AR
08	Delete Empty Invert	N
09	File Containing Additional Display Information	INVOICES

10 Dictionary names for Additional Display Info
    01> CUST.NBR   02> INVOICE.AMOUNT

Fig. 8.10 Using CUSTOMERS file as index file

There are several things to notice about these entries. First of all, notice that the inverted lists will go into field 5 of the

CUSTOMERS file. Previously this field was not defined, but now you could name it INV.NO using BUD. (Remember that it will be a multi-value field.) Also notice at prompt 8, "Delete Empty Invert", that although the default is "Y", you answered "N" because if there are no invoice numbers for this customer, you certainly don't want to delete the customer's record from the CUSTOMERS file.

You can now enter your invoice data using INV.ENTRY and an inverted list of invoice numbers will be placed into the INV.NO field of the CUSTOMERS file. Now whenever you list the CUSTOMERS file, every customer record will display the invoices for that customer as shown in **Figure 8.11.**

CUST.NO (RECORD KEY)	NAME	ADDRESS	CITY	ST	INV.NO.
			CUSTOMERS		
6	KENNY SMITH	2A PINE HILL	PORTSTOWN	CA	
7	GEORGE HARRIS	331 MARKS	HOUSTON	TX	
1	JOSEPH SMITH	123 MAIN	BAKERSVILLE	CA	003
2	MARILYN HARRIS	43 MAPLE	ORLANDO	FL	
4	JOSEPH CAPONE	421 5TH	EUREKA	CA	001
					004
3	MARGIE SMITH	8765 OAK	NEW YORK	NY	002
5	MARILYN POLSTER	3333 BROADWAY	PARKER	NY	005

Fig. 8.11

Maintaining cross-references in this manner serves three functions. It reduces the need for additional files, it allows you to retrieve invoice numbers in the invoice data entry screen through CUST.NBR, and it provides an easy way to reference all the invoices of a particular customer.

USING THE FORM-LIST COMMAND WITH CROSS REFERENCES

Until now, we have only discussed using cross-references during record retrieval in a data entry screen. However, you can also utilize these inverted lists to speed up processing during a report.

Suppose you want to list the INVOICES file, but only those pertaining to a particular customer. You could use the following command (generating reports is covered in the next chapter):

:LIST INVOICES WITH CUST.NBR = 3

Revelation would sequentially search every record in the INVOICES file looking for all those records having a CUST.NBR of 3. If the file contained hundreds or thousands of invoices this search would take a long time.

This search time can be shortened significantly using the inverted lists of invoice numbers you are maintaining in the 5th field of the CUSTOMERS file. Using the FORM-LIST command (see PART III: COMMAND REFERENCE), you could enter:

:FORM-LIST CUSTOMERS 3 5
>LIST INVOICES

The FORM-LIST command instructs Revelation to go to the CUSTOMERS file and find a record with the key (CUST.NO) = 3. The 5th field (the inverted list of invoice numbers) is then extracted from this record to create a select list of invoice numbers.

This select list is then passed on to the >LIST INVOICES command and only those invoice records in the select list are listed from the INVOICES file. This procedure is much faster than searching every invoice record for a CUST.NBR = 3.

ADVANCED TOPICS

It might be instructive to explain what happens during each phase of the cross reference procedure. This description is only for advanced users who are familiar with the record layout in the RDES file. See the Appendix VII for this layout.

Building XREF:

When you file the data entry screen after using SCR to define the cross reference, three things occur to the RDES file:

1) Another record is created in RDES with the key equal to **"XR*filename*fieldname"** (called the cross reference parameter record) where file name and field name correspond to the cross referenced dictionary record defined in the Prompt Editor.

2) Field 6 of the data entry screen's RDES record has the **filename$fieldname** inserted to indicate the default cross reference parameter record to use. Field 10 is flagged "Y" for the invert logic to be inserted if the GEN process is ever used.

3) Field 24 of the inverted data field in the RDES program record is flagged to indicate that an index should be updated for this field whenever the data entry screen is filed to disk.

To invoke the cross reference maintenance logic, R/DESIGN calls the program **V44**, stored as object code in the VERBS file. The source code for this program is in the PROG file which comes with the Utilities disk.

Accessing XREF:

1) If a field has key.flag = "K" (field 23 of the prompt layout in the RDES program record) indicating that it is the key field, and a cross reference is attempted, then R/DESIGN (PROMPTER subroutine) looks for the **"XR*filename*fieldname"** record in the RDES file based on

field 6 of the RDES record. If it is not found then a message is displayed saying that XR*filename*fieldname is not found in RDES.

2) If the field does not have key.flag = "K" (field 23 of the prompt layout in RDES program record) and field 27 of the prompt layout record (DISPLAY.XREF) is null, then you will see a message saying the field is not set up for cross reference. Otherwise the cross reference parameter record in RDES (obtained from field 27 -- file name,field name) is retrieved and the cross reference information is displayed.

3) To invoke the cross reference display logic, the R/DESIGN, PROMPTER program calls the program **V62** (the compiled object code is in the VERBS file, however the source code is actually in the PROG file that comes with the UTILITIES disk.)

CHAPTER NINE: DISPLAYING DATA AND GENERATING REPORTS

This chapter discusses how to generate reports from the data in your database file. Most of this chapter is spent explaining how to construct a LIST command (an entire output report can be defined with this one command). We also explain how R/DESIGN generates a report program by constructing a LIST command and converting it into R/BASIC code.

Since this is the first chapter in which we use TCL and R/LIST extensively, the following is a quick review of these portions of Revelation.

1. TCL is the command level from which you run programs, perform file operations, and perform various system functions. R/LIST is an ad hoc report generator accessed through a set of 6 TCL commands. The most important R/LIST commands are LIST and SELECT.

2. R/LIST is said to be "dictionary driven". The words that comprise R/LIST commands must be contained in one of two dictionaries. The first word of an R/LIST command must be an entry in the VOC file. The rest of the words in the R/LIST command must be either a file name, an entry in the dictionary of that file, or an entry in the dictionary of VOC.

3. There is a lot of flexibility in the order of the phrases in an R/LIST command.

4. An R/LIST command can be up to 256 characters long; however, if it is longer than the screen width the line will scroll like a tickertape.

5. Non-numeric record IDs and any other String literals used in R/LIST commands must be enclosed in quotes; numeric values need not be.

6. Compare operators must be separated from the surrounding words with spaces, for example:

AMOUNT > 100 not **AMOUNT>100**

LISTING A FILE

The information contained in a file can be displayed with the LIST command. LIST is an extremely powerful command which can define an entire report by combining numerous descriptive phrases. The basic format for the command is the word LIST followed by the filename of the file whose contents are to be displayed. For example, :LIST CUSTOMERS would list information from the CUSTOMERS file.

For large files the LIST display may take up many screens; in which case you will be shown the first screen full of information with a prompt at the bottom, "Press <E> to continue?". If you do not want to page through the rest of the screens of the LIST output, you can just enter "END" which will take you back to the TCL prompt.

Selecting Which Fields to Display

Assume you have created the database file, INVOICES, as shown in **Figure 9.1** with the key field INV.NO.

INV.NO	CUSTOMER	DATE	UNITS
100	ALLIED ELECTRIC	21 SEP 86	14
101	UNIVERSAL FANS	19 SEP 86	5
102	ALLIED ELECTRIC	25 AUG 86	32
103	CITY HARDWARE	07 SEP 86	8
103A	CITY HARDWARE	08 SEP 86	5
104	CITY HARDWARE	30 AUG 86	24
105	UNIVERSAL FANS	28 SEP 86	12
106	ALLIED ELECTRIC	01 OCT 86	19

Fig. 9.1 Example data file, INVOICES

You can select which fields to display by including their names in the LIST command. For example:

:LIST INVOICES CUSTOMER

would produce the screen shown in **Figure 9.2**. You can see that the INV.NO and the CUSTOMER fields are displayed. The record key is always displayed unless you specifically direct that it not be (suppressing the record key is covered later in this chapter). You can display as many fields on your report as you wish; but if they cannot fit on one line they will wrap around to the next line and the report will no longer line up in neat columns. If you want to list the record keys only, use the following format:

:LIST ONLY INVOICES

```
PAGE 1                                22:15:59  18 SEP 86


INVOICES    CUSTOMER........


   100   ALLIED ELECTRIC
   101   UNIVERSAL FANS
   102   ALLIED ELECTRIC
   103   CITY HARDWARE
   103A  CITY HARDWARE
   104   CITY HARDWARE
   105   UNIVERSAL FANS
   106   ALLIED ELECTRIC


8 Records processed



Press <E> to continue
```

Fig. 9.2 :LIST INVOICES CUSTOMER

Using Group Field Names

A group field name will display several fields without your
having to enter each field name in the LIST command. For
example, if you defined a group field, DAILY.RPT, to include
the data fields CUSTOMER, DATE, and UNITS, you could
then list the database with:

:LIST INVOICES DAILY.RPT

This would produce a report displaying the CUSTOMER,
DATE, and UNITS fields (as well as the record key) for every
record in the INVOICES file.

@CRT and @LPTR

What happens if you use the LIST command without any field names (e.g. :LIST INVOICES)? There is a special group field which determines which fields will be displayed in this situation. Every time you create a data file with R/DESIGN, this special group field, @CRT, is placed in the dictionary of the file. This is the default group field for listing a file to the screen. Similarly, you can create @LPTR, which would be the default group field for listing a file to the printer (if no @LPTR exists, @CRT is used).

Initially, @CRT and @LPTR do not include any fields, but you can define them to include any fields you wish by invoking BUD, entering @CRT or @LPTR for the field name, defining it as a "G" type field, and entering the names of the fields for the group in parameter 13.

If, for some reason, there is no @CRT record in the dictionary of a file, R/LIST will default to the @CRT record from the VOC file to determine what fields to display.

R/LIST only uses @CRT or @LPTR if no display field names are included in the LIST command.

SELECTING WHICH RECORDS TO BE DISPLAYED

There are several ways to select which records to display. One way is to include record keys in the LIST command. For example:

:LIST INVOICES 100 101 102

would list the first three records from the data file shown in **Figure 9.1** (in this example, the display fields would be determined by @CRT).

You can also list a specified number of records by using:

:LIST 3 INVOICES

This would list 3 records; which three depends on how the records are stored in the file, but it will generally not be the first three records you entered. This variation of the LIST command is useful for getting a quick sampling of a database.

The WITH Phrase

The most powerful way of selecting records is the "WITH" clause, for example:

:LIST INVOICES WITH UNITS > 10

would list the five records in the database (from Figure 9.1) with a value of UNITS greater than 10. The phrase consists of the word "WITH" followed by a field name, a comparison expression, and a value. *Note that comparison operators must be separated from the other words in the expression by spaces.* **Figure 9.3** is a list of comparison operators, along with some synonym expressions which can be substituted for them (additional synonyms are shown in Appendix IV).

The last few comparison operators listed in **Figure 9.3** need additional explanation. The operator "]" (or "STARTING IN") locates records with the specified literal string at the front of the field. Using our example database from **Figure 9.1**,

:LIST INVOICES WITH CUSTOMER STARTING IN "UNIV"

or

:LIST INVOICES WITH CUSTOMER]"UNIV"

would list invoices 101 and 105. Likewise,

:LIST INVOICES WITH CUSTOMER ENDING IN "ELECTRIC"

would list invoices 100, 102 and 106.

The CONTAINING comparison will locate records if the specified string appears anywhere in the field. Note that the string fields must be enclosed in quotes.

:LIST INVOICES WITH CUSTOMER "[D]"

or

:LIST INVOICES WITH CUSTOMER [ ] "D"

would list all invoices except 101 and 105

The last comparison operator, MATCHES, uses the concept of pattern matching which is explained in Chapters 4 and 7. For example,

:LIST INVOICES WITH INV.NO MATCHES "3N1A"

would list all the records whose INV.NO contained three numbers followed by an alphanumeric (i.e. invoice 103A).

COMPARISON OPERATORS	SYNONYMS
=	EQ, EQUAL TO (The "=" operator may be ommitted since it is implied, as in :LIST FN WITH COMPANY "PBS")
<	LT, LESS THAN
<=	LE, LESS THAN OR EQUAL TO
#	NE, NOT EQUAL TO
>	GT, GREATER THAN
>=	GE, GREATER THAN OR EQUAL TO
]	STARTING IN, STARTING WITH
[	ENDING IN, ENDING WITH
[...]	CONTAINING
MATCHES	MATCH

Fig. 9.3 R/LIST comparison operators

Comparing Date Fields

If you have a field which contains date information and you are storing it internally as a "date" and not just as a literal string, you can apply some special comparisons. (See the "Input and Output Conversions" section of Chapter 4).   The LIST command recognizes the following special variables: YESTERDAY, TODAY, TOMORROW, SUNDAY, MONDAY, TUESDAY, etc. It calculates their date value from the computers internal clock/calendar for making comparisons.   For example, if you were performing a LIST command on 13 SEP 1986, and used:

:LIST INVOICES WITH DATE >= YESTERDAY

all of the the invoices entered with dates since 12 SEP would be listed. The day of the week variables evaluate to that past day of the week (e.g. if you used the variable WEDNESDAY on Friday, 12 September, it would evaluate to 10 September). Remember that you can only compare dates with each other if they are stored in the computer as integers through the use of an input conversion.

"WITHOUT" Phrase

You can use the word WITHOUT instead of WITH to select the records which do not meet the specified comparison condition. For example:

:LIST INVOICES WITHOUT CUSTOMERS = "ALLIED"

would list all the invoices except those of ALLIED. There are a number of words which can be substituted for WITH and WITHOUT; they are listed in Appendix IV.

Combining Comparison Phrases

Several WITH or WITHOUT phrases can be combined using the connector words "OR" or "AND". AND will only list records which meet both expressions while OR will list records meeting either condition.

> **:LIST INVOICES WITH CUSTOMER = "ALLIED"**
> **AND WITH DATE = TODAY**

would list all of ALLIED's invoices from today.

> **:LIST INVOICES WITH CUSTOMER = "ALLIED"**
> **OR WITH DATE = TODAY**

would list all of today's invoices plus all of ALLIED's invoices regardless of date. You can include as many comparison expressions as you want in a LIST command, subject to the overall length constraint of 256 characters.

Range Comparisons

Another variation of the WITH phrase is expressing a range of values with the "FROM ... TO" clause. For example:

> **:LIST INVOICES WITH UNITS FROM 10 TO 20**

would list the records with a value of UNITS between 10 and 20. Likewise,

> **:LIST INVOICES WITH CUSTOMERS FROM "A"**
> **TO "M"**

would list the invoices for customers whose names start with A through L. Note that MACK'S ELECTRIC would not be included since it comes after "M" in an alphabetical listing. Also note that the literals "A" and "M" must be in quotes but the numeric values 10 and 20 need not be.

SORTING RECORDS

A listing of records can be sorted by using a BY phrase:

:LIST INVOICES BY CUSTOMER

would display the invoices in alphabetical order of the customers. To have the sorting done in descending order, use BY-DSND instead of BY. You can have as many BY phrases in the command as you want and the records will be sorted in the order of the BY phrases. For example:

:LIST INVOICES BY CUSTOMER BY DATE

would sort the invoices first by customer and then by date within each customer. See **Figure 9.4.**

PAGE 1		17:14:30	06 SEPT 1986
INV.NO	CUSTOMER	DATE	UNITS
102	ALLIED ELECTRIC	25 AUG 86	32
100	ALLIED ELECTRIC	21 SEP 86	14
106	ALLIED ELECTRIC	01 OCT 86	19
104	CITY HARDWARE	30 AUG 86	24
103	CITY HARDWARE	07 SEP 86	8
103A	CITY HARDWARE	08 SEP 86	5
101	UNIVERSAL FANS	19 SEP 86	5
105	UNIVERSAL FANS	28 SEP 86	12

Fig. 9.4   LIST INVOICES BY CUSTOMER BY DATE

The SORT Command

The records from a data file can also be displayed in sorted order using the SORT command. The sort command is essentially identical to the LIST command except that it always does a final sort by the key field. Thus the following two commands are equivalent:

:LIST INVOICES WITH DATE = TODAY BY CUSTOMER BY INV.NO

:SORT INVOICES WITH DATE = TODAY BY CUSTOMER

Note that the above example combines WITH and BY phrases.

Neither the LIST nor SORT command changes the order in which the data is stored in the data file; they only determine the order of the data displayed with this particular command.

Sorted fields do not automatically get displayed. They must be specified separately in the R/LIST command or else be part of the @CRT group field. Thus,

:LIST INVOICES BY DATE CUSTOMER

will display all invoices sorted by date, but the only fields displayed in the report will be INVOICE.NO and CUSTOMER.

TOTALING FIELDS

Fields which contain numeric data can be totaled with the TOTAL phrase. Once again using the example data file from **Figure 9.1**, you could total the UNITS field with the following command:

:LIST INVOICES TOTAL UNITS

the result of the above command is shown in **Figure 9.5**.

Notice that only the key field and the totaled field are displayed. But we said earlier that if you do not include any display fields in the LIST command, it will default to the @CRT group field. Well, the LIST command treats the TOTAL phrase (and the BREAK-ON phrase described in the next section) as display fields. Therefore, the UNITS field is displayed and @CRT is not used. To display other fields along with the totaled field, just include their names as additional display fields.

You can include as many TOTAL phrases in the command as you like.

```
PAGE 1                          22:19:15  18 SEP 1986


INVOICES     UNITS


100          14
101          5
102          32
103          8
103A         5
104          24
105          12
106          19
***          114


8 Records Processed


Press <E> to continue
```

Fig. 9.5 :LIST INVOICES TOTAL UNITS

BREAKING UP A LISTING

Using a BREAK-ON phrase will cause the listing to break
(skip a line) each time the value of the specified field changes.
This is generally used in conjunction with a BY phrase. For
example:

**:LIST INVOICES BY CUSTOMER BREAK-ON
CUSTOMER DATE TOTAL UNITS**

will produce the screen display shown in **Figure 9.6.** Notice
that DATE is included in the command as a display field.

Inserted at each break in the report is a break line consisting of
three asterisks in the BREAK-ON field and a subtotal in the
field being totaled. A grand total is printed at the bottom of
the display.

(Figure 9.6 shown on next page.)

```
PAGE 1                                    22:21:33  18 SEP 86

INVOICES        CUSTOMER           DATE            UNITS

100             ALLIED ELECTRIC    21 SEP 86       14
102             ALLIED ELECTRIC    25 AUG 86       32
106             ALLIED ELECTRIC    01 OCT 86       19

                ***                                65

103             CITY HARDWARE      07 SEP 86       8
103A            CITY HARDWARE      08 SEP 86       5
104             CITY HARDWARE      30 AUG 86       24

                ***                                37

101             UNIVERSAL FANS     19 SEP 86       5
105             UNIVERSAL FANS     28 SEP 86       12

                ***                                17


                ***                                119


8 Records Processed

Press <E> to continue
```

Fig. 9.6 Example of BREAK-ON phrase

BREAK-ON Options

BREAK-ON can be modified by adding BREAK-ON options to the BREAK-ON phrase. The options consist of text and/or special characters. The entire option must be enclosed in double quotations and the special characters must be enclosed in single quotes. The allowed option characters are shown as follows:

'U' UNDERLINE: prints a line between the data being subtotaled and the subtotal amount. This will insert an extra line at each break unless the 'L' option is used.

'UU' DOUBLE UNDERLINE: prints the same line as 'U' plus a line under each subtotal.

'P' PAGE: causes a new page to be started at each break.

'L' LINE: eliminates the blank line between the group of records and the break line.

'D' DATA: eliminates the break line and supresses subtotaling if there is only one record in the break group.

'V' VALUE: prints the value of the breaking field in place of the three asterisks on the break line. This is used with the text part of the option to print a subtitle on the break line (see example).

'B' BREAK: allows the value of the breaking field to be printed in the heading of each page (see explanation of HEADING below).

The results of the following command are shown in **Figure 9.7.**

:LIST INVOICES BY CUSTOMER BREAK-ON CUSTOMER "TOT FOR 'ULV'" DATE TOTAL UNITS

```
PAGE 1                                    22:21:33  18 SEP 86


  INVOICES         CUSTOMER                DATE          UNITS


  100              ALLIED ELECTRIC         21 SEP 86     14
  102              ALLIED ELECTRIC         25 AUG 86     32
  106              ALLIED ELECTRIC         01 OCT 86     19
                                                         ___
          TOT FOR ALLIED ELECTRIC                        65


  103              CITY HARDWARE           07 SEP 86     8
  103A             CITY HARDWARE           08 SEP 86     5
  104              CITY HARDWARE           30 AUG 86     24
                                                         ___
          TOT FOR CITY HARDWARE                          37


  101              UNIVERSAL FANS          19 SEP 86     5
  105              UNIVERSAL FANS          28 SEP 86     12
                                                         ___
          TOT FOR UNIVERSAL FANS                         17
                                                         ___

  ***                                                    119


  8 Records Processed



  Press <E> to continue
```

Fig. 9.7 Example of BREAK-ON options

Labeling Grand Totals

When a TOTAL phrase is used, the grand total of the specified field is shown at the bottom of the report with three asterisks in the record ID column (see **Figure 9.7**). This line can be modified with GRAND-TOTAL followed by options similar to the BREAK-ON format. The allowed options are:

'U'   **UNDERLINE:** places a double line (===) above the grand total.

'UU'   **DOUBLE UNDERLINE:** places double lines (===) above and below the grand total.

'P'   **PAGE:** causes the grand total to be printed on a separate page.

'L'   **LINE:** eliminates the blank line which usually precedes the grand total.

The following is an example of a command with a Grand Total modifier:

LIST INVOICES BY CUSTOMER BREAK-ON CUSTOMER "TOT FOR 'ULV'" DATE TOTAL UNITS GRAND TOTAL "TOT UNITS 'UU'"

HEADINGS AND FOOTINGS

HEADING and FOOTING phrases are used in a LIST command to specify text to be printed at the top and bottom of each page of the report. Following the word HEADING or FOOTING are options consisting of text and/or special characters. The whole option must be in double quotes and the special characters must be in single quotes. The format for the HEADING and FOOTING phrases is similar to the BREAK-ON phrase. But in this case, the order of the text and special characters within the option is significant. Additionally, you can alternate text and special characters. The special characters are as follows:

'B'   BREAK: is only used when a new page is started at each break (the 'P' BREAK-ON option). 'B' causes the value of the break field to be inserted in the header/footer. For this option to work, the 'B' option must also been used in the BREAK-ON phrase.

'D'   DATE: inserts the current date.

'F'   FILENAME: inserts the name of the file being listed.

'L'   LINE: specifies a line feed.

'N'   NO HEADING: is used by itself to eliminate the default heading which consists of page, date, and time.

'P'   PAGE: inserts page number.

'PP'   PAGE JUSTIFIED: inserts page number right justified in a field four spaces wide.

'Sn'   SPACE: will enter n spaces.

'T'   TIME: inserts current time.

For example, in a LIST command the phrase:

HEADING " 'F' REPORT DATED 'DL'PAGE 'PL'CUSTOMER 'BL'"

would print the following at top of the first page:

INVOICES REPORT DATED 13 SEP 1986
PAGE 1
CUSTOMER ALLIED ELECTRIC

If you want one of your text words to appear in quotation marks, surround it by two single quote marks on each side.

For example,

HEADING "TODAYS "DATE" IS 'D'"

would print the header:

TODAYS 'DATE' IS 13 SEP 1986.

REPORT MODIFIERS

There are several modifiers which can be included in a LIST statement to change the output format. These modifiers are described below:

ID-SUPP: suppresses the printing of the key field. Normally the key field is displayed on all reports generated with the LIST command.

DBL-SPC: double space; causes the report to double space.

SUPP: suppresses the end message (indicating how many records were processed) which normally follows the listing, and also suppresses the default header (page, date, and time).

HDR-SUPP: same as SUPP.

COL-HDR-SUPP: suppresses the end message, the default header, and the column headings.

DET-SUPP: eliminates displaying of the actual record information, leaving just the subtotal and grand total lines.

DIRECTING THE REPORT OUTPUT

There are three command options used to direct the report output. The command option is enclosed in parentheses () and can be placed anywhere in the command statement. The valid command options are described below:

(P)   sends the output to the printer. The line width and lines per page for the printer are set with the TCL command SET-LPTR (see the COMMAND REFERENCE).

(N)   When the output is sent to the screen, it pauses at the end of each page. Using (N) will cause the report to scroll straight through to the end.

(S)   When an R/LIST command is executed, Revelation actually creates a program in R/BASIC, compiles it, and then runs it. The (S) option stores this R/BASIC source code in the DOS file with the record name RLIST (the DOS file is explained in Chapter 10). You can then access it with **:TEXT DOS RLIST** for editing (see USING GEN in the advanced topics at the end of this chapter).

You may compile this program and actually run it from TCL. Be warned, however -- you must first either pass a select list to the program or place a select command in the source code itself.

(SX) The same as (S) except the command is not executed.

SAVING A LIST COMMAND TO PRODUCE STANDARD REPORTS

When you are experimenting with a database or refining the design of a report, you might use the same or similar commands time and again. As you can tell, some LIST commands can get quite long. Fortunately, you can save yourself a lot of time with the Dot Processor which was described in Chapter 5. In fact, this is how you create a report program, by naming and saving a LIST command with the Dot Processor.

After executing a LIST command, enter from TCL: **.:S1 report name**. Now, instead of retyping the entire LIST command to produce the report, just enter whatever you typed for report name in the dot processor command above.

COUNTING RECORDS

The records in a file can be counted with the R/LIST command COUNT. You can also use this command to count only those records which meet certain conditions. For example:

> **:COUNT INVOICES**
> 145 Records Counted

counted all of the records in the INVOICES file.

> **:COUNT INVOICES WITH CUSTOMER = "ALLIED ELECTRIC"**
> 34 Records Counted

counted only those invoices sent to ALLIED ELECTRIC.

CREATING AND USING SELECT LISTS

Select lists are created with the SELECT command. There is no display output from a SELECT command, instead a list of record IDs is created which can be used in other operations (see "Select List" section of Chapter 4). The command can be used without conditional phrases,

> **:SELECT INVOICES**

in which case all the records in the file are selected. But it is usually used in conjunction with a conditional phrase:

> **:SELECT INVOICES WITH UNITS > 10**

Select lists can also be placed in a sorted order using a BY phrase.

> **:SELECT INVOICES WITH UNITS > 10 BY CUSTOMER**

The select list is then passed to the very next command entered from TCL. To emphasize this, the normal TCL prompt (:) is replaced with a (>) prompt after you execute a SELECT command.   This reminds you that if your next operation involves the same file, only the records in your select list will be used. After that, the prompt reverts back to the (:) prompt.

To suppress the message indicating the number of records selected, use the (S) option.

Saving and Retrieving Lists

A select list can be saved with the SAVE-LIST command so that you can perform an operation with the same group of selected records in the future; for example:

```
:SELECT INVOICES WITH UNITS > 10
28 Record(s) Selected
>SAVE-LIST LARGE.INV
:
```

would create a select list and save it with the name LARGE.INV in the LISTS file. This select list could be recalled with the GET-LIST command:

```
:GET-LIST LARGE.INV
28 Record(s) Selected
>LIST INVOICES (P)
:
```

would recall the saved select list and then display to the printer the 28 selected records.

If you have created a select list and are at the > prompt but then decide you do not want the select list to be used in the next command, just enter >CLEAR and you will return to the colon prompt.

BROWSING RECORDS FROM A DATA FILE

You can easily browse through records from a data file using the following procedure. Call up the data entry screen for the data file as if you were going to edit a record. At the record ID prompt, use PERFORM to execute a SELECT command; for example:

PERFORM SELECT INVOICES WITH AMOUNT > 100

This will form a select list of IDs of the INVOICE records with amount > 100. The first ID from the list is fed to the record ID prompt on the data entry screen and that record's information is displayed on the screen. If you press <E> at the CHANGE prompt, the next ID from the list is entered and the second record's information is displayed. This process will continue until the select list is exhausted or until you press Ctrl-E to exit the screen.

You can also select the records directly from TCL, and then at the ">" prompt enter the name of the data entry screen. The select list will still be passed to the data screen.

MERGING DATA FROM A FILE WITH A FORM DOCUMENT

A common use of a database is to merge information from a data file with a standard form. This is accomplished with the FORM command as explained in the following example.

Assume you want to merge a mailing list data file containing names and addresses with a form letter. Use the text editor to compose the form letter and store it as a record in a file (it will help keep your application organized if you put all of your form documents in one file). Where you want information from the data file to appear in the form letter, insert the field name in braces {}. When you execute the FORM command, the form letter will print out as many times as there are records in the data file; each time with a different name and address. The use of the FORM command is described in detail in the COMMAND REFERENCE.

GENERATING A REPORT PROGRAM WITH R/DESIGN

In this chapter we have shown you how to construct a LIST statement to produce a report. You can save that LIST statement with the dot processor and execute it in the future. Alternatively, R/DESIGN provides a prompt-driven routine for generating an R/BASIC program which can then be compiled and run. This program will produce a report in exactly the same format as an R/LIST command.

You might ask how this is different from using the (S) option with the LIST command. The answer is that it is not very different at all! There are two distinctions to be made, however:

1)   Whereas the LIST (S) option does not include a
      SELECT command in the source code it generates, the
      R/DESIGN process *does* include the SELECT
      statement. (There is nothing, however, to prevent you
      from editing the program generated by LIST and
      inserting a SELECT or PERFORM SELECT yourself.)

2)   Whereas you must construct the LIST command
      yoUrself from TCL, the R/DESIGN routine prompts
      you each step of the way.

It is our belief that very little utility is had from R/DESIGN's routine since you still need to understand the LIST command in order to follow R/DESIGN's prompts! But, for those readers who still insist on trying this process, we present a discussion in the following section.

Naming a Report Program

The first step in generating a report program is to define the program with PGMR. Enter PGMR from the RDESIGN menu or from TCL and answer its prompts as follows:

01 Program Name
> Enter the program name. It can be any length of alphanumeric characters, but must begin with an alphabetic character and may not contain any spaces.

02 Type of Program
> Enter REPORT

03 Short Title for Heading
> Enter a short descriptive program name. It will be used for application documentation and for heading information in source code generated by R/DESIGN. An input here is mandatory and there is no default value. We usually use the same value as the program name.

04 Language Used
> Enter BASIC since all report programs are R/BASIC programs.

05 Major File Used
> Enter the name of the data file which will provide the data for the report.

06 Additional Files Read
> Skip this prompt by pressing <E>.

07 Additional Files Written
> Skip this prompt by pressing <E>.

Constructing the LIST Statement

The SEL portion of R/DESIGN will help you construct a LIST statement. Enter SEL from either the RDESIGN menu or the TCL prompt. You will then see a screen similar to the example shown in **Figure 9.8**.

```
SEL      INV.RPT  (INV.RPT)      FILE = INVOICES   PAGE = 1

01> *0 INV.NO
02> CUSTOMER
03> DATE
04> UNITS




ENTER NEXT "BY" STATEMENT (I)? (#1)
```

Figure 9.8   SEL Screen for Report Program

You will be prompted to input five parts of the LIST statement starting with a BY phrase. The other four parts are: WITH phrases, display fields, modifiers, and heading. You can make as many entries to each prompt as you like. When you have made all of the entries you wish for one prompt, press <E> twice to go to the next prompt.

Notice that the fields from the data file are displayed in the upper portion of the screen. Instead of typing in the field name at each prompt, you can just enter the reference number next the field you are selecting (these reference numbers are not the same as the FMC numbers assigned in BUD). The exception to this is the WITH phrase where you must type out the whole phrase, including the field name. The " (I) " in the prompt at the bottom of the screen indicates when you can use the reference number instead of typing the field name.

To sort our example by the CUSTOMER field, you would enter either of the following:

BY CUSTOMER
or

BY 2

At the "WITH" prompt, just enter the same phrase you would include in a LIST statement. At the "display" prompt, enter the fields you want to appear on the report. BREAK-ON and TOTAL phrases cause their subject fields to be displayed; therefore, they are entered at this prompt.

At the "modifier" prompt you can enter any of the modifiers that apply to the LIST command except GRAND-TOTAL. This is also where you indicate if the report is to go to the printer -- but instead of entering the command option (P), enter LPTR.

The last prompt is "heading". Enter the heading you want to appear at the top of each page, including any special characters in single quotes (you cannot enter a footing). Do not enter the word HEADING nor enclose your entry in double quotes as you would in a LIST statement.

After entering the last prompt, you will be returned to either the R/DESIGN menu or the TCL prompt. You have essentially "built" a LIST command which is now stored as a record in the RDES file (see Appendix VII for the RDES record structure).

Compiling and Saving the Report Program

Before you can run your report program, your LIST command must be turned into R/BASIC source code and compiled. This is done with the GEN routine of R/DESIGN. Call GEN from either the R/DESIGN menu or by entering GEN at the TCL prompt (if you get an error message or cannot get to GEN see the Advanced Topics at the end of this chapter).

GEN will prompt you for the name of your program and for the name of a file where it will be stored. Enter the same report program name as you entered in PGMR and designate a file to hold the program. The file must have already been created using the CREATE-FILE command (see CREATE-FILE in PART III: COMMAND REFERENCE). We generally use one file to hold all of our R/BASIC programs (named BP for Basic Programs).

You will then be asked if you want to compile and run the program. You want the program compiled, answer "Y". Your program is now compiled and saved. Using INV.RPT as an example, there would now be a record in the BP file with an ID of INV.RPT containing the R/BASIC code. There would be another record in the BP file with an ID of $INV.RPT containing the compiled code. This report program could then be run by entering.

:RUN BP INV.RPT

DISPLAYING A DIRECTORY OF FILES AND PROGRAMS

You can display a listing of the files which are attached to your account by using the command LISTFILES. This will display all of the files which you can access from the current account including the files you created, the files placed in the account when it was created, and any global files (assuming the media where all these files are located have been attached).

You can list all of the Revelation files located on a medium with the LISTMEDIA command.

You can list the data entry screens you have created by listing the RDES file with :LIST RDES. The names of the entry and report programs as well as any cross references and menus you have created with R/DESIGN will be displayed.

BUILDING MENUS

Menus link your application together and are built with R/DESIGN's BLD.MENU routine. The selections on your menu can perform TCL commands, run R/BASIC programs, display other menus or even perform DOS commands. The BLD.MENU routine makes an entry in the VOC file so that the menu can be called by just entering its name at the TCL prompt.

Invoke BLD.MENU by selecting option (10) of the R/DESIGN Menu or entering BLD.MENU at the TCL prompt. The screen shown in **Figure 9.9** will be displayed.

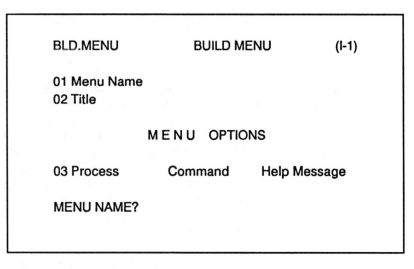

```
BLD.MENU            BUILD MENU            (I-1)


01 Menu Name
02 Title


              M E N U   OPTIONS


03 Process        Command      Help Message


MENU NAME?
```

Fig. 9.9 BLD.MENU screen

The following is a description of the prompts on the BLD.MENU screen.

01   **Menu Name**
      Enter the name of the menu; this will be the ID of the record in RDES containing the menu's parameters (and also a VOC entry).

02   Title

Enter the title that you wish to appear at the top of the menu. You have two options for locating all of the text which will appear on the menu. You can rely on the default values of BLD.MENU or you can specify screen locations using the format "(column, row)". For example, "(10,5)ACCOUNTING MENU" would position the title "ACCOUNTING MENU" at column 10 and row 5. Note that if you use the screen location format for the title then you must also use this format for the process descriptions in the next prompt.

03   Process

Enter the description of the option as you wish it to appear on the menu. This and the next two prompts are associated multi-values. If you used a screen location for the title, you must use one here also.

Command

Enter a TCL command, R/LIST sentence, cataloged program name, or another menu name. When the respective process description is selected, this command will be executed. To include a password with a command option, place the password within "@" signs before the command; e.g. "@XYZ@MENU ACCT.MENU" would prompt for the password XYZ before calling the ACCT.MENU menu.

Help Message

Enter a description up to 79 characters in length which will be displayed at the bottom of the screen when the option is highlighted.

You can exit a menu without selecting any of the options by using the function keys, Ctrl F5. Normally this will take you to the TCL prompt. Instead of going to the TCL prompt, you can have a TCL command executed by using the following procedure:

- if you are not using the screen location format, enter the TCL command as the last <u>process</u>, enclosed in "@" (e.g. @OFF@ would log off of Revelation if Ctrl F5 was entered at the menu).

- if you use screen location format, enter (0,0) as the last <u>process</u> and the TCL command enclosed in "@" as the last <u>command</u>.

REVELATION'S INTERNALLY GENERATED DOCUMENTATION

Revelation will generate documentation for applications developed with R/DESIGN. This documentation is generated with the DOC routine which is invoked from the RDESIGN Menu or by entering DOC at the TCL prompt. You will be prompted for the name of a data entry program and whether you want the documentation sent to the printer or the monitor.

This useful feature is not commonly found on database management systems. If you spend the little amount of time it takes to enter information into the Description fields of the R/DESIGN routines when you are building your application, you can easily generate thorough documentation which is very helpful for someone who needs to understand how your application works.

ADVANCED TOPICS

Prompting for inputs to a TCL command

You can use two question marks to prompt the user for inputs to any TCL command. TCL will display whatever text is included between the question marks as a prompt. For example:

:LIST ?ENTER FILE NAME?

will prompt the user:

ENTER FILE NAME?

Then when an entry is made, the command will be performed using that entry in the command. This format works on all TCL commands, not just with the LIST command. For example:

DELETE BP ? WHICH RECORDS?

You can insert a dictionary item within the question marks and the bottom screen prompt (parameter 12 from the BUD screen) will be used as a prompt for the operator. For example:

:LIST INVOICES WITH CUST.NO = ?CUST.NO?

will prompt the operator with "ENTER CUSTOMER NUMBER" if that was the parameter stored in the CUST.NO dictionary record for the bottom screen prompt.

The last example will only work if the CUST.NO is numeric data. Since all non-numeric data must be enclosed within quotes in the LIST command, use quotes inside the question marks. For example:

:LIST INVOICES WITH CUST.NAME = ?'ENTER CUSTOMER NAME'?

would prompt:

ENTER CUSTOMER NAME

Then if you entered ACE APPLIANCE, the command that would be performed would be:

:LIST INVOICES WITH CUST.NAME = 'ACE APPLIANCE'

A single question mark at the end of the command will prompt the user using the system prompt character:

LIST ?

would prompt:

?

One small problem with this entire feature is that it leaves a space in the command where the question mark appeared. This prevents you for prompting for data which <u>must</u> go right next to another character in the command line. For example, consider the COPY command:

COPY CUSTOMERS 103 TO: (?filename?

This command will <u>not</u> work because the file name that is entered <u>must</u> be right next to the parenthesis, but the question prompting leaves a blank space.

How Select Lists are Stored

In a previous example, we saved a select list of 28 records and gave it the name LARGE.INV. This would create a record in the LISTS file with an ID of LARGE.INV. Each field in a record will contain a selected ID. You can view the names of saved select lists with :LIST LISTS.

Using GEN

You may have problems invoking GEN. GEN uses a utility file named CN which is located on the SYSPROG account. If you have installed the Utilities Disk as described in Chapter 5, then this file should already be on your hard disk in the SYSPROG account. If you try to use GEN from another account, you will get an error message saying you need to attach CN.

The best solution is to make CN a a global file so that all accounts can access it. Use the MOVE command to copy CN from the SYSPROG account to the "NULL" account.

:MOVE SYSPROG CN C TO: NULL CN C

This creates a global copy of CN (check this by doing a LISTMEDIA; you should see two CN files, one in SYSPROG and one with no account). Then delete the unnecessary copy of CN from the SYSPROG account with DELETE-FILE. (First make sure that you are logged into the SYSPROG account.)

If CN is attached by your account but it still cannot be invoked, you may not have the updated version of CN (it was changed with some recent revisions to Revelation). Delete the old CN file and then MOVE the updated version to your hard disk.

CHAPTER TEN: FILE OPERATIONS

This chapter explains how to perform various file operations such as copying, moving and deleting records and files.

Insofar as Revelation overlays its own file structure and disk maintenance on top of DOS, Revelation can almost be viewed as having its own operating system. For instance, if you tried to list your Revelation data files from anywhere in DOS, all you would get is a list of cryptic file names beginning with the three letters "ROS" followed by five numbers.

This confusing state of affairs stems from the heart of Revelation's power -- its unique file structure. It is this file structuring system that allows for easy dynamic string handling, Local Area Network record locking, and virtually unlimited fields per record and records per file. (Actually, there is a limit of 64k characters per record, but if you ever legitimately reach this limit, send us a copy of your application notes and we'll reimburse you for the price of this book!)

There is a penalty to bear for this powerful and flexible file structure, however. It comes in the form of the confusing and sometimes difficult task of manipulating files and records. And if things aren't perplexing enough, there is the additional issue of what to do about the dictionary records of files.

This chapter uses a number of TCL commands -- for a complete syntax and description of all of the TCL commands, see PART III: COMMAND REFERENCE.

REVIEW OF HOW REVELATION STORES DATA: MEDIA, ACCOUNTS, AND FILES

1. The word "volume" is used in Revelation to refer to the storage medium where files are placed. This volume may be a disk drive or a DOS path name which includes the disk drive and directory path such as C:\REV\DATA. You must name a medium with the NAMEMEDIA command before you can store Revelation files on it. That will set up a DOS file named ROSMEDIA.MAP to keep track of the Revelation files on that medium. The default volume always refers to the drive and directory which contains REV.EXE.

2. An account is a group of related files used for a particular application. You can only be logged into one account at a time. The SYSPROG account is the only defined account when you first start Revelation, but you may create as many accounts as you need. Each account may have its own password, and each account has its own set of files. Some files may be in the global (or null) account, thereby allowing access to these files from all accounts.

Each account must also have its own VOCabulary file. (The VOC file is automatically created whenever you create a new account. This VOC file is placed in the default volume and must remain there since Revelation will only look in the default volume for the vocabulary.)

When you log into an account, Revelation automatically "attaches" the files for that account located on the default medium. You must tell Revelation to attach files located on other media.

3. When you create an account, Revelation creates a LISTS file (for select lists) and a VOC (vocabulary) file. If you want to use R/DESIGN with this account, you will need to create an RDES file.

4. When you create a file using R/DESIGN's DEF program, or with the TCL CREATE-FILE command, you must always define the file name. DEF only allows you to create files on the default drive in the currently logged account. The CREATE-FILE command, on the other hand, allows you to create files on any drive, but limits creation of files to the current account only. Revelation database files consist of a dictionary part and a data part. The dictionary part contains the information which defines the fields of the data part.

COPYING RECORDS

Copying Records Within a File

Often you will want to duplicate a record in a file. For example, this is useful when you want to create a record which is similar to an existing record. You'll find it easier to copy the old record and make modifications to it rather than start from scratch.

Records are copied within a file with the **COPY** command. In the following example, the record for customer number 1543 (CUST.NO is the key field) is copied to a new record and given the number 1556:

:COPY CUSTOMERS 1543 TO: 1556

Changing the Record Key

What if you need to change the record key of a particular record? This is accomplished by copying that record to another record in the file with a different name and using the delete option of the COPY command:

:COPY CUSTOMERS 1543 (D) TO: 1556

Using a Data Entry Screen to Duplicate Records in a File

There is another way to duplicate records within a file if you are using an R/DESIGN data entry screen. At the record key prompt, retrieve the record you wish to copy by entering its key (the rest of the prompts will be automatically filled in). From the CHANGE prompt, edit the key prompt and type in a new record ID. After pressing <E> at the CHANGE prompt, you will be asked if you want to delete the original record. If you answer "yes", you will rename the record. If you answer "no", you will have two records that are identical except for the record ID.

Copying Records Between Different Files of the Same Account

Copying records from one file to another is rather simple when the files are in the same account. Just decide whether you just want the record copied to another file or whether you want it moved. "Move" in this context means deleted from the original file and moved to the target file. Use the COPY command and include the "D" option if the record is being moved. In the following example, the CUSTOMERS record with a key of 1543 will be copied to the file OLD.CUSTOMERS and deleted from the file CUSTOMERS.

:COPY CUSTOMERS 1543 (D) TO:
(OLD.CUSTOMERS 1543

Notice that the target file is preceded by a left parenthesis "(" to indicate that record 1543 is to be copied to the **file**

OLD.CUSTOMERS. The parenthesis and file name are omitted when copying to the same file, as in the previous examples.

The second "1543" on the command line is optional; when records are copied to a different file the default record key is the old key. Of course, if you wanted the record to have a different key when it was copied to OLD.CUSTOMERS, you could have entered a different ID on the command line.

Copying Records Between Files in Different Accounts

What if either the source file or the destination (target) file is *not* in the current account? In this case, use the **SET-FILE** command to create a qfile pointer called QFILE to point to the file in the other account. Then use the COPY command. In the following example, the two records with customer numbers of 1543 and 1567 will be copied to the file pointed to by QFILE.

:COPY CUSTOMERS 1543 1567 TO: (QFILE

Another example:

COPY QFILE 341 TO: (CUSTOMERS 1546

copies record 341 of the file pointed to by the qfile pointer, to record 1546 of the CUSTOMERS file.

In the unlikely case when both files are in a different account, only one of the files can be pointed to using the SET-FILE command. Therefore we recommend that you logto one of the accounts and use one of the above procedures.

Copying an Entire File to Another File

All of the records from one file can be copied to another file by using the wildcard character "*" with the COPY command.

:COPY CUSTOMERS * TO: (OLD.CUSTOMERS

This process, however, is *not* the same as copying the entire file for two reasons:

a)   The target file must already exist when using the COPY command, and

b)   You have only copied the *data records* and not the dictionary records.

Of course, you could then copy all the dictionary records (see below), but there is a faster method for copying an entire file using the MOVE command.

Copying a Select List of Records

In the previous examples of the COPY command, the record(s) to be copied were placed on the command line. You can also pass a list of selected records to the COPY command for processing as follows:

:SELECT CUSTOMERS WITH CITY = "ST. LOUIS"
>COPY CUSTOMERS TO: (OLD.CUSTOMERS

A list of customers living in St. Louis will be passed to the COPY command and only these records will be copied to the OLD.CUSTOMERS file.

COPYING FILES

One of the more confusing file operations in Revelation involves copying files from one account to another or from one volume to another volume. To add to the confusion is the misnaming of the command used to perform this function.

While the COPY command is used to copy records from one file to another, the MOVE command is used to copy files from one place (from one account or from one volume) to another. The MOVE command copies both the data records and the dictionary records; there is no option that allows you to selectively copy one or the other. The MOVE command also does not have a delete option such as the one with COPY that allows you to delete the original file.

The source and destination files of a MOVE command can be in any account. If you are moving a file within the same account and volume, the file must be given a unique name, otherwise you will be told that the file already exists. The following example copies the CUSTOMERS file in the SYSPROG account located on the C drive to a file on the same account and volume with the name OLD.CUSTOMERS:

> **:MOVE SYSPROG CUSTOMERS C TO: SYSPROG OLD.CUSTOMERS C**

Several files can be moved by separating their names with semicolons:

> **:MOVE SYSPROG CUSTOMERS;INVOICES C TO: SYSPROG OLD.CUSTOMERS;OLD.INVOICES C**

Copying Files to a Different Volume

To copy a file within the same account but to a different volume use:

> **:MOVE SYSPROG CUSTOMERS C TO: SYSPROG OLD.CUSTOMERS B**

or

> **:MOVE SYSPROG CUSTOMERS C TO: B**

In the second example, note that the name of the file being copied is used as the name of the target file. This name repetition is only allowed when copying a file to a different volume or to a different account. In order to understand why this is the case, you need to understand what actually happens during the MOVE command.

How the Move Command Works

1) The ROSMEDIA.MAP of the destination volume is checked to determine that no existing file in the destination account on that volume already has the destination file name .

2) The new file is assigned a DOS file name with the next sequential file number stored in the ROSMEDIA.MAP on the designated volume (see Appendix V).

3) The file is physically copied to the designated volume.

4) The ROSMEDIA.MAP is updated to show the account and name of the new file, the corresponding DOS name, and the modulo of the file.

Thus, if a file is being copied to the same account and the same volume it must have a unique name. In all other cases, the target file may have the same name.

Note that even when a file is copied to the current account, it is not available for immediate access and will not appear in the list of files generated by the LISTFILES command because it has not yet been ATTACHed. Although the name of the file was placed into the ROSMEDIA.MAP during the MOVE operation, it is up to you to attach the file by using the ATTACH command.

What happens if you create two files in the same account with the same name, but on different volumes? Revelation will not attach two files with the same name at the same time, instead it will attach the last one you specified to be attached. For example if you entered the command:

:MOVE SYSPROG CUSTOMERS C TO: SYSPROG CUSTOMERS A

and then entered **:LIST CUSTOMERS**, you would still be listing the CUSTOMERS file on the C drive. However, if you then ATTACH the A drive, the CUSTOMERS file on that drive becomes the current CUSTOMERS file. Any operation that you now perform on the CUSTOMERS file will be performed on the file on the A drive.

In other words, only one file with a particular name may be attached at any one time. An account may have several files with the same name, but they will have to exist on different volumes. Only the file from the last volume attached will be the current file listed by the LISTFILES command and, therefore, used by Revelation.

Moving Files to Other Computer Systems with a Floppy Diskette

Often you will want to copy a file and take it to another system. The process for this procedure involves the following steps:

1) Use the NAMEMEDIA command to create a ROSMEDIA.MAP on a formatted floppy diskette.

2) Use the MOVE command to copy the Revelation file(s) to the floppy. For example:

      :MOVE SYSPROG CUSTOMERS;INVOICES C TO: A

In this example, the CUSTOMERS and INVOICES files will both be copied to the A drive.

3) When you get to the other Revelation system, simply MOVE the files from the diskette to the desired account on the hard disk.

CAUTION! You must be careful when moving files using the actual DOS names of the files. It is tempting, for example, to perform a LISTFILES to view the DOS names of a Revelation file and then copy these DOS files to another directory or disk drive. You must ensure that no other DOS files with that name exist (each Revelation system assigns the same DOS file names) and that the ROSMEDIA.MAP is updated with the

Revelation file name, DOS file name, and modulo for that file. This risky process is only recommended for advanced users.

Changing the Account of a File

Three methods exist for changing the account to which a file belongs. Each method is used for different circumstances.

Method 1: For files residing in the currently logged account and default volume, use the RENAME-FILE command.

Method 2: When the file resides on the current volume, but **not** in the currently logged account, use the MOVE command to copy the file to the new account and volume. Then, making sure that you are logged into the original account, perform the DELETE-FILE command to delete the original file. You may use Method 1 above instead if you first log to this new account.

Method 3: When the file resides on a volume that is **not** attached, editing the ROSMEDIA.MAP becomes necessary. This method should only be attempted by advanced users.

1) Invoke the text editor for the ROSMEDIA.MAP of the volume where the file resides, for example:

:TEXT DOS C:\REV\DATA\ROSMEDIA.MAP

2) Find the correct account and file name on the third line of the record and carefully change the sub-value corresponding to the name of the account for that file.

3) Save the ROSMEDIA.MAP and then ATTACH the appropriate volume in order to reflect this change.

DELETING RECORDS AND FILES

Revelation provides two commands for deleting records and files. Some confusion may occur when you delete a file from an account and that file also exists on another account or volume; but we shall discuss these situations.

Deleting Records from a File   .

Use the DELETE command to delete records from a specific file. For example, to delete customer 1546 from the CUSTOMERS file, use:

:DELETE CUSTOMERS 1546

You may also delete records through an R/DESIGN data entry screen by typing "DELETE" or pressing Ctrl-D from the CHANGE prompt.

There is a third method for deleting records from a file. If you are using the TEXT editor, pressing Ctrl-D will delete the record you are currently editing. Again, you will first be prompted to verify this action.

You may also pass a select list to the DELETE command:

:SELECT CUSTOMERS WITH STATUS =
"INACTIVE"
>DELETE CUSTOMERS

To delete all the data records from a particular file while leaving the dictionary intact, use the CLEAR-FILE command. Or, if you wish the data records to remain while still deleting the dictionary records, use the CLEAR-FILE command with the word "DICT" preceding the file name. For example:

:CLEAR-FILE CUSTOMERS
:CLEAR-FILE DICT CUSTOMERS

When you delete a record, the actual space occupied by the file on the disk may or may not be reduced -- this depends on whether the file uses a ROS or LINK file structure. ROS files expand and contract as files are added and deleted. However, LINK files are pre-allocated disk space at file creation time; they will expand as the need arises but will not contract. When records are deleted from LINK files, the file does not change size but the space freed by the deleted record is now available for use by another record.

Deleting Files

Use the DELETE-FILE command from TCL to delete files in the current account, for example:

:DELETE-FILE CUSTOMERS

You will be asked to verify this operation.

Remember, to delete a file in another account, you must first logto that account. Also, to delete a file which exists in the current account but on a volume that has not been attached, you must first attach that volume.

You may also delete files with R/DESIGN by using the DEF program. After retrieving the file's information on the screen, type "DELETE" or press Ctrl-D from the CHANGE prompt to delete the file.

MERGING FILES

Many other database management systems have special commands for merging or joining two files. Before we discuss how Revelation handles this function, let's define what we might mean by merging files.

Two files may be joined to form a third database file, with all the records from both files now in this new file. Or, we might want to create a third file by merging the records from two other files but limit which fields from each record get copied.

Records in Revelation files must all have unique keys. This requirement, although bearing many advantages, proves to be an important consideration when merging files. At first, it seems quite trivial to join two files. Simply use the COPY command to copy all the records from one file to the other.

For example:

:COPY INVOICES.OLD * TO: (INVOICES.NEW

would copy all the records in the INVOICES.OLD file to the INVOICES.NEW file. If some of the records in INVOICES.OLD have the same IDs as records in INVOICES.NEW, you will get a message saying that these records cannot be copied because they already exist in the destination file. If you want to overwrite these records on INVOICES.NEW, you must use the (O) option (see the COPY command in the COMMAND REFERENCE).

You must also ensure that the structures of the data records being merged are the same. For example, if in one file the customer's name is in field 2 while in the second file the name is in field 3, watch out -- you will not be given any warning during the COPY process, but just wait until you start reporting or retrieving records. If the merged data does not correspond to the data dictionary of the destination file, there will be plenty of confusion.

The level of complication quickly escalates when you want to join only specified fields from the data records of two or more files. Because there are no TCL commands for this purpose, you will need to use R/BASIC programming to accomplish this task.

SORTING RECORDS WITHIN A FILE

Sorting files is another common concept defined by other database management packages, but doesn't have any real meaning with Revelation. Most other database packages sequentially place each new record into a data file. Since they use sequential searches to retrieve a record, it sometimes helps to have the file in some kind of sorted order.

Revelation, on the other hand, uses a unique method called "hashing" for adding and retrieving records to a database file. An algorithm is performed using the record key and the modulo of the file to come up with a group number for that record.   (There are as many groups as the value of the modulo.) The record is then added to the end of this group. When records are deleted from the file, the group is dynamically restructured to replace the void left by the record.

Since the hashing algorithm uniquely determines the placement of a record, physically sorting the stored records becomes impossible. But this doesn't mean we can't get the illusion of a sorted file. Revelation's LIST processor gives the user tremendous flexibility for *displaying* the data in virtually unlimited numbers of sorted sequences.

RENAMING FILES

Earlier in this chapter we explained how you can rename a file by using the MOVE command to copy the file to a new name and then deleting the original file.   The RENAME-FILE command is a faster way of changing the name of a file. For example, enter :RENAME-FILE INVOICES and Revelation will prompt you for the new file name.

One of the important reasons for renaming a file is that two files with the same name cannot be attached at the same time. One solution is to rename one of the files.

What happens when a file is renamed using the RENAME-FILE command? Nothing more than that the information pertaining to that file in the ROSMEDIA.MAP is changed. With this information, you should see that another way to change a file's name is to edit the third field of the ROSMEDIA.MAP and change the Revelation file name directly.

CAUTION! You must be careful; this method will not report errors such as entering a duplicate name for a file that already exists on that volume in that account.

FILE POINTERS

Qfile pointers are discussed extensively earlier in this book. In this section we only want to cover the use of qfile pointers in relation to file operations.

We have already seen that qfiles may be used with the COPY command. In this capacity, qfiles are simply synonyms for the actual file to which they point. When records are copied to or from a qfile, they are actually being copied to or from the file to which the qfile points. Likewise, if you delete records from a qfile, the records are deleted from the file to which the qfile points. Even select lists may be generated from qfiles.

However, the MOVE command will NOT work with qfiles and you may not use the qfile pointer to delete a file. If you use the DEF program in R/DESIGN and press Ctrl-D from the CHANGE prompt after retrieving a qfile record, you will delete the qfile pointer itself and not the file to which it points.

DICTIONARY RECORDS

One of the powerful features of Revelation is the data dictionary in every file. We have discussed dictionaries in other parts of this book; therefore, this section will only discuss how the concepts discussed in this chapter pertain to a file's dictionary.

The COPY command can be used to act on dictionary records in the same way as it acts on data records if you precede the file name with the word "DICT" in the command. For example, to copy the dictionary record NAME from the CUSTOMERS file to the dictionary of the file OLD.CUSTOMERS enter:

:COPY DICT CUSTOMERS NAME TO: (DICT OLD.CUSTOMERS

CAUTION! If you are copying a dictionary item to another file and you omit the "DICT" after the parenthesis, you will end up copying the dictionary record as a data record to the target file.

Another method for copying dictionary records from one file to another is to use the BUD program in R/DESIGN. After retrieving a dictionary record, edit the file name prompt by entering "1" at the CHANGE prompt. Enter the name of the file where you want to copy the dictionary item.

Suppose you want to copy just the dictionary structure from one file to another. One way to do this would be:

1) Use the CREATE-FILE command to create the new file.
2) COPY all the dictionary records from the original file to the new file.

A second method, which is significantly faster on files with many dictionary items, is:

1) Use the MOVE command to copy the entire file to a new file.
2) Use the CLEAR-FILE command to clear the data portion of this new file.

It is important to understand that deleting a dictionary record does NOT delete the information stored in the corresponding field of the data records. This fact rests on the idea that dictionary records and data records are stored in separate frames within the file, and that data records are nothing more than strings of dynamic arrays (see Appendix V).

In a data record, the only thing that separates one data field value from another is the field marker (ASC 254 = ■). A dictionary record is only necessary if you want to refer to that value by name and to control its input and output requirements. Of course, to gain access to that field in an R/DESIGN screen requires that a dictionary record exist.

If you happen to have a file that has data records but no dictionary records, you might wonder what happens when you try to LIST the file. The LIST processor first searches for a dictionary record named @CRT, the group field containing the names of the default display fields. If that dictionary field is absent, R/LIST will refer to the dictionary of the VOC file and use the information in its @CRT dictionary record. Usually this dictionary record is defined to list the first five fields in a record.

BACKING UP THE SYSTEM

Backing up a Revelation system presents its own special set of unique considerations. Consider what occurs if you just use the DOS copy command to backup a Revelation file to diskette. If the file is a ROS file, then you must copy all of the associated DOS files. This is fairly easy to accomplish; just determine the native DOS file name for the Revelation file using the LISTMEDIA or LISTFILES command and then use the DOS copy command:

COPY ROS10016.* A:

But now the trouble begins. What if you can't fit all the files onto one floppy? No problem -- use the DOS BACKUP command instead. In fact, once you know the native file names of the Revelation files you want to backup, you could create a DOS batch file that performs this backup. The one warning here is that if you modify your Revelation system by recreating or copying your files and then renaming them, the DOS file names in the batch file may become obsolete. Once again, use caution.

CAUTION! When it comes time to restoring these files, there are other dangers. The DOS restore command only places the files from the floppy back into the directory from which they were backed up. You still have the task of ensuring that the ROSMEDIA.MAP knows the files are there, with the appropriate Revelation file name and the correct modulo.

Furthermore, if you backup the native DOS files for the purpose of moving them to another system, you must be very careful that the restore process does not wipe out any files with the same DOS names on the other system!

Consider this next possibility. Suppose you have a Revelation file that was copied onto a floppy by the DOS copy command.

Let's assume that it is the Revelation file CUSTOMERS with the DOS native filename of ROS10016. If you somehow corrupt the original CUSTOMERS file, what do you have to do to restore it from the floppy?

If you know that the original file has a DOS filename of ROS10016, and you are certain that the modulo of the file has not been changed since copying it to the floppy, it is possible to use the DOS erase command to delete any ROS10016.* files, and then just copy ROS10016.* from the floppy back to the volume of the original file. (It is necessary to first erase ROS10016.* because there may be more ROS10016 files on the disk than on the backup copy).

A somewhat simpler method exists for backing up most Revelation files. For smaller files, using the MOVE command to copy files from a volume to a floppy disk is much more convenient. You must be certain, however, to use the NAMEMEDIA command to create a ROSMEDIA.MAP on every target floppy diskette that you use.

One big advantage to backing up Revelation files in this manner is that you have the option of restoring specific records rather than the whole file at once. Furthermore, you don't have to worry about the DOS native file names.

The only drawback with this last method is that you may run out of room on the floppy diskette. You will therefore have to calculate how much room is needed for each Revelation file by looking at the size of the corresponding DOS files.

Finally, perhaps the easiest method for backing up your Revelation data files (and therefore the safest, since if it is easy you will be sure to perform the backup!) is to purchase a tape backup system and perform daily backups on your disk.

If you only want to backup your Revelation files, then create a VOC entry that batch performs the MOVE command and copies all the desired Revelation files to an empty subdirectory with a ROSMEDIA.MAP. The tape system can then backup only this subdirectory. The advantage to this method is that it allows you to restore your files to a subdirectory without the worry of writing over other files.

DOS FILE OPERATIONS

There are at least three entry points to DOS and DOS files from Revelation:

1) **The TCL command :PC** temporarily suspends execution of Revelation and places the user into DOS. Enter "EXIT" from the DOS prompt to return to Revelation.

Alternatively, you could enter **:PC command,** where "command" is any valid DOS command. In this case, the DOS command will execute and then return you to Revelation.

2) **R/BASIC DOS file commands.** These special R/BASIC commands allow you to directly manipulate DOS files. They are covered in Part III, Command Reference.

3) **The DOS file.** Revelation allows the user to treat all of DOS as if it were one big file with all DOS files viewed as records within the Revelation "DOS" file. Thus, you can use the COPY command to copy "records" from the DOS file into Revelation files. For example,

:COPY DOS A:PORTER TO: (BP

will copy the DOS file PORTER, located on the A-drive, to a record in the BP file with the name "PORTER".

Similarly, you may use the DELETE command to delete a DOS file:

:DELETE DOS TEMPORARY

ADVANCED TOPICS

Recovering a Deleted File

Generally speaking, once a Revelation file has been deleted, there is no way to recover it. However, if you have the good fortune to know what the DOS file name was, as well as the modulo of the file before it was deleted, you might be able to restore the file.

Use a file recovery utility to attempt recovering the DOS file or files associated with the lost Revelation file. If it is a LINK file there will only be one DOS file. If it is a ROS file, things can get a little tricky since there will be n+1 or more DOS files for a Revelation file with modulo n, depending on how many records were in the file and whether there were any additional overflow frames.

For example, if you know that the ROS file corresponds to the DOS files ROS10015.???, try to recover all DOS files beginning with "ROS10015". If the operation is successful, you will then modify the ROSMEDIA.MAP in the appropriate volume to recognize this recovered file. Three associated multi value fields must be modified:

Field 3:   Append the account and Revelation file name as sub-values. (account^{n}filename)

Field 4:   Append the DOS file name without the extension.

Field 5:   Append the modulo of the file.

As usual, remember to attach this volume in order to reflect the changes to the ROSMEDIA.MAP.

Recreating Files -- Overflows and Networks

There are two reasons to recreate files in Revelation: to convert ROS files to LINK files for use on a network, or to correct severe frame overflow problems in a file. This section discusses the latter problem. Setting up a network system will be discussed in the next chapter.

The difference between ROS and LINK file structures, as well as the definition of groups and frames, is discussed in detail in Appendix V. Briefly, the modulo of a file is determined according to the number of records and bytes per record estimated at file creation. This modulo number is the number of groups used to store all the records of the file. Records are placed in frames within each group, and if too many records are entered in that group, a frame overflow situation is created, resulting in less efficient disk access.

Determining if a file has reached the frame overflow situation and is degrading the performance of the system can be a tricky problem.

Determining frame overflow status for ROS files is quite different from determining the status for LINK files. For ROS files, you must look at the corresponding DOS files to make this determination. To discover the DOS filename, use the LISTFILES command. (Alternatively, you may compile and catalog the WHERE program in the PROG file that comes with the Utilities Disk and then run this program from TCL. The native DOS file name for any given Revelation file is printed on the screen.)

After finding the DOS file name, get a partial directory of that volume containing the file by issuing the following command from TCL:

:DIR ROS10016.*

where "ROS10016" is the DOS file name. This command will produce all the DOS files associated with the Revelation file in question. To determine the number of frame overflows, check the extensions of the DOS files. Any file with an extension containing a number other than "0" as the last digit is considered an overflow frame. Thus, the file "ROS10016.041" would be an overflow frame, while "ROS10016.030" would not. An excessive number of these frames will probably result in a loss of disk efficiency.

LINK files prove to be a little more tricky. Revelation comes with a utility in the PROG file called RECOVER.LINK. Catalog this utility,

:CATALOG PROG RECOVER.LINK

then run it from TCL. It will show the number of overflow frames for each group of a LINK file .

It's very common to have some frame overflow with LINK files since their frames are only 1k in length. A record larger than 1k will automatically create an overflow frame. You then need to determine how many groups are in frame overflow, how many overflow frames there are, and if this number is too big -- when compared to the average record size -- to warrant taking action.

Unfortunately, for both ROS and LINK files, there is no easy way to determine if the overflow situation is critical. If you suspect that the efficiency of your system is being affected by frame overflow, we suggest you experiment with the modulo of the file.

To change the modulo of a file, use the RECREATE-FILE command which uses the same syntax as the CREATE-FILE command (see PART III: COMMAND REFERENCE). Also, see the discussion on determining the modulo of a file in Appendix V.

CHAPTER ELEVEN: NETWORKING

Increasingly, Local Area Networks are becoming familiar sights in many microcomputer environments. Whether as gateways to larger computer systems or as stand alone networks, LANs provide a way to share centralized data and peripheral hardware equipment.

But using LANs requires that your database management system have a way to preserve the integrity of the database when more than one user tries to access a file.

Cosmos has built networking capabilities into the single-user version of Revelation so that when you decide to run an application on a network, all you have to do is purchase a Network Revelation "bump" disk. One copy of the bump disk needs to be installed for every four Revelation users.

Whether or not you have a Network version now, understanding its capabilities will help you develop single-user applications that are designed for the possibility of later using them on a network.

CONSIDERATIONS WHEN CHOOSING A NETWORK

Choosing the right local area network is nearly as important as choosing the right database management software. It is important to realize that database management applications frequently access large amounts of data on the network file server. Therefore file server speed can be a crucial factor in determining the right LAN to use with Revelation.

In choosing the topology of the network and the network software, you should consider:

1) Price per network node,

2) Number of users on the network during peak use,

3) Number of network users of Revelation at any one time,

Among the LAN vendors, the following manufacturers have been approved for use with Revelation:

> Anex
> AT&T StarLAN
> EtherNet
> HP Office Share
> IBM PC Network
> IBM PC Token Ring
> Nestar Plan
> Novell
> 3COM Ethershare
> 3COM 3Plus
> Tapestry
> Ungermann-Bass

File Structures

There are several factors to consider when using Revelation in a LAN environment. First, you must determine which files are to be shared among the users. This includes both program files and data files. Second, those data files which will be shared must be able to prevent two or more users from retrieving the same record at the same time.

Why is record locking important? To see why, it is first important to understand how a workstation interfaces with a file server.

When a record is retrieved, it is copied from the disk to the memory of the user's workstation. When the user files the record to disk, it is copied from the user's workstation back to the file server disk.

Now suppose User #1 retrieves a record and begins making changes to it. While this is happening, suppose User #2 is also allowed to retrieve that same record and also make changes to it. User #2 completes the modifications and files the record to disk, thinking that these changes will be saved. But when User #1 files the record, it will overwrite whatever is already there, thus negating any changes User#2 has made -- and User#2 will have no idea that his/her changes have been lost.

As you know, Revelation provides two different file management systems. Files with the ROS structure do not have the ability to lock records as they are being used. Therefore, if you want to prevent two users from gaining access to the same record at the same time, you *must* use the LINK file structure.

It should be pointed out that ROS files may still be used on a LAN. In fact, for relatively small files that are *not used* for writing or updating records, the ROS structure is preferred since it provides faster access. Several users may retrieve the same record simultaneously -- as long as the record is for *reading purposes only*, there is no danger of data loss.

HOW REVELATION LOCKS RECORDS

Record locking is not magic. When a record in a LINK file is retrieved, the network operating system can flag that record through a device called a semaphore. Network Revelation has the ability to check that flag. Other workstations will see this and not access the record until the flag is removed.

Applications developed with R/DESIGN automatically use the semaphore flag system. An attempt to retrieve a record that has been flagged will cause R/DESIGN to display a message indicating that the record is in use. This automatic locking and unlocking of records occurs throughout R/DESIGN data entry screens. In addition, you will not be able to use the Revelation text editors on a record nor COPY a record that is flagged. However, the LIST command will still report records that are already in use because it does not attempt to modify those records.

Note that applications designed exclusively with R/DESIGN will be portable between single-user and LAN environments.

PROGRAMMING WITH NETWORKING IN MIND

It is very important that applications employing R/BASIC programming adhere to the requirements for record locking if the application is to be used in a networking environment.

Although a LAN operating system provides the ability to flag a record semaphore, Network Revelation still has the responsibility to tell the operating system which records to flag. Two commands in R/BASIC are used to control this function.

The LOCK command tells the network which record in a file to flag, while the UNLOCK command resets this flag.

IMPORTANT! Even if a record has been flagged as LOCKed, there is nothing to prevent an R/BASIC program from retrieving that record. The record locking function is a logical process, and if the program developer does not abide by that logic, record lockout can be ignored.

Record LOCKing does not actually prevent someone from retrieving a record. The LOCK command only tries to set a record's semaphore flag. If the flag is already set, the ELSE clause of the statement is executed. This conditional branching allows the programmer to decide what to do if the record *is* already in use.

If you try to retrieve a record without first attempting to lock it, nothing will stop you even though the record is already "locked". It is up to each program to obey the status of the LOCK command. Therefore, the programmer must use the LOCK command whenever a record is retrieved if the application will be used in a LAN environment. The LOCK command should include an ELSE statement to be performed if the record is already flagged. This is illustrated with the following program (skip this example if you are not yet familiar with programming):

```
* This routine will attempt to read a record
* from the CUSTOMERS file and write it to
* the TEMP file
OPEN "", "CUSTOMERS" TO CUST.FILE ELSE STOP
OPEN "", "TEMP" TO CUST.TEMP ELSE STOP
TOP:
PRINT "Which Customer do you wish to archive? ":
INPUT CUST.NO
READ CUST FROM CUST.FILE,CUST.NO ELSE
   PRINT CUST.NO:" is not in the Customers file"
   GOTO TOP
END
LOCK CUST.FILE,CUST.NO ELSE
   PRINT CUST.NO:" is being used by someone else."
   GOTO TOP
END
WRITE CUST TO CUST.TEMP,CUST.NO
UNLOCK CUST.FILE,CUST.NO
```

Notice that the LOCK command provides an alternative program logic if the record is already locked. However, again, there is nothing to prevent the programmer from excluding this logic and going ahead and retrieving the record even though it is being used by someone else.

Developers should be aware that a workstation may not lock the same record twice. If this is atttempted, it will result in the ELSE condition of the LOCK statement being executed. You may test for this condition by examining the value of the STATUS() function immediately after the LOCK is executed. If the LOCK is unsuccessful, STATUS() will have one of the following values:

0   record locked by another workstation.
1   record previously locked by current workstation.

Consider the following example:

```
LOCK:
INPUT CUST.NO
LOCK CUST.FILE, CUST.NO ELSE
  IF STATUS() = 0 THEN
    PRINT CUST.NO:" is locked by another user"
    GO TO LOCK
  END
END
READ CUST FROM CUST.FILE, CUST.NO ELSE STOP
```

Notice that the ELSE condition tests the value of STATUS(). If STATUS() does not equal 0, then the record is already locked by the current workstation, so there is no danger in reading the record. Thus, if the record is not already locked, or if it is locked by the current workstation, then the record is read from the file. If the record is locked by another user, the operator is asked to input another customer number.

It is very important that a program UNLOCK a record when finished with it; this allows other workstations access to that record.

Developers designing applications for single-user environments should consider using this record locking logic for the eventuality of moving the application to a LAN. Applications employing the LOCK and UNLOCK commands will run on single user and network versions of Revelation.

We should discuss the concept often referred to as the **"dreaded deadlock"**. Suppose User #1 has one record locked and attempts to retrieve another record which is already locked by User #2. User #1 has a logic which causes it to loop until this record is unlocked:

```
LOCKED = 0
LOOP UNTIL LOCKED
    LOCK CUST.FILE,CUST.NO THEN LOCKED = 1
REPEAT
```

In this example, the attempt to lock the record is continued until the LOCK is successful. But what if User #2 is in a similar loop trying to lock User #1's record?! Both programs will vainly sit there forever (or until the electricity is shut off).

The moral of the story is -- be careful when developing these kinds of locking routines. Specifically, programmers should consider how many times a LOCK should be attempted before a message is either displayed to the user, or some alternate action is taken. Below is an example of this type of logic. This program makes ten attempts at locking a record. On the tenth failure, it prompts you if you want to keep trying.

```
* Another example of record locking logic
*
OPEN "", "CUSTOMERS" TO CUST.FILE ELSE STOP
OPEN "", "TEMP" TO CUST.TEMP ELSE STOP
TOP:
PRINT "Which Customer do you wish to archive? ":
INPUT CUST.NO
LOCKED = 0
COUNT = 10 ; * Try to lock a record only 10 times
```

```
LOOP
  IF NOT(COUNT) THEN
    PRINT CUST.NO:' is locked.  Keep trying? ':
    INPUT TRY
    IF TRY='Y' THEN
      COUNT = 10
    END ELSE
      LOCKED = 1
    END
  END
UNTIL LOCKED
  LOCK CUST.FILE,CUST.NO THEN
    LOCKED = 1
  END ELSE
    COUNT-=1
  END
REPEAT
* If LOCKED=1 and COUNT<>0 then read the record
IF LOCKED AND COUNT THEN
  READ CUST FROM CUST.FILE,CUST.NO ELSE STOP
  WRITE CUST ON CUST.TEMP,CUST.NO
  UNLOCK CUST.FILE,CUST.NO
END
GOTO TOP
```

System developers designing applications to run on networks should consider placing all compiled R/BASIC programs in ROS files as the ROS file structure provides faster disk access. As long as this compiled code is only being read, there is no problem with multiple access of these records. Since the ROS file structure is more efficient for small files, try to keep the size of these files below 64k in length. See Appendix V for a detailed discussion of ROS vs. LINK file structures.

CONVERTING SINGLE USER APPLICATIONS TO RUN ON NETWORKS

Certainly part of the appeal and power of designing an application with Revelation is the portability from single user systems to Local Area Networks. If R/DESIGN is used to develop an application, the conversion process is minimal. This ease is also true for applications where the developer has used the LOCK and UNLOCK commands.

In these situations the only real step to converting single-user applications to run on LAN's is to change the Revelation file structure to the LINK system for those files which will be sharing data. The RECREATE-FILE file command is used to perform this conversion.

RECREATE-FILE CUSTOMERS 50 100 10 (L)

This command will recreate the CUSTOMERS file to the LINK file structure. Revelation will calculate the modulo of this new file by using the parameters passed in the command line. In this case, 50 records with an average record size of 100 bytes and 10 dictionary items will be used in the calculation.

There is a TCL command that comes with the networking version of Revelation that automatically converts system and the tutorial database files to the LINK file structure. Simply enter the command :NETWORK.SETUP from the TCL prompt. If this record is not in your VOC file, you may enter the following commands to make the appropriate LINK files.

RECREATE-FILE LISTS 5 900 2 (L)
RECREATE-FILE RDES 7 900 2 (L)
RECREATE-FILE VOC 200 30 56 (L)
RECREATE-FILE SYSTEM 20 35 2 (L)

The tutorial database files should also be recreated in a similar fashion if you want to share these tutorial files on the LAN.

It is important that you do NOT make the SYSOBJ file a LINK file, as this file contains the program necessary to access files with the LINK structure. Obviously, you would not want to ever lock out another workstation from using this program!

SPEED CONSIDERATIONS

It is common for developers to place all Revelation files -- system files, program application files, and database files -- onto the file server of the LAN. The reasoning is that all users may then have access to these files. But for networks that have extremely heavy workloads with many users vying for access to the shared files, overall system performance will surely erode.

This is particularly easy to understand when you consider that each user must not only tie up the network to read and write shared data, but also use the file server to retrieve R/DESIGN screens and R/BASIC programs.

Once an application is ready to install on a network, the developer should consider placing all *application program* files (which are never written to) onto each local workstation's hard disk. This would include the RDES file, the LISTS file, and all the files containing the application's R/BASIC programs. Thus, when any workstation loads Revelation from the file server, the local hard disk is ATTACHed also. This process reduces the read attempts made on the network to only those files which have constantly changing shared data. Network efficiency will thus be maximized.

A word of warning: The disadvantage to this method is that the developer must update each workstation's files whenever modifications are made to the application. Developers should consider the tradeoff between network speed and ease of system maintenance.

Placing all compiled R/BASIC programs in small ROS files instead of LINK files will also increase speed. As long as these program files are only read from, and not written to, there is no need to provide security against multiple access of these records.

CHAPTER TWELVE: INTRODUCTION TO PROGRAMMING WITH R/BASIC

Revelation's fourth generation programming language, R/BASIC, is inappropriately named. Although R/BASIC employs a command syntax which often resembles other BASIC languages, its database manipulation capabilities are far more powerful than any of its namesakes. Furthermore, it has structured programming abilities rivaling some of the most sophisticated programming languages.

In many ways, R/BASIC can be viewed as a generic language, allowing programmers to write code with logical structures resembling the coder's favorite language.

This chapter covers some of the fundamental concepts of R/BASIC including: when to use programming; how to store, compile, and run programs; and understanding variables, constants, and expressions.

We do not attempt to teach general programming concepts. That task is more appropriately left to the many books that specifically focus on that task. We will cover, however, the meaning of many programming concepts within the context of R/BASIC. For the ambitious programming neophyte, these explanations may indeed serve as an adequate learning tool if used in conjunction with this book's reference section and a fearless attitude towards experimentation.

SITUATIONS WHICH REQUIRE PROGRAMMING IN R/BASIC

It is quite possible to create a complete database system with little or no R/BASIC programming because R/DESIGN is a powerful, and in many cases completely adequate, applications development tool. But even R/DESIGN is not used to its fullest power without a knowledge of R/BASIC.

There are three situations which require the use of R/BASIC: symbolic fields, sophisticated applications, and utility operations.

Symbolic Fields

Symbolic fields can be used to perform complex tasks in ways that at first may not be obvious. During R/DESIGN data entry, symbolic fields can be used to display the result of calculations based on other data already input. They can also be used to perform data input checking routines or to update other files with data from the current screen. Just about any task or routine that you can write in R/BASIC can be used as code in a symbolic field.

When using symbolic fields to display calculated results, it is necessary to equate the special variable "@ANS" to the final result; it is the value of this variable which R/DESIGN and R/LIST use as the value of the symbolic field.

Sometimes during data entry you may want to use a symbolic field to check the status of other R/DESIGN system variables in order to determine a course of action. For example, you might decide to print some information on the screen only if you are adding a record rather than just retrieving an old record for display. A symbolic field can be used to determine the status of the add/change mode and then perform the appropriate action.

To check the status of the add/change mode, you will have to insert the R/DESIGN common variables into your symbolic field in order to check the value of the common variable CHANGE (not to be confused with the CHANGE prompt). To do this, use the statement:

$INSERT PROG,RDESIGN.COMMON

at the beginning of your code to gain access to these R/DESIGN variables.

Sophisticated Applications

Nothing prevents a developer from completely ignoring R/DESIGN and writing program code from scratch. However, even for the most sophisticated applications, a middle course between R/DESIGN and R/BASIC programming is often the best approach.

In certain situations, you may want to customize a data entry screen in a way that is just not possible through R/DESIGN's Prompt Editor. Furthermore, you may require capabilities not possible with the R/LIST processor. In these situations R/BASIC becomes quite essential.

Certainly you are free to write these programs from scratch. However, Revelation provides a utility to generate R/BASIC code for either an R/DESIGN screen or an R/LIST sentence. From this generated code you can then make your own customized program. Of course, you will have to become familiar with the conventions and variables used in this generated code. The effort and time may be worth it -- not only because of the decreased programming for any future generated programs, but also as an opportunity to see an example of R/BASIC programming.

But we offer the following advice: If you think you need to generate R/BASIC code in place of an R/DESIGN screen, think hard about it. There is a very high probability that whatever it is you want to do, it can be done through the use of a symbolic field or a cataloged program during one of the R/BASIC entry points in the data entry screen.

Utilities

Perhaps you need to merge only certain fields from one file to another or quickly locate specific information throughout all of your files. Maybe you need to develop a backup procedure based on user-defined criteria, or compare two versions of a file in order to determine what has changed. These are examples of utilities that would require R/BASIC programming. The power is limited only by your imagination.

WHAT IS AN R/BASIC PROGRAM?

Let's first distinguish between an R/DESIGN data entry screen and an R/BASIC program. The former consists of a set of parameters that are defined using the various R/DESIGN routines such as PGMR, SEL, and SCR. These parameters are stored in a record in the RDES file -- one record for each data entry screen. When you run a data entry "program" these parameters are fed to the R/DESIGN ENTER program which uses them for displaying the data entry screen and prompting for data.

A program created in R/BASIC is quite different. Each program is a set of commands performed in a logical sequence; each statement is very specifically defined by the programming language called "R/BASIC".

Consider an example of a "program" in the language called "TRASH". These statements (or commands)   must be performed one at a time. The execution of the program results in very specific action.

TAKE GARBAGE OUT
THROW INTO BARREL
CALL SANITARY ENGINEER
WASH HANDS

In R/BASIC each line consists of a programming statement that instructs the computer to perform a certain operation. These statements can be broken into categories according to their function:

1) **Input and output statements** determine how data is collected and how it will be displayed.

2) **Assignment statements** assign values to variables.

3) **Calculation statements** manipulate the value of variables.

4) **Control statements** redirect the sequence of program instructions. Since statements are normally executed one after the other, control statements are often called branching and looping statements.

5) **Comment statements** have no effect on the program, but are very helpful in explaining the logic and flow of commands. For complicated programs, providing comments is an essential part of programming. Anyone who will read your code will need them as a road map. And if you return to your own program in the future, you will be grateful to yourself for providing a reminder of what you originally had in mind.

Usually, each statement is placed on a separate line, however you can place several statements on the same line by separating them with semicolons. This makes the program run slightly faster but can make debugging more difficult.

In addition to statements, there are other important "players" in an R/BASIC program. We will discuss variables, expressions, functions, and arithmetic and logical operations before we are finished with this chapter.

Creating a Program

The first step in creating a program is to make a place to store it. Unlike many other programming languages where each program is stored as a separate file in DOS, each R/BASIC program is stored as a record in some Revelation file. We recommend placing programs in special files created just for the purpose of storing R/BASIC programs. Create a file from TCL:

:CREATE-FILE BP 1 1

This command will create a file called "BP" (for "Basic Program"). It makes no difference what you name the files used to store your programs. Since you do not yet know how many programs will be stored in this file nor the average size of the programs, you may have to recreate the file later to provide for faster disk access (see Appendix V).

Revelation provides two separate tools for creating and editing a program. Usually you will use the full-screen TEXT editor for this purpose; the line editor is also available -- although tedious to use in comparison.

:TEXT BP PROG1

will invoke the full-screen editor, creating or editing the PROG1 record in the BP file.

Then just enter your program statements (it is not necessary to precede each program statement with line numbers). To save your program, press the Shift-F2 keys and your sequence of statements will be filed as the PROG1 record in the BP file (see Chapter 14 for more information on the editors).

Compiling a Program

The set of statements you have saved as the PROG1 program is often referred to as "source code". Revelation does not provide an interpreter for R/BASIC which would allow you to run the program directly from this collection of sequential statements.

In fact, when you create a program with the editors, everything you type will be accepted and saved. No "interpretation" or error detection occurs during the editing process.

To prepare your program for execution, you must first compile the source code. Compiling your program results in the creation of another record in the same file where the source code is stored. The record has the same record key name as your program, except for a "$" appended to the beginning of the name. Thus, if you compiled the PROG1 record in the BP file from the above example, you would create another record in the BP file with the record key of $PROG1.

There are three ways to compile a program.

1) From within the TEXT editor, press the Ctrl-F2 keys when you save your code (instead of Shift-F2). This sequence of key strokes first saves the source code and then attempts to compile it. Or from the line editor, enter the command "FIC" to file and compile the program.

2) From the TCL prompt enter the command "COMPILE BP PROG1". This command will compile the PROG1 record in the BP file and place the compiled code in the "$PROG1" record.

3) The TCL command **BASIC** is identical to the **COMPILE** command.

In all three cases, the source code is first saved to the file and an attempt is made to compile the program. If no errors are detected during compilation, the compiled program is saved to disk. If an error is detected, it is reported to the screen and the compiler continues to look for and report any other errors in the program. After the error search is complete, if any errors have been detected, the compiler aborts without saving any compiled code to disk. (The original source code is left untouched, however.)

If you attempt to edit a compiled record with the editors, all you will see is something that looks like garbage. Maybe your program is trash (!), but the reason it looks so weird in the editor has to do with what happens during compilation.

The R/BASIC compiler transforms your program into more efficient machine language that will run faster than a program which is executed one line at a time by an interpreter. Therefore, your compiled program becomes a bunch of non-printable characters and what you see if you try to edit a compiled record is a bunch of garbage. There's really no reason to look at a compiled record; all changes to a program should be done to the original source code.

ADVANCED TOPIC: Those readers who insist on viewing the compiled code should do so with the line editor. Certain non-printable characters have special meaning to Revelation (see Appendix) and the TEXT editor interprets these characters, causing the screen to clear or the cursor to move wildly. The line editor, however, prints an ASCII character for these normally non-printable values between ASCII 1 and ASCII 31.

Running a Program

There are several ways to run your PROG1 program after it is stored in the BP file.

1) From the TCL prompt enter the command:

RUN BP PROG1

2) Catalog the program so that it becomes one of the commands in the VOC file.

CATALOG BP PROG1

This command will create an entry in the VOC file called PROG1. Now all you have to do is enter the word "PROG1" from TCL and the program will execute.

3) You may CALL this CATALOGed program from any other program. Or you may call this program from any one of

the five entry points to R/BASIC in an R/DESIGN data entry screen prompt as described in Chapter Seven, Advanced Topics.

For all these methods to work, there must be a compiled program in the stated file (as indicated by the record key name beginning with the "$").

ADVANCED TOPIC: There is one exception to the rule that only CATALOGed programs may be called directly from R/BASIC or R/DESIGN. If the compiled program is a record in the VERBS file, then it may be called from another routine even if it has not been cataloged.

DEBUGGING A PROGRAM

Some day in the far future we will be able to write the following four-line program:

```
TURN ERRORS OFF
LOOP
  PERFORM WHAT I AM THINKING
REPEAT
```

Until that time, an essential step in creating any program will be the process of ridding the program of errors. There are two species of these "bugs", as they are often called, and debugging an R/BASIC program is handled in two ways.

The first kind of bug is an error in the statement syntax or construction of an R/BASIC statement. Most of these errors are detected by the R/BASIC compiler during compilation. If errors are encountered, the errant line number and a cryptic error message is displayed. Compilation will be aborted after all lines have been checked and any errors detected.

Be forewarned that it may be difficult finding the detected error. Most of the time, if you edit the source file and examine the bad line, the incorrect syntax will be obvious. But some errors such as a missing statement label or END statement make it difficult to pinpoint the exact cause of the problem.

The other type of error is not detected by the compiler. These errors usually involve an oversight by the programmer and produce incorrect screen displays or unexpected results. These errors may be caused by improper logic within the code, typos, or not understanding the proper use of an R/BASIC statement.

To help locate errors in your program, Revelation provides an interactive symbolic debugger.

There are three ways to invoke the debugger:

1)   Press the Ctrl and Break keys together.
2)   Insert a DEBUG statement into your program at the point where you wish to call the debugger.
3)   Use the (D) option with the RUN command, or when executing any cataloged R/BASIC program from TCL.

When the debugger is called, program execution is suspended and the debugger exclamation prompt (!) is displayed. The debugger commands allow you to display the value of a variable, step through the program a line at a time, and return to program execution, to name just a few possible actions. (See Appendix XI.)

System developers wishing to prevent end-users from accidentally or maliciously entering the debugger may turn off the break key as an entry point into the debugger by issuing the BREAK KEY OFF statement in their programs.

When programs are compiled, each line of source code is automatically preceded with a line mark. This allows the exact line number to be displayed to indicate where execution was halted when the debugger is invoked by the Ctrl-Break keys. However, to compress the compiled code you may suppress the line marks by using the "S" option with compilation:

COMPILE BP PROG1 (S).

This will still allow interruption of the program by the Ctrl-Break keys; you just won't know exactly where execution was halted. Using LINEMARK statements in your program will force the compiler to generate line marks at those points in the program.

Infinite Loops

All this talk about interrupting the execution of a program brings us to the topic of infinite loops. If you have programmed before, you undoubtedly have experienced infinite loops. These dreaded loops occur when the same set of statements are executed over and over without stopping. There are only a few ways to stop this infinite loop:

1) Reboot the computer.
2) Turn off the computer.
3) Press Ctrl-Break and hope that you have allowed for this exit.

If you haven't suppressed the line marks during compilation, you are probably in good shape. However, there is an exception to this rule -- Ctrl-BREAK will not interrupt a loop contained solely on one line; for example:

```
A=5 ; B=6
LOOP J+=1 UNTIL A=B REPEAT
```

The moral of this lesson is that if you are trying to achieve faster processing time by placing several statements all on one line, be very careful to avoid loops with no escape.

LISTING PROGRAMS

There are two functions that will be important to you once you start creating R/BASIC programs: getting a list of all your programs, and printing a program listing.

Listing Programs You Have Written

There is no sure fire way to list all of your R/BASIC programs since they may be scattered throughout many files. (In fact, there is nothing preventing you from placing an R/BASIC program as a record in a standard database file -- other than your wise sense of restraint and desire to avoid confusion!)

However, a little forward planning can help. By placing all your programs in special files reserved only for R/BASIC programs, all you will have to do is LIST those files to see a listing of your programs. If you only wish to see a listing of the compiled programs, select only those record keys beginning with "$"; for example:

:LIST ONLY BP WITH @ID STARTING WITH "$"

Notice that this LIST command includes the word ONLY. This modifier suppresses the display of all fields except the record ID, thus preventing the actual object code from disrupting the screen display.

It is advised that all files used to store R/BASIC programs have the letters "BP" (or some such mnemonic) somewhere in their name in order to quickly determine which files you want to list. Examples are: AR.BP, UTIL.BP

Printing a Program Listing

To get a statement listing of a particular program, use the BLIST command from the TCL prompt:

:BLIST BP PROG1

This command will print a listing of the source program PROG1. The BLIST command automatically sends the output to the printer. To route the output to the screen, use the "T" option (for Terminal):

BLIST BP PROG1 (T)

The BLIST command will automatically place line numbers before each line for reference purposes. In addition, it will indent each line according to the imbedded nesting logic in your program (see BLIST in the COMMAND REFERENCE).

STATEMENT LABELS

To pass execution of a program to another part of the program, you must be able to identify where to direct control. Statement labels may be used for this purpose.

Four rules must be followed:

1) Labels may be either numeric or alphanumeric.
2) Valid labels can be one word, or several words separated by a period (.) or dollar sign ($).
3) Blank spaces within the label are not allowed.
4) Alphanumeric labels must be terminated with a colon (:).

Examples:

BEGIN:
1000:
1000
SCREEN.PRINT:

So, for example, one statement in a program could be:

GOTO SCREEN.PRINT

VARIABLES AND CONSTANTS

There are several types of variables used in R/BASIC. In general, variables are data expressions which may change value during the execution of a program.

At any given time during the course of a program a variable will have a particular value.

Constants

Constants are either **numeric** or **string**. Numeric constants are, simply put, numbers. In R/BASIC, numbers may range from -9999999999999.9999 to +99999999999999.9999, and they may get as close to 0 as -.000000000000000001 or +.000000000000000001. Calculations are limited to plus or minus 10 raised to the plus or minus 4932 power.

Numeric constants may not include a dollar sign or comma.

String constants are a string of characters which may include letters, numbers, or any other keyboard character. References to string constants are enclosed in single or double quotes. Some examples:

> **"This is an example of a string"**
> **'So is "this" example'**

In Revelation, all inputs are considered character strings. If the string happens to be all numbers, then calculations may be performed on it since it can also be viewed as a number. For instance, if we write:

> **X="345"**
> **PRINT X+1**

the result will be 346.

The longest string that may appear in quotes is 254 characters in length. The longest string that can be created during program execution is 65530 characters in length. These longer strings may be created, for example, by concatenating several strings together.

The null string is a little different than the actual number 0. A null string is '""' or ". Although the null string, if used in a calculation, will be given a value of 0, if it is compared to 0, the null string will not be equal (it is considered less than 0). For example,

> **X=""**
> **PRINT 5+X**

will print the value 5, whereas,

X=""
IF X = 0 THEN PRINT "THIS WORKS"

will NOT print

"THIS WORKS".

Variables

Variable names must begin with an alphabetic character, but then may be followed by any letter, number, periods or dollar signs. Spaces and dashes (-) may not be used. Certain names may not be used for variable names since they have special meaning to the system: CASE, ELSE, END, NEXT, REPEAT, UNTIL, and WHILE.

The value of a variable may change during program execution, and it may change between being numeric or string, and even change length.

Variable Types

Variables may be scalar (that is, equated to single value constants) or expressions:

X=5
X=Y
X=C+3

or they may be assigned to a matrix, or even to a dynamic array.

Chapter Four covers the fundamental concepts of dynamic arrays. In contrast to dynamic arrays, matrices could be considered static arrays.

A **matrix** is an array consisting of many data elements. Unlike dynamic arrays, matrices pre-allocate blocks of space in memory. Therefore, regardless of the size of the matrix, data can be retrieved very quickly just by specifying the exact location in the array. Dynamic arrays, on the other hand, must be sequentially searched for specific data elements.

Matrices may have more than one dimension. Thus the matrix DIMENSIONed as A(5,3) will have five rows and three columns.

Before a matrix may be used in a program, it must be named in a **DIMENSION** or **COMMON** statement in order to pre-allocate the storage space in RAM. All matrices are allocated space for a "zero element". Thus the matrix dimensioned as A(5,3) has 5*3=15 plus 1=16 elements. (A(0,0) is this zero element.)

Assigning Variables

A variable must be assigned a value during program execution otherwise any reference to an unassigned variable will result in the display of an error message. Variables may be assigned values in many different ways including:

1) The assign statement: variable = expression
The variable must always be on the left side of the equal sign and it will take on the current value of the expression. The expression may be any constant, variable, or arithmetic or logical expression such as

```
AMOUNT = 5
AMOUNT = TOTAL.DUE
AMOUNT = TOTAL.DUE*20
```

2) The EQUATE statement: EQUATE X TO AMOUNT
This statement is used to equate all occurrences of the variable X to the value of AMOUNT during compilation. No storage in memory is allocated to X since it is replaced everywhere in the program by the value of AMOUNT.

3) The COMMON statement: COMMON AMOUNT
This statement is used to pass the value of AMOUNT to any subroutine program which also has COMMONed the variable AMOUNT.

The calling program must still assign a value to AMOUNT. But the subroutine, by declaring the variable COMMON, automatically assigns AMOUNT the value passed from the calling program.

4) The DIMENSION and MAT statements: DIM X(5) and MAT X = 0
These statements declare and allocate space in memory for six data elements, X(0) - X(5), and assign them all the value of 0.

Special Variables

Certain variables are used by Revelation and can also be used in your program. These variables (which are explained in Appendix II) are used for such values as the name of the current LOGON account, the most recently executed TCL sentence, and many of the R/DESIGN values used during data entry.

Many of these special variables may be redefined by R/BASIC programs while others can only be "read", that is, programs may only extract the value of the variable for other calculations or decision branching.

EXPRESSIONS AND OPERATORS

Working with variables and constants requires an understanding of how these elements may be put together in expressions and what sort of operations may be performed within these expressions.

Expressions

There are four different types of expressions that may be used in an R/BASIC statement: arithmetic, comparison, pattern match, and logical.

1) **Arithmetic expressions** perform calculations that produce a single numeric result. They combine variables, constants, or R/BASIC internal functions with any combination of arithmetic operators such as addition and multiplication to produce a numeric result.

Example: S+3*24/(Y+2)

2) A **comparison expression** is the result of separating two arithmetic expressions by a comparison operator such as GT, >, or = (see below). A comparison expression will always evaluate to either a one (1) if true or zero (0) if false.

EXAMPLE: Y=6+(Z>3).

In this example, (Z>3) is a comparison expression. If the value of Z is greater than 3 then the expression evaluates to 1 and Y=7, otherwise Y=6.

3) A **pattern match** expression is a type of comparison expression and is the result of trying to match a string value to a matching pattern. If there is a successful match then the expression evaluates to one (1), otherwise it evaluates to zero (0). The matching pattern must be enclosed in quotes or it must be a variable.

There are five different matching patterns. In the first four, n stands for an integer:

a)   nA - tests for that number of alphabetic characters.
b)   nN - tests for that number of numeric characters.
c)   nX - tests for that number of any characters.
d)   nZ - tests for up to that number of any characters.
e)   "string" - tests for exact text enclosed in quotes.

Examples:

```
SSN = "491-64-9750"
Y = SSN MATCH "3N'-'2N'-'4N"
```

HJ = "49ER"
DD = "2N2A"
Y = HJ MATCHES DD

In both examples the value of Y evaluates to 1.

4) A **logical expression** is the result of comparing two or more expressions with the logical operators AND or OR. True logical expressions evaluate to one (1), false expressions evaluate to zero (0).

Examples:

Z = (X>3) OR (Y-2)

If X is greater than 3, or Y does not equal 2, then, in either case, Z=1.

Z = (X>3) AND (Y-2)

In this example, it must be the case that both X is greater than 3 AND Y does not equal 2 for Z to equal 1.

Operators

There are many different types of operators in R/BASIC. Not only are there operators used with each of the different type of expressions -- arithmetic, comparison, pattern matching, and logical -- there are additional operators used with strings, dynamic arrays, and assignment expressions.

1) **Arithmetic operators** - These operators are used to form arithmetic expressions. The priority order of operators is shown in **Figure 12.1**. This priority determines the order in which expressions are calculated.

PRIORITY	OPERATION	KEYBOARD SYMBOL
1	positive	+
1	negative	-
2	scientific notation	E
2	exponentiation	** or ^
3	multi-valued multiplication	***
3	multi-valued division	///
3	multiplication	*
3	division	/
4	multi-valued addition	+++
4	multi-valued subtraction	---
4	addition	+
4	subtraction	-
5	multi-valued concatenation	:::
5	concatenation	:

Fig. 12.1 Arithmetic operators

The four multi-valued operators, ***, ///, +++, ---, are provided to allow for multiplication, division, addition, and subtraction of two multi-valued strings. For example, if

$$X = "2^2 4^2 6^2 3"$$

$$Y = "3^2 5^2 7^2 1"$$

then X+++Y = $"5^2 9^2 13^2 4"$, where each value in the first data element is added to the corresponding value in the second data element.

2) **Comparison operators** - These operators compare the values of two expressions and returns that evaluation as true or false (1 or 0). The comparison operators are:

EQ	=	Equal to
NE	# <>	Not equal to
GT	>	Greater than
LT	<	Less than
GE	>= =>	Greater than or equal to
LE	<= =<	Less than or equal to
MATCH or		
MATCHES		Pattern Matching

3) **Logical operators** - These two operators, AND and OR, logically compare two expressions and return a true or false value (1 or 0). These operators have the lowest priority order of all operators. The following truth table shows the result of using these operators on two expressions with various truth values.

p	q	p AND q	p OR q
T	T	T	T
T	F	F	T
F	T	F	T
F	F	F	F

Table 12.2 Logical operators

Consider, for example, the statements

AGE=15
IF AGE GT 10 AND AGE LT 20 THEN PRINT "Teenager"

According to the above truth table, the two expressions "AGE GT 10" and "AGE LT 20" must both be true in order for the conjunction of the expressions to be true. In the stated example, the message "Teenager" would print out.

4)   **String operators** - There are two operators for manipulating strings of characters.

a) **Concatenation operator (CAT or :)** used to join two or more strings.

FNAME = "JOHN"
LNAME = "MORGAN"
PRINT FNAME:" ":LNAME

The above statements would print
"JOHN MORGAN".

b) **bracket [ ] function** used to extract substrings from strings. The format for this function is [b,l], where b=the beginning position, and l=length of substring. (See [ ] bracket function in the COMMAND REFERENCE.)

Y = "JOHN MORGAN"
Z = Y[2,6]

In this example, Z = "OHN MO".

5) **Dynamic string operator** - The angle bracket operator (<>) is used to extract and replace data within dynamic arrays. The general format is:

variable<field.expression, value.expr, sub-value.expr>

Neither the value.expr nor the sub-value.expr are necessary arguments; for example:

REC = "BOB DOE■123 MAIN^{2}APT 2■HOUSTON■TEXAS"
A = REC<3>

The variable A would equal "HOUSTON". By contrast, in the following example the second value of the second field would be replaced by "APT 4".

REC<2,2> = "APT 4"

If there are only 4 fields in a dynamic array and a statement says

REC<7>=256

the appropriate number of field markers will be added until the seventh field is reached, at which point 256 will be inserted.

REC<0> always refers to the entire dynamic array.

REC<-1> = 256 will add a field marker to the end of the dynamic array and then add the value 256.

6)   **Assignment operators** - In addition to the general assignment operator "=" which is used to assign a value to a variable, there are three special assignment operators,
+=, -=, :=.

These operators may be used to replace expressions such as the following:

Y = Y+2	replace with	Y += 2
Y = Y-2	replace with	Y -= 2
Y = Y:@FM	replace with	Y := @FM

ADVANCED TOPICS

Cataloging an R/BASIC Program

When you CATALOG an R/BASIC program, a record is created in VOC with a record ID equal to the program name.

:CATALOG BP PROG1

Field one of this VOC record equals "RBASIC". Field three equals the file name where the program is stored (in this case, BP), and field four is equal to the record name (PROG1).

CHAPTER THIRTEEN: PROGRAMMING OPERATIONS

R/BASIC has a wealth of features which make it one of the most powerful microcomputer programming languages for database management. But tapping the full power of this language requires understanding the concepts behind many of the commands. This chapter discusses some of these R/BASIC concepts, including internal system functions, program control, subroutines, common variables, recursion, and select lists.

FUNCTIONS

A function is a routine that is performed and returns a value which may be used by the program. R/BASIC has already defined many internal functions for common routines; these are listed in the COMMAND REFERENCE. These internal functions may be used in R/BASIC statements wherever an expression is appropriate.

Most of the internal functions are dependent on user-specified arguments which are passed to the function for evaluation. For example, the LEN() function calculates the character length of the expression between the parentheses, such as LEN(NAME), or LEN("1234567"). Any valid expression may appear between the parentheses; you may even have a function within a function: LEN(TRIM(NAME)).

As expressions, all functions must appear on the right hand side of the assignment statement. You may not use, for example, LEN(NAME)=6; however, Y=LEN(NAME) is valid.

PROGRAM CONTROL

At some point, most programs require a deviation from the normal sequential processing of statements. This program control can take many forms: branching on certain conditions, jumping to other parts of the program (or even other programs), or continuous looping through a group of statements.

Unconditional Branching

Unconditional jumping to another statement in the program is performed by the GOTO statement. For example, GOTO AGAIN, will cause program execution to unconditionally jump to the statement label "AGAIN:".

Conditional Branching

Often during program execution you will want to test or compare two values, and depending on the outcome, branch to separate statements. R/BASIC provides several vehicles for performing this conditional branching.

The logic of the IF ... THEN ... ELSE statements is one method for executing conditional branching. These statements are discussed at length in the COMMAND REFERENCE.

Additional conditional branching is achieved by using the ON GOTO statement. Depending on the value of an expression, branching will proceed to an associated statement label. For example,

ON AGE GOTO INFANT,TODDLER,PRE.SCHOOL

will cause program execution to go to the statement label INFANT if AGE=1, TODDLER if AGE=2, and PRE.SCHOOL if the value of AGE is any other value.

One more set of statements used to execute conditional branching is the **BEGIN CASE ... END CASE** framework which performs various statements depending on the value of the expressions being tested. This framework differs from the other two methods in that there may be several different test expressions:

```
BEGIN CASE
  CASE AGE=3
    GOTO 300
  CASE NAME="SMITH"
    GOTO 100
  CASE 1
    PRINT "NEITHER SMITH NOR 3"
END CASE
```

Program Loops

One method for creating a loop in a program is to use a conditional GOTO statement until a tested value is true:

```
X=1
START:
PRINT "PRINTING COUNTER = ":X
X+=1
IF X <= 10 THEN GOTO START
```

Fortunately, R/BASIC provides two tools which are more efficient for program looping than the relatively slow IF conditional.

> 1) FOR ... NEXT
> 2) LOOP ... UNTIL ... REPEAT

The FOR and NEXT statements specify the beginning and ending points of a program loop, which is repeated until an incremental counter reaches a specific value:

```
FOR X=1 TO 10
  PRINT "COUNTER = ":X
NEXT X
```

Each time the NEXT statement is performed, X gets incremented by 1 and program control is sent back to the FOR statement until X is greater than 10.

The most efficient method for controlled looping is to use the structured programming framework provided by the LOOP ... UNTIL ... REPEAT statements.

```
COUNT=0
LOOP
 INPUT X
 UNTIL X = "END"
  COUNT+=1
  PRINT "COUNTER = ":COUNT
REPEAT
```

In this example, the INPUT and PRINT statements are executed repeatedly until the word "END" is input.

SUBROUTINES

A subroutine is a separate set of statements that handles a particular function or operation. The subroutine is invoked by a calling statement; and after the execution of the subroutine, control is returned back to the point in the main program where the call was initiated. Large complicated programs often are organized into smaller, more manageable chunks which can be tested independently from the other parts of the program. There are two type of subroutines: internal and external.

Internal Subroutines

An internal subroutine is contained within the program which calls it. Control is passed from the main body of the program to the internal subroutine by a GOSUB statement. Thus, GOSUB GETNAME will pass control to the statement label "GETNAME:". The statements following the statement label are executed until a RETURN statement is encountered and control is passed back to the next statement after the GOSUB.

```
BEGIN:
* First get mailing label before printing
*
GOSUB GETNAME
PRINT NAME
PRINT ADDRESS
PRINT CITY
* Start over for next label
GOTO BEGIN:
*
* Begin GETNAME subroutine
*
GETNAME:
INPUT NAME
INPUT ADDRESS
INPUT CITY
RETURN
```

Notice that whereas the GOTO statement causes program control to pass to another part of the program, the GOSUB/RETURN statements only temporarily pass control to another part of the program.

External Subroutines

External subroutines are separate programs that have been previously compiled and cataloged. There are several ways to call external subroutines and pass values (or "arguments" as they are often called) back and forth between the programs.

Calling Subroutines

The CALL statement is used to transfer control from the calling program to an external subroutine. The arguments to be passed are enclosed within parentheses of the CALL statement.

CALL PROG2(X,Y)

PROG2 must be a cataloged program whose first line is a SUBROUTINE statement declaring the name of the subroutine and possessing the same number of arguments as the CALL statement. For example:

SUBROUTINE PROG2(A,CNT)

Notice that the same variable names do NOT have to be used in the calling program and the subroutine. Only the order of the passed variables is important. In the above example, the value of X in the calling program will be passed to A in PROG2, while the value of Y is passed to CNT. Similarly, when control is returned to the calling program, the values are passed in the other direction, A to X and CNT to Y.

```
* PROG1
PRINT "HERE AT PROG1"
INPUT X
CALL PROG2(X)
PRINT "HERE AT PROG1 AGAIN. X=":X

SUBROUTINE PROG2(H)
* PROG2
PRINT "HERE AT PROG2. H= ":H
H=H*2
RETURN
```

After cataloging these programs and executing PROG1, the following will be displayed:

```
HERE AT PROG1
?5
HERE AT PROG2. H=5
HERE AT PROG1 AGAIN. X=10
```

A subroutine may be called without passing arguments. For example,

```
CALL PROG3
```

will execute PROG3, but no values will be passed back and forth. In this case, the subroutine is NOT required to have a SUBROUTINE statement. This type of call is used to perform certain actions that do not require returning new values to the calling program. An example of this type of call might be when you want to call a routine from several different screen programs to display static information such as the time and date.

Declaring Subroutines and Functions

The DECLARE statement is used in a calling program to allow user-defined subroutines and functions.

When you DECLARE SUBROUTINE, no CALL is necessary. All you have to do is use the name of the subroutine as an R/BASIC statement.

```
* PROG1
DECLARE SUBROUTINE PROG2
PRINT "HERE AT PROG1"
INPUT X
PROG2(X)
PRINT "HERE AT PROG1 AGAIN. X=":X

SUBROUTINE PROG2(H)
* PROG2
PRINT "HERE AT PROG2. H= ":H
H=H*2
RETURN
```

After cataloging these programs and executing PROG1, the same display as before will result:

```
HERE AT PROG1
?5
HERE AT PROG2. H=5
HERE AT PROG1 AGAIN. X=10
```

Declaring Functions

User-defined functions may also be defined in R/BASIC programs. These functions can be used in exactly the same way as the internal system functions. When a program statement uses the declared function, the FUNCTION subroutine is executed and returns a value to the calling program. This value must be passed back explicitly on the RETURN statement.

Whereas declared subroutines can be used as an R/BASIC statement, declared functions may only be used as expressions on the right side of an assignment operator.

Also notice in this example that the function program's first line is a FUNCTION statement .

```
* PROG1
DECLARE FUNCTION PROG2
PRINT "HERE AT PROG1"
INPUT X
Y=PROG2(X)
PRINT "HERE AT PROG1 AGAIN. Y=":Y

FUNCTION PROG2(H)
* PROG2
PRINT "HERE AT PROG2. H= ":H
H=H*2
RETURN H
```

After cataloging these programs and executing PROG1, the same display as before will result:

```
HERE AT PROG1
?5
HERE AT PROG2. H=5
HERE AT PROG1 AGAIN. Y=10
```

COMMON VARIABLES

There is yet one more way to share data back and forth between programs and subroutines. The **COMMON** statement provides a common area for storing variables shared by both the main calling program and any external subroutines.

When two programs declare certain variables as COMMON, one program may CALL the other without having to explicitly pass the shared values in an argument list.

The COMMON block must be declared in the main program if the common variables are to be shared with the main program's subroutines (even if the main program does not use any of the common variables itself).

```
* PROG1
COMMON X
PRINT "HERE AT PROG1"
INPUT X
CALL PROG2
PRINT "HERE AT PROG1 AGAIN. X=":X

SUBROUTINE PROG2
* PROG2
COMMON H
PRINT "HERE AT PROG2. H= ":H
H=H*2
RETURN
```

After cataloging these programs and executing PROG1, the following will be displayed:

```
HERE AT PROG1
?5
HERE AT PROG2. H=5
HERE AT PROG1 AGAIN. X=10
```

Notice that the name of the variables used in the COMMON statement need not be the same. It is the relative order of the variables listed in the COMMON statements that determines the correspondence between shared common values in each program.

Subroutines called from R/DESIGN data entry screens may use the COMMON variables defined by R/DESIGN. This block of common variables can be inserted into your own programs for access to the values used by R/DESIGN (see Appendix III). To make these variables COMMON to your program without having to retype all of the COMMON statements, use the following statement near the beginning of your program:

$INSERT PROG,RDESIGN.COMMON

This will insert the RDESIGN.COMMON record from the PROG file into your program during the compilation process. The RDESIGN.COMMON record in the PROG file is nothing more than a set of COMMON statements for all the variables used by R/DESIGN.

Labeled Common

A familiar feature to FORTRAN programmers, also available with R/BASIC, is the labeled common area. This common block differs from the COMMON area discussed above because the block is made available to ALL programs, subroutines, and functions, not just to a specific program and its subroutines. Once a labeled common area is defined and given a label, it is available until you log off; for example:

COMMON /ADMIN/AMOUNT,TOTAL

establishes a common area named ADMIN with two values in it. Any program can now access the values in this common block by simply having the statement

COMMON /ADMIN/VAR1,VAR2

at the beginning of the program. Notice once again that it is only the relative order of the variables listed in the named COMMON area -- and not the actual names -- that determines the association between shared common values.

Unlike the normal COMMON blocks which may use as many COMMON statements in a program as memory allows, a labeled common area may only use one COMMON statement and is limited to 254 characters in length.

```
* PROG1
COMMON /TEST/X
PRINT "HERE AT PROG1"
INPUT X
END

* PROG2
COMMON /TEST/H
PRINT "HERE AT PROG2. H= ":H
H=H*2
END

*PROG3
COMMON /TEST/X
PRINT "HERE AT PROG3. X= ":X
END
```

In this example, there is no CALL to a subroutine. Instead, PROG1 initializes the first value in the labeled common area.

Then, any program executed after PROG1 may have access to this value and even replace it with another value.

HERE AT PROG1
?5

Running BP PROG2 from TCL yields:

HERE AT PROG2. H= 5

And running BP PROG3 produces:

HERE AT PROG3. X= 10

RECURSION

One of the great features of Revelation lies in its ability to suspend operation and perform other functions and programs without losing the values of variables from the original routine. Revelation provides several tools for performing recursive operations.

Programs may make recursive calls. That is, a program that performs some operation on a set of variables may call itself to again perform that same operation on the new values. This second set of values is passed back to the program's first level of execution without altering the original values.

From an R/BASIC program, the editors, or the debugger, you can suspend operations and perform a TCL command with the **EXECUTE** command (this is conceptually like operating at the TCL level of an entirely separate system). Revelation recognizes that you are at the second "recursive level" of TCL (the first level was running the R/BASIC program, the editor, or the debugger). Sometimes you may notice after the completion of the second level of execution that the TCL colon prompt is replaced with a double colon prompt (::) indicating that you are still at the second level. To return to the next higher recursive level, you use the RETURN command. You can use EXECUTE to perform up to 10 levels of recursion.

Recursion is also important in understanding the difference between two sets of system variables that may be used throughout your R/BASIC programs. The first set is **@USER0** through **@USER4**; the second set is **@RECUR0** through **@RECUR4**. Both sets of variables are automatically set equal to null ("") during logon to Revelation. These variables may be used for any purpose by the user. For example, if you have passwords that will be used throughout an application, you can enter them into the @USER variables at the beginning of the application and access the passwords through these variables from any program.

The difference between @USER and @RECUR is reflected in how they behave with the EXECUTE and PERFORM statements. The @USER variables may be modified during the execution of a program and this modification will be passed back to the original program. @RECUR variables, however, are saved before the EXECUTE, and even if the variable is modified during the second level, the variable will retain its original value upon return to the first level of execution.

SELECT LISTS

A list of record keys in a program can be built in two ways. One way is to use the R/BASIC statement SELECT.

**OPEN ",'INVOICES" TO INV ELSE STOP
SELECT INV**

But this selects all of the records in a file. To specify selection criteria or sort order you must use the TCL SELECT command in a PERFORM statement:

PERFORM "SELECT INVOICES WITH AMOUNT > 100"

will create a smaller select list meeting the specified condition.

Once you have created a select list, you can sequentially read its values to a variable with a READNEXT statement. Then, you can use this variable to read the entire record and assign it to another variable. You may use any variables you wish for the current ID and current record, but it's good practice to assign these values to the system values @ID and @RECORD in case you want to tie your program to R/DESIGN, R/LIST, and the dictionaries; for example:

```
OPEN ",̈"INVOICES" TO INV ELSE STOP 'CANT
    OPEN INVOICES'
OPEN 'DICT','INVOICES' TO @DICT ELSE STOP
SELECT INV
LOOP WHILE 1
    READNEXT @ID ELSE
    PRINT 'FINISHED LISTING INVOICES'
    STOP
END
READ @RECORD FROM INV, @ID THEN
    PRINT {INV.NO}, {CUST.NAME}, {AMOUNT}
END ELSE
    PRINT 'NO RECORD FOR ' :@ID
END
REPEAT
END
```

This program opens the data and dictionary portion of the INVOICES file (it's necessary to open the dictionary to the variable @DICT because we are going to refer to some of the dictionary records in our print statement). After selecting all the record keys in the file, the current ID and record are assigned to special variables. Each ID is read in turn and information from that record is printed out.

Note that Revelation does not assign the values of a select list to any system variable, so the only way you can access them is through the READNEXT statement. Also, the most recently formed select list remains the current list until it is cleared or another SELECT is performed.

DICTIONARY NAMES VS. DYNAMIC ARRAY

You may refer to data elements in a data file either by their dictionary name or by their location in the dynamic array that constitutes the actual data record.

For example, in the above program, notice that the PRINT statement refers to the dictionary name. The {} function will calculate the value of these fields in the current record stored in @RECORD. (We could have used any name for this variable. @RECORD just conforms to the name used by R/DESIGN.)

But suppose that INV.NO, CUST.NAME, and AMOUNT are the first, third, and fourth fields in every record (defined in BUD with FMC equal to 1,3,4 respectively.) Then our print statement could directly reference these locations in the dynamic array without ever referring to the dictionary name.

PRINT @RECORD<1>, @RECORD<3>, @RECORD<4>

TRANSLATING DATA BETWEEN TWO FILES

When you display data in a data entry screen or in an output report, you are usually limited to displaying data from one file. It is quite common, however, to want to retrieve data from a second file, based on the values in the first file. Revelation provides a powerful tool for translating data between two files.

To see how this process works, consider the following example. Suppose you are designing a system for tracking customer invoices. You might decide to create a single database file with one record for each invoice. This file could have fields for INVOICE.NO and INVOICE.AMT, as well as fields for the customer name and address.

The only drawback to this system is that you may end up entering repeat customers' names and addresses many times, wasting disk space and operator input time.

A better solution is to create a second file, the CUSTOMERS file, with a unique customer number for each customer record. The INVOICES file then only needs to have a field for the customer number. Now whenever you want to print out the invoices from this file, you can use the customer number to translate to the CUSTOMERS file to retrieve the customer name and address.

Consider the following partial dictionary layouts for these two files:

DICT of CUSTOMERS		DICT of INVOICES	
Field Name	FMC	Field Name	FMC
CUST.NBR (record key)	0	INVOICE.NO (record key)	0
CUST.NAME	1	INVOICE.AMT	1
ADDRESS	2	INVOICE.DATE	2
CITY	3	CUST.NO	3
ST	4		

Figure 13.1

Notice that each invoice record is stored with a customer number. This customer number can be used to translate over to the corresponding record in the CUSTOMERS file and retrieve the customer name. Just create a symbolic field called

NAME in the INVOICES file with the following R/BASIC formula:

@ANS=XLATE("CUSTOMERS",{CUST.NO},1,"X")

Whenever this symbolic field is displayed, the customer number stored in the CUST.NO field of the INVOICES file is used as the record ID in the CUSTOMERS file to find the correct customer. The variable @ANS is assigned the customer name from the value in field 1 of this record in the CUSTOMERS file. Similarly, you could set up another symbolic field in the INVOICES file to retrieve the address from the CUSTOMERS file.

@ANS=XLATE("CUSTOMERS",{CUST.NO},2,"X")

CHAPTER FOURTEEN: TEXT AND LINE EDITORS

THE TEXT EDITOR

The TEXT editor is Revelation's full screen editor which resembles a complete word processor. With the TEXT editor you can easily insert, delete, and move text. When editing is complete, the record being edited is saved back to its file (and in the case of a program, it can also be compiled).

The TEXT editor is primarily used for three purposes:

1) to create and edit R/BASIC programs.
2) to enter or update large text fields.
3) to create a complex symbolic field in a data file.

Invoking The TEXT Editor

There are three ways of invoking the TEXT editor. One way is with the TCL command TEXT; this method is used to create

R/BASIC programs. It can also be invoked automatically when you are entering data into a "text" field in your data entry screen. Finally, it can be invoked for entering multivalued field entries.

Invoking the TEXT editor with the TEXT command

From the TCL prompt invoke the TEXT editor as follows:

:TEXT <DICT> filename <record.id...>

> where:
> **DICT** is an optional command word.
> **filename** is the name of the file holding the
>   records to be edited.
> **record.id**(s) are the record IDs to be edited.

Using DICT in the command will edit a record from the dictionary portion of the file. Notice that the record ID is optional; if you leave it out, you will be prompted for the name of the record to edit. You can also edit more than one record by including several record IDs in the command, or by using an asterisk (*) for the record.id which will edit all the records in the file. If more than one record is to be edited, each will be called by the TEXT editor as the previous record is filed.

For example, to create a program named TAX.CALC and store it in your BP (Basic Programs) file, start by calling the TEXT editor:

:TEXT BP TAX.CALC

You will see the TEXT editor screen along with the message "YOU ARE ADDING A NEW RECORD" at the top. Then enter your R/BASIC statements and when you are finished, save and compile the program by hitting Ctrl F2.

CAUTION: When you create a *record* in the Revelation file DOS, you are actually creating a *DOS* file with that record name (see Chapter 10 for a discussion of the DOS file). Do not use any of the following characters in that record name:

$$. \quad : \quad " \quad \wedge \quad - \quad *$$
$$, \quad ; \quad [\ ] \quad ? \quad = \quad /$$

It will appear as if the file has been created and the information stored; but when you go to retrieve it, it won't be there. The file was actually never saved -- not a pleasant experience!

Automatically Invoking the TEXT Editor for "Text" Fields

You may want to use the TEXT editor for entering data to a field in a data entry screen. To do this, modify that field's data entry prompt using SCR to change the format justification to T for "Text". But before the format justification can be changed, the Text Depth Parameter in the Prompt Editor screen must contain a value greater than 1. Then every time you enter data at this data entry prompt, the TEXT editor will be automatically invoked.

Invoking the TEXT Editor at Data Entry Prompts for Multi-Value Fields.

Finally, the TEXT editor can be called to enter data into multi-valued fields. At the WHICH VALUE? prompt, pressing Ctrl-T will invoke the TEXT editor and each value will be displayed on a separate line on the TEXT editor screen. Alternatively, you could enter "TEXT" for one of the multi-values and the TEXT editor would also be invoked.

To disable access to the TEXT editor for a multi-valued field prompt, enter "NOTEXT" as one of the Edit Patterns for this data entry prompt in the SCR Prompt Editor.

You may find that a few of the TEXT editor keys described later in this chapter will not work when the TEXT editor is invoked with either of these last two methods.

Status Line

When the TEXT editor is invoked, a status line with the following information is displayed on the bottom line of the screen:

File	The name of the file containing the record being edited.
Item	The ID of the record being edited.
Line	The number of the line where the cursor is located.
Col	The column where the cursor is located.
L	Displayed when line insert is on. Line insert causes a new line to be inserted whenever the return key is pressed. SHIFT F4 will toggle line insert on/off.
W	Displayed when automatic line wrap is on. SHIFT F3 toggles line wrap off/on.
INS	Displayed when character insert is on. Character insert causes data entered from the keyboard to be inserted into the text of the record. When character insert is off, entered data will overwrite existing data. The INS key toggles character insert on/off.

Help

Pressing the F1 key while in the TEXT editor (if you invoked it with the TCL command) will display at the top of your screen the reference guide shown in **Figure 14.1**. This will remain on your screen while you are using the TEXT editor and will serve as a quick reference. To remove it from your screen, press F1 again.

KEY:	F1	F2	F3	F4	F5	F6
	HELP	RESTRT	FRFRMT	INSLIN	RPTLOC	PRTRPL
(W/SHIFT)	DSPSIZ	FILE	WRAP	LINSMD	CPYMOV	SAVRST
(W/CTRL)	EXHELP	FIC	DELWRD	DELLIN	LOCATE	REPLACE
(W/ALT)		SAVE		DFNWN	RSTLIN	

KEY:	F7	F8	F9	F10
	CLRBOL	CLREOL	VMARK	SHFTWN
(W/SHIFT)	DELETE	DFNBLK	CLRDFN	GOTOLN
(W/CTRL)	INCLUD	EDIT	ABORT	CENTER
(W/ALT)	CHGWDD	DFNTAB	MERGLN	SPLTLN

Fig. 14.1 Help Functon Key Guide

For more detailed help with a TEXT editor function key, press CTRL F1. You will then receive a detailed explanation of the next function key you press. Pressing the space bar will return you to the record you were previously editing.

Cursor And Screen Control Keys

The TEXT editor uses the same keys for cursor control and basic editing as are used on most Personal Computer word processors. Remember that the NUMERIC LOCK at the right of your keyboard must be turned off to use the numeric keypad.

ARROW KEYS - Moves the cursor one space in the indicated direction.

INS - Toggles character insert on/off.

DEL - Deletes the character at the current cursor position.

HOME - Moves the cursor to the left most column on the screen. If you are editing lines which are longer than your screen is wide, successive HOME keys will scroll your screen to the left.

END - Moves the cursor to the end of the current line. If your line is longer that your screen, successive END keys will scroll the screen to the right.

TAB - Moves cursor to the next tab stop.

BACKSPACE - Deletes the character to the left of the cursor.

ESCAPE - Will execute the current line as if it were entered as a TCL command. (e.g. if the current line were LIST CUSTOMERS, pressing the ESC key would execute that command).

RETURN - moves the cursor to column 1 of the next line; inserts a new line if Line Insert is on.

PAGE-UP and PAGE-DOWN - Scrolls the screen up or down one page.

CTRL HOME and CTRL END - Moves the cursor to the first or last line of the current page.

CTRL LEFT ARROW and CTRL RIGHT ARROW - Moves the cursor one word left or right.

CTRL PAGE-UP and CTRL PAGE-DOWN - Moves the cursor to the beginning or end of the current record.

CTRL D - Deletes the entire record.

CTRL Q - Quits a multi-record edit.

Function Key Description

F1   Displays the FUNCTION KEY REFERENCE
             GUIDE at the top of your screen.

F2   Restart Edit. Restarts the TEXT editor in the
             same record without saving any changes.

F3   Reformat text. Reformats a block of text
             (defined with the block function keys) to a new
             line width for which you are prompted.

F4   Insert a line. Inserts a line before the current
             line.

F5   Search again. Locates the next occurrence of a
             value specified in the last use of the Search
             function key, CTRL F5. If no value is found, a
             beep will sound. If the text is found in the
             current record, the cursor will move to that
             value.

F6   Replace again. Searches for next value specified
             by the last use of the Replace function key,
             CTRL F6, and replaces the value as directed.

F7   Erase to the beginning of line. Erases the
             current line from the beginning to the cursor
             location.

F8   Erase to end of line. Erases current line from
             the cursor location to the end of the line.

F10   Shifts the screen display horizontally. It
             alternates between displaying column 1 at the
             left of the screen and displaying the column you
             specify with ALT F5 at the left of the screen.

SHIFT F1   Display record size. Displays size of record
             being edited.

SHIFT F2   File item. Saves the edits you have made and exits the TEXT editor.

SHIFT F3   Toggle word wrap. Turns word wrap on/off. With word wrap off, all data is entered on a single line until you press return. With word wrap on, text will automatically wrap to the next line when it reaches the set line width and a "W" is displayed on the command line. You are prompted for line width when word wrap is turned on.

SHIFT F4   Toggle line insert. Turns Line Insert on/off. With Line Insert on, a line is inserted each time you press the return key. The cursor will be positioned on this new line at the first column in the previous line which has text. When Line Insert is on, a "L" will be displayed on the status line.

SHIFT F5   COPY or MOVE a block of text.   After marking a block of text with SHIFT F8 and positioning the cursor where you want the block to go, SHIFT F5 is pressed and you are prompted for whether it is a MOVE or a COPY; then the function is executed.

SHIFT F6   SAVE, RESTORE, or APPEND a block of text.   You can save a block of text to a temporary buffer, retrieve and insert the saved text, or append text to the block which is already saved.

SHIFT F7   Delete a block of text. Deletes a block of text marked with SHIFT F8.

SHIFT F8   Define a block of text. Pressing this key once will mark the beginning of a block of text. After moving the cursor, pressing again will mark the end of the block. The block can then be moved, copied, deleted, or saved.

SHIFT F9   Clear the current block.   Clears the current
             marked block so that another can be marked.
             Alternatively, marking a new block with SHIFT
             F8 also clears the previous block.

SHIFT F10   Go to a line. Moves the cursor to a specified
             line. You will be prompted for a line number.
             In addition to a line number, you may enter a
             +n or -n to move the cursor n lines up or down.

CTRL F1   Extended help display. A description will be
             shown of the next function key pressed after
             this one. Press "S" for a summary of all cursor
             control keys. Press "F" for a summary of all
             function keys. Press SPACEBAR to exit.

CTRL F2   File and compile. Stores the program you are
             editing and attempts to compile the code. If the
             compilation is successful, the compiled code is
             stored as another record in the file. The name
             of this compiled record is the program name
             preceded by a "$". For example, if you compile
             a program named PROG1, the record ID of the
             compiled record will be $PROG1.

CTRL F3   Delete word. Deletes from the cursor to the
             end of the word.

CTRL F4   Delete line. Deletes the current line.

CTRL F5   Search for text. Prompts for the text for which
             to search and then moves the cursor to the first
             occurrence of that text.

CTRL F6   Search and replace text. Prompts you for text
             to replace, the text with which to replace it, and
             whether all occurrences of the text should be
             replaced.

CTRL F7	Include text from another record. Prompts you for a file name, record ID, starting line number, and ending line number. The indicated text will be inserted after the current line.
CTRL F8	Edit another record. Prompts you for another record to edit. The current record will not be cleared. Instead, the screen will be split, with another window displaying this second record. To return to the first record, save or exit the second record. Blocks of text may be passed back and forth between the records using Shift F6.
CTRL F9	Abort edit. Aborts the edit without saving changes.
CTRL F10	Center current line. Moves the text of the current line so it will be centered on the page.
ALT F2	File and continue. Saves changes made so far and remains in the current record.
ALT F5	Shifts the screen display horizontally; prompts for the column number you want displayed at the left of the screen. F10 will toggle between this screen display and a display with column 1 at the left of the screen.
ALT F6	Restore a line. Restores a line to the condition it was in when it last became the current line.
ALT F7	Change word definition character. This allows you to change the character which the CTRL LEFT ARROW and CTRL RIGHT ARROW keys use for determining how far to move the cursor (normally the space which separates words). For example, setting it to a value mark would allow you to move to the next value using CTRL RIGHT ARROW.

	ALT F8	Define tab stops. Default tabs are every 10 columns. A format line will be displayed with asterisks marking the tab stops. Edit this line to change the tab settings.

ALT F8 — Define tab stops. Default tabs are every 10 columns. A format line will be displayed with asterisks marking the tab stops. Edit this line to change the tab settings.

ALT F9 — Merge lines. Merges the current line and the next line into one line.

ALT F10 — Split a line. Splits the current line at the cursor position.

FUNCTION KEY SUMMARY

KEY	HELP ABBR	EXPLANATION
F1	HELP	HELP DISPLAY CURRENT RECORD.
F2	RESTRT	ABORT CURRENT EDIT AND RESTART WITH SAME RECORD.
F3	REFRMT	REFORMAT TEXT.
F4	INSLIN	INSERT LINE.
F5	RPTLOC	DO LAST LOCATE AGAIN.
F6	RPTRPL	DO LAST REPLACE AGAIN.
F7	CLRBOL	ERASE FROM CURSOR TO BEGINNING OF LINE.
F8	CLREOL	ERASE FROM CURSOR TO END OF LINE.
F10	SHFTWN	TOGGLE DISPLAY WINDOW BETWEEN COLUMN 1 AND WINDOW START
SHIFT F1	DSPSIZ	DISPLAY SIZE OF CURRENT RECORD.
SHIFT F2	FILE	EXIT AND FILE RECORD.
SHIFT F3	WRAP	TURN WORD WRAP ON/OFF.
SHIFT F4	LINSMD	TURN LINE INSERT ON/OFF.
SHIFT F5	CPYMOV	COPY OR MOVE A BLOCK OF TEXT.
SHIFT F6	SAVRST	SAVE OR RETRIEVE A BLOCK OF TEXT.
SHIFT F7	DELETE	DELETE A BLOCK OF TEXT.
SHIFT F8	DFNBLK	DEFINE THE START AND END OF BLOCK OF TEXT.
SHIFT F9	CLRDFN	CLEAR THE BLOCK DEFINITION.
SHIFT F10	GOTOLN	GOTO LINE N OR +N, -N LINES.

(continued on next page)

CTRL F1	EXHELP	EXTENDED HELP DISPLAY.
CTRL F2	FIC	COMPILE AND FILE R/BASIC PROGRAM RECORD.
CTRL F3	DELWRD	DELETE WORD.
CTRL F4	DELLIN	DELETE LINE.
CTRL F5	LOCATE	LOCATE STRING.
CTRL F6	REPLACE	REPLACE STRING.
CTRL F7	INCLUD	INCLUDE TEXT FROM ANOTHER RECORD AND/OR FILE.
CTRL F8	EDIT	EDIT ANOTHER RECORD.
CTRL F9	ABORT	ABORT EDIT.
CTRL F10	CENTER	MOVE CURRENT LINE TO CENTER OF SCREEN.
ALT F2	SAVE	FILE CHANGES AND CONTINUE EDIT.
ALT F5	DFNWN	CHANGE COLUMN NUMBERS.
ALT F6	RSTLIN	RESTORE CURRENT LINE TO VALUE BEFORE CHANGE.
ALT F7	CHGWDD	CHANGE WORD DEFINITION CHARACTER.
ALT F8	DFNTAB	DEFINE TAB STOPS.
ALT F9	MERGLN	MERGE CURRENT LINE WITH FOLLOWING LINE.
ALT F10	SPLTLN	SPLIT CURRENT LINE.

THE LINE EDITOR

The line editor is used to edit one line of text from a record at a time. It can be used to create a program and to add, delete or modify R/BASIC code, data records and dictionary records. Like the TEXT editor, it edits text; but the commands and procedures are entirely different.

One situation when you will use the line editor instead of the TEXT editor is for editing a record which has a field containing compiled code (which includes various non-printable ASCII characters). If the TEXT editor tries to print this compiled code, the monitor will receive some random control characters, making the display useless. Using the line editor, you can edit this record without worrying about the compiled code because the line editor does not try to print the non-printable characters.

Another reason for using the line editor is that it has a feature for converting records between Revelation format and DOS format (Revelation uses a field mark to mark the end of lines while DOS uses the carriage return and line feed characters).

Invoking The LINE Editor

The line editor is invoked from the TCL prompt with the ED command. The format for the ED command is:

:ED <DICT> file.name <record.id record.id ...>

where,
DICT is an optional command word which
specifies that a dictionary is to be edited.
file.name is the name of the file containing the
record to be edited.
record.id(s) are optional record IDs of the
records to be edited.

If more than one record is listed, the first record will be brought up for edit. After you are finished editing it, the second record will automatically be brought up, etc. An asterisk (*) may be used to specify all the records in a file. After the line editor is invoked, the screen will display the name of the record being edited, the word "TOP" to indicate that you are at the top line of the record, and the line editor prompt, a period. For example:

:ED BP DATA.ENTRY

will edit the DATA.ENTRY record of the BP file.

:ED BP *

will edit each record of the BP file in turn.

The line editor will display a record line by line, using sequential line numbers for each line and an internal line pointer to keep track of the current line. When the line pointer is at the top of the record the message TOP will be displayed; when it points to the last line, EoR (End of Record) will be displayed.

You can create a new record by just entering a new value for record ID when invoking the editor from TCL. The line editor will display the message NEW RECORD in this case.

Line Editor Commands

Ln   displays the next n lines starting with the next line after the current line.

Nn   moves the line pointer down n lines; displays EoR (End of Record) if it runs out of lines. If n is omitted, moves down one line.

Gn   moves the current line pointer to line n.

T   moves the line pointer to the top of the record, just before line one.

B   moves the line pointer to the bottom of the record and displays the last line.

Un   moves the line pointer up n lines; if n is omitted, moves up one line.

I   inserts a line of data into the record. If I is used by itself, the line editor will prompt you with the line number 0001 followed by a plus sign. The data you enter will be inserted after the current line. If you include data with the I command, that data will be inserted after the current line.

C   displays a "ruler" line on the screen below the current line; this is useful for positioning a piece of information on the screen.

Ln/string locates a string in the next n lines after the current line and displays all the lines in which the string occurs. If n is omitted, then the next occurrence of the string is located and that line is displayed. If the string includes the character "/", then you cannot use this character to separate the "n" and "string" in the command; use any character which does not appear in the string instead (except space or a minus sign).

A repeats the last **Ln/string** command.

DEn deletes n lines starting with the last line displayed on the screen; the remaining lines are renumbered.

Rn/string1/string2 searches the next n lines and replaces the first occurrence of string1 with string2. If an asterisk is included in the command (Rn/string1/string2/*), all occurrences will be replaced. If n is omitted, the current line is searched. The lines where the replacement takes place will be displayed. If the strings include the character "/", then do not use this character as a delimiter in the command; instead, use any other character which does not appear in the string (except space or a minus sign). EX: **R*W/O*without**

RA repeats the last **Rn/string1/string2** command.

MEn/record.id/n merges lines from another record into the current record. "record.id" is the ID of the source record; a null (") will use the current record as the source. The first n is the number of lines to merge; the second n is the line number of the first line to be merged. If either n is omitted, it is assumed to be 1. The merged lines will be inserted after the current line.

FI files the current record to disk along with the changes you have made. If the record is a dictionary record, the dictionary compiler is invoked. If the compilation is not successful, you will be returned to the line editor so that the problem can be fixed.

FIC files the record and attempts to compile it.

FS   files the record to disk and returns you to the same record for additional editing.

FD   deletes the current record; you will be prompted to make sure you really want to delete the record.

EX   exits the editing session without saving any changes.

EXT exits a multi-record edit; the changes to the current record are not saved and you are returned to the TCL prompt.

P   is a program command which can be assigned the value of any line editor command. It consists of P followed by a space and any line editor command; e.g. **.P L4/TEST** would store the locate command **L4/TEST**, which could then be run by just using the **.P** command. Only one p command can be used at a time, and the default value is L22.

REV is used to convert an entire record to Revelation format from DOS format. DOS uses a carriage-return, ASCII CHAR(13), and line feed, ASCII CHAR(10), to mark the end of a line; while Revelation uses a field mark, ASCII CHAR(254). This command just replaces the DOS characters with field marks so that the record can be edited with the line editor.

PC   (or PCDOS) converts a record from Revelation format to DOS format; the opposite of the REV command.

?   Displays the last TCL command, the current line number, and the size of the current record.

A summary of line editor commands is given in **Figure 14.2.** A similar summary will be displayed by the line editor if you enter the word 'HELP' at the dot prompt.

Command	Explanation
Ln	Displays n lines.
Nn	Moves down n lines.
Gn	Goes to line n.
T	Goes to top of record.
B	Goes to bottom of record.
Un	Moves up n lines.
I(or I data)	Inserts information.
C	Displays ruler line.
Ln/string	Locates string in next n lines.
A	Repeats last Ln/string command.
DEn	Deletes n lines.
Rn/str1/str2	Replaces string 1 with string 2.
RA	Repeats last Rn/str1/str2 command.
MEn/rec.id/n	Merges first n lines from a record starting with the second n line number.
FI	Files the record to disk.
FIC	Compiles and files the record.
FS	Files the record and returns to the record.
FD	Deletes the record.
EX	Exits without saving changes.
EXT	Exits multi-record edit without saving changes.
P	Programs a line editor command.
REV	Converts end of line characters from DOS to Revelation format.
PC	Converts end of line characters from Revelation to DOS format.
?	Last TCL command, and current record size.
HELP	Displays this command summary.

Fig. 14.2 Summary of Line Editor commands

ADVANCED TOPICS

Calling The Editors From An R/BASIC Program

Revelation provides programmers access to the two text processors for use in R/BASIC programs.

The editor used by TCL and R/DESIGN is called RTP22, while the editor used by Revelation's TEXT editor is called RTEXT.

This section will describe the variables that must be passed to these routines from an R/BASIC program. The R/BASIC CALL statement must pass these variables in the order specified below. For an example of how to use these programs, view the PROMPTER program in the PROG file. R/DESIGN uses PROMPTER during data entry screen prompting.

RTP22

DATA.IO	Actual data passed between the calling program and RTP22.
COLM	Column position where data is to be displayed.
ROW	Row position where data is to be displayed.
MLEN	Maximum length of window display. A value of 30, for example, will only show 30 characters before "tickertaping" starts.
MAXLEN	Maximum length of character string (65536).
CSTART	Column position where cursor will be positioned after data is displayed.
FLAG	Flags whether in R/DESIGN or not. 1 = RTP22 called from R/DESIGN. 0 = RTP22 called from non-R/DESIGN program.
MSG	Used with R/DESIGN. Prompt message at bottom of screen.
REENTER.SW	Flags where initial data is to be retrieved. 1 = Retrieve from DATA.IO 0 = Used with R/DESIGN. Retrieve data from @RECORD. RTP22 determines the correct field no. in @RECORD from ITEM.RDES<9>.
PROMPT.FOR	Used with R/DESIGN. Name of data entry field being processed.
DUP	Used by R/DESIGN.
ITEM.RDES	Used by R/DESIGN. RDES record containing data entry screen prompt information.

IN.SCREEN Used by R/DESIGN.
1 = Prompting occurs in screen.
0 = Prompting occurs at bottom of screen.

VALUE.NO Used by R/DESIGN. Holds value of multi-value being processed.

DIS.VAL Used by R/DESIGN. Template of data to be displayed, with screen locations.

SCREEN Used by R/DESIGN. Data entry screen template.

All variables must be assigned a value -- even if it is only the null value (") -- before being passed to RTP22. This particularly applies to those values that are only used by R/DESIGN.

RTEXT

RTEXT is the full screen TEXT editor. While this editor is normally invoked for the entire screen, you may actually define the window size for displaying text in your own programs.

TYPE Type of data being passed to RTEXT. 'STRING' = String of text information. 'R/DESIGN' = Data passed from R/DESIGN.

TEXT.DELIM Type of delimiter to use for separating each line of the text. Multi-value fields are delimited by @VM, while text fields are delimited by CHAR(251), the text marker.

DATA.IO Actual data passed to the text editor from the R/BASIC program. RTEXT does not modify this value.

STORE.IT2 Used to test if the data passed to RTEXT has been modified. If the data passed to RTEXT has been changed, then STORE.IT2 will contain this new data. Otherwise, STORE.IT2 retains its initial value. You are advised to give STORE.IT2 some unusual initial value, such as "%%%%", since it is highly unlikely that this string of characters would be entered as the data in RTEXT.

ROW Starting row position where data is to be displayed.

COLM   Column position where data is to be displayed.
SIZE   Maximum length of line being displayed. A
             value of 30 for example, will display only 30
             characters before "tickertaping" starts. Of
             course, you could invoke the wrap function by
             pressing Shift-F3 from the text editor.
STATUS.LINE   Specify where text editor status line will be
             displayed.
PROMPT.FOR   Used by R/DESIGN. Name of data entry
             field being processed.
RESERVED1   Used internally by RTEXT.
RESERVED2   Used internally by RTEXT.
HELP.KEY   Used by R/DESIGN. Determines whether
             RTEXT help screen or data entry field
             description must be displayed.

PART THREE: COMMAND REFERENCE

INTRODUCTION TO COMMAND REFERENCE

Part III, "Command Reference", consists of four sections:

Reference Commands grouped by function
TCL commands
R/BASIC statements
R/BASIC internal functions

The first section is a functional grouping of the commands with a brief description of each. This is a quick reference for locating a command to accomplish some specific task.

The next three sections give detailed descriptions of the TCL commands, R/BASIC statements, and R/BASIC internal functions in alphabetical order. Each description consists of: the name, short description, complete syntax, rules for using the expression, allowable options, examples, and some helpful notes on using the expression.

The conventions used in Part III when writing the expressions are as follows:

Mandatory expression words	UPPER CASE
Optional expression words	<UPPER CASE BRACKETS>
Mandatory input parameters	lower case
Optional input parameters	<lower case brackets>
Options	(lower case)

for example:

COPY <DICT> sourcefile <source.rec...> (DONPTSIRX)

where:
COPY is the command word,
<DICT> is an optional command word,
sourcefile is the mandatory input parameter,
<source.rec...> is an optional parameter, and
(DONPTSIRX) are the options letters available for this command. Several of these one-letter codes can be entered at once and they do not need to be separated by spaces.

Three dots (...) following a parameter means that as many values can be entered as desired. Values should be separated by a space unless otherwise indicated.

REFERENCE COMMANDS GROUPED BY FUNCTION

TCL COMMANDS

All TCL commands are stored as records in the VOC file. Therefore, synonyms may be created for any of these commands by using the COPY command:

COPY VOC command TO: new.command.name

Also, all references to record.ID or record may be replaced with an asterisk (*) to designate action on all records in a file. For example,

BLIST BP *

would BLIST all the records in the BP file.

ACCOUNT OPERATIONS

ATTACH <medium> <filename...> (S)
      (attaches files in a media)
CHANGE-PASSWORD
      (changes account's password)
CREATE-ACCOUNT accountname
      (creates a new account)
DELETE-ACCOUNT accountname
      (deletes an account)
DETACH medium <filename>
      (detaches files from a medium)
DIR <dos.directory or filename>
      (runs DOS DIR command)
LISTFILES (P)
      (lists the attached files)
LISTMEDIA <medium> (P)
      (lists Revelation files on a medium)
LOGTO accountname <password>
      (logs from one account to another)
MLIST
      (same as LISTFILES)
NAMEMEDIA medium mediumname
      (sets up a DOS drive/directory for Revelation files)
NETWORK.SETUP
      (converts system files to LINK structure)
OFF
      (logs off of Revelation)
SET-FILE account filename medium
      (sets special qfile pointer)

FILE OPERATIONS

CLEAR-FILE <DICT> filename
      (deletes data or dictionary portion of a file)
COPY <DICT> sourcefile source.rec ... (DONPETSIRXL)
  TO:< (<DICT> destinationfile> destination.rec ...
      (copies records)
CREATE-FILE filename #records rec.size <#fields> <med>
  (LRS)
      (creates a new file)

DELETE <DICT> filename record.id
>   (deletes record from a file)

DELETE-FILE filename
>   (deletes a file from the system)

DELETE-LIST listname
>   (deletes a select list from the LISTS file)

MOVE <acct> filename <filename ...> <med> TO: <newacct>
>   <newfilename; newfilename ...> newmed
>   (copies a file to another name, account, or medium)

RECREATE-FILE filename #records rec.size <#fields> <med>
  (LRS)
>   (changes file management system)

RENAME-FILE filename <newaccountname> newfilename
>   (renames a file or changes file's account)

PROGRAMMING

BASIC
>   (same as COMPILE)

BLIST filename record.id (T)
>   (formats an R/BASIC program listing for output)

CATALOG filename record.id
>   (sets pointer to R/BASIC program or subroutine)

COMPILE filename record.id ... (CPS)
>   (compiles R/BASIC program)

DELETE-CATALOG program.name
>   (deletes the catalog reference to an R/BASIC program)

RUN filename record.id (DP)
>   (executes an R/BASIC program)

DATA MANIPULATION

FORM-LIST filename record.id field
>   (creates a select list from a multi-valued field)

GET-LIST listname
>   (retrieves a select list)

SAVE-LIST listname
>   (saves a select list)

SELECT <DICT> filename <with clause> <by clause ...>
> (creates a list of record IDs meeting specified
> conditions)

SSELECT <DICT> filename <with clause> <by clause ...>
> (creates a sorted list of record IDs)

DISPLAYING INFORMATION

COUNT filename <with clause>
> (counts records in a file)

DUMP filename
> (examines a link file frame by frame)

EDIT <DICT> filename record.id ...
> (invokes line editor)

ENTER program.name
> (runs R/DESIGN data entry screen)

FORM formsfile form.record datafile
> (merges data from a datafile with a template form)

HELP <command>
> (accesses the on-line help program)

LIST <n> <ONLY> <DICT> filename <'rec.id' ...> <with clause>
> <by clause ...> <fieldname ...> <total clause ...>
> <break-on clause ...> <heading clause> <footing clause>
> <modifier clause ...> (NPSE)
> (produces ad hoc reports)

LOOKDICT filename
> (lists dictionary records)

SET-COLOR <esc.seq> <COLOR> <DEFAULT> <NONE>
> (specifies the terminals video characteristics)

SET-CRT, SET-LPTR <width> <,height>
> (sets display/page width and height)

SORT <n> <ONLY> <DICT> filename <'rec.id ...'> <with clause>
> <by clause ...> <fieldname ...> <total clause ...>
> <break-on clause ...> <heading clause> <footing clause>
> <modifier clause ...> (NP)
> (produces sorted ad hoc reports)

SUM filename fieldname <with clause>
> (sums the amounts of specified field)

TEXT <DICT> filename record.id ...
> (invokes the text editor)

MISCELLANEOUS

CD filename fieldname
> (compiles the dictionary record of a symbolic field)

FLUSH
> (clears inactive file buffers)

LOAD-TEXT-PARMS
> (loads parameters of VERBS TEXT record)

PC <dos command> .... EXIT
> (runs DOS commands from within Revelation)

PORT <-LOOK> <-DEVICE devname> <-BAUD n> <-STOP n>
<-BITS n> <-PARITY E/O/N/M/S> <-XOFF YES/NO>
> (configures computer as a terminal of a mini or
> mainframe. Used in conjunction with TERMINAL.)

RDESIGN
> (calls R/DESIGN Menu)

RMENU menu.name
> (calls menu processor for displaying menus)

SET-OPTIONS (DOPTXIRNSCLEWU)
> (sets default options)

TERMINAL <-LOOK> <-DEVICE devname> <-BAUD
n> <-STOP n> <-BITS n> <-PARITY E/O/N/M/S> <-
XOFF YES/NO>
> (configures computer as a terminal of a mini or
> mainframe. Used in conjunction with the PORT
> command.)

TIME
> (displays current time)

UTILITY.MENU
> (calls Utility Menu)

WHO
> (provides info on user)

R/BASIC STATEMENTS

INPUT AND OUTPUT PARAMETERS

COLHEADING "string1" :@FM: "string2" :@FM: "string3" ...
> (sets column headings for an output report)

COLLENGTH length1 :@FM: length2 :@FM: length3 ...
> (sets column width for an output report)

FOOTING "exp1 'options' exp2 'options' ..."
      (prints footer at bottom of each page or screen)
HEADING "exp1 'options' exp2 'options' ..."
      (prints header at top of each page or screen)
INPUT var <,length><:>
      (reads from a data statement or prompts for keyboard
      input)
OUT port#, char#
      (sends a single character to a communications port)
PAGE
      (advances the screen or printer a page)
PRINT <exp1, exp2, exp3, ...> (:)
      (prints to the printer or screen)
PRINTER ON/OFF
      (directs output to the printer or video display)

ASSIGNMENT OF VARIABLES

CLEAR/CLEAR COMMON
      (assigns all variables to a value of null)
CLEARDATA
      (clears data stored by a DATA statement)
CLEARSELECT
      (clears the current select list)
COMMON var1, var2, var3 ...
      (allows variables to be used by main program and
      subroutine)
DATA exp1, exp2, exp3...
      (assigns data for a subsequent INPUT statement)
DIM mat1(row<,col>) mat2(row<,col>) mat3(row<,col>) ...
      (names and dimensions a matrix variable)
EQUATE var1 TO var2
      (equates one variable to another)
INPUT var <,length><:>
      (reads from a data statement or prompts for terminal
      input)
LET
      (optional assignment word)
MAT matrix1 = expression
      (assigns values to a matrix variable)

MATPARSE array INTO mat
>   (assigns values from dynamic array to matrix variable)

MATREAD matrix FROM file.var, rec.id ELSE statements
>   (inputs data from a record into a matrix variable)

MATWRITE matrix TO file.var, rec.id
>   (writes values from a matrix variable to a record)

READ var FROM file.var, rec.id ELSE statements
>   (assigns the information from a record to a variable)

READNEXT id.var ELSE statements
>   (reads record ID from a select list)

READV var FROM file.var, rec.id, field# ELSE statements
>   Assigns the value from a specified field to a variable)

TRANSFER var1 TO var2
>   (transfers value of one variable to another)

WRITE exp TO file.var, rec.id
>   (writes to a record)

WRITEV exp TO file.var, rec.id, field#
>   (writes to a specified field within a record)

MANIPULATION OF INFORMATION

CONVERT exp1 TO exp2 IN var
>   (replaces characters in a string)

DELETE file, rec.id
>   (deletes a record from a file)

LOCATE exp1 IN exp2 <BY seq> <USING dlm> SETTING var
>   ELSE statements
>   (locates a value within a dynamic array)

REMOVE var FROM string.exp AT col.exp SETTING flag.var
>   (extracts a sub-string from a dynamic array)

SELECT file.var
>   (creates a list of record IDs)

SWAP exp1 WITH exp2 IN var
>   (exchanges all occurrences of a literal string with
>   another string)

PROGRAM CONTROL

ABORT
>   (returns control to TCL)

BEGIN CASE
> CASE test.expr
> statements
> CASE test.expr
> statements
> END CASE
>   (provides conditional branching)

CALL subname <(arg1, arg2,...)>
>   (calls an external subroutine)

CHAIN program.name
>   (transfers control to another program)

END
>   (marks the end of a program or multi-line statement)

FOR count.var = exp1 TO exp2 <STEP exp3> <WHILE/UNTIL
>   test>
>   statements
> NEXT count.var
>   (loops a specified number of times)

GOSUB label
> RETURN
>   (transfers program control to an internal subroutine)

GOTO label
>   (transfers control of the program to any statement)

IF test.exp THEN statements <ELSE statements>
>   (conditional branching)

LOOP <statements>
>   WHILE/UNTIL test.exp
>   <DO statements>
> REPEAT
>   (creates a structured program looping)

ON exp GOSUB label#1, label#2, label#3 ...
>   (transfers control to one of several subroutines)

ON exp GOTO label#1, label#2, label#3 ...
>   (transfers control to one of several statement labels)

RETURN
RETURN TO statement.label<:>
>   (returns to the main program from internal or external
>   subroutines)

STOP <expression>
>(stops the program)

INTERFACE WITH OUTSIDE FILES/PROGRAMS

DEBUG
>(activates the program debugger)

DECLARE FUNCTION f1, f2, f3 ...

DECLARE SUBROUTINE s1, s2, s3 ...
>(allows user defined functions and subroutines)

EXECUTE "TCL command"
>(recursively executes a TCL command from inside a program)

FUNCTION name (arg)
>(identifies a program as a function)

INITRND value
>(initializes random number generator)

$INSERT <filename,> rec.id
>(inserts source code from another program during compilation)

OPEN dictionary.exp, filename TO file.var ELSE statements
>(opens a file to be read or written)

OSBREAD var FROM file.var AT byte.start LENGTH byte.length
>(breaks large dos file into sections)

OSBWRITE exp TO file.var AT start.byte
>(writes data into a DOS file in sections)

OSCLOSE file.var
>(closes a DOS file opened with OSOPEN)

OSDELETE dos.filename
>(deletes a DOS file)

OSOPEN dos.filename TO file.var ELSE statements
>(opens a DOS file for OSBREAD and OSBWRITE)

OSREAD var FROM dos.filename ELSE statements
>(reads data from a DOS file into a variable)

OSWRITE exp TO dos.filename
>(writes information to a DOS file)

PCEXECUTE
>(same as PCPERFORM)

PCPERFORM dos.command
>(performs a DOS command from inside your program)

PERFORM "command"
> (performs a TCL command from inside a program)

SUBROUTINE name <(arg1,arg2,...)>
> (identifies a program as a subroutine)

MISCELLANEOUS

BREAK ON/OFF/expression
> (turns break key on and off)

REM <statement>
 * <statement>
 ! <statement>
> (inserts remarks into the program)

ECHO OFF/ON
> (suppresses the displaying of input data on the screen)

FLUSH
> (clears inactive file buffers)

GARBAGECOLLECT
> (recovers unused string space)

LINEMARK
> (places debugger linemarks in the program)

LOCK file.var, rec.id ELSE statements
> (attempts to lock a record so only one user
> can have access at a time)

NULL
> (no-action statement; used for readability)

PROMPT char
> (sets the prompt character)

STARTLINECOUNT
> (starts putting linemarks in a program)

STOPLINECOUNT
> (stops placing linemarks in a program)

STORAGE val
> (specifies number of ROS file buffers)

UNLOCK file.var, rec.id
UNLOCK ALL
> (unlocks records on a multi-user network)

R/BASIC INTERNAL FUNCTIONS

Most functions require arguments placed between the parentheses of the function as the expressions to operate on. Some functions, however, do not require these expressions. We have preceded these functions with an asterisk (*).

MATHEMATICAL

ABS(number)
> returns the absolute value of a number

ATAN(number)
> arctangent

BITAND(EXP1,EXP2)
BITOR(EXP1,EXP2)
BITXOR(EXP1,EXP2)
BITNOT(EXP1)
> performs binary operations

COS(number)
> trigonometric cosine

EXP(number)
> natural exponent

INT(number)
> converts to whole integer

LN(number)
> natural log

NEG(number)
> negative of the number

PWR(base,power)
> raises a number to a power

RND(number)
> random number

SIN(number)
> triginometric sine

SQRT(number)
> square root

SUM(expression)
> adds the lowest delimited elements of a dynamic array

TAN(number)
> tangent

STRING OPERATIONS

[ ]   var [start.exp,length]
         extracts a sub-string from a variable
ALPHA(exp)
         tests for only alphabetic characters
COUNT(string,substring)
         counts occurrences of substring
DCOUNT(string,substring)
         same as COUNT
DELETE(exp,field#,value#,subvalue#)
         deletes an element from a dynamic array
EXTRACT(exp,field#,value#,subvalue#)
         extracts an element from a dynamic array
FIELD(exp,delimiter,occurrence)
         returns specified substring
FIELDSTORE(exp,delimiter,n,x,substring)
         replaces, deletes, inserts substrings
INDEX(string,substring,occurrence)
         locates a specified occurrence of a substring
INSERT(exp,field#,value#,subvalue#,element)
         inserts an element into a dynamic array
INVERT(expression)
         inverts ASCII characters
LEN(string)
         length of string expression
MATUNPARSE(matrix variable)
         assigns values from matrix variable to dynamic array
REPLACE(exp,field#,value#,subvalue#,element)
         replaces an element in a dynamic array
SPACE(number)
         blank spaces
STR(string,number)
         repeats a string
TRIM(expression)
TRIMF(expression)
TRIMB(expression)
         trims excess spaces

GENERAL

@(column,<row>)
        positions cursor
CALCULATE(field.name)
        calculates field value from current record
CHAR(number)
        converts a number to ASCII character
* COL1()
        returns the starting position of a substring
* COL2()
        returns the ending position of substrings
* DATE()
        current system date
DIR(dos.filename)
        file information
* DRIVE()
        current drive
FMT(expression,format.pattern)
        converts an expression into another format
HASH(rec.id,modulo,offset)
        returns the group number a record will hash into
* GETBREAK()
        BREAK key status
* GETECHO()
        ECHO status
* GETPRINTER()
        PRINTER status
* GETPROMPT()
        PROMPT status
ICONV(exp,conv.code)
        converts data for internal storage
* INMAT()
        modulus of a file or number of matrix elements
INP(port)
        input from communications port
MOD(exp1, exp2)
        modulo or remainder of two numbers
NOT(expression)
        tests for zero value
NUM(expression)
        tests for numeric string

OCONV(exp,conv.code)
>output conversion

QUOTE(expression)
>places quotation marks

SEQ(character)
>converts ASCII character to number

* SERIAL()
>Revelation serial number

* STATUS()
>set by other operations

* TIME()
>internal time

* TIMEDATE()
>internal time and date

XLATE(filename,rec.id,field#,cont)
>retrieves data from a record field

TCL COMMANDS

ATTACH
(ATTACHES FILES IN A VOLUME)

Purpose

The ATTACH command is used to make the files in a media (DOS drive/directory) other than the default media available to the system. ATTACH scans the ROSMEDIA.MAP of the specified medium for files belonging to the current account. Any files found are made accessible for the current work session. It also checks for any file pointers which can be used with this account.

Syntax

:ATTACH <med> <filename...> (S)

med is the medium to be attached, expressed as a DOS drive/directory.

filename is the name of a specific file to be attached

Rules

1. Only one account can be attached at a time.

2. If the medium is not given, the default medium is assumed.

3. The medium must be given if a filename is given.

4. Two files in different volumes can have the same name. The last one attached will be used by the system. When you attach a file with the same name as one already attached you receive the following message:

Changing file "filename" to drive "med"

5. You cannot attach two volumes with the same ROSMEDIA name at the same time.

Options

S   Suppresses the display of messages.

Example

The current account is PERSONNEL. The default medium is C:\REV. The subdirectory C:\REV\RECORDS is a Revelation medium with the following files:

Filename	Account
EMPLOYEES	PERSONNEL
WAGE.SCALE	PERSONNEL
UNITS.PRODUCED	MANUFACTURING
LABOR.HOURS	MANUFACTURING

There is also a file pointer, LAB.HRS, located in the VOC file of the PERSONNEL account which points to the LABOR.HOURS file.

Using the command:

:ATTACH \REV\RECORDS

would make the following files available for the current work session:

EMPLOYEES
WAGE.SCALE
LAB.HRS

Notes

1. A medium must first be named with the NAMEMEDIA command before it can be attached.

2. See the LISTFILES and DETACH commands.

3. The default medium is attached when you log onto an account. You would want to reattach it with the ATTACH command when another user on your network has created a file

on the default medium since you logged on, or if you want to re-ATTACH a file on this medium which has the same name as a file in another more recently attached volume.

BASIC
(same as COMPILE)

BLIST
(FORMATS AN R/BASIC PROGRAM LISTING)

Purpose

BLIST prints out an R/BASIC program in a format which makes it easier to see the structure of the program. This is accomplished by indenting the loop and multi-line statements such as FOR/NEXT, IF, CASE, etc.

Syntax

:BLIST filename <record.id...> (options)

filename is the file containing the program(s).

record.id is the record(s) containing the program(s) to be listed.

Rules

1. Leave the record.id blank to BLIST a SELECT list of the file.

2. Use an asterisk (*) for the record.id to BLIST all of the records in a file.

Options

T   Outputs to the Terminal instead of the printer.

Examples

:BLIST BP EXAMPLE.RPT

would print a formatted list of the EXAMPLE.RPT record in the BP file.

:BLIST BP *

would list all of the records in the BP file.

:SELECT BP WITH @ID CONTAINING "RPT"
32 Record(s) selected
>BLIST BP

would list the 32 records whose ID contained the text "RPT".

Assume we created the following sample program using the text editor:

```
* EXAMPLE PROGRAM
TOP:
PRINT "NUMBER OF LABELS ":
INPUT NUM
COUNTER = 0
LOOP
PRINT
UNTIL COUNTER = NUM DO
PRINT; PRINT "NEW NAME AND ADDRESS"
FOR X = 1 TO 4
INPUT LINE
IF LINE <> "" THEN
PRINT LINE
END
NEXT X
COUNTER += 1
REPEAT
PRINT; PRINT "GO AGAIN":
INPUT AGAIN
IF AGAIN = "Y" THEN GOTO TOP
STOP
```

But if this program were listed with the BLIST command it would look like this:

```
0001        * EXAMPLE PROGRAM
0002    TOP:
0003        PRINT "NUMBER OF LABELS ":
0004        INPUT NUM
0005        COUNTER = 0
0006        LOOP
0007        | PRINT
0008        UNTIL COUNTER = NUM  DO
0009        | PRINT;PRINT "NEW NAME AND ADDRESS"
0010        | FOR X = 1 TO 4
0011        |   INPUT LINE
0012        |   IF LINE <> "" THEN
0013        |   | PRINT LINE
0014        |   END
0015        | NEXT X
0016        | COUNTER += 1
0017        REPEAT
0018        PRINT; PRINT "GO AGAIN":
0019        INPUT AGAIN
0020        IF AGAIN = "Y" THEN GOTO TOP
0021        STOP
```

Notes

1. This kind of listing is very useful for a structured programming language like R/BASIC. In fact, you should get into the habit of indenting your loops and multi-line statements when writing programs of any complexity.

CATALOG
(SETS VOC POINTER TO R/BASIC PROGRAM)

Purpose

The CATALOG command sets up a file pointer in the VOC file which points to an R/BASIC program. That program can then be executed by typing the program name at the TCL prompt rather than using the RUN command. It is also used to set up a pointer to an external subroutine so that the subroutine can be called from inside a program. (See R/BASIC statement CALL).

Syntax

:CATALOG filename <record.id...>

filename is name of file holding the program or subroutine.

record.id is the ID of the record containing the program or subroutine.

Rules

1. Leave record.id blank to CATALOG a SELECT list.

2. Use an asterisk (*) for the record.id to catalog all records in a file.

3. The program must have been compiled before it can be cataloged. The compilation would normally be performed when the program was written and saved with the Text Editor.

4. A CATALOGed program will still not run if the file holding the program has not been attached.

5. Subroutines are cataloged just like other programs.

Examples

```
:CATALOG BP EXAMPLE.RPT
'EXAMPLE.RPT' cataloged
:EXAMPLE.RPT
```

would catalog the EXAMPLE.RPT record in the BP file and then run the program.

```
:CATALOG BP *
```

would catalog all of the records in the BP file.

```
:SELECT BP WITH @ID "[RPT]"
32 Record(s) selected
>CATALOG BP
```

would catalog the 32 records in the BP file whose ID contained the text "RPT".

Notes

1. Programs are usually written with the Text Editor and stored as a record in a file which you set up to hold your programs. You can think of the record ID as the name of the program. (See Chapter 12 for more discussion on creating programs).

2. External subroutines are essentially special programs which are called from inside another program to run as a subroutine of that program (see Chapter 13).

CD
(COMPILES A DICTIONARY RECORD)

Purpose

The CD command is used to compile the dictionary record of a symbolic field after you have used the line editor to change the R/BASIC formula of that field.

Syntax

CD file.name field.name

file.name is the name of the data file containing the symbolic field which has been edited.

field.name is the name of the symbolic field which has been edited.

Examples

:CD CUSTOMERS TOTAL.AMOUNT

would recompile the R/BASIC formula for the symbolic field TOTAL.AMOUNT in the CUSTOMERS FILE.

Notes

1. When you define the structure of a file with BUD, it creates a dictionary record for each of the data fields you define. For a symbolic data field, the dictionary record has a field containing

the R/BASIC statements for the field's formula. When you file the dictionary record, BUD compiles the R/BASIC formulae and stores this compiled code in another field in the dictionary record (see Appendix IX). There is no problem changing the R/BASIC statements with BUD. But if you change them with the line editor, you must recompile the R/BASIC code using the CD command; otherwise the old compiled code will still be used by Revelation.

2. We mention the R/BASIC code being edited with the line editor and not the text editor. That is because the dictionary record which is being edited has a field containing compiled code. Remember that if you try to edit the compiled code with the text editor, it will go nuts trying to display the compiled code. Thus the reason for using the line editor.

3. Since most users will change a symbolic field's formula with BUD, the CD comand is mainly for those developers who might need to change a dictionary formula on-the-run in a separate R/BASIC program.

CHANGE-PASSWORD
(CHANGES ACCOUNT'S PASSWORD)

Purpose

The CHANGE-PASSWORD command changes an account's password by prompting for the account name, the old password (if there is one), and the new password.

Syntax

:CHANGE-PASSWORD

Rules

1. Passwords can be as long as you like and contain any characters, including spaces.

2. You must be in the SYSPROG account to use this command -- even if you want to change the password for some other account.

CLEAR-FILE
(DELETES DATA OR DICTIONARY PORTION OF A FILE)

Purpose

The CLEAR-FILE command is used to delete all the records in either the DATA or DICT portion of a file.

Syntax

:CLEAR-FILE <DICT> filename

filename is the name of the file to be cleared.

Rules

1. If DICT is used in the command, then only the dictionary portion of the file is cleared. If DICT is omitted then only the data records are deleted.

2. The file to be cleared must be attached.

3. An alternate syntax is **:CLEAR-FILE DATA** filename.

COMPILE
(COMPILES R/BASIC PROGRAMS)

Purpose

The COMPILE command is used to compile an R/BASIC program which was not already compiled using one of the text editors.

Syntax

:COMPILE filename <record.id...> (options)

filename is the name of the file containing the program to be compiled.

record.id is the ID of the record(s) to be compiled.

Rules

1. Leave the record.id blank to compile a SELECT list of the file.

2. To compile all the records of a file, use an asterisk (*) for the record.id.

3. COMPILE displays an asterisk (*) as it successfully compiles each line. If it encounters any errors, the errant line number is displayed and the compiler continues looking for other errors. After the last line is checked the following error message is displyed:

Line (n) Compilation Aborted; No object produced.

Options

C   Cuts off the symbol table. This reduces the space occupied by the object code, but the DEBUGGER will not not be able to trace any variables.

P   Prints the output messages from COMPILE to the printer.

S   Suppresses the generation of linemarks in the object code, thus reducing the amount of disk space needed for storage. This option also prevents the debugger from reporting the correct line number where execution was halted, since the debugger will now see the entire program as line 1.

Example

:COMPILE BP REPORT23 (P)

compiles a program stored as REPORT23 in the BP file and sends any compiler messages to the printer.

:COMPILE BP *

compiles all the records in the BP file.

:SELECT BP WITH @ID CONTAINING REPORT
24 Record(s) selected
>COMPILE BP

compiles the 24 selected BP records.

Notes

1. After successful compilation of a program, the compiled code is stored in the same file as the source code, but with a record ID of "$" followed by the program name. Thus, in the first example above, the compiled record would have an ID = $REPORT.

2. The COMPILE and BASIC commands are completely interchangeable.

COPY
(COPIES RECORDS)

Purpose

The COPY command copies records within the same file or to another file.

Syntax

:COPY <DICT> sourcefile <source.rec...> (options)
TO:< (<DICT> destinationfile> <destination.rec...>

sourcefile is the name of the file containing the records to be copied.

source.rec is the record ID(s) to be copied

(destinationfile is the name of the file where the copied record will be located.

destination.rec is the ID(s) of the record(s) which will hold the copied information.

Rules

1. The command word DICT is used if the records are to be copied from or copied to the dictionary portion of a file.

2. Leave the source.rec blank to copy a SELECT list.

3. Use an asterisk (*) for source.rec to copy all the records in a file.

4. If no destination filename is given, the records are copied within the same file.

5. An open parenthesis, "(", must be placed in front of the destination filename if one is used. This tells Revelation that the expression to follow is a file name and not a record ID.

6. You can either type the expression "TO:" and the subsequent information all on the first line, or press <E> after entering the source line, in which case Revelation will prompt you with "TO:".

7. If there is more than one source record, they are copied to the destination records in the order listed. If no destination records are listed, then the new records are given the same names as the old records.

8. If the destination record already exists, it will not be written over unless either the O or N options are used (see below).

Options

D   deletes the source records after they have been copied to the destination file; has no effect if used with a P or T option.

O   allows the source record to be written over an already existing destination record if one exists.

N   copies the source record only if a record with the destination name exists. No new records will be written.

P   copies the source record to the Printer (no TO: prompt). **PE** suppresses form feed at start of report.

T   copies the records to the terminal (no TO: prompt).

S   suppresses the output of messages.

I   converts the copied record(s) to DOS format. Field marks are converted to carriage returns-line feeds and the record is terminated with Ctrl Z.

R   converts the source record(s) from DOS format into Revelation format by converting carriage return-line feeds into field marks (the opposite of option I).

X   copies the source record(s) into hexadecimal format (advanced users only).

L   performs record locking logic during COPY procedure.

Examples

:COPY INVOICE 482 (D) TO: 583

copies record 482 in the INVOICE file to record 583 and deletes the old record.

> **:COPY INVOICE 482 (O) TO: (RECEIPTS 285**

copies invoice 482 to record 285 in the RECEIPTS file. If this record ID already exists in the RECEIPTS file, the COPY command will write over it.

:COPY DICT ORDERS * TO: (DICT NEW.ORDERS

copies all the dictionary records from the ORDERS file to the dictionary of the NEW.ORDERS file.

> **:SELECT INVOICES WITH DATE EQ "10/11/86"**
> 32 Record(s) selected
> **>COPY INVOICES TO: (OLD.INVOICES**

would copy 32 invoice records with an invoice date from October 11, 1986, to another file named OLD.INVOICES.

Notes

1. The P and T options are useful in getting a list of a program.

2. You can copy DOS files by using the special Revelation file "DOS" (see Chapter 10). Revelation treats all of your DOS files as one big Revelation file named "DOS", in which each actual DOS file is seen as a record. A DOS file can be copied by substituting its drive/directory and filename for the record ID in the COPY command. For example,

> **:COPY DOS C:\ADMIN\LETTERS TO: B:LETTERS**

would copy the DOS file, LETTERS, in the ADMIN subdirectory of the C drive to the B drive. Likewise:

> **:COPY INVOICE AMOUNT (I) TO: (DOS C:INV.AMT**

would copy the AMOUNT record from the INVOICE file to the DOS file INV.AMT on the C drive, first converting it into DOS format.

COUNT
(COUNTS RECORDS IN A FILE)

Purpose

The COUNT command counts the number of records which meet a specified condition.

Syntax

:COUNT <DICT> filename <with clause>

filename is the name of the file containing the records to be counted.

with clause is the selection phrase consisting of the word WITH followed by a field name and comparative expression (see Chapter 9).

Rules

1. If no with clause is used, the total number of records is returned.

Example

:COUNT MAILLIST WITH STATE = "CA"
54 record(s) counted

CREATE-ACCOUNT
(CREATES A NEW ACCOUNT)

Purpose

The CREATE-ACCOUNT command is used to create and name a new account.

Syntax

:CREATE-ACCOUNT accountname

accountname is the name of the new account.

Rules

1. You will be prompted for a password. Hit return if you do not want a password for this account; otherwise enter the password, which can be as long as you desire and contain any characters including spaces.

Notes

1. You can log into the new account with the LOGTO command.

2. When you create a new account, a VOC file and LISTS file are created for this new account and stored on the default medium. See Chapter 3 for additional information about accounts.

CREATE-FILE
(CREATES A NEW FILE)

Purpose

The CREATE-FILE command is used to create and name a new Revelation file.

Syntax

:CREATE-FILE filename #records rec.size <#fields> <med> (LRS)

filename is the name of the new file. The name can be up to 50 characters long and include any characters except open/close parentheses or spaces.

#records is the estimated number of records to be placed in the file.

rec.size is the estimated average number of characters per record.

#fields is the estimated number of dictionary records. This parameter is only used with the LINK file structure.

med is the DOS drive and directory which will contain the new file.

L or **R** forces the file into either the LINK or ROS file management structure.

Rules

1. If #records and rec.size are not given in the command line, you will be prompted for their entry. You will also be prompted for #fields for LINK files.

2. If you do not enter a medium, the default medium will be used. Other media must already be named using the NAMEMEDIA command before they can hold Revelation files.

3. Entering the L or R option forces that file structure on the new file. Use only one letter. Do not use R for a file which will be shared on a network.

Option

S   Suppresses the display of messages.

Example

:CREATE-FILE INVOICES 200 600 10 C:\REV\ACCTG (L)

creates the INVOICES file in the ACCTG subdirectory of the REV subdirectory on the C drive, with a file size approximated from 200 records of 600 characters each and 10 dictionary items. The LINK file structure will be used.

:CREATE-FILE INVOICES

This will create the INVOICES file and force Revelation to prompt for the additional information required to complete the file creation process.

Notes

1. Usually it will suffice to just give the new filename in the command and let Revelation prompt for information to determine if the file should use ROS or LINK structure.

2. Don't worry if your estimate of the file size is way off; you can always change it (and the file structure) using the RECREATE-FILE command if you notice that disk access of the file becomes slow.

3. The following rules will be used to determine which type of file structure to employ:

> ROS - If the file is small (less than 200k bytes) and it will not be shared on a network.

> LINK - If the file will be shared on a network.

> LINK - If the file will not be shared but is calculated to be greater than 200k bytes in size, Revelation will ask if you want to make the file a LINK file. The LINK file structure provides maximum efficiency for large files.

4. The rules for specifying directories and subdirectories are the same as for DOS.

DELETE
(DELETES RECORD FROM A FILE)

Purpose

The DELETE command removes a record or records from a file.

Syntax

:DELETE <DICT> filename <record.id...>

filename is the name of the file containing records to be deleted.

record.id is the ID of a record to be deleted.

Rules

1. Leave record.id blank to delete a SELECT list.

2. Use an asterisk (*) to delete all the data records in a file. (This would be the same as the CLEAR-FILE command.)

Examples

:DELETE INVOICE 482

deletes record 482 from the INVOICE file.

:DELETE DICT INVOICE *

deletes all of the dictionary records from the INVOICE file.

:SELECT INVOICE WITH AMOUNT > 300
30 Record(s) selected
>DELETE INVOICE

deletes the 30 selected invoice records.

Notes

1. Be careful when using this command as the deleted records cannot be recalled.

DELETE-ACCOUNT
(DELETES ALL THE FILES IN AN ACCOUNT)

Purpose

Deletes the specified account as well as all of the files assigned to the account.

Syntax

:DELETE-ACCOUNT account.name

account.name is the name of the accout to be deleted.

Examples

:DELETE-ACCOUNT ADMIN

Notes

1. There are two steps to this process. Phase One deletes all the files in the named account that are located on the default medium. Revelation then prompts you to enter other drives/directories where there may be additional files associated with this account in order to delete those files also.

DELETE-CATALOG
(UN-CATALOGS A PROGRAM)

Purpose

The DELETE-CATALOG is used to un-CATALOG a program which you had previously cataloged with the CATALOG command.

Syntax

:DELETE-CATALOG prog.name

prog.name is the name of the R/BASIC program which you no longer want cataloged.

Examples

:DELETE-CATALOG LIST.SAMPLE

Notes

1. The program itself is not deleted. Only the entry in the VOC file is deleted. This VOC entry allows you to run the program by just entering its name at the TCL prompt. By removing the VOC entry you may only execute the program with the RUN command.

DELETE-FILE
(DELETES A FILE FROM THE SYSTEM)

Purpose

DELETE-FILE deletes a currently attached Revelation file from the system.

Syntax

:DELETE-FILE filename

filename is the name of the file to deleted.

Rules

1. The file must be attached before it can be deleted.

2. You cannot delete a file by using its qfile name with the DELETE-FILE command. To delete the file which is pointed to by the qfile, you must use that file's actual name.

Examples

:DELETE-FILE INVOICE

deletes the INVOICE file.

Notes

1. To delete a qfile *pointer* you will have to delete the qfile record from the VOC file, or if you have created the special QFILES file (see Chapter 5), then you will have to delete the qfile record from this file.

DELETE-LIST
(DELETES A SELECT LIST)

Purpose

DELETE-LIST deletes a SELECT list from the LISTS file which has been previously saved.

Syntax

:DELETE-LIST listname

listname is the name of the SELECT list to be deleted.

Examples

:SELECT INVOICE WITH AMOUNT > 300
3 Record(s) selected
>SAVE-LIST SAMPLE
"SAMPLE" saved on 'LISTS' file
:DELETE-LIST SAMPLE
"SAMPLE" deleted from the 'LISTS' file

Notes

1. See the SAVE-LIST and GET-LIST commands.

DETACH
(DETACHES FILES FROM A MEDIUM)

Purpose

The DETACH command is used to disconnect files on a medium (DOS drive/directory) from the system. (It is the opposite of the ATTACH command.)

Syntax

:DETACH <medium> <filename...>

medium is the DOS drive/directory whose files are to be detached.

filename is the name of the file(s) to be detached.

Rules

1. If no filenames are listed, all of the files on the medium are detached.

2. If no medium is listed, the default medium will be detached.

3. The VERBS and VOC files cannot be detached.

Examples

:DETACH C:\REV\ADMIN

detaches all of the Revelation files on the ADMIN subdirectory.

:DETACH C:\REV\ADMIN PERS.REC EMP.DATA

detaches the PERS.REC and EMP.DATA files.

DIR
(EXECUTES THE DOS DIR COMMAND)

Purpose

Using the DIR command you can execute the DOS command DIR from the TCL prompt. The syntax is the same as if you were entering the command from the DOS prompt.

Examples

:DIR C:\ADMIN

would display the DOS directory of the ADMIN subdirectory.

Notes

1. You can include any DOS command as a TCL command by creating a VOC entry with the DOS command as the record key and PCPERFORM as the first field.

DUMP
(EXAMINES A LINK FILE FRAME BY FRAME)

Purpose

The DUMP command is for advanced users. It displays a LINK file, group by group and frame by frame.

Syntax

:DUMP filename

filename is the name of the LINK file to be displayed.

Rules

1. The file must have been created with the LINK file management system.

2. The right and left cursor arrow keys move from frame to frame. The up and down cursor arrow keys move from group to group.

3. To edit a byte in the displayed frame, press Ctrl-E to enter edit mode. In this mode the cursor keys move you around the displayed frame. Pressing the ESC key returns you to viewing mode.

4. To view segments of the frame in hexidecimal form, press Ctrl-H. In this mode the cursor keys move you around the displayed frame, showing 16 bytes at a time in hexidecimal form. Pressing the ESC key returns you to normal viewing mode.

Notes

1. You should only attempt to edit a file with the DUMP command if you have received a Format Error and are not able to recover important records.

2. Be very careful when editing a frame. Each frame contains overhead information used for maintaining group number, frame number, and pointers to any overflow frames. If you accidentally corrupt these numbers the integrity of your data will be violated or you will receive a format error when you later try to use the file.

EDIT
(INVOKES LINE EDITOR)

Purpose

The EDIT command invokes the Line Editor which allows editing, creating, or viewing of records.

Syntax

:EDIT <DICT> filename <record.id...>

DICT causes the dictionary portion of the file to be edited instead of the data portion.

filename is the name of the file to be edited.

record.id is the ID of the record(s) to be edited.

Rules

1. Leave record.id blank to edit a SELECT list.

2. Use an asterisk (*) for record.id to edit all records in a file.

Examples

:EDIT INVOICES 358 953

edits records 358 and 953 of the INVOICES file. Record 953 will be displayed for editing after you exit record 358.

:EDIT INVOICES *

will edit all of the records in the INVOICES file.

:SELECT INVOICES WITH AMOUNT > 300
32 Record(s) Selected
>EDIT INVOICES

will successively edit the 32 selected records.

Notes

1. See Chapter 14 for more information on using the Line Editor. The Line Editor is used much less frequently than the Text Editor.

ENTER
(RUNS AN R/DESIGN DATA ENTRY PROGRAM)

Purpose

The ENTER command is used to run an R/DESIGN created data entry screen for which, for whatever reason, a VOC entry has not been made.

Syntax

:ENTER pgrm.name

pgrm.name is the name of the data entry program.

Rules

1. ENTER invokes the R/DESIGN interpreter to display the data entry screen created with R/DESIGN. The ENTER program uses the parameters stored in the RDES file.

Notes

1. Normally, when you create a data entry program with R/DESIGN an entry is automatically made in the VOC file which allows you to run the data entry screen by just entering its name at the TCL prompt. However advanced users might copy an RDES record and modify it to create another screen. In this case no VOC entry will exist. The ENTER command may be used to run that program.

2. The ENTER command will first look in the RDES file for the record containing the data entry screen parameters. If the record is not in that file, then the VERBS file will be searched. R/DESIGN, however, will automatically store this record in the RDES file when the screen is first designed.

FLUSH
(CLEARS INACTIVE FILE BUFFERS)

Same as the the R/BASIC statement FLUSH - see the R/BASIC statement section.

FORM
(MERGES DATA FROM A DATAFILE WITH A TEMPLATE FORM)

Purpose

The FORM command takes data stored in a data file and inserts it one record at a time into a template form. An example would be merging a datafile of addresses into a form letter to produce a custom mailing.

Syntax

:FORM formsfile form.record datafile

formsfile is the name of the file containing the template form.

form.record is the ID of the record in the formsfile which contains the template to be used.

datafile is the name of the file containing the data records to be merged with the template form.

Rules

1. Create a formsfile to hold your template forms. Then, using the Text Editor, create the template as a record in the formsfile (see Chapter 14 on using the Text Editor).

2. Lay out the template with literal text as you want it to print out. Where you want to insert data from the datafile, type the name of the field in braces { }. The fields you are inserting can be single or multi-valued data fields, as well as single or multi-valued symbolic fields.

3. When the command is executed, the template will be printed as many times as there are records in the datafile. Each time it is printed, the next sequential record will be used to insert the values for the field names you used in the template.

4. When field names are used in the template, the output conversion, justification, and display length are determined by the dictionary definition of that field. You can override these dictionary parameters by using the following convention when typing the field in braces:

{ fieldname; <conversion>; <display>; <maxvalues> }

>   where

>>   **fieldname** is the dictionary name of the field to be inserted.

>>   **conversion** is the output conversion to be used.

>>   **display** is the justification and length to be used.

>>   **maxvalues** is the maximum number of values to be displayed in the template if the field is multi-valued..

>   Note that the three parameters are optional and are separated by semicolons (;). If a parameter is left blank, its semicolon must still be inserted so that the FORM program will know which parameter you are entering (see examples).

5. **Form Control Statements** may be placed at the top of the template to redefine field names and to control the formatting of the template. Each Form Control Statement begins with two back slashes (\\) so that the FORM program will know that the line is a control statement and not part of the template to be printed. There must be a space between the \\ and the command word that follows it. The Form Control Statements are:

\\ DEFINE name = <fieldname>; <conv>; <disp>; <maxval>

>>   **name** is the name that will be used in the template to replace the field's dictionary name. This name may be an existing dictionary name. You might

use this Form Control Statement because a long fieldname might otherwise take up too much space in the template.

fieldname is the actual dictionary record that is being redefined for the FORM template. You may still use this dictionary name in the template, as well as the new name being defined with this Form Control Statement.

conv is the output conversion to be used on the field in the template.

disp is the display format and length to be used for the field in the template.

maxval is the maximum number of values to display in the template if this field is multi-valued.

Note that the four parameters are all optional, but that they must appear in this order; if one is left out, the semicolon used as a delimiter must still be entered. However, parameters can be left off the *end* of the string without needing to enter their delimiters (see examples).

Each DEFINE statement must be on a separate line.

\\ MOUNT.FORM = form#

form# is the name of any special paper forms which you want inserted into your printer before the FORM command is executed. The FORM program will stop and prompt you to insert the special paper before it begins printing. If you enter *STD for form# then there will be no prompt (system default is *STD).

\\ PAUSE = NO/YES

YES will cause FORM to pause after each page is printed to allow you to manually feed another blank form into the printer. NO is used for continuous feed paper and printers with automatic cut sheet paper feeders (system default is NO).

\\ MV = n/ALL

n is the maximum number of values you want to print from a multi-value field. **ALL** will print all of the multi-values (system default is ALL).

\\ WIDTH = n

n is the number of characters per line (system default is 132).

\\ LENGTH = n

n is the number of lines per page (system default is 66).

\\ PRINTER = ON/OFF

ON directs output to the printer. **OFF** sends output to the terminal (system default is ON).

\\ MARGIN = n

n is the number of spaces for the left margin.

\\ ALIGN = YES

YES prompts the operator to set the top of form on the printer.

\\ SELECT = TCL SELECT with clause

Provides a method for selecting records from the file entered on the FORM command that meet the specified criteria. Only those records selected will be used in producing the forms.

\\ SPACEOUT = YES/NO

> NO causes each field, when inserted, to take up the exact number of spaces as are defined in the field's display width parameter, regardless of whether the actual information takes up the allocated width. A YES will take out blank spaces from the fields (system default is YES). Inserting a space in column 1 of any line will cause the FORM command to treat that line as if it has a SPACEOUT opposite to the value set in the Form Control Statement.

\\ INSERT.MV = YES/NO

> Multi-values are printed one value to a line. If YES is entered, the rest of the text is pushed down as the values are inserted into the template. If NO is entered, the text is not pushed down by multi-values. Therefore enough room must be left for the maximum number of multi-values or they will write over the text that follows (system default is YES).

\\ FORMS.UP = n

> n is the number of forms to be printed across the width of the page; e.g. n = 2 might be used to print two columns of mailing labels per page (system default is 1).

Examples

Examples of **Form Control Statements:**

\\ **DEFINE A = AMOUNT; MD2; R#5; 3**
defines A to mean the AMOUNT field with output conversion MD2, right justified, display length 5, and a maximum of 3 values per multi-value.

\\ DEFINE ADDRESS = ;L#25
defines the ADDRESS field to have the same name, but
a different justification and display length. Note the
semicolon before L#25 must be included, but those
following can be dropped.

As an example of an application using the FORM command,
assume you have a mailing list stored in a file named MAILLIST
with the following fields: MR.MS, FIRSTNAME, LASTNAME,
TITLE, COMPANY, and ADDRESS. The ADDRESS field is
multi-valued. You want to send a standard letter addressed by
name to each person from Missouri. Create a template letter
with a record ID of EXAMPLE.LTR in a file called FORMS.
Use the TEXT editor to design this template. The beginning of
the EXAMPLE.LTR template might look like this:

\\ DEFINE LN = LASTNAME
\\ DEFINE FN = FIRSTNAME
\\ MOUNT.FORM = STATIONARY
\\ PAUSE = YES
\\ SELECT = WITH ST = "MISSOURI"
\\ SPACEOUT = YES

{MR.MS} {FN} {LN}
{TITLE}
{COMPANY}
{ADDRESS}

Dear {MR.MS} {LN}:

I am just writing to thank you for coming to our
gallery opening last Monday. It was good to see...

You would generate your semi-custom letters by using the
following command:

:FORM FORMS EXAMPLE.LTR MAILLIST

Notes

1. The FORM command is similar to the "mail merge" capability of any standard word processor. This allows you to merge data in your database with a standard output form. The FORM command has the added power of being able to use symbolic fields.

2. The file which holds your form templates can be named anything you desire; we just use FORMS as an example.

3. The default values of the Form Control Statements can be changed by creating a FORM.DEFAULT record in the file which holds your template forms. In this record, insert the Form Control Statements you want the FORM program to use each time it uses a template from that file. If you want different default values for different groups of templates, just put them in separate files, each file having its own FORM.DEFAULT record.

4. The \\ DEFINE statement is useful if you have a long field name which you do not want to type every time it occurs in the template, particularly if you are changing the field's display and output conversion. It is also useful for field names which take up more space than their actual values. Using a shorter definition for the field will allow you to space everything where you what it in the template.

5. The \\ SPACEOUT statement takes out unwanted spaces from fields; e.g. where you insert a field into the text of a sentence. If the actual information stored in the field is shorter than the display length, you would have extra spaces in the middle of the sentence. On the other hand, when you are lining data up in columns, you want each item to take up the same width, no matter what length the actual data, so that your columns will line up.

FORM-LIST
(CREATES A SELECT LIST FROM A MULTI-VALUED FIELD)

Purpose

The FORM-LIST command creates a select list from the values in a multi-valued field.

Syntax

:FORM-LIST filename record.id field

filename is the name of the file containing the multi-valued field to be selected.

record.id is the ID of the record containing the information to be selected.

field is either the FMC number or the dictionary name of the field containing the multi-values.

Rules

1. The field can be specified by either giving the field's FMC number or giving the dictionary name for the field.

Examples

Assume you have a datafile named INVOICES with the record key equal to the the invoice number. Furthermore, this file is cross referenced to the CUSTOMERS file so that every time an invoice is entered in the INVOICES file, the invoice number is added to the customer's record in a multi-valued field named INV.NO. To display the invoices of the customer named JONES you would use the following commands:

:FORM-LIST CUSTOMERS JONES INV.NO
4 Record(s) selected
>LIST INVOICES

Notes

1. The FORM-LIST is most commonly used to make select lists from multi-value fields which are cross referenced from another file. Then when you make a list out of the values in the multi-valued field, each value corresponds to a record ID in the cross-referenced file.

GET-LIST
(RETRIEVES A SELECT LIST)

Purpose

The GET-LIST command retrieves a select list which was previously saved with a SAVE-LIST command. The select list, which is stored as a record in the LISTS file, consists of a list of record IDs.

Syntax

:GET-LIST listname

listname is the name of the list to be retrieved.

Rules

1. The list must have been previously named and saved using the SAVE-LIST command. Alternatively, the list may be created with one of the editors.

Examples

:SELECT INVOICES WITH AMOUNT > 300
32 record(s) selected
>SAVE-LIST SAMPLE

creates a select list of 32 record IDs.

:GET-LIST SAMPLE
32 record(s) selected
>LIST INVOICES

lists the 32 selected records of the INVOICE file.

HELP
(ACCESSES THE ON-LINE HELP PROGRAM)

Purpose

The HELP command takes you either to the HELP menu or directly to the HELP message for one of the TCL commands included in the HELP file.

Syntax

:HELP <command>

command is the name of one of the TCL commands.

Rules

1. If no command is entered, the HELP MENU, showing all indexed commands, is displayed.

2. To bypass the HELP MENU, enter the name of the command with which you want help directly on the HELP command line.

Notes

1. You may press the F1 key from the TCL prompt to invoke the HELP menu. If you have already started typing a command when the F1 key is pressed, the HELP program will provide information on that command.

2. For additional information see the description of the on-line HELP program in Chapter 5.

3. To add additional items to the HELP menu, you must edit two different records in the HELP file. The first record is the COMMANDS record which contains the name of all the commands displayed on this menu. The second record is COMMANDS.DESC which contains the information to be displayed when help is invoked.

LIST
(PRODUCES AD HOC REPORTS)

Purpose

The LIST command allows you to generate an ad hoc listing of a file and includes the following features: record selection, sorting, display field selection, and heading/footing text.

Syntax

:LIST <n> <ONLY> <DICT> filename <'rec.id...'> <WITH clause> <BY clause...> <fieldname...> <TOTAL clause...> <BREAK-ON clause...> <HEADING clause> <FOOTING clause > <modifier clause...> (options)

n is the number of records to list.

ONLY is used to list the record IDs only (no other fields will be displayed)

DICT lists records from the dictionary portion of the file.

filename is the name of the file containing the information to be listed

'rec.id' is the ID of the record(s) to be listed; must be enclosed in quotes if non-numeric.

WITH clause is a selection phrase starting with the TCL word WITH or WITHOUT.

BY clause is a sort expression starting with the TCL word BY.

fieldname is the name of the field(s) to be displayed in the listing.

TOTAL fieldname displays a numeric field to be totaled.

BREAK-ON fieldname clause causes breaks in the report when the value of that field changes.

HEADING clause provides text which will appear at the top of each page of the report.

FOOTING clause provides text which will appear at the foot of each page of the report.

modifier clause modifies the format of the report format, using ID-SUPP, DBL-SPC, COL-HDR, HDR-SUPP, SUPP.

Rules

1. The LIST command can contain up to 256 characters and will automatically ticker tape.

2. Using "n" to list only a certain number of records will list the first n records as Revelation stores them, not as they were entered.

3. ONLY causes only the record IDs to list. Specifying fieldnames will cause those fields to list in addition to the record IDs. Using a TOTAL or BREAK-ON clause causes those fields to list also. If none of the above expressions are used, the fields specified in the group field @CRT (or @LPTR if appropriate) will be listed.

4. If both a BREAK-ON clause and a TOTAL clause are used, sub-totals will be generated for each break in the report.

5. In a WITH clause, alphanumeric strings used as comparison values must be enclosed in quotes; numeric values need not be.

6. LIST will normally display the information from one record on one line. If the information from a record is too long to fit on one line, it will line wrap to the next line and the output report will no longer line up in nice columns.

7. See Chapter 9 for a detailed explanation of how to use the LIST command.

Options

N   No page. When the output of a LIST command is displayed on the terminal it pauses at the end of each page. This option does away with that pause and scrolls straight to the end of the report.

P   causes the output to go to the Printer.

S   generates R/BASIC Source code from the LIST command (see chapter 9).

E   suppresses initial formfeed.

Examples

:LIST 3 CUSTOMERS NAME ADDRESS PHONE

:LIST ONLY INVOICES

:LIST INVOICES WITH AMOUNT > 300 BY CUSTOMER BREAK-ON CUSTOMER TOTAL AMOUNT (P)

:LIST MAILLIST BY LASTNAME HEADING "MARKETING PROSPECTS"

Notes

1. Including a "group" fieldname in the command will cause a group of fields to be listed.

2. Normally, the LIST command displays only information from one file. However, data in other files may be displayed by defining a symbolic field with a formula containing the XLATE function (see Chapter 13).

3. LIST may be used to view the field structure of a datafile using **:LIST DICT filename DICT.INFO.** (DICT.INFO is a group field name in the dictionary of the VOC file.)

LISTFILES
(LISTS THE ATTACHED FILES)

Purpose

The LISTFILES command is used to list all of the "attached" files, in other words, the files which you have access to while logged into the current account. It will also list the qfile pointers in the account.

Syntax

:LISTFILES (options)

Options

P   sends output to the Printer

Examples

:LISTFILES

```
REVELATION              NATIVE
FILENAME      VOLUME    FILENAME      MODULO

VERBS         C:        ROS00001      04
VOC           C:        ROS10035      LNK7
LISTS         C:        ROS10036      LNK7
QFILE         C:        ROS10035      LNK7
MD            C:        ROS10035      LNK7
EMPLOYEE  C:\REV\ADMIN  ROS10041      LNK334
PAYROLL   C:\REV\ADMIN  ROS10042      02
```

Notes

1. The VOLUME on the LISTFILES output is the DOS drive/directory you specified when you created the file.

LISTMEDIA
(LISTS REVELATION FILES ON A MEDIUM)

Purpose

The LISTMEDIA command lists all the Revelation files on the specified medium. These will be all the files in the Revelation directory, ROSMEDIA.MAP, for that volume.

Syntax

:LISTMEDIA <medium> (options)

medium is the DOS drive and directory.

Rules

1. The medium does *not* have to be attached in order to list its files.

2. All the Revelation files on the medium will be listed regardless of the account they are in.

3. If no medium is given, the default medium is used. The default medium is the volume containing the Revelation system files.

4. The LISTMEDIA command will only work on those volumes containing the ROSMEDIA.MAP file created with the NAMEMEDIA command.

Options

P   sends output to the Printer.

Examples

:LISTMEDIA C:\REV\ADMIN

```
Medium name for Volume "C:\REV\ADMIN" is ADMINISTRATION

        Revelation      Native
Account Filename        filename        Modulo

ADMIN   TASKS           ROS10000        01
ADMIN   FORMS           ROS10001        01
ADMIN   ACCOUNT         ROS10002        03
AR      INVOICES        ROS10003        LNK10
```

Notes

1. If no account is listed for a file, it means that the file is a global file and can be accessed from any account.

LOAD-TEXT-PARMS
(LOADS SYSTEM PARAMETERS FROM THE VERBS TEXT RECORD)

Purpose

This command is used if you modify the parameters in the TEXT record in the VERBS file and want these changes made effective during the current Revelation session. This file holds parameters used by the text editor, the TCL processor and V57 (the menu program). The parameters are read into a Labeled Common area, %%TEXT%%, when you first load Revelation. Therefore, if you modify this record, the changes will not become effective until you logon again or use this command.

Syntax

:LOAD-TEXT-PARMS

Notes

1. The TEXT record in the VERBS file may be modified to customize your keyboard and certain other system parameters. See Appendix VIII.

LOGTO
(MOVES TO ANOTHER ACCOUNT)

Purpose

The LOGTO command is used to log straight to another account without having to log off of the current account and then log into the new account.

Syntax

:LOGTO accountname <password>

accountname is the name of the account you want to log into.

password is the password of the new account.

Rules

1. If the account has a password and it is not given in the command then you will be prompted for it.

2. You can only be logged into one account at a time.

3. When you LOGTO an account, Revelation will attach the files for this account located in the default medium. If additional files for this account are located on other media, those media will have to be attached using the ATTACH command.

4. The VOC file for every account must be on the default medium so Revelation can attach it when logging into the account.

Notes

1. You can have a program execute automatically upon logging into an account. This is useful for attaching other media, running a data entry screen, or displaying a custom logon menu (see Chapter 5).

LOOKDICT
(DISPLAYS DICTIONARY LAYOUT)

Purpose

This command is used to display some of the fields from the dictionary records of a data file. Thus, it will tell you information about the structure of the data fields.

Syntax

:LOOKDICT filename

filename is the name of the data file whose dictionary records you wish to display.

Rules

1. LOOKDICT displays the FMC, NAME, FORMULA, CONVERSION, and JUSTIFICATION fields of the dictionary records.

Examples

:LOOKDICT CUSTOMERS

Notes

1. This command is similar to using the **:LIST DICT filename DICT.INFO** command except that the output is displayed in two columns, which is ideal for displaying the layout of a dictionary with many records.

MLIST
(SAME AS LISTFILES)

MOVE
(COPIES A FILE TO ANOTHER NAME, ACCOUNT, OR MEDIUM)

Purpose

The MOVE command can be used to make a copy of a file on a different medium, in a different account, or with a different name.

Syntax

:MOVE <acct> filename <;filename...> <med>
TO: <newacct> <newfilename; newfilename...>
newmed

acct is the account where the file is currently located.

filename is the name of the file(s) to be copied. If more than one file is to be copied, the names must be separated by semicolons.

med is the DOS drive and directory of the file to be moved.

newacct is the name of the account to which the file is being copied.

newfilename is the file name(s) of the new files. If more that one name is being used they must be separated by semicolons.

newmed is the DOS drive and directory where the new file will be located.

Rules

1. The filename and new medium are mandatory input parameters.

2. The medium must be the DOS terminology; you cannot use the medium name defined with the NAMEMEDIA command.

3. If you want to move a file to a new account, you must also give the new file a name, even if it is the same as the current name; otherwise, MOVE will mistake your new account as the new file name for the current account.

4. You must leave a space after "TO:".

5. The files you copy into the current account may not show up on a LISTFILES command until you log off and log back onto the account. (Or until you re-ATTACH the current volume.)

6. You cannot copy over an already existing file; if you try to you will get an error message saying the file already exists.

Examples

        :MOVE INVOICES TO: \ACCTG

        :MOVE ADMIN INV \REV\ADM TO: SALES INV \REV\ADM

        :MOVE INV;RECPT; TO: SALES INV.1;RECPT.1 \REV

Notes

1. MOVE does not delete the old file; it just makes a copy.

2. The MOVE command always copies both the dictionary and data parts of a file.

3. See Chapter 10 for a detailed discussion on file operations.

NAMEMEDIA
(INITIALIZES A DOS DRIVE/DIRECTORY FOR REVELATION FILES)

Purpose

The NAMEMEDIA command prepares a medium (DOS drive/directory) so that it can be used for storing Revelation files. A DOS file named ROSMEDIA.MAP is created on the medium to act as a directory of the Revelation files on that medium.

Syntax

:NAMEMEDIA med medname

med is the DOS drive/directory to be named.

medname is the name you want to give to the medium (2 to 25 characters).

Examples

:NAMEMEDIA \REV\ADMIN ADMINISTRATION

Notes

1. The NAMEMEDIA command can be used to rename a previously named media.

2. See Chapter 5 for a descripion of the layout of the ROSMEDIA.MAP.

NETWORK.SETUP
(CHANGES SYSTEM FILES TO LINK STRUCTURE FOR USE ON A NETWORK)

Purpose

This command will convert some of the system files to the LINK structure so that they can be used on a network without causing problems when two operators try and access them at the same time.

Syntax

:NETWORK.SETUP

Rules

1. This command converts the tutorial files and the LISTS, RDES, VOC, and SYSTEM files to the LINK structure.

OFF
(LOGS USER OFF OF REVELATION)

Purpose

OFF is used to log off of Revelation.

Syntax

:OFF

PC, EXIT
(ALLOWS USER TO RUN DOS COMMANDS FROM WITHIN REVELATION)

Purpose

The PC command allows you to suspend Revelation while you perform DOS functions.

Syntax

:PC dos.command

or

:PC
 .
 .
C:>EXIT

dos command is any valid DOS command.

Rules

1. When the DOS command completes execution, control is passed back to Revelation. If no DOS command is given with the PC command, you will be shown the DOS prompt, at which time you may enter whatever DOS commands you wish. To return to Revelation, enter EXIT from the DOS prompt.

2. This command only functions on DOS versions 2.0 or later.

3. The DOS file COMMAND.COM must exist on the default drive for this command to work. (Alternatively, the DOS COMSPEC could be set.)

4. You can change the current directory while in DOS; but when you return to Revelation, the default directory will reset to the same as before you went to DOS.

PORT
(CONFIGURES YOUR COMPUTER AS A TERMINAL OF A MINI OR MAINFRAME)

Purpose

The PORT command, in conjunction with the TERMINAL command, allows you to set up your computer to act as a terminal of a mini or mainframe computer. This is useful for downloading data from the larger computer to a Revelation application.

Syntax

:PORT <-LOOK> <-DEVICE devname> <-BAUD n>
<-STOP n> <-BITS n> <-PARITY E/O/N/M/S>
<-XOFF YES/NO> <-BREAK> <-MARK>

devname is the name of the communications driver to be used by PORT.
-BAUD n baud rate for data transmission.
-STOP n number of stop bits.
-BITS n number of data bits.
-PARITY E/O/N/M/S Parity: even, odd, none, mark, or space.
-XOFF YES/NO XOFF/XON protocol.
-MARK 7 bit data transmission retains system delimiter marks.
-BREAK n break signal sent to host may be n times longer than normal when break is requested. (n is between 1 and 255.)

Rules

1. PORT -LOOK will display the current protocol settings.

2. If no device name is given, the COMM driver will be used.

RDESIGN
(CALLS THE R/DESIGN MENU)

Purpose

This command is used to bring up the R/DESIGN menu.

Syntax

:RDESIGN

RECREATE-FILE
(CHANGES FILE MANAGEMENT SYSTEM)

Purpose

The RECREATE-FILE command is used to change a file's management system between the ROS and LINK structure, or to change the file's modulo.

Syntax

:RECREATE-FILE filename #records rec.size <#fields> <med> (LRS)

filename is the name of the file to be recreated.

#records is the estimated number of records in the file.

rec.size is the estimated number of characters per record.

#fields is the estimated number of dictionary records.

med is the DOS drive/directory where the file is located.

L or **R** forces the file into either the LINK or ROS file
management structure.

Rules

1. The number of records and record size are prompted for if
not given in the command.

2. The number of fields is only needed if the file is going to be a
LINK file.

3. The medium to hold the new file must have already been
named using the NAMEMEDIA command.

4. RECREATE-FILE will prompt you whether this file will be
shared if you have a networking version of Revelation.

5. If the file will be shared it will be a LINK file. If it will be
smaller than 200k and not shared, it will be a ROS file. If it is
not shared but is calculated to be greater that 200k you will be
prompted to make it a LINK file.

6. Do not use this command if you have a network and someone
else is accessing this file at the same time.

Options

S   Suppresses the display of messages.

Examples

:RECREATE-FILE CUSTOMERS 30 900

Notes

1. See Appendix V for a discussion on the ROS and LINK file
structures and how to determine the best parameters to use with
the RECREATE-FILE command.

RENAME-FILE
(RENAMES A FILE)

Purpose

The RENAME-FILE command is used to rename a file or change the account of a file in the current account.

Syntax

:RENAME-FILE old.filename <new.acctname> new.filename

old.filename is the name of the file to be renamed.

new.acctname is the account to which the file is to be changed.

new.filename is the new name the file will have.

Rules

1. The file to be renamed must be attached.

2. If you do not enter either filename, you will be prompted for it. You can abort by entering END or hitting the return key.

3. The file cannot have the same name as a file already attached.

Notes

1. The RENAME-FILE command automatically updates the ROSMEDIA.MAP. Furthermore, the new name becomes immediately accessible for use without having to ATTACH the medium.

RETURN
(RETURNS TO PREVIOUS LEVEL OF EXECUTION)

Purpose

Revelation has the ability to interrupt a program and run another program or perform TCL functions. These other programs or functions are performed on another "level" of

Revelation as indicated by the TCL prompt of two or more colons (::) instead of one. The RETURN command returns you back to the previous level of execution.

Syntax

:RETURN

Rules

1. The EXECUTE command may be run from the editor, the debugger, R/BASIC, and any R/DESIGN screen. The RETURN is only needed if you are at TCL on a level greater than 1.

Notes

1. See Chapter 13 for a detailed explanation of this feature under the EXECUTE command.

2. Use the TCL command WHO to determine your current level.

RUN
(EXECUTES AN R/BASIC PROGRAM)

Purpose

The RUN command is used to execute an R/BASIC program which has already been compiled.

Syntax

:RUN filename record.id (options)

filename is the name of the file containing the R/BASIC program.

record.id is the ID of the record which is the program to be executed.

Rules

1. The compiled code should exist as a record in the file with an ID of $record.id. If the program was compiled with the editors or with the TCL commands COMPILE or BASIC, this will be the case.

Options

D   enter the Debugger immediately upon execution of the program.

P   sends output to the Printer.

Examples

:RUN BP PROG1

SAVE-LIST
(SAVES A SELECT LIST)

Purpose

The SAVE-LIST command is used to save a list of record IDs which was created with the SELECT or SSELECT command. The list can then be quickly retrieved.

Syntax

:SAVE-LIST listname

listname is the name given to the select list.

Rules

1. SAVE-LIST can only be used directly after the SELECT/SSELECT command from the ">" prompt.

2. Lists are retrieved with the GET-LIST command and deleted with the DELETE-LIST command.

Examples

```
:SELECT INVOICES WITH AMOUNT  >  300
32 Record(s) selected
> SAVE-LIST SAMPLE
'SAMPLE' saved on 'LISTS' file
```

Notes

1. Lists are stored as records in the LISTS file.

SELECT
(CREATES A LIST OF RECORD IDs MEETING SPECIFIED CONDITIONS)

Purpose

The SELECT command is used to "select" a group of records meeting certain conditions. This list of record IDs is then available for performing other functions.

Syntax

:SELECT <DICT> filename <WITH clause> <BY clause...>

filename is the name of the file from which the selected records will come.

WITH clause is the WITH expression which determines the selection criteria.

BY clause sorts the list by the record's fields.

Rules

1. After a SELECT list is generated, the list is available for processing by the very next command only. This is indicated by the ">" prompt. The SELECT list may be passed to other TCL commands, to the LIST command, or to R/DESIGN data entry screens.

2. Selected lists are saved using the SAVE-LIST command, retrieved with the GET-LIST command, and deleted with the DELETE-LIST command.

Examples

:SELECT INVOICES WITH AMOUNT > 300
32 Record(s) selected
> LIST INVOICES

would list the 32 selected records.

:SELECT INVOICES WITH AMOUNT > 300
32 Record(s) selected
> SAVE-LIST INVO.BIG

would save the selected list so it could be accessed later.

SET-COLOR
(SPECIFIES THE TERMINAL'S VIDEO CHARACTERISTICS)

Purpose

The SET-COLOR command allows you to adjust the video characteristics of your system. You can change the background and foreground colors, as well as the display attributes, of four display modes: normal, reverse, highlight, and reverse highlight.

Syntax

:SET-COLOR <esc.seq> <COLOR> <DEFAULT> <NONE>

esc.seq are the escape codes which set the four display modes: normal, reverse, highlight, reverse highlight (in this order and separated by commas).

Rules

1. Using the command SET-COLOR alone will display the current settings and show the syntax for the command.

2. Using the command with the escape sequences will specify the background and foreground colors (for a color monitor) or other characteristics for a monochrome monitor (brightness, reverse video, blinking). The escape codes are given in Appendix VI.

3. Using COLOR will set the escape sequences to the default values for a color monitor.

4. Using DEFAULT will set the escape sequences to the default values for a monochrome monitor.

5. Using NONE sets all the parameters to null.

Examples

        :SET-COLOR

displays the current escape sequences.

        :SET-COLOR 0H,,01

sets the normal and highlight display modes.

        :SET-COLOR COLOR

sets the escape codes to the default values for a color monitor.

Notes

1. SET-COLOR modifies the value of the system variabale @COLOR. This variable is a dynamic array consisting of 5 fields:
        1 = "COLOR", "DEFAULT", or "NONE"
        2 = Normal video attributes
        3 = Reverse video attributes
        4 = Highlight attributes
        5 = Reverse highlight attributes

2. R/DESIGN uses this variable to determine what colors and attributes to use when displaying data entry screens and values.

SET-CRT, SET-LPTR
(SETS TERMINAL/PRINTER WIDTH AND HEIGHT)

Purpose

These commands set the number of columns across and the number of lines down which will be displayed on the screen and printed out on your printer.

Syntax

:SET-CRT <width> <,height>
:SET-LPTR <width> <,height>

width is the number of characters per line.

height is the number of lines per screen/printer page.

Rules

1. Using SET-CRT/LPTR alone will display the current settings of width and height.

2. Either width, height, or both can be entered. If height is entered it must be preceded by a comma so that the command will distinguish it from the width parameter.

Examples

    :SET-CRT
    CRT WIDTH 80
    CRT HEIGHT 24

    :SET-LPTR 80,60

    :SET-CRT ,15

sets height of CRT display to 15 lines.

Notes

1. These parameters can be accessed in R/BASIC with the following R/BASIC variables:

    @CRTWIDE
    @CRTHIGH

@LPTRWIDE
@LPTRHIGH

2. Setting these parameters only affects the way certain
Revelation commands will format output display, such as BLIST,
LIST, COPY (PT parameters).

SET-FILE
(SETS QFILE POINTER)

Purpose

The SET-FILE command sets the QFILE pointer to point to
any file in any account and volume. This allows access to the file
through the QFILE file name.

Syntax

:SET-FILE account filename <med>

account is the account in which the actual file resides.

filename is the name of the actual file to which the QFILE will
point.

med is the medium (DOS drive/directory) where the file being
pointed to is stored.

Rules

1. If no medium is given, the default medium is assumed.

Examples

:SET-FILE ADMIN PERSONNEL \REV\ADMIN
"QFILE" set

sets QFILE to point to the PERSONNEL file in the ADMIN
account. This file may be LISTed just like any other file:

:LIST QFILE FOR STATE = "CA"

Notes

1. QFILE is just the name of the special qfile pointer which can be set using this command. You can create other qfile pointers with any names you desire (see Chapter 4).

2. Most TCL file operations will work through a qfile pointer. One exception is the DELETE-FILE command: you may not delete a file using :DELETE-FILE QFILE.

SET-OPTIONS
(SETS DEFAULT OPTIONS)

Purpose

The SET-OPTIONS command allows you to "set" an option so that whenever you use a TCL command for which that option is valid, the option will be assumed.

Syntax

:SET-OPTIONS (option...)

option is the letter code of the option to be set.

Rules

1. If SET-OPTIONS alone is used, currently set options will be displayed.

2. The options which can be entered are all of the options from the various TCL commands plus one other option, the W option. The W option is for **WRITE-IMMEDIATE** and is discussed below.

3. Using **:SET-OPTIONS ()** will turn off any set options.

Options

Valid options are: **DOPTXIRNSCLEWU.**

Examples

:SET-OPTIONS (P)
:COPY BP DATA.ENTRY

would be the same as

:COPY BP DATA.ENTRY (P)

:SET-OPTIONS (PSC)
:SET-OPTIONS
The following options are now always implied: (PSC)

Notes

1. The WRITE-IMMEDIATE mode only affects ROS files and how quickly data is written to disk. In the normal FAST-WRITE mode, ROS files are buffered in memory (see Appendix V). This means that when you modify records in ROS files, they are only written back to disk when:

1. Control passes to TCL,
2. No key has been pressed for 30 seconds,
3. An R/BASIC FLUSH command has been entered, or
4. The memory occupied by the buffered file is required for other immediate purposes.

The WRITE-IMMEDIATE option causes ROS files to be immediately written to disk any time a record is changed.

SORT
(PRODUCES SORTED AD HOC REPORTS)

Purpose

The SORT command allows you to generate an ad hoc listing of a file in exactly the same manner as the LIST command. The only difference is that the SORT command sorts by record ID after all the other BY clause sorts. See the LIST command and Chapter 9.

Examples

:SORT CUSTOMERS WITH ST = "CA"

This command is identical to:

:LIST CUSTOMERS BY @ID WITH ST = "CA"

SSELECT
(CREATES A SORTED LIST OF RECORD IDs MEETING SPECIFIED CONDITIONS)

Purpose

The SSELECT command is used to "select" a group of records from a file in exactly the same manner as the SELECT command. The only difference is that the SSELECT command sorts the selected records by record ID after completing any other BY clause sorts. See the SELECT command and also Chapter 9.

Examples

:SSELECT CUSTOMERS WITH ST = "CA"

This command is identical to:

:SELECT CUSTOMERS BY @ID WITH ST = "CA"

SUM
(TOTALS THE SPECIFIED FIELD FOR SPECIFIED RECORDS)

Purpose

The SUM command totals the values of a specific numeric field for all records meeting specifed criteria.

Syntax

:SUM filename fieldname <WITH clause>

filename is the name of the file containing the field to be
summed.

fieldname is the name of the field to be summed.

WITH clause is the WITH phrase which selects the records
to be summed.

Examples

:SUM INVOICES AMOUNT WITH AMOUNT > 300

Total AMOUNT is $39,300.00

Notes

1. Do not try to SUM a field which is not numeric. The SUM
command will print an error message for every non-numeric
value it encounters!

TERMINAL
(CONFIGURES YOUR COMPUTER AS A TERMINAL OF A MINI OR MAINFRAME)

Purpose

The TERMINAL command, in conjunction with the PORT
command, allows you to set up your computer to act as a
terminal of a mini or mainframe computer.

Syntax

:TERMINAL <-LOOK> <-DEVICE devname>
<-BAUD n> <-STOP n> <-BITS n>
<-PARITY E/O/N/M/S> <-XOFF YES/NO>

Refer to the PORT command for an explanation of these
parameters.

Rules

1. The appropriate communications driver must be specified in the DOS CONFIG.SYS file with the command

DEVICE = commdrv.sys size,port

commdrv.sys is one of the communication drivers that resides on the Revelation Utility disk.
size is the size of the data buffer in bytes (default = 2K).
port is the communications port (com1,com2, etc.).

2. To download data from the host to Revelation when the system is in TERMINAL mode, enter the following command:

ESC RF filename, rec.id, rec.size, data

filename is the Revelation file.
rec.id is the record key.
rec.size is the length of the item (in bytes) being downloaded.
data is the actual data in the item specified.

3. To escape from the TERMINAL mode, press **F9**.

Notes

1. The TERMINAL and PORT commands are most often used to communicate with PICK based computers. This is useful for downloading data from a larger computer to a Revelation application.

TEXT
(INVOKES THE FULL-SCREEN TEXT EDITOR)

Purpose

The TEXT command invokes the TEXT Editor so you can edit one or more records from a file.

Syntax

:TEXT <DICT> filename <record.id...>

filename is the name of the file holding the records to be edited.

record.id is the record ID to be edited.

Rules

1. If more than one record is to be edited, each will be called into the Text Editor as the previous record is filed.

2. Using an asterisk (*) for the record.id will edit all the records in the file.

3. Using DICT will edit a record from the dictionary portion of the file.

Examples

:TEXT BP ENTRY.DATA

will invoke the Text Editor and display the ENTRY.DATA record from the BP file.

Notes

1. See Chapter 14 for a detailed discussion.

TIME
(DISPLAYS SYSTEM TIME)

Purpose

This command will display the current system time.

Syntax

:TIME

UTILITY.MENU
(CALLS UTILITY MENU)

Purpose

This command brings up the Utility Menu so the operator can choose one of its options.

Syntax

:UTILITY.MENU

Rules

1. The utilities disk must first have been installed by running the INSTALL.UTL program (see Chapter 5).

WHO
(DISPLAYS USER INFORMATION)

Purpose

This command is used to display information about the user; i.e. account, recursive level, and station (network only).

Syntax

:WHO

R/BASIC STATEMENTS

ABORT
(RETURNS CONTROL TO TCL)

Purpose

The ABORT statement stops any processing which is occurring and returns the operator to the TCL prompt.

Syntax

ABORT <ALL>

Examples

ABORT

IF X = "END" THEN ABORT

Notes

1. An R/DESIGN Menu option which calls a one line R/BASIC program containing the ABORT statement will **not** return the user to TCL. ABORT ALL must be used in this instance.

BREAK
(TURNS BREAK KEY ON AND OFF)

Purpose

When the break key is turned "on", you can hit the CTRL and BREAK keys simultaneously to interrupt a program and call the program Debugger. When the break key is turned off, this keyboard function is disabled.

Syntax

BREAK ON/OFF/expression

expression is any expression

Rules

1. BREAK ON is the default value, thus the break key is operational when you first turn on the computer.

2. BREAK OFF turns the break key off.

3. BREAK *expression* turns the break key **off** if the expression evaluates to zero and **on** if expression evaluates to non-zero.

Examples

BREAK ON

BREAK OFF

BREAK TESTB

where the value of the variable TESTB will determine the status of the break key.

Notes

1. Some programs must not be interrupted during execution, such as during a long sorting routine. Disabling the break key should be considered an important part of the routine's process.

2. The break key is reset whenever a program is terminated.

CALL
(CALLS AN EXTERNAL SUBROUTINE)

Purpose

The CALL statement allows you to exit your program to run a subroutine which is stored as a separate program, then return to your original program where you left off. It also allows you to pass variables back and forth between the subroutine and the main program.

Syntax

CALL subname <arg1, arg2,...>

subname is the name of the subroutine.

arg1, arg2 are variables, constants, or expressions whose values are passed to the subroutine.

Rules

1. The subroutine must have been previously compiled and cataloged on the current account.

2. The number of arguments in the CALL statement must be equal to or less than the number of arguments in the SUBROUTINE statement. The arguments are paired up in order; the first argument in the CALL statement with the first argument in the SUBROUTINE statement, the second with the second, and so on. One or both of the arguments in a pair should be a variable. When control shifts to the program/ subroutine whose argument is a variable, that variable is assigned the value of its counterpart.

3. If there are more arguments in the SUBROUTINE than in the CALL statement, the excess will be assigned a null value.

4. The subroutine may be called directly by specifying its name in the CALL statement or it may be called indirectly by using the "@variable" syntax (see example below).

Examples

MAIN PROGRAM:
.
.
CALL TAX.CALC(Y,INC)
.
.
END

```
SUBROUTINE TAX.CALC(X,I)
        .
        .
RETURN
END
```

calls the subroutine TAX.CALC and passes two variables between them.

```
CALC = "TAX.CALC"
CALL @CALC(A,B)
```

would also call the subroutine TAX.CALC.

Notes

1. The CALL statement is not required to pass variables to the subroutine.

2. See the DECLARE, SUBROUTINE, and RETURN statements.

3. For a detailed discussion on subroutine calls, refer to Chapter 13.

CASE
(PROVIDES CONDITIONAL BRANCHING)

Purpose

The CASE statement sets up a set of conditions. Depending on which condition is met, the program will execute specified statements.

Syntax

BEGIN CASE
  CASE test.expr
    statements
  CASE test.expr
    statements

    .
    .

END CASE

test.expr can be any expression, but is usually a comparison expression (see Chapter 12).

statements are the statements which will be executed if the preceding test expression is true.

Rules

1. The program will evaluate each test expression in turn until it finds one which is true, then it executes the statements immediately following.

2. Any expression can be entered for test.exp. If the expression evaluates to 0, it is considered false; it it evaluates to anything else, it is considered true.

3. If several test expressions are true, only the statements following the *first* true expression will be executed. The program will then proceed to the next statement after END CASE.

4. If all of the test expressions are false, the program proceeds to the next statement after END CASE.

Examples

```
BEGIN CASE
  CASE A < 5
    GOTO 100
  CASE A = 5
    GOTO 200
  CASE 1
    GOTO 300
END CASE
```

```
BEGIN CASE
   CASE AMOUNT.DUE
      GOTO 100
   CASE AMOUNT.PAID > 500
      GOTO 200
END CASE
```

In the first example, notice that the third case has a test expression of 1. This forces program control to 300 for any passes through this branch that don't evaluate to true in the other two test expressions.

Notice in the second example that the test expressions don't even have to be related.

CHAIN
(TRANSFERS CONTROL TO ANOTHER PROGRAM - NO RETURN)

Purpose

CHAIN is used to transfer control to another program with no provision for returning to the original program.

Syntax

CHAIN pgmr.name

pgrm.name is the name of the program to which control is being transferred.

Rules

1. The program must be cataloged.

Notes

1. This is different from the CALL statement where control is transferred to an external subroutine and then returned to the original program with a RETURN statement.

CLEAR/CLEAR COMMON
(ASSIGNS ALL VARIABLES TO A VALUE OF NULL)

Purpose

The CLEAR statement assigns all variables which are not in the common area a value of null. The CLEAR COMMON statement assigns all variables which are in the common area a value of null.

Syntax

CLEAR
CLEAR COMMON

Rules

1. The CLEAR statement may be used anywhere in a program.

Notes

1. If the CLEAR statement is used at the beginning of a program, it will "assign" all of the variables in the program a value of null. This will prevent the "variable not assigned" error if you use a variable before assigning it a value.

2 The CLEAR COMMON statement is useful for clearing all of the variables which may have been set in previously run external subroutines.

3. For information on common variables and external subroutines see Chapter 13.

CLEARDATA
(CLEARS DATA STORED BY A DATA STATEMENT)

Purpose

The CLEARDATA statement clears out all of the data which was set by a previous DATA statement.

Syntax

CLEARDATA

Notes

1. The CLEARDATA statement sets the special system variable @DATA to null.

CLEARFILE
(CLEARS ALL THE DATA FROM A FILE)

Purpose

CLEARFILE is used to clear all data from a file, leaving the dictionary records intact.

Syntax

CLEARFILE filevar

filevar is the name that the file was opened to.

Examples

```
OPEN "","INVOICES" TO INV ELSE STOP
CLEARFILE INV
```

CLEARSELECT
(CLEARS THE SELECT LIST)

Purpose

The CLEARSELECT statement sets the current select list to null.

Syntax

CLEARSELECT

COLHEADING/COLLENGTH
(SETS COLUMN WIDTHS AND HEADINGS FOR A REPORT)

Purpose

These two statements are used together. COLHEADING specifies the column headings which will appear at the top of each page of a report. COLLENGTH specifies how wide each of the columns of the report will be.

Syntax

COLHEADING "string1" :@FM: "string2" :@FM: "string3" ...

string1, string2, string3 are the column headings for columns 1, 2, 3.

COLLENGTH length1 :@FM: length2 :@FM: length3 ...

length1, length2, length3 are the lengths (or widths) of columns 1, 2, 3 of the report.

Examples

```
TITLES = "NAME" :@FM: "PHONE" @FM:
"COMPANY"
HEADING  "CUSTOMER LIST"
COLHEADING  TITLES
COLLENGTH  15 :@FM: 8 :@FM: 25
```

would create the following at the top of each page of the report (see also HEADING statement):

CUSTOMER LIST
NAME...........PHONE...COMPANY..................

Notes

1. Multi-value marks (CHAR(253) or @VM) may be used to produce multi-lined column headings.

COMMENTS
(PLACES DOCUMENTATION REMARKS IN A PROGRAM)

Purpose

COMMENT statements are used to place internal documentation statements anywhere in your written program. They are useful for identifying the program at the top and for explaining the program's logic throughout the body.

Syntax

* <statement>
! <statement>
REM <statement>

statement is whatever remarks you want to make.

Rules

1. The statement can have whatever characters you wish but must be contained on one line. If you want to make a longer remark, break it into several lines all starting with *, !, or REM.

2. The comment statements can occur anywhere in a program except preceding a SUBROUTINE statement, which must be the first line of an external subroutine.

Notes

1. Good programmers use comments throughout their programs because it inevitably will save time when someone comes back to

that program months or years later and needs to understand how it works.

2. Comments do not affect the size of the compiled code because the compiler ignores them during the compilation process.

COMMON
(ALLOWS VARIABLES TO BE SHARED BETWEEN A MAIN PROGRAM AND ITS SUBROUTINES)

Purpose

The COMMON statement places any number of variables into a "common area" so that they can be shared between a main program and its external subroutines.

Syntax

COMMON var1, var2, var3 ...
        or
COM var1, var2, var3 ...

var1, var2, var3 are the variables to be use in common by the
        main program and its subroutines.

Rules

1. The variables which will be used by both the main program and a subroutine must be defined by the COMMON statement before they are first used in the program.

2. If a matrix variable is in the common statement, it can be dimensioned here rather than with a DIMENSION statement (see example).

3. The COMMON variables must be defined in the main program even if the main program does not use the variables. Both the main program and subroutines must use the COMMON statements to access the common variables.

4. Each main program has its own common area. Thus, main programs do not share common areas, they only share them with their external subroutines.

5. The CLEAR COMMON statement is used to set all of the variables in the common area to null.

6. The external subroutine is identified with a SUBROUTINE statement and is called by the main program with the CALL statement.

Examples

COMMON X,Y,Z(5),RATE,COUNTER

places the variables X,Y,Z,RATE,COUNTER in the common area, and dimensions the matrix variable Z. Thus, the variable X can be used in an external subroutine and it will have the same value it had in the main program when the external subroutine was called.

Notes

1. This is one way of linking the variables of a main program and an external subroutine. Another is by using the arguments of the CALL and SUBROUTINE statements.

2. Internal subroutines do not need to have these links made since they are part of the program and automatically share the same variables.

3. Revelation now provides a feature for labeled COMMON areas. This allows defining a common area that can be shared among whole groups of programs, not just between main programs and their subroutines. See Chapter 13 for a detailed discussion on common areas.

CONVERT
(REPLACES CHARACTERS IN A STRING WITH OTHER CHARACTERS)

Purpose

The CONVERT statement searches a string and replaces specified characters with other characters. The replace is performed on a character-by-character basis. String-for-string replacements are done with the SWAP statement.

Syntax

CONVERT "ch1 ch2..." TO <"ch1r ch2r..."> IN var

ch1 ch2... are the characters to be replaced. You do not need to separate the characters with spaces as we have shown in the syntax (see example).

ch1r ch2r... are the replacement characters.

var is the variable which will be searched for the specified characters.

Rules

1. The characters are replaced in order; i.e. ch1r replaces ch1, ch2r replaces ch2, etc.

2. This command replaces character-by-character, not string-by-string (see example).

3. If the number of replacement characters is fewer than the characters to be replaced, the extra characters will be deleted from the variable.

Examples

TITLE = "OVER THE HILL"
CONVERT "THE" TO "AN" IN TITLE

replaces each T with an A , each H with N, and every E is deleted, so that TITLE would now become
"OVR AN NILL".

DATA
(STORES DATA FOR AN INPUT STATEMENT)

Purpose

The DATA statement stores data values which can subsequently be read into the program by any number of INPUT statements.

Syntax

DATA exp1, exp2, exp3...

exp1, exp2, exp3 are any valid expressions (variables, functions, or literals).

Rules

1. The data stored by the DATA statement is used in order by the input statements until all of the data is exhausted.

2. Once all of the stored data has been exhausted, any additional requests for data from INPUT statements will result in a prompt on the screen requesting input from the keyboard.

3. If a variable used in the DATA statement is later given a new value, it is the original value that is used as the INPUT value. In other words, it is the value of the variable at the time of the DATA statement, rather than at the time of the INPUT statement, that is used. This is because once a variable is read in a DATA statement, its *value* is immediately placed in line for the INPUT statement. The variable has no further meaning.

Examples

```
X = 5
Y = 12
DATA 7,X,Y,"FIVE"
Y = 25
INPUT A
INPUT B
```
(continued on next page)

```
INPUT C
INPUT D
PRINT A: B: C: D
```

would print: 7512FIVE

DEBUG
(ACTIVATES THE PROGRAM DEBUGGER)

Purpose

DEBUG is used if you want to interrupt a program and call the Debugger to help you solve a problem with a program. It can be placed after an IF statement so that the debugger will be called only if some condition exists which indicates something is wrong with the program.

Syntax

DEBUG

Rules

1. The debugger can also be called by hitting the CTRL BREAK key combination while the program is running (assuming the break key has not been turned off with a BREAK statement).

Notes

1. See Appendix XI for more information on using the Debugger.

DECLARE
(ALLOWS USER-DEFINED FUNCTIONS AND SUBROUTINES)

Purpose

The DECLARE statement is used at the beginning of a program to allow a user-defined function in the program. The function itself is defined and stored as a separate program. This command can also "declare" external subroutines so that they can be "called" by just using their name instead of using a CALL statement.

Syntax

DECLARE FUNCTION f1, f2, f3 ...
DECLARE SUBROUTINE s1, s2, s3 ...

f1,f2,f3 (s1,s2,s3) are the names of user defined functions (subroutines).

Rules

1. The user-defined function must either be stored in the same file as the program declaring it, or it must be cataloged using the TCL CATALOG command.

Examples

The following program calculates the factorial of any number by employing a user-defined function named FACT.

```
DECLARE FUNCTION FACT
INPUT Y
PRINT FACT (Y)
END
```

The function FACT is stored as a separate program and is shown below.

```
FUNCTION FACT (X)
A=1
FOR N=1 TO X
  A=A*N
NEXT N
RETURN A
END
```

Notes

1. See the FUNCTION, SUBROUTINE, and CALL statements and also refer to Chapter 13.

DELETE
(DELETES A RECORD FROM A FILE)

Purpose

The DELETE statement deletes a record from a file which was previously opened with an OPEN statement.

Syntax

DELETE file, rec.id

file is the variable name assigned to the file in the OPEN statement.

rec.id is the ID of the record to be deleted.

Rules

1. The file must have been opened with the OPEN statement before a record can be deleted.

Examples

```
OPEN '','INVOICES' TO INV.FILE ELSE STOP
FOR N=1 TO 4
  REC = "INV":N
  DELETE INV.FILE,REC
NEXT N
```

This program will delete records INV1, INV2, INV3, and INV4 from the INVOICES file.

Notes

1. See the OPEN statement for information on opening a file.

DIM
(NAMES AND ALLOCATES SPACE FOR MATRIX VARIABLES)

Purpose

The DIM statement names a matrix variable before it is used and allocates the space it requires.

Syntax

DIM mat1(row<,col>), mat2(row<,col>), mat3(row<,col>) ...

mat1, mat2, mat3 are the names of matrix variables.

row is a numeric expression for the number of elements in the first dimension of the matrix.

col is a numeric expression for the number of elements in the second dimension and must be separated by a comma from the first dimension.

Rules

1. You can dimension as many matrix variables as you like with a DIM statement.

2. Each matrix variable can be one or two dimensional (i.e. the col expression is optional).

3. Once the dimensions of a matrix have been set, they cannot be changed.

4. The number of elements in a one-dimensional matrix is equal to the value of row plus one more, the (0) element. The number of elements in a two-dimensional matrix is equal to (row * col) plus one more, the (0,0) element.

5. The DIM statement only names the matrix and defines its dimensions. It does not assign values to the elements.

6. You can use the word DIMENSION in place of DIM.

Examples

```
ROW = 4
DIM ACCOUNT(ROW,3), CODE(8)
MAT ACCOUNT = 1
FOR X = 1 TO ROW
  FOR Y = 1 TO 3
    PRINT ACCOUNT(X,Y)
  NEXT Y
NEXT X
```

Notes

1. For more information on matrix variables see Chapter 12.

2. The COMMON statement can also be used to dimension matrix variables.

ECHO
(SUPPRESSES THE DISPLAY OF INPUT DATA ON THE SCREEN)

Purpose

The ECHO statement controls whether to display data which is input to a program from the keyboard. Input data is normally displayed but can be turned off if desired.

Syntax

ECHO OFF/ON

Rules

1. ECHO OFF will suppress the display of subsequent data input.

2. ECHO ON re-enables the echo feature.

END
(MARKS THE END OF A PROGRAM OR BLOCK OF STATEMENTS)

Purpose

END can mark the physical end of a program, terminate the program, or mark the end of a block of statements started with statements such as IF, READ, or OPEN.

Syntax

END

Rules

1. See IF, READ, or OPEN statements.

2. A program need not end with the END statement.

EQUATE
(EQUATES ONE VARIABLE TO ANOTHER)

Purpose

EQUATE allows you to equate a variable name to another variable, reducing the amount of required computer memory during run time.   R/BASIC accomplishes this by replacing every occurrence of the first variable name with the second variable during compilation.

Syntax

EQUATE var.symbol TO var.name
                   or
EQ var.symbol TO var.name

var.symbol is the variable name you would like replaced during
           compilation.

var.name is the variable that will be used in place of var.symbol.

Examples

EQUATE VM TO CHAR(253)

makes VM equivalent to ASCII character 253. During compilation, every occurrence of the variable VM will be replaced by "²", the ASCII character 253.

EXECUTE
(RECURSIVELY EXECUTES A TCL COMMAND FROM INSIDE A PROGRAM)

Purpose

EXECUTE allows you to execute a TCL command from within a program and then return to the program. EXECUTE does not pass information to or from the calling program. CALL or PERFORM statements can run other programs and pass information back and forth.

Syntax

EXECUTE "command"

command is the TCL command just as it would be entered at the TCL prompt.

Rules

1. When an EXECUTE statement is used, Revelation suspends all current processing, internally saves all variables, and goes to a second "level" to execute the new command. Upon return to the calling program, all variables are restored to the values they had before the EXECUTE was performed.

Examples

EXECUTE "ACCPAY.ENTRY"

would execute the ACCPAY.ENTRY program and then return to the current program.

Notes

1. EXECUTE is useful for running several programs in the same application which do not need to pass information among themselves.

2. The number of levels that may be recursively executed is limited by the amount of RAM in the computer.

FLUSH
(CLEARS INACTIVE FILE BUFFERS)

Purpose

The FLUSH statement is used to clear any inactive file buffers in order to recover additional memory string space.

Syntax

FLUSH

Notes

1. The ROS file management system is a buffered system which stores groups of records in a temporary buffer. This makes for greater disk efficiency since whenever a record in a group of records is retrieved from the disk, the entire group of records is temporarily stored in memory. That way, if any other record in that group is retrieved, Revelation won't have to go to the disk to get it. The group of records stays in memory until Revelation needs that space for another group. If the space is not needed, the group will remain in the buffer until control is passed to TCL. The FLUSH statement forces these buffers to clear out any unused records. Any records that have been modified will be written back to disk.

2. If you use the W option with the SET-OPTION command, Revelation will immediately write ROS file records back to disk as soon as it is finished modifying them. This alleviates the need to use the FLUSH command.

3. The GARBAGECOLLECT statement is usually used immediately after FLUSH to recover unused string space. These two statements will provide more RAM for your program.

4. Normally, you will not worry about FLUSHing the memory buffers since Revelation takes care of this task for you. It will only become a concern if your programs need additional string space in memory to perform complex operations or use large matrix variables.

5. For additional information, see the SET-OPTION command and refer to Appendix V.

FOOTING
(PRINTS FOOTER AT BOTTOM OF EACH PAGE OR SCREEN)

Purpose

The FOOTING statement places a footer at the bottom of each page of a report generated by your program.

Syntax

FOOTING "exp1 'options' exp2 'options' ..."

exp1, exp2 ... are text expressions to be inserted in the footer.

options are:

    B BREAK: inserts the name of the field which is being used to break the report.

    D DATE: inserts current date as DD MMM YYYY.

    F FILENAME: inserts the name of the file being read.

    L NEW LINE: causes a line feed and carriage return.

    N NO PAGE: suppresses automatic paging.

P PAGE: inserts current page number.

PP PAGE JUSTIFY: right justifies current page number.

Sn SPACE: enters n spaces.

T TIME: inserts current time and date.

" inserts a single quote.

Examples

FOOTING "Page 'P' of the 'F' file -- 'D' "

would generate a footing which looked like:

Page 12 of the INV.RPT file -- 21 AUG 1986

Notes

1. See Chapter 9 for additional details.

FOR/NEXT
(PROGRAM LOOP SPECIFIED NUMBER OF TIMES)

Purpose

The FOR/NEXT statements provide the structure for designating a program loop.

Syntax

FOR count.var = exp1 TO exp2 <STEP exp3>
<WHILE/UNTIL test.exp>
  statements
      .
      .
NEXT count.var

count.var is the variable used as a counter to determine how many times the program will go through the loop exp1, exp2, exp3 are expressions which evaluate to numeric values.

test.exp is any expression,but usually a comparison expression.

statements are any valid statements.

Rules

1. The counter variable is initially set equal to exp1. Each time through the loop, the counter is increased in increments of exp3 until it exceeds exp2. At this point the program exits the loop and continues with the statement following NEXT.

2. If "STEP exp3" is left out, the step increment is assumed to be 1.

3. If the WHILE/UNTIL parameter is used, each time through the loop, the test expression is evaluated. Program control stays within the loop if a WHILE test expression is true, or if an UNTIL test expression is false.

4. Any expression can be entered for test.exp. If the expression evaluates to 0, it is considered false; if it evaluates to anything else, it is considered true.

5. FOR/NEXT loops can be nested within each other.

6. Program control can be directed out of the loop with a GOTO or GOSUB statement. However, do not use these statements to enter the middle of a loop.

Examples

```
FOR N = 2 TO 10  STEP 2
   PRINT N
NEXT N
```

would print the numbers 2,4,6,8,10.

```
Y = 1
FOR N = 1 TO 10 WHILE Y <= 15
   Y = Y*2
   PRINT N,Y
NEXT N
```

would print:

1	2
2	4
3	8
4	16

and then exit because Y is now greater than 15.

Notes

1. Any expressions in the FOR statement which do not change value within the loop should be calculated before the loop is entered. This provides improved efficiency.

FUNCTION
(IDENTIFIES A PROGRAM AS A FUNCTION)

Purpose

A FUNCTION statement must be the first line in a program written as a user-defined function.

Syntax

FUNCTION name (arg1, arg2, ...)

name is the name of the function as stated in the DECLARE statement of a calling program .

arg1 is a variable (or set of variables) used to pass values from the program using the function to the program performing the function.

Rules

1. The FUNCTION statement must be the first line of the function program.

2. The function program must be compiled and cataloged before it can be called. The function program need not be cataloged if its compiled code is stored in the same file as the calling program.

3. The program performing the function sends the function value back to the calling program via the RETURN statement.

Notes

1. See the DECLARE statement and refer to Chapter 13.

GARBAGECOLLECT
(RECOVERS UNUSED STRING SPACE AFTER A FLUSH)

Purpose

At regular intervals Revelation clears out unused string space in memory. Sometimes additional string space is required for complex operations such as manipulating matrix variables. At these times you may wish to *force* Revelation to clear out any unused data from the memory buffers. The FLUSH command will clear out the buffers and the GARBAGECOLLECT command recovers this cleared out memory for immediate use in your program.

Syntax

GARBAGECOLLECT

Notes

1. This statement is normally used just after a FLUSH statement.

2. Refer to the FLUSH command for a more detailed discussion.

GOSUB
(TRANSFERS THE PROGRAM TO AN INTERNAL SUBROUTINE)

Purpose

GOSUB sends program control to an internal subroutine. Once the subroutine is completed, control passes back to the main program either where it left off or wherever the subroutine specifies.

Syntax

GOSUB label#1
.
.
.

label#1:
.
.
.

RETURN
    or
RETURN TO label#2

label#1 is the statement label marking the beginning of the subroutine.

label#2 is any statement label in the program.

Rules

1. GOSUB sends the program to the subroutine statement label where it continues executing until a RETURN or RETURN TO statement is reached. A RETURN statement sends the program back to the statement following the GOSUB statement. The RETURN TO statement also terminates the subroutine, but sends the program to the specified statement label.

2. The statement label must end in a colon (:) unless it consists of just numeric characters.

Examples

The following program has two internal subroutines:

```
* This program prompts for the unit cost and
*  quantity sold and then calculates the sales
*  tax and prints the statement.
TOP:
PRINT "ENTER QUANTITY SOLD": ; INPUT QTY
IF QTY = "END" THEN STOP
PRINT "ENTER UNIT COST": ; INPUT UNIT.COST
SUBTOTAL = QTY * UNIT.COST
GOSUB TAX.CALC
TOTAL = SUBTOTAL + TAX
GOSUB PRINT.STMT
*
* Tax calculation subroutine
*
TAX.CALC:
PRINT "ENTER STATE": ; INPUT STATE
IF STATE = "CA" THEN
  TAX = .06 * SUBTOTAL
END ELSE
  TAX = 0
END
RETURN
*
* Statement printing routine
*
PRINT.STMT:
PRINT QTY:" @ ":UNIT.COST:" =  ":SUBTOTAL
PRINT "TAX        ":TAX
PRINT "TOTAL      ":TOTAL
RETURN TO TOP
END
```

Notes

1. It is better to use subroutines in programs rather than GOTO statements because it will be easier to keep track of the structure of the program.

GOTO
(UNCONDITIONAL BRANCHING)

Purpose

GOTO sends the program to whatever statement label you designate.

Syntax

GOTO label

label is a statement label in the program.

Rules

1. When the GOTO statement is encountered, program control is unconditionally transferred to the specified location in the program.

2. Statement labels must be followed by a colon unless they are numeric. A colon may be included after the "label" in the GOTO statement for clarity, but has no effect.

3. GOTO statements can transfer control of the program to statements either preceding or following the GOTO statement.

Examples

```
FOR COUNTER = 1 TO 10
  IF AMOUNT < 125
    GOTO SALES
  END
  PRINT CUSTOMER, AMOUNT
NEXT COUNTER
SALES:
IF SALES86 > 2 * SALES85 THEN
  PRINT CUSTOMER, AMOUNT
END
```

Notes

1. The TO in GOTO may be omitted, as in GO SALES.

HEADING
(PRINTS HEADER AT TOP OF EACH PAGE OR SCREEN)

Purpose

The HEADING statement places a header at the top of each page of a report.

Syntax

HEADING "exp1 'options' exp2 'options' ..."

exp1, exp2 ... are text to be inserted in the header.

options are:

B   BREAK: inserts the field name which is being used to break the report.

D   DATE: inserts current date as DD MMM YYYY.

F   FILENAME: inserts the name of the file being read.

L   NEW LINE: causes a line feed and carriage return.

N   NO PAGE: suppresses automatic paging.

P   PAGE: inserts current page number.

PP PAGE JUSTIFY: right justifies page number.

Sn SPACE: inserts n spaces.

T   TIME: inserts current time and date.

"   inserts a single quote

Examples

HEADING "Page 'P' of the 'F' file 'LD' "

would generate a HEADING as follows:

Page 12 of the INV.RPT file
12 AUG 1986

Notes

1. With LIST statements, if the 'B' option is inserted in the HEADING clause, a 'B' must also be used with the BREAK-ON option clause to indicate which value should be inserted into the heading. In R/BASIC, the value of the @BREAK variable is used. This variable is automatically maintained if the 'B' option is also used with the BREAK-ON clause.

2. Refer to Chapter 9 for a detailed discussion on the use of HEADING in reports.

IF
(CONDITIONAL BRANCHING)

Purpose

The IF statement evaluates a test expression and executes one set of statements if the expression evaluates true and another set if it evaluates false.

Syntax

IF test.exp THEN statements <ELSE statements>
> or

IF test.exp THEN
  statements
END
> or

IF test.exp THEN statements ELSE
  statements
END
> or

IF test.exp THEN
  statements
END ELSE
  statements
END

or

IF test.exp THEN
  statements
END ELSE statements

test.exp is any expression, but normally a comparative expression.

statements are any valid R/BASIC statements. Several statements can be located on a line, but they must be separated by semicolons.

Rules

1. The IF statement first evaluates the test expression. If it is a comparison statement, the comparison is either true or false. For all other expressions, if the expression has a value of 0 it is interpreted as false; if its value is anything else it is true.

2. If the test expression is true, the program transfers to the statements following THEN; if false, program control transfers to the statements following ELSE.

3. Another IF clause may be included in the statements following THEN or ELSE, resulting in nested IF clauses.

Examples

```
IF AMOUNT > 300
  ACCOUNT = "MAJOR"
  PRINT CUSTOMER, ACCOUNT, AMOUNT
END ELSE
  IF AMOUNT > 100
    ACCOUNT = "NORMAL"
    PRINT CUSTOMER, ACCOUNT, AMOUNT
  END ELSE
    PRINT CUSTOMER: " MINOR"
  END
END
```

Notes

1. When the statements do not appear on the same line as the key words THEN or ELSE, but follow on the next lines instead, a terminating END must be used.

INITRND
(INITIALIZES THE RND() FUNCTION)

Purpose

INITRND is used to initialize the RND() internal function, which is used to generate random numbers.

Syntax

:INITRND val

Notes

1. The RND function is a very simple random number generator (in fact, not very random). The RND() function will return an integer between 0 and n-1, where n is the numeric argument passed to the RND() function. The sequence of numbers will always be the same for a given argument. Thus, RND(50) always returns values between 0 and 49 in the following order: 8,9,13,36,....

To create a more random list each time RND(50) is used, you could use the INITRND statement which resets the random number generator. RND(50) will produce a completely different set of numbers for each different value of INITRND. Thus,

INITRND 1

will cause RND(50) to generate numbers in the following order: 33,9,38,36,....

INPUT
(READS FROM A DATA STATEMENT OR PROMPTS FOR KEYBOARD INPUT)

Purpose

INPUT either reads the next data element stored by a DATA statement, or pauses program execution and prompts the operator for an input from the keyboard.

Syntax

INPUT var <,length><:>

var is the name of the variable which will be given the value of the entered data.

length is any numeric expression and specifies the maximum number of characters which can be entered at the input prompt. It must be separated from the variable with a comma.

Rules

1. When the INPUT statement is encountered and there is no data stored from a previous DATA statement, the program prompts you with a "?" and waits for an entry from the terminal.

2. If a length is given, the program will automatically execute a carriage return and line feed (same as pressing <E>) when the specified number of characters has been entered.

3. A colon placed at the end of the input statement suppresses the carriage return/line feed which normally gets sent to the screen after the operator enters a response and presses <E>.

4. You can type ahead in a program and the characters you enter will be "waiting" when the program reaches an INPUT statement.

5. A special version of INPUT is used if the length expression evaluates to -1. There is no pause or prompt; instead the program checks to see if there are any characters from the

keyboard waiting. If there are, the variable is assigned the next keyboard character.

Examples

PRINT "ENTER THE ZIP CODE":
INPUT ZIP,5

will prompt you to enter the zip code and then display a question mark. After you have entered 5 digits the program assigns the data to the variable ZIP without your having to press <E>.

Notes

1. If the length is set to -1 and one of the special keys is pressed (such as the function keys or cursor control keys) the variable is assigned the values CHAR(0) followed by the MS DOS scan code.

$INSERT
(INSERTS SOURCE CODE FROM ANOTHER PROGRAM DURING COMPILATION)

Purpose

Many programs will have some lines of source code in common, particularly statements used to initialize program parameters. Instead of entering them each time you write a program, you can store these common statements in a single program and insert them with the $INSERT statement. When the program is compiled, the statements from this common program will be inserted into your program.

Syntax

$INSERT <filename,> rec.id

filename is the name of the file containing the source code to be inserted.

rec.id is the ID of the record containing the code to be inserted.

Rules

1. If a filename is used it must be followed by a comma.

2. If no filename is given the record containing the source code must be in the same file as the program which contains the $INSERT statement.

Examples

$INSERT PROG, RDESIGN.COMMON

would insert the R/BASIC statements stored in the RDESIGN.COMMON record of the PROG file.

Notes

1. The $INSERT statement is often used to insert COMMON statements which apply to a group of programs.

2. Program line numbers referenced by the compile and run-time errors are not affected by the inserted source code.

LET
(OPTIONAL FIRST WORD IN ASSIGNMENT STATEMENT)

Purpose

LET may be used as the first word of an assignment statement.

Syntax

LET var = exp

var is the variable being assigned a value.
exp is the value being assigned to the variable.

Examples

LET X = 5

means the same as:

X = 5

LINEMARK
(PLACES DEBUGGER LINEMARKS IN THE PROGRAM)

Purpose

When a program is compiled with the S option, no linemarks are placed in the object code. This means that the Debugger sees the entire program as one big line of code, stripping the Debugger of some of its power. LINEMARK statements place linemarks at specified locations throughout the program, allowing the Debugger to display the line number at those points.

Syntax

LINEMARK

Notes

1. See Chapter 12 and Appendix XI.

LOCATE
(LOCATES A VALUE WITHIN A DYNAMIC ARRAY)

Purpose

The LOCATE statement is used to locate the position of any value within a dynamic string array. If it finds the value you specify, the value's position in the dynamic array will be assigned to a variable.

Syntax

LOCATE exp1 IN exp2 <BY seq> <USING dlm> SETTING var ELSE
statements   (all on one line)
or

LOCATE exp1 IN exp2 <BY seq> <USING dlm> SETTING var ELSE
       statements
END

    exp1 is the value to be located. It can be a literal, variable, or other valid expression.

    exp2 is the string expression to be searched, usually a designation for a dynamic array.

    seq is the order sequence in which LOCATE expects to find the elements:
        AL - ascending, left justified (alpha)
        AR - ascending, right justified (numeric)
        DL - descending, left justified
        DL - descending, right justified

    dlm is the delimiter which LOCATE uses to divide the string expression into elements.

    var is the variable which will be set to the position number of the search value.

    statements are any valid statements.

Rules

1. If a dynamic array is being searched, the specified delimiter should be for a specific field, value, or subvalue (i.e. a field mark, CHAR 254; value mark, CHAR 253; or subvalue mark, CHAR 252).

2. When the value is found in the searched expression, the position where it was found will be assigned to the SETTING variable (for example, if the delimiter is the value mark, and exp1 is found in the fourth value, var would be assigned the value 4).

3. If the BY phrase is used, LOCATE will expect elements of the array already to be sorted in the specified order. Therefore it will only look for the search value where it should occur in the sorted string of elements.

4. @VM is the default delimiter if USING is ommitted.

5. If the value being located cannot be found in the search string, the ELSE statements will be executed. If a BY phrase was used, the SETTING variable will be assigned the position where exp1 should have been located, given the sorting order of the array. This allows easy updating of the dynamic array.

Examples

STR = "ABC^{2}DEF■GHR■TKD■POY"
VALUE = "GHR"
LOCATE VALUE IN STR USING @FM SETTING N ELSE
  PRINT "GHR NOT FOUND"
END

In this example, N would be assigned the value of 2.

Notes

1. If the value is not found in the string, the SETTING variable will be equal to a value one greater than the total number of delimited elements.

2. Using the BY phrase will make your program run faster if you are frequently locating elements in a very large dynamic array. Of course, the elements must be sorted first.

3. The LOCATE statement never changes the dynamic array. It only scans the array and leaves the updating of the array to the programmer. The SETTING variable may be used to determine what and where to modify the array.

LOCK
(LOCKS A RECORD ON THE NETWORK FILE SERVER)

Purpose

The LOCK statement locks a specified record in a file so that no other user on the network can lock that record until you unlock the record with the UNLOCK statement.

Syntax

LOCK file.var, rec.id ELSE statements
> or

LOCK file.var, rec.id ELSE
> **statements**

END

file.var is variable assigned to the file with an OPEN statement.

rec.id is the ID of the record to be locked.

statements are any valid statements.

Rules

1. The file must have been previously opened with the OPEN statement.

2. If the record which you are attempting to lock has been locked already by another user, the ELSE statements will be executed.

3. Terminating the program will not unlock the record. The record will be unlocked when your program uses the UNLOCK statement or you log off of the system.

Examples

```
OPEN "","INVOICES" TO WORK.FILE ELSE STOP
PRINT "INPUT INVOICE NUMBER": ; INPUT INV
LOCK WORK.FILE, INV ELSE
  PRINT "INVOICE ":INV:" IS ALREADY LOCKED"
  STOP
END
```

Notes

1. A locked record can still be changed simultaneously by another user if both users do not abide by the locking protocol.

2. The LOCK statement has no effect unless used on a local area network. Thus, developers should follow record locking logic even on a single user system. This precaution will minimize

development time if the application should ever be ported to a LAN environment.

3. If a LOCK attempt is unsuccessful, the STATUS() function is flagged. This flag indicates whether the record is locked by another user or previously locked by the current workstation.

4. For a more thorough discussion on record locking, see Chapter 11.

LOOP
(CREATES A STRUCTURED PROGRAM LOOP)

Purpose

The loop statement is used to create a structured program loop which is repeated until a specified condition is met.

Syntax

LOOP <statements> WHILE/UNTIL test.exp <DO statements> REPEAT

statements are any valid statements

test.exp is any expression but normally a comparison expression.

Rules

1. Once the loop is entered, the program will continue to loop until the conditional (WHILE/UNTIL test.exp) is not met and then it exits the loop.

2. Statements can be placed in the loop either before the test expression, after the test expression, or both.

3. Any expression can be used as a test expression. An expression which evaluates to 0 is false; an expression which evaluates to anything else is considered true.

4. Statements can be all on one line or broken into several lines. If several statements are on a line next to each other, they must be separated by semicolons.

5. The DO word in the command is optional. But if it is omitted and a statement is placed on the same line as the test expression, the expression and statement must be separated by a semicolon.

Examples

X=0
LOOP X=X+1 WHILE X<10 DO PRINT X: REPEAT

will print 123456789.

LOOP
  INPUT AMOUNT
  WHILE AMOUNT <> 0
    PRINT AMOUNT+TAX
REPEAT

will continue prompting for AMOUNT and printing it until an AMOUNT equal to 0 is encountered.

MAT
(ASSIGNS VALUES TO A MATRIX VARIABLE)

Purpose

MAT can assign the same value to all the elements of a matrix variable, or it can assign each element in the matrix a corresponding value from another matrix.

Syntax

MAT matrix1 = expression
          or
MAT matrix1 = MAT matrix2

matrix1 and **matrix2** are matrix variables.

expression is any valid expression.

Rules

1. The matrix variables must have been dimensioned in previous DIM or COMMON statements.

2. The expression assigned to matrix1 will be assigned to all the elements of the matrix.

3. In the second format, matrix1 is assigned the values of matrix2. The number of elements of matrix1 must be the same as matrix2; however, they can have different dimensions (e.g. X(3,4) and Y(12) and Z(2,6) all have 13 elements counting the (0) or (0,0) element).

4. Elements are assigned values in order; e.g. X(3,4) would be assigned in the following order:
(0,0),(1,1),(1,2),(1,3),(1,4),(2,1),(2,2)...

Examples

```
MAT TABLE = 0
```

assigns all the elements of the matrix TABLE to 0.

```
DIM X(3,4), Y(12)
FOR N = 0 TO 12
  Y(N) = N
NEXT N
MAT X = MAT Y
END
```

would set X(0,0)=0; X(1,1)=1; X(1,2)=2; etc.

MATPARSE
(CONVERTS DYNAMIC ARRAY INTO MATRIX)

Purpose

MATPARSE is used to assign the values of fields from a dynamic array to a one dimensional matrix.

Syntax

MATPARSE array INTO mat

array is a dynamic array.
mat is a one dimensional matrix variable.

Rules

1. The matrix must have been previously dimensioned with a DIM or COMMON statement.

Examples

The following example shows the use of the MATPARSE statement and the related internal function, MATUNPARSE.

```
DIM X(5), Y(5)
FOR COUNT=1 TO 5
  X(COUNT)= COUNT*2
NEXT COUNT
ARRAY= MATUNPARSE(X)
PRINT "FROM MATRIX TO DYNAMIC ARRAY: ":ARRAY
PRINT
MATPARSE ARRAY INTO Y
PRINT "FROM DYNAMIC ARRAY TO MATRIX: ":
PRINT Y(1):' ':Y(3):' ':Y(5)
```

would print:

FROM MATRIX TO DYNAMIC ARRAY: 2■4■6■8■10

FROM DYNAMIC ARRAY TO MATRIX: 2 6 10

MATREAD
(INPUTS DATA FROM A RECORD INTO A MATRIX VARIABLE)

Purpose

MATREAD sequentially assigns the contents of each field from a data record to an element of a matrix.

Syntax

MATREAD matrix FROM file.var, rec.id ELSE statements
or

MATREAD matrix FROM file.var, rec.id ELSE
  statement
  statement
END

matrix is the matrix variable which will receive the data fields.

file.var is the variable that the file containing the record to be read was opened to.

rec.id is the ID of the record whose fields will be assigned to the matrix.

statements are any valid statements.

Rules

1. The matrix variable must have been dimensioned previously with a DIM or COMMON statement.

2. The file.var and rec.id must be separated by a comma.

3. The data from each field in the record is assigned to each element of the matrix in order (see example).

4. If there are more elements in the matrix than fields in the record, the leftover matrix elements are assigned a null value. If there are more fields than matrix elements, all of the leftover fields are placed as one big string into the last matrix element.

5. If the record cannot be read, the ELSE statements are executed and the matrix is left unassigned.

6. The file must have been opened previously with an OPEN statement.

Examples

```
DIM INV(4,3)
OPEN "","INVOICES" TO INV.FILE ELSE STOP
MATREAD INV FROM INV.FILE, ID ELSE
    PRINT "INVOICE ":ID:" IS NOT ON FILE"
    STOP
END
```

would assign the first field to INV(0,0); the second to INV(1,1); the third to INV(1,2); the fourth to INV(1,3); the fifth to INV(2,1); the sixth to INV(2,2); etc.

Notes

1. The data record is left unchanged after the assignment of its fields to the matrix.

MATWRITE
(WRITES VALUES FROM A MATRIX VARIABLE TO A RECORD)

Purpose

MATWRITE writes each element of a matrix variable to a field of a specified record in a Revelation file.

Syntax

MATWRITE **matrix** TO **file.var, rec.id**
                        or
MATWRITE **matrix** ON **file.var, rec.id**

matrix is the matrix variable whose values are to be written to the record.

file.var is the variable that the file containing the record to hold the values was opened to.

rec.id is the ID of the record to contain the values of the matrix.

Rules

1. Each element of the selected matrix is written to the record as a separate field (see the example for the order in which the matrix elements are read).

2. The file must have been opened already by a previous OPEN statement.

3. Note that there must be a comma between the file.var and the rec.id. If there is no record with this ID, one will be created.

Examples

Matrix variable INV(4,3) has been dimensioned and assigned values.

MATWRITE INV TO INVOICES, 758

would assign values to record 758 of the INVOICES file in the following order: element INV(0,0) to the first field; element INV(1,1) to the second field; element INV(1,2) to the third field; element INV(1,3) to the fourth field; element INV(2,1) to the fifth field; element INV(2,2) to the sixth field; etc.

Notes

1. MATWRITE is usually used after you have read a data file record to a matrix with MATREAD and manipulated the values with your program. You will use MATWRITE when you are ready to put the values back into the record.

NEXT
(see FOR/NEXT statement)

NULL
(NO-ACTION STATEMENT)

Purpose

NULL can be entered where a statement is required but no operation or action is desired.

Syntax

NULL

Examples

OPEN "","INVOICES" TO INV.FILE ELSE NULL

Notes

1. NULL may *not* be used as an expression as in
IF NULL THEN GOTO 100.

ON GOSUB
(CONDITIONAL BRANCHING TO INTERNAL SUBROUTINES)

Purpose

ON GOSUB transfers program control to one of several subroutines depending on the value of an expression in the GOSUB statement.

Syntax

ON exp GOSUB label#1, label#2, label#3 ...

exp is any valid expression.

label#1, label#2, label#3 are statement labels marking the beginning of subroutines.

Rules

1. The expression is evaluated and truncated to an integer value. If the value is equal to one, program control passes to the first subroutine; a value of two passes control to the second subroutine; a value of three passes control to the third subroutine; and so on.

2. If the value is less than one, an error message is displayed and control passes to the first subroutine. If the value is greater than the number of subroutines, an error message is displayed and control passes to the last subroutine.

3. Colons may be inserted after each statement label in the ON GOSUB statement to increase readability.

4. As in all subroutines, program control will return to the main part of the program when a RETURN or RETURN TO statement is encountered.

5. Using a statement label that does not exist in the program will result in an error message.

6. ON GOSUB must be written on one line, with statement labels separated by commas.

Examples

```
BEGIN CASE
   CASE AMOUNT < 100
      N = 1
   CASE AMOUNT < 200
      N = 2
   CASE AMOUNT > 200
      N = 3
END CASE
ON N GOSUB SMALL:, MED:, LARGE:
```

will send program control to one of the three subroutines depending on the value of the AMOUNT variable.

ON GOTO
(CONDITIONAL JUMP TO ANOTHER STATEMENT LABEL)

Purpose

ON GOTO transfers program control to one of several statement labels depending on the value of an expression in the GOTO statement.

Syntax

ON exp GOTO label#1, label#2, label#3 ...

exp is any valid expression.

label#1, label#2, label#3 are statement labels.

Rules

1. The expression is evaluated and truncated to an integer value. If the value is equal to one, program control passes to the first statement label; a value of two passes control to the second statement label; a value of three passes control to the third statement label; and so on.

2. If the value is less than one, an error message is displayed and control passes to the first statement label. If the value is greater than the number of statement labels, an error message is displayed and control passes to the last statement label.

3. Colons may be inserted after each statement label in the ON GOTO statement to increase readability.

4. Using a statement label that does not exist in the program will result in an error message.

5. ON GOSUB must be written on one line with statement labels separated by commas.

Examples

```
BEGIN CASE
  CASE AMOUNT < 100
    N = 1
  CASE AMOUNT < 200
    N = 2
  CASE AMOUNT > 200
    N = 3
END CASE
ON N GOTO SMALL:, MED:, LARGE:
```

will send program control to one of the three statement labels depending on the value of the AMOUNT variable.

Notes

1. The letters TO may be omitted from ON GOTO, as in
ON X GO SMALL, MED, LARGE.

OPEN
(OPENS A FILE FOR READING OR WRITING)

Purpose

Before a program can access a file to read or write information to it, that file must be "opened" and given a variable name with the OPEN statement.

Syntax

OPEN "DICT"/", "filename" TO file.var ELSE statements
    or
OPEN "DICT"/", "filename" TO file.var ELSE
  statements
END

filename is the Revelation name of the file to be opened, enclosed in quotation marks.

file.var is any variable expression.

statements are any valid statements.

Rules

1. The first expression in the statement must be either the word DICT, which indicates the dictionary portion of the file will be opened; or null as indicated by two quotation marks ("or "") to open the data portion of the file.

2. The filename must be separated from the preceding expression by a comma.

3. The file.var is how you will refer to this file in other statements in your program such as READ, READV, WRITE, MATREAD, MATWRITE, and DELETE.

4. The ELSE statements are mandatory and will be executed if the file does not exist or cannot be opened.

5. Each file you use in your program must be opened with its own OPEN statement.

Examples

```
OPEN ", "INVOICES" TO INV ELSE
     PRINT "INVOICES FILE CANNOT BE OPENED"
END
```

opens the data portion of the INVOICES file and assigns it the variable name INV.

```
OPEN "DICT",INVOICES TO DICT.INV ELSE NULL
```

opens the dictionary of the INVOICES file and assigns it the variable name DICT.INV. If the dictionary cannot be opened no action is taken and the program continues to the next line.

Notes

1. There is no limit to the number of files which can be opened and there is no need to close a file. In fact, there is no way of "closing" a file. This is because the OPEN statement doesn't

really open a file, it justs assigns a variable name to the file so
that all statements in the program can use the same variable to
refer to the file.

OSBREAD
(READS LARGE DOS FILES IN SMALL SECTIONS)

Purpose

OSBREAD breaks DOS files larger than 64k characters into
smaller sections and reads these smaller sections. Normally,
R/BASIC will read DOS files with OSREAD and write to them
with OSWRITE. However, files larger than 64K must be
handled in smaller sections. The file must first be opened with
OSOPEN, then read in sections with OSBREAD, written in
sections with OSBWRITE, and closed with OSCLOSE. DOS
files can be deleted with OSDELETE.

Syntax

OSBREAD var FROM file AT byte.start LENGTH length.exp

var is the variable name to be assigned a portion of the larger
DOS file.

file is the variable name given to the DOS file in an OSOPEN
statement.

byte.start is the byte number where reading should begin. The
beginning of the file is byte 0.

length.exp is how much data to read into var in bytes (must be
less than 65,530).

Rules

1. The OSBREAD statement assigns a portion of a large DOS
file to the variable starting with byte.start and continuing for
length.exp.

2. The DOS file must have been previously opened with the OSOPEN statement.

3. After the execution of the OSBREAD statement, a value is assigned to the STATUS() function as follows:
> 0 = no errors
> 1 = bad DOS file
> 2 = access denied by DOS
> 4 = file does not exist
> 5 = undefined error

Examples

```
* This routine reads a DOS file of 250,000 bytes
*    containing ASCII fixed length records and
*    prints out the first five characters from each record.
OSOPEN "MAGNUM" TO PI ELSE STOP
START=0
FOR X=0 TO 249,999 STEP 250
   OSBREAD REC FROM PI AT X LENGTH 250
   PRINT REC[1,5]
NEXT X
OSCLOSE PI
```

Notes

1. This statement is not normally used with Revelation files. OSBREAD just provides the R/BASIC programmer with a tool for reading any type of file.

OSBWRITE
(WRITES DATA INTO A DOS FILE AT A SPECIFIED POINT)

Purpose

OSBWRITE writes data into DOS files which are larger then 64k characters. Normally, R/BASIC will read DOS files with OSREAD and write to them with OSWRITE. However, files larger than 64K must be handled in smaller sections. The file must first be opened with OSOPEN, then read in sections with

OSBREAD, written in sections with OSBWRITE, and closed
with OSCLOSE. DOS files can be deleted with OSDELETE.

Syntax

OSBWRITE exp TO file.var AT start.byte
                        or
OSBWRITE exp ON file.var AT start.byte

exp is the data which will be written back into the DOS file.

file.var is the variable name given to the DOS file in an
                OSOPEN statement.

start.byte is the byte number where writing should begin. The
                beginning of the file is byte 0.

Rules

1. OSBWRITE writes the exp data back to the DOS file
beginning at start.byte in the file.

2. The DOS file must have been previously opened with the
OSOPEN statement.

3. After the execution of the OSBWRITE statement, a value is
assigned to the STATUS() function as follows:
   - 0 = no errors
   - 1 = bad DOS file
   - 2 = access denied by DOS
   - 3 = disk or directory full
   - 4 = file does not exist
   - 5 = undefined error
   - 6 = attempt to write a read only file

Examples

```
* This routine reads a DOS file of 250,000 bytes
*   containing ASCII fixed length records and
*   changes the state data to "CA" in certain records
*   before writing the data back to the file.
*

OSOPEN "MAGNUM" TO PI ELSE STOP
START=0
```
(continued on next page)

```
FOR X=0 TO 249,999 STEP 250
  OSBREAD REC FROM PI AT X LENGTH 250
  IF REC[10,2]="ca" THEN
    REC[10,2]="CA"
  END
  OSBWRITE REC ON PI AT X
NEXT X
OSCLOSE PI
```

Notes

1. This statement is not normally used with Revelation files. OSBWRITE just provides the R/BASIC programmer with a tool for writing to any type of file.

OSCLOSE
(CLOSES A DOS FILE OPENED WITH OSOPEN)

Purpose

OSCLOSE closes DOS files previously opened with the OSOPEN statement. Normally, R/BASIC will read DOS files with OSREAD and write to them with OSWRITE. However, files larger than 64K must be handled in smaller sections. The file must first be opened with OSOPEN, then read in sections with OSBREAD, written in sections with OSBWRITE, and closed with OSCLOSE. DOS files can be deleted with OSDELETE.

Syntax

OSCLOSE file.var

file.var is the variable name assigned to the file when it was opened.

Rules

1. After the execution of the OSCLOSE statement, a value is passed to the STATUS() function as follows:
   0 = no errors
   1 = undefined error

Examples

See examples with OSBREAD and OSBWRITE.

OSDELETE
(DELETES A DOS FILE)

Purpose

OSDELETE deletes the specified DOS file.

Syntax

OSDELETE file.exp

file.exp is the full DOS path name of the file to be deleted, including the drive, directory, name, and extension. The expression may be a variable or a literal string placed in quotes.

Rules

1. If no drive/directory is given, the default medium is assumed.

2. After the execution of the OSDELETE statement, a value is assigned to the STATUS() function as follows:

    0 = no errors
    1 = bad DOS file
    2 = access denied by DOS
    4 = file does not exist
    5 = undefined error

Examples

```
OSDELETE "TEST.DTA"
PRINT STATUS()
FILE="TEST.TXT"
OSDELETE FILE
```

OSOPEN
(OPENS A DOS FILE FOR OSBREAD AND OSBWRITE)

Purpose

R/BASIC provides several tools for reading from and writing to a DOS file. Normally, you will read from a DOS file with OSREAD and write to it with OSWRITE. However, files larger than 64K must be handled in smaller sections. The file must first be opened with OSOPEN, then read in sections with OSBREAD, written in sections with OSBWRITE, and closed with OSCLOSE. DOS files can be deleted with OSDELETE.

Syntax

OSOPEN dos.filename TO file.var ELSE statements

dos.filename is the full DOS file name to be opened including the drive, directory, name, and extension.

file.var is the variable name assigned to the DOS file.

statements are any valid statements.

Rules

1. Once the file is opened, OSBREAD and OSBWRITE refer to the file by file.var.

2. Files opened with an OSOPEN statement should be closed with an OSCLOSE statement to ensure proper updating of the file on disk.

3. After the execution of the OSOPEN statement, a value is assigned to the STATUS() function as follows:
   0 = no errors
   1 = bad DOS file
   2 = access denied by DOS
   4 = file does not exist
   5 = undefined error

Examples

```
            TOP:
            INPUT FILE.NAME
            OSOPEN FILE.NAME TO PI ELSE
              BEGIN CASE
                CASE STATUS()=1
                  PRINT "BAD DOS FILE NAME
                CASE STATUS()=2
                  PRINT "ACCESS DENIED BY DOS"
                CASE STATUS()=4
                  PRINT FILE.NAME:" DOES NOT EXIST"
                CASE 1
                  PRINT "ERROR"
              END CASE
              GOTO TOP
            END
            PRINT FILE.NAME:" SUCCESSFULLY OPENED"
            OSCLOSE FILE.NAME
```

OSREAD
(READS DATA FROM A DOS FILE INTO A VARIABLE)

Purpose

Your R/BASIC program can read from and write to a DOS file. Normally, you will read it with OSREAD and write to it with OSWRITE. However, files larger than 64K must be handled in smaller sections. The file must first be opened with OSOPEN, then read in sections with OSBREAD, written in sections with OSBWRITE, and closed with OSCLOSE. DOS files can be deleted with OSDELETE.

Syntax

OSREAD var FROM dos.filename ELSE statements

var is the variable name to which you are assigning the information from the DOS file.

dos.filename is the full path name of the DOS file to be read, including its drive, directory, name, and extension. The dos.filename may be a variable expression or a literal string enclosed in quotes.

statements are any valid statements.

Rules

1. When the OSREAD statement is executed, the data from the DOS file is read into the variable you specified.

2. If no drive and directory location are given, the default drive/directory are assumed.

3. After the execution of the OSREAD statement, a value is assigned to the STATUS() function as follows:
   0 = no errors
   1 = bad DOS file
   2 = access denied by DOS
   4 = file does not exist
   5 = undefined error

Examples

```
OSREAD NOTES FROM "\WORD\NOTES.DOC" ELSE
   PRINT STATUS()
   STOP
END
```

Notes

1. This statement is not normally used with Revelation files. OSREAD just provides the R/BASIC programmer with a tool for reading from any type of file.

OSWRITE
(WRITES DATA TO A DOS FILE)

Purpose

Your R/BASIC program can read from and write to a DOS file. Normally, you will read it with OSREAD and write to it with OSWRITE. However, files larger than 64K must be handled in smaller sections. The file must first be opened with OSOPEN, then read in sections with OSBREAD, written in sections with OSBWRITE, and closed with OSCLOSE. DOS files can be deleted with OSDELETE.

Syntax

OSWRITE exp TO dos.filename
           or
OSWRITE exp ON dos.filename

exp is the expression containing the data to be written to the DOS file.

dos.filename is the full path name of the DOS file to be read including its drive, directory, name, and extension. The dos.filename may be a variable expression or a literal string enclosed in quotes.

Rules

1. When the OSWRITE statement is executed, the data from the variable is written to the DOS file.

2. If the DOS file exists, it will be overwritten with the new data. If the DOS file does not exist, it will be created.

3. If no drive and directory location are given, the default drive/directory are assumed.

4. After the execution of the OSWRITE statement, a value is assigned to the STATUS() function as follows:
   - 0 = no errors
   - 1 = bad DOS file
   - 2 = access denied by DOS
   - 3 = disk or directory full

4 = file does not exist
5 = undefined error
6 = attempt to write a read only file

Examples

OSWRITE NOTES TO "\WORD\NOTES.DOC"
PRINT STATUS()

writes the information in the variable NOTES to the DOS file NOTES.DOC on the WORD directory. A "0" will be printed if no errors occurred.

Notes

1. This statement is not normally used with Revelation files. OSWRITE just provides the R/BASIC programmer with a tool for writing to any type of file.

OUT
(SENDS A SINGLE CHARACTER TO A COMMUNICATIONS PORT)

Purpose

OUT is used to send a single ASCII character to a communications port.

Syntax

OUT port#, char#

port# is an expression which evaluates to a number between 0 and 65535, representing the communications port number.

char# is an expression which evaluates to a number between 0 and 255, indicating the ASCII character to be sent to the communications port.

Rules

1. When the statement is executed, the single ASCII character is sent to the communications port.

Examples

OUT 3,27

sends ESC to port 3.

FOR N = 65 TO 70
** OUT 1387, N**
NEXT N

sends ABCDEF to port 1387.

PAGE
(ADVANCES THE SCREEN OR PRINTER ONE PAGE)

Purpose

PAGE forces the current output device (screen or printer) to advance one page.

Syntax

PAGE

Notes

1. The PAGE statement obeys the setting for the current page as determined by the PRINTER statement.

2. The PAGE statement forces the printing of any specified HEADING and FOOTING.

PCEXECUTE
(same as PCPERFORM)

PCPERFORM
(PERFORMS A DOS COMMAND FROM INSIDE YOUR PROGRAM)

Purpose

Your program can execute DOS commands using the PCPERFORM statement.

Syntax

PCPERFORM dos.command

dos.command is any DOS command. It may be a variable expression or a string literal enclosed in quotes.

Rules

1. This statement will only work with DOS versions 2.0 or later.

2. The DOS command will be executed as if it had been entered at the DOS prompt of the default drive/directory. The DOS file COMMAND.COM must be accessible from that directory.

3. After the DOS command is executed, control passes back to the program.

Examples

```
PC:
PRINT "INPUT DOS COMMAND":
INPUT COM
IF COM <> "END" THEN
  PCPERFORM COM
  GOTO PC
END
```

will keep executing DOS commands until you enter END at the prompt.

PERFORM
(PERFORMS A TCL COMMAND FROM INSIDE A PROGRAM)

Purpose

PERFORM allows you to perform a TCL command from within a program and then return back to the program.

Syntax

PERFORM "command"

command is the TCL command just as it would be entered at the TCL prompt.

Rules

1. When a PERFORM statement is used, Revelation goes to a second "level" to perform the new command. PERFORM statements are recursive, that is, all of the current variables are saved before execution of the TCL command and then restored upon return to the program. The one exception to this rule is if you perform a SELECT. In this case, the select list *is* passed backed to the program.

Examples

```
OPEN "","CUSTOMERS" TO FILE.VAR ELSE STOP
OPEN "DICT","CUSTOMERS" TO @DICT ELSE STOP
PERFORM "SELECT CUSTOMERS WITH ST = 'CA'"
LOOP
   READNEXT @ID ELSE STOP
   READ @RECORD FROM FILE.VAR,@ID ELSE STOP
   PRINT @ID,{NAME}
REPEAT
```

This program will perform the SELECT command and then pass back the record IDs for processing customers in California.

Notes

1. If you want a completely recursive call to TCL, including the current select list, use the EXECUTE statement.

PRINT
(PRINTS TO THE PRINTER OR SCREEN)

Purpose

PRINT causes an expression or group of expressions to be printed on the current output device.

Syntax

PRINT <exp1, exp2, exp3, ...>

exp1, exp2, exp3 are any expressions

Rules

1. The print expressions can be variables, literals, or any valid expression. If literals are used they must be enclosed in quotation marks unless the literal consists solely of numeric characters.

2. The output will go to the screen unless the printer is made the current output device with a PRINTER statement.

3. When each expression is separated by a comma, the expressions are printed in "print zones" which are 16 characters wide. Alternatively, the expressions can be separated by colons, and the expressions will be attached to each other.

4. A "dangling" comma or colon following the last expression will cause the next print statement to continue to print on the same line.

5. If no expression is given, a blank line will be printed.

Examples

```
PRINT "Today's Date is ":OCONV(DATE(),"D")
PRINT "How are you":
INPUT HEALTH
```

PRINTER
(DIRECTS OUTPUT TO THE PRINTER)

Purpose

PRINTER ON directs output from subsequent PRINT statements to the printer until a PRINTER OFF statement is encountered.

Syntax

PRINTER ON/OFF

Examples

PRINTER ON
PRINT "THIS IS A TEST OF THE PRINTER"
PRINTER OFF

Notes

1. The default output device for all PRINT statements is the display screen.

PROMPT
(SETS THE PROMPT CHARACTER)

Purpose

PROMPT is used to set the character which will be displayed when your program is prompting the operator for input.

Syntax

PROMPT char

char is a single character or an expression which evaluates to a single character.

Rules

1. If more than one character is specified, only the first is used as the prompt.

2. The default prompt is a question mark.

Examples

PROMPT "$"
PRINT "Enter the dollar amount ":
INPUT X

would prompt the operator with: **Enter the dollar amount $.**

READ
(ASSIGNS DATA READ FROM A RECORD TO A VARIABLE)

Purpose

The READ statement reads a specified record in a file and assigns the data stored in it to a variable so that the data is accessible to your program.

Syntax

READ var FROM file.var, rec.id ELSE statements
or

READ var FROM file.var, rec.id ELSE
  statements
END

var is the name of the variable assigned to the data.

file.var is the variable name assigned to the file in an OPEN
    statement.

rec.id is the ID of the record to be read. The record ID may be a
    variable expression or a literal string enclosed in quotes.

statements are any valid statements.

Rules

1. Note that a comma is required between file.var and rec.id.

2. If the record does not exist, the ELSE statements are executed. If the file cannot be accessed, the program will abort and an error message will be displayed.

3. The record must be less than 65,531 bytes.

Examples

```
OPEN "","CUSTOMERS" TO FILE.VAR ELSE STOP
PERFORM "SELECT CUSTOMERS WITH ST = 'CA'"
LOOP
  READNEXT REC.ID ELSE STOP
  READ RECORD FROM FILE.VAR,REC.ID ELSE STOP
  PRINT REC.ID,{NAME}
REPEAT
```

This program will process a list of customers by assigning each record ID from the select list to the variable REC.ID and then reading each corresponding record from the CUSTOMERS file.

READNEXT
(READS RECORD ID FROM A SELECT LIST)

Purpose

READNEXT will extract the next record ID from the current select list and assign that value to a specified variable.

Syntax

READNEXT id.var ELSE statements

or

READNEXT id.var THEN
  statements
END ELSE
  statements
END

id.var is the variable which will be assigned the value of the next record ID from the select list.

statements are any valid statements.

Rules

1. Each time the READNEXT statement is encountered, it extracts the next ID from the select list.

2. When the select list is exhausted, the ELSE statements are executed.

Examples

```
OPEN ", "INVOICES" TO INV ELSE STOP
PERFORM "SELECT INVOICES WITH INV.NO > 10"
LOOP
  READNEXT X ELSE
    PRINT "END OF INVOICES"
    GOTO FINISH:
  END
  READ INVREC FROM INV, X ELSE STOP
  PRINT INVREC
REPEAT
FINISH:

    .

    .
```

Notes

1. The select list may be passed to the program in several ways. From TCL, either execute the SELECT command or the GET-LIST command and then immediately run the program.

```
:GET-LIST FLORIDA
>RUN BP PROG1
        or
:SELECT CUSTOMERS WITH ST = "FL"
>PROG1
```

2. The R/BASIC SELECT statement may be used to generate a complete list of all the record IDs in a file. To generate a more refined select list, use the PERFORM statement.

READV
(READS DATA FROM A SPECIFIED FIELD)

Purpose

READV assigns the data in a specified record field to a variable.

Syntax

READV var FROM file.var, rec.id, field# ELSE statements
or

READV var FROM file.var, rec.id, field# ELSE
  statements
END

var is the name of the variable which will be assigned the field's value.

file.var is the variable name given to the file in an OPEN statement.

rec.id is the ID of the record containing the field to be read.

field# is the FMC number of the field to be read.

Rules

1. The file.var, rec.id, and field# must be separated by commas.

2. If the file cannot be accessed, an error message will result.

3. If the record cannot be read, the ELSE statements will be executed.

Examples

```
OPEN ", "INVOICES" TO INV ELSE STOP
FOR N = 1001 TO 1010
  READV AMT FROM INV, N, 2 ELSE STOP
  PRINT N, AMT
NEXT N
```

This program will print the record ID and field #2 from invoice records 1001 to 1010.

REM
(see COMMENTS)

REMOVE
(EXTRACTS A SUB-STRING FROM A DYNAMIC ARRAY)

Purpose

The REMOVE statement extracts a sub-string from a dynamic array and assigns it to a variable. It searches a specified array and finds the sub-string located between any of the seven ASCII string delimiters from ASCII 249 to ASCII 255.

Syntax

REMOVE var FROM string.exp AT col.exp SETTING flag.var

var is the name of the variable which will be assigned the value of the sub-string.

string.exp indicates the dynamic array from which the sub-string will be extracted. Often this dynamic array is a variable assigned the value of a record or field from a previous READ or READV statement.

col.var is an expression which evaluates to a number indicating the starting position in the string where the next search should begin.

flag.var is a variable which will be assigned a value depending on which delimiter marked the end of the sub-string. The possible delimiters are:

0 = end of dynamic array
1 = record mark: ASCII CHAR(255)
2 = field mark: ASCII CHAR (254)
3 = value mark: ASCII CHAR(253)
4 = subvalue mark: ASCII CHAR(252)
5 = text mark: ASCII CHAR(251)

6 = ASCII CHAR(250)
7 = ASCII CHAR(249)

Rules

1. REMOVE scans the specified string starting from the **col.var** position and assigns to **var** the first sub-string it encounters. REMOVE does not differentiate between delimiters except for setting the value of **flag.var**.

2. When a sub-string is assigned to the variable, the value of **col.var** will change to point to the next sub-string.

Examples

```
FM=@FM
VM=@VM
STRING="ONE":FM:"TWO":VM:"THREE":VM:"FOUR"
COL = 0
MARK=1
LOOP WHILE MARK <> 0
  REMOVE NUM FROM STRING AT COL SETTING MARK
  PRINT NUM,COL,MARK
REPEAT
```

This program will display the following output:

ONE	5	2
TWO	9	3
THREE	15	3
FOUR	20	0

RETURN/RETURN TO
(TERMINATES INTERNAL OR EXTERNAL SUBROUTINES)

Purpose

Internal and external subroutines must return to the main or calling program when completed. RETURN is used to return to the next line in the main program after the GOSUB or CALL statement. RETURN TO is used only with internal subroutines and returns to some other statement label in the main program.

Syntax

RETURN

or

RETURN TO statement.label<:>

statement.label is any statement label in the main program.

Rules

1. A RETURN statement can be used after calling an internal subroutine with GOSUB, or after calling an external subroutine with CALL.

2. A RETURN TO statement is only used with internal subroutines.

Examples

```
MAIN PROGRAM:
SIZE = "SMALL"
INPUT Z
IF Z = "END" THEN STOP
IF Z>100 THEN CALL LGE(Z,SIZE)
PRINT Z, SIZE
END

SUBROUTINE LGE(Z,SIZE)
  IF Z>1000 THEN
   GOSUB PRINTSIZE
  END
  SIZE = "LARGE"
FINISH:
  Z=Z*10
  RETURN
PRINTSIZE:
  PRINT Z:" IS NOT ":SIZE
  SIZE="VERY LARGE"
  RETURN TO FINISH
RETURN
END
```

This program and its subroutine demonstrate the use of the RETURN statement. Notice that in the external subroutine there is an internal subroutine which uses the RETURN TO statement.

NOTES

1. The RETURN TO statement should be used carefully as it makes debugging and modifying the program more difficult.

2. If the RETURN is omitted from an external subroutine, control will still be returned to the main program when the END statement is encountered. It is still good programming practice to include the RETURN statement.

SELECT
(CREATES A COMPLETE LIST OF A FILE'S RECORD IDS)

Purpose

SELECT will create an exhaustive list of IDs from the file you specify. This list can then be read by the READNEXT statement to access each record in the file. This is very similar to forming a select list with the TCL SELECT command. The major difference is that with the R/BASIC SELECT, no selection criteria are allowed.

Syntax

SELECT file.var

file.var is the variable assigned to a file with an OPEN statement.

Examples

```
OPEN ", "INVOICES" TO INV ELSE STOP
SELECT INV
LOOP
   READNEXT INV.NO ELSE STOP
   READ REC FROM INV,INV.NO THEN
      PRINT INV.NO,{INV.AMOUNT}
```

(continued on next page)

```
END
REPEAT
```

This program reads every invoice record from the INVOICES file and reports the invoice number and amount.

STARTLINECOUNT
(STARTS LINEMARKS)

Purpose

The compiler usually places linemarks before every line during the compilation process. When the debugger is called it is then able to correctly report the line number where execution was halted. The suppress option of the COMPILE statement will suppress all linemarks in order to compress the code. In this case, use of the STARTLINECOUNT statement will force the compiler to still place linemarks at every line following this statement until a STOPLINECOUNT statement is encountered.

STOP
(TERMINATES THE PROGRAM)

Purpose

STOP can be used anywhere in the program to terminate the program.

Syntax

STOP <expression>

expression is any expression

Rules

1. When a STOP is encountered, the program is terminated and the expression is printed on the screen.

Examples

IF X>100 THEN STOP "TERMINATED WITH X = ":X

STOPLINECOUNT
(STOPS LINEMARKS FROM OCCURING IN THE PROGRAM)

Purpose

STOPLINECOUNT is used to stop linemarks from occuring from this point in the program until a STARTLINECOUNT statement is encountered.

Syntax

STOPLINECOUNT

Notes

1. Eliminating linemarks reduces the amount of space the compiled program occupies, but it means that the debugger will not be able to correctly report the line number where execution was halted.

STORAGE
(SPECIFIES NUMBER OF ROS FILE BUFFERS)

Purpose

STORAGE sets the number of ROS file buffers to be used.

Syntax

STORAGE no

no is the number of storage buffers from 1 to 10.

Notes

1. The more buffers, the more ROS files will be stored in RAM and disk access time will be reduced. However they take up RAM space which could possibly be used for other purposes.

SUBROUTINE
(IDENTIFIES A PROGRAM AS A SUBROUTINE)

Purpose

A SUBROUTINE statement must be the first line of an external subroutine so that Revelation can identify the subroutine when it is called by the main program. It is also used to pass data between the subroutine and the main program.

Syntax

SUBROUTINE name <(arg1,arg2,...)>

name is the name of the subroutine (used in the CALL statement).

arg1,arg2,... are expressions used to pass information between the main program and the subroutine; separated by commas and enclosed in parentheses.

Rules

1. The subroutine program must be compiled and cataloged before it can be called.

2. The number of arguments in the SUBROUTINE statement must be equal to the number of arguments in the CALL statement. The names of the arguments are not required to be identical in the main and subroutine programs. It is the relative position in the argument list that determines what value each variable receives. The arguments are paired up in order; the first argument in the CALL statement with the first argument in the SUBROUTINE statement, the second with the second, and so

on. At least one of the arguments in each pair should be a variable.

Examples

See Chapater 13 for several examples of subroutines.

SWAP
(REPLACES A LITERAL STRING WITHIN A VARIABLE)

Purpose

SWAP replaces a specified literal string with another string wherever it occurs in a variable. SWAP looks for the entire literal string; which is different from the CONVERT statement which does character by character replacements.

Syntax

SWAP exp1 WITH exp2 in var

exp1, exp2 are literal strings

var is the variable where the replacement takes place.

Rules

1. Wherever exp1 occurs in the variable, exp2 will be put in its place.

Examples

```
STR = "MANTLE: THE GLORY DAYS"
SWAP "MANTLE" WITH "MICK" IN STR
PRINT STR
```

This program will print the following line:

MICK: THE GLORY DAYS

Notes

1. Whereas the CONVERT statement performs a character by character replacement, the SWAP statement replaces an entire

sub-string with another literal string. SWAP might replace a 12 character string with a 5 character string. CONVERT only replaces one character with another.

STRING="THE HEN IN THE BED"
CONVERT "THE" TO "MY" IN STRING
PRINT STRING

This program yields "MY YN IN MY BD" because every "T" is replaced with "M", "H" with "Y", and "E" is deleted. If we say instead **SWAP "THE" WITH "MY" IN STRING** the program would print "MY HEN IN MY BED" because only the word "THE" will be replaced with "MY".

TRANSFER
(TRANSFERS THE VALUE OF ONE VARIABLE TO ANOTHER)

Purpose

TRANSFER assigns the value of one variable to another and then sets the original variable to null.

Syntax

TRANSFER var1 TO var2

var1 is the variable whose value is being transferred.
var2 is the variable receiving the value.

Examples

INPUT X
TRANSFER X TO Y

is equivalent to:

Y = X
X = ''

UNLOCK
(RELEASES PREVIOUSLY LOCKED RECORDS FOR OTHERS TO USE)

Purpose

The UNLOCK command unlocks records which were previously set with a LOCK statement.

Syntax

UNLOCK file.var, rec.id
> or

UNLOCK ALL

file.var is the variable name assigned to a file with an OPEN statement.

rec.id is the ID of the record to be unlocked.

Rules

1. Depending upon which form of the statement you use, either the record specified or all of the records which have been locked from your workstation since you logged on will be unlocked.

2. After a record is unlocked, other users on the network may have access to it.

3. Records which are locked will not be automatically unlocked when a program is terminated. They must be unlocked with an UNLOCK command or they will be unlocked when you log off of the account.

4. When you exit the Debugger with an END command, the Debugger executes an UNLOCK ALL command.

Examples

```
OPEN ", "INVOICES" TO INV ELSE STOP
INPUT INV.NO
LOCK:
```

(continued on next page)

```
LOCK INV, INV.NO ELSE
  PRINT INV.NO:" IS ALREADY LOCKED"
  PRINT "DO YOU WISH TO TRY AGAIN":
  INPUT AGAIN
  IF AGAIN="Y" THEN GOTO LOCK: ELSE STOP
END
READ REC FROM INV,INV.NO ELSE GO UNLOCK
REC<2>="UPDATED"
WRITE REC TO INV, INV.NO
UNLOCK:
UNLOCK INV, INV.NO
```

Notes

1. The LOCK and UNLOCK statements have no effect unless used on a local area network. Therefore an application may be written for a LAN environment and still run on a single user system as well.

2. Even if a record has not been UNLOCKed, there is nothing preventing a programmer from ignoring the lock placed on a record. This practice is not recommended. All users should abide by the record-locking logic to ensure the highest data integrity.

3. See the LOCK statement and refer to Chapter 11.

WRITE
(WRITES TO A RECORD)

Purpose

WRITE is used to update or create a record in a file which has been opened with an OPEN statement.

Syntax

WRITE exp TO file.var, rec.id
            or
WRITE exp ON file.var, rec.id

exp is the expression which will replace the contents of the record or become the new record.

file.var is the variable name given to the file in an OPEN statement.

rec.id is the ID of the record to be replaced or created.

Rules

1. The file must have been previously opened and assigned to a variable using an OPEN statement.

2. If no record with the ID of rec.id exists, one will be created.

Examples

```
OPEN ", "INVOICES" TO INV ELSE STOP
INPUT INV.NO
READ RECORD FROM INV,INV.NO THEN
  RECORD<5>="UPDATED"
END ELSE
  INPUT NAME
  INPUT ADDRESS
  RECORD<1>=NAME
  RECORD<2>=ADDRESS
END
WRITE RECORD TO INV, INV.NO
```

This program tries to read a record in the INVOICES file. If the record exists then it is updated and written back to disk. If the record is new, new data is entered and the record is filed.

Notes

1. If there are any trailing null field marks in the record, these are not deleted by the WRITE statement. In the above example, if RECORD=SMITH■123 MAIN■HOUSTON■■■, the trailing field marks would not be deleted by the WRITE statement.

WRITEV
(WRITES TO A SPECIFIED FIELD WITHIN A RECORD)

Purpose

WRITEV is used to update a specified field within a record.

Syntax

WRITEV exp TO file.var, rec.id, field#
        or
WRITEV exp ON file.var, rec.id, field#

exp is the value to be inserted into the field

file.var is the variable name assigned to the file in an OPEN statement.

rec.id is the ID of the record.

field# is the FMC number of the field to be updated.

Rules

1. The file must have been previously opened with an OPEN statement.

2. WRITEV will replace the existing value of the specified record with the value of **exp**. If there is no record with the ID of **rec.id**, one will be created and the specified field number will be assigned the value of **exp**.

Examples

```
OPEN ", "INVOICES" TO INV ELSE STOP
INPUT ID
READV AMOUNT FROM INV, ID, 3 ELSE STOP
WRITEV AMOUNT*2 TO INV, ID, 3
```

This program will prompt for the record ID containing the invoice amount that needs to be updated and then write the updated amount back to the record.

R/BASIC FUNCTIONS

INTRODUCTION

R/BASIC has more than 60 pre-defined functions which you can use in your programs. A function is a defined operation, usually a mathematical or string operation, which operates upon one or more values and returns a final value. The generic syntax for a function is:

function.name(arg1,arg2,...)

where

function.name is the name of the function.

arg1,arg2,... are the arguments which are operated upon by the function. Several of the R/BASIC functions do not allow any arguments, but the parentheses are always shown even if they are empty so that R/BASIC will know that **function.name** is a function and not a variable.

There is one exception to this generic syntax, the bracket function, which is the first one listed in this section.

Functions are used in statements just like other expressions. For example, SQRT is a function which requires a single argument and evaluates to the square root of that argument. For example:

PRINT SQRT(9)

would print: **3**

Unless stated otherwise, the arguments in a function can be any valid expression: a literal string, a variable, mathematical operation, etc.

For example:

X = 9
PRINT SQRT(X)

would also print: **3**

Functions are also recursive. You can use the same function as its own argument without losing the calculated value at each recursive level.

X = 81
PRINT SQRT(X)
PRINT SQRT(SQRT(X))

would print: **9**
               3

[ ]

(EXTRACTS A SUB-STRING)

Purpose

The bracket function [ ] extracts a sub-string from a variable.

Syntax

var[start.position,length]

var is the variable string from which the sub-string is extracted.

start.position is the character position in the string where the extraction starts.

length is the length of the extracted substring.

Rules

1. If start.position is a negative number, the start position is that many characters from the end of the string.

2. If the length is a negative number, the characters are extracted from right to left, (and thus will appear in reverse order).

3. A special case of the length expression consists of the letter B or F followed by a second letter. An "F" causes the function to extract from the starting position forward until a character is found which matches the character following the "F". The position where it is found is assigned to the value of COL2(), another function to be discussed later. A "B" causes the function to search backwards until it finds a character matching the character following the "B", and then extracts up to the start.position. The position where this is found is assigned to COL1().

Examples

Expression	Evaluates to
A =	"THIS IS A LONG STRING"
A[6,9]	IS A LONG
A[-3,2]	IN
A[14,-4]	GNOL
A[3,"FL"]	IS IS A
A[14,"BH"]	IS IS A LONG

@
(POSITIONS VIDEO CURSOR)

Purpose

The @ function positions the cursor on the screen in conjunction with a print statement.

Syntax

@(column,<row>)

column is column number.

row is row number.

Rules

1. If the row is left out, the cursor will be positioned to the indicated column of the current row.

2. Special cursor controls:
   @(-1) clears screen
   @(-2) sends cursor to upper left corner
   @(-3) clears from current position to end of
         screen
   @(-4) clears to end of current line

Examples

PRINT @(-1):@(15,10):"Please wait ...."

This PRINT statement will clear the screen and then print a message starting at column 15, row 10.

Notes

1. The screen rows run from 0 to 24, while the columns are numbered from 0 to 79. Thus, the upper left corner of the screen is (0,0) while the lower right corner is (79,25).

ABS
(ABSOLUTE VALUE)

Purpose

ABS always returns the absolute value of the expression between the parentheses.

Syntax

ABS(expression)

Examples

Statement	Evaluates to
ABS(40)	40
ABS(-40)	40

Notes

1. The absolute value of a number is its distance from 0 on the number line. Thus the absolute value of a number is never negative.

ALPHA
(ALPHABETIC CHARACTERS ONLY)

Purpose

ALPHA returns a 1 (true) if the argument contains only alphabetic characters and returns 0 (false) if it contains any other characters.

Syntax

ALPHA(exp)

Examples

Expression	Evaluates to
ALPHA("DIXIE")	1
ALPHA("TST4")	0
VAR=123	
ALPHA(VAR)	0

Notes

1. ALPHA is the opposite of the NUM function.

ATAN
(ARCTANGENT)

Purpose

ATAN returns the arctangent of the argument in degrees.

Syntax

ATAN(tangent)

Examples

Statement	Evaluates to
Y=ATAN(-5)	-78.6901
Y=ATAN(-1)	-45.0000
Y=ATAN(0)	0
Y=ATAN(1)	45.0000
Y=ATAN(3)	71.5651

BITAND, BITOR, BITXOR, BITNOT
(BITWISE OPERATIONS)

Purpose

The BIT functions perform bit-wise logical operations.

Syntax

BITAND(exp1,exp2)
BITOR(exp1,exp2)
BITXOR(exp1,exp2)
BITNOT(exp1)

Rules

1. These functions perform logical operations based on the binary representation of numbers. Thus BITNOT(31) = BITNOT(00011111) = 11100000 = 224 and BITAND(6,3) = BITAND(0110,0011) = 0010 = 2.

Examples

The following table demonstrates the result of the BIT functions operating on two different expressions.

EXP1	EXP2	BITAND	BITOR	BITXOR
0	0	0	0	0
1	0	0	1	1
1	1	1	1	0
5	1	1	5	4
63	31	31	63	32

Consider the last example. If we convert decimal 63 and decimal 31 into their binary notation we get:

63 111111
31 011111

Apply the rules given in the above table, comparing each corresponding bit, and you can understand the results of this last example in the table. The BITXOR may not be as obvious. The BITXOR calculates a 1 only if two bits are diferent. Thus, BITXOR(63,31) is 100000, or decimal 32.

Notes

1. These functions are particularly useful with the OUT statement and the INP function.

CALCULATE
(CALCULATES FIELD VALUE)

Purpose

The CALCULATE function returns the value of a data field when the argument is the dictionary name for that field.

Syntax

CALCULATE(exp)

exp is any expression that is equal to a valid dictionary record ID.

Rules

1. If the argument is an actual dictionary name, you must also enclose it in quotes, as in CALCULATE("COMPANY").

2. The CALCULATE function may be used in place of the { } functions for returning the value of a data field in the current record.

3. If the argument of the CALCULATE function is a *variable* that evaluates to a dictionary name, rather than the actual name itself, you *must* use the CALCULATE function instead of the { } function. For example,
> **X="CUST.NAME"**
> **PRINT CALCULATE(X)**

In this example you could not have opted to use {X}.

4. The dictionary of the data file must have been previously OPENed to the variable @DICT, and the current record must be assigned to the variable @RECORD. Otherwise R/BASIC will not know how to evaluate the data field, and either unexpected results will occur or a not-too-meaningful error message could be displayed.

5. When the dictionary item is calculated, the output conversion, display format, and column heading are returned in the system variables @CONV, @FORMAT, and @HEADER respectively. You may use these variables in R/BASIC PRINT statements.

Examples

```
OPEN "","CUSTOMERS",TO CUST ELSE STOP
OPEN "DICT","CUSTOMERS" TO @DICT ELSE STOP
PERFORM "SELECT CUSTOMERS WITH ST = 'MA'"
X="PHONE"
LOOP
  READNEXT @ID ELSE STOP
  READ @RECORD FROM CUST,@ID ELSE STOP
  PRINT @ID,CALCULATE("COMPANY") @FORMAT:"   "
  PRINT CALCULATE(X) @FORMAT:"   "
  PRINT {INVOICE.AMT} @CONV
REPEAT
```

CHAR
(CONVERTS NUMBER TO ASCII CHARACTER)

Purpose

CHAR converts a number to its corresponding ASCII character.

Syntax

CHAR(expression)

Rules

1. The expression must evaluate to an integer between 0 and 255. Values outside that range will be adjusted to be within the range, e.g, CHAR(260) =CHAR(4).

Examples

Statement	Evaluates to
Y=CHAR(37)	%
Y=CHAR(72)	H
Y=CHAR(254)	(field marker)
X=27	
Y=CHAR(X)	ESCape

COL1()
COL2()
(COLUMN POSITIONS)

Purpose

These functions can be used after the FIELD and [] functions to define the beginning and ending position of the substring found by the FIELD and [] functions.

Syntax

COL1()
COL2()

Notice that these two functions will not operate on an argument. Instead, they are assigned their values by two other system functions.

Examples

Statement	Evaluates to
X = FIELD("999/888/777","/",2)	
PRINT X	888
Y=COL1()	4
Y=COL2()	8
S = "THIS IS A LONG STRING"	
Y = S[14,"BH"]	IS IS A LONG
Y=COL1()	2
Y=COL2()	15

COS/SIN
(TRIGONOMETRIC COSINE/SINE)

Purpose

COS and SIN return the trigonometric cosine or sine of the argument.

Syntax

COS(expression)
SIN(expression)

The expression must evaluate to an angle between 0 and 360. Values outside this range are adjusted before calculation of the functions, e.g. SIN(405) = SIN (45).

Examples

Statement	Evaluates to
Y=SIN(0)	0
Y=SIN(45)	.7071
Y=SIN(90)	1
Y=COS(0)	1
Y=COS(45)	.7071
Y=COS(90)	0

Notes

1. Since the arguments must be in degrees of an angle, you will have to convert radians to degrees. This conversion is: degrees = radians * 180 / 3.14159 degrees.

COUNT
(COUNTS OCCURRENCES OF A STRING)

Purpose

COUNT returns number of times a string appears in another string.

Syntax

COUNT(string,sub.string)

string is the string which will be searched.

sub.string is the string whose occurrences will be counted

Rules

1. If the sub.string is null, the function returns the total number of characters in the first string.

2. During the scan of the first string, each character is matched to the substring defined in the second expression only once.

Examples

Statements	Evaluates to
Y=COUNT("753-7594-4759","75")	3
Y=COUNT("SSSSSSSS","SS")	4

DATE
(CURRENT SYSTEM DATE)

Purpose

returns the current system date of your computer. The value returned is the number of days since December 31, 1967 (the method Revelation uses to store date information). To convert to a useful display date, see OCONV and TIMEDATE() functions.

Syntax

DATE()

Examples

Date	Internal Representation
December 31,1967	0
July 1, 1979	4200

DCOUNT
(COUNTS OCCURENCES OF SUBSTRING IN A STRING)

Purpose

See COUNT function

DELETE
(DELETES AN ELEMENT FROM A DYNAMIC ARRAY)

Purpose

DELETE returns a dynamic array with one element deleted.
See Chapter 3 for an explanation of dynamic arrays.

Syntax

DELETE(exp, field#, value#, subvalue#)

exp designates the dynamic array to to searched.

The second,third,and fourth expressions are the delimiter expressions. Their respective numeric values determine whether the data to be deleted is a field, value, or sub-value.

Rules

1. If the subvalue# is non-zero, then the specified subvalue from the value and field is deleted. If the subvalue# is zero, the specified value from the field is deleted. If both the subvalue and value expressions are zero, the specified field is deleted.

2. There is no 0th field, value, or subvalue. Therefore, the function interprets DELETE(A,0,0,2) as DELETE(A,1,1,2).

3. The corresponding character mark is automatically deleted.

Examples

Statement	Evaluates to
Y=DELETE(A,2,3,4)	deletes a sub-value
Y=DELETE(A,2,3,0)	deletes a value
Y=DELETE(A,3,0,0)	deletes a field

DIR
(RETURNS INFORMATION ON A DOS FILE)

Purpose

DIR returns a dynamic array whose fields are the file size, creation date, and creation time.

Syntax

DIR("dos.name")

dos.name is the DOS name of a file on the system medium; e.g. ROS10000.010

Examples

```
Y=DIR("REV.EXE")
PRINT Y<1>:SPACE(3):
PRINT OCONV(Y<2>,"D"):SPACE(3):
PRINT OCONV(Y<3>,"MTH")
```

This would print **76158   10 AUG 86   10:43AM**.

DRIVE()
(CURRENT DRIVE)

Purpose

DRIVE( ) returns the full DOS path name of the default drive and directory.

Syntax

DRIVE()

Examples

Statement	Evaluates to
Y=DRIVE()	C:\REV\

EXP
(NATURAL EXPONENT)

Purpose

EXP calculates the mathematical base "e" raised the the power indicated in the argument.

Syntax

EXP(expression)

Examples

Function	Evaluates to
EXP(1)	2.718
EXP(2)	7.389

Notes

1. If the expression evaluates to zero or less, an error message is displayed.

2. The EXP function is the inverse of LN function.

EXTRACT
(EXTRACTS AN ELEMENT FROM A DYNAMIC ARRAY)

Purpose

EXTRACT extracts an element from a dynamic array. See Chapter 3 for an explanation of dynamic arrays.

Syntax

EXTRACT(exp, field#, value#, subvalue#)

exp is the dynamic array.

The next three arguments determine which element to extract.

Rules

1. If the subvalue# is non-zero, then the specified subvalue from the specified value and field is extracted. If the subvalue# is zero, the specified value from the specified field is extracted. If both the subvalue and value expressions are zero, the specified field is extracted.

2. There is no 0th field, value, or subvalue; therefore the function interprets EXTRACT(A,0,0,2) as EXTRACT(A,1,1,2).

Examples

Statement	Evaluates to
Y=EXTRACT(A,2,3,4)	extracts a sub-value
Y=EXTRACT(B,1,2,0)	extracts a value
Y=EXTRACT(C,5,0,0)	extracts a field

Notes

1. There is a dynamic string operator which accomplishes the same effect as the EXTRACT function. It is the angle bracket < > which is discussed in detail in Chapter 12. The above examples could have been written:

    Y=A<2,3,4>
    Y=B<1,2>
    Y=C<5>

FIELD
(SUBSTRING DELIMITER SEARCH)

Purpose

FIELD returns a substring from a string expression. The function counts the occurrences of a delimiter and returns the element just prior to the specified occurrence of that delimiter.

Syntax

FIELD(exp, delimiter, occurrence, <fields>)

exp is the string being searched.

delimiter is the character which delimits the elements of the string.

occurrence is the number of occurrences of the delimiter before the function extracts an element. The element extracted is the one just prior to the number entered here.

fields is an optional parameter that specifies the number of successive fields after the specified occurrence of the delimiter that are to be extracted with the sub-string.

Rules

1. If the specified delimiter does not exist in the string expression, the entire string is returned if the first occurrence of the delimiter was specified. If any other occurrence was specified, and either the delimiter or the specified occurrence do not exist, a null value is returned.

Examples

Statement	Evaluates to
A = FIELD("#25#35#76#92","#",3)	35
Y=COL1()	4
Y=COL2()	7
B=FIELD("NAJJK","$",3)	JJK
F=FIELD("NAJJK","$",5)	""
C=FIELD("NAJJK","#",1)	NAJJK
D=FIELD("NAJJK$HC","$",1,2)	N$A

Notes

1. See the COL1() and COL2() functions. These functions will hold the absolute string position of the delimiters directly preceding and following the extracted substring.

FIELDSTORE
(REPLACES, DELETES, INSERTS SUBSTRINGS)

Purpose

FIELDSTORE replaces, deletes, or inserts a specified substring into another string expression. It defines a delimiter to divide the string expression into elements and specifies the location and operation to be performed on the string.

Syntax

FIELDSTORE(exp,delimiter,n,x,substring)

exp is the string expression upon which the operations will be conducted.

delimiter is the character which separates the elements.

n is the number of the element where the operation takes place.

x evaluates to a number and determines what operation will occur. A positive x will replace the next x elements of exp with the first x elements of the substring. A negative x will delete the next x elements of exp and insert the entire substring. X equal to 0 will not delete any elements but will insert the substring at the n position.

Examples

Function	Evaluates to
X = "415-384-8735" FIELDSTORE(X,"-",2,1,392)	415-392-8735
X = "415-384-8735" FIELDSTORE(X,"-",1,-2,554)	554-8735

```
X = "415-384-8735"
FIELDSTORE(X,"-",3,0,"6688")          415-384-6688-8735
```

FMT
(OUTPUT FORMAT)

Purpose

FMT converts an expression into another display format. It is useful for changing the way you want a value displayed.

Syntax

FMT(exp,jms)
            or
exp jms

exp is the expression to be converted.

j is the justification code:
> L left justification
> R right justification
> C center justification
> T text justification

m is a mask, or template. The "#" symbol, or a combination of "#" characters with other characters can be used as a pattern template. If more than one "#" is used in the template, the "#"s will be replaced with the characters in the expression to be converted while the other characters in the mask will be left as is.

s is size. If the mask character is a single "#", the size character will determine the size of the resulting expression.

Rules

1. The format function is implied every time you use an expression in an R/BASIC statement, all you need to do is

include the format description after the expression. For
example:

    PRINT FMT(TEST,L#7)
    PRINT TEST "L#7"

mean the same thing.

Examples

Function	Evaluates to
X = "123456789"	
FMT(X,L#3)	"123"
FMT(X,R#3)	"789"
FMT(X,L###-##-####)	"123-45-6789"
X = "123"	
FMT(X,L#5)	"123 "
FMT(X,R#5)	" 123"

GETBREAK()
(STATUS OF BREAK KEY)

Purpose

GETBREAK returns the status of the break key, 1 is on, 0 is off
(see BREAK KEY statement).

Syntax

GETBREAK()

GETECHO()
(ECHO STATUS)

Purpose

GETECHO returns the status of ECHO; 1 = on, 0 = off (see ECHO statement).

Syntax

GETECHO()

GETPRINTER()
(PRINTER STATUS)

Purpose

GETPRINTER returns the status of the printer; 1 = on, 0 = off (see PRINTER statement).

Syntax

GETPRINTER()

GETPROMPT()
(CURRENT PROMPT CHARACTER)

Purpose

GETPROMPT returns the current prompt character.

Syntax

GETPROMPT()

HASH
(HASHING FUNCTION TO DETERMINE ROS FILE GROUP)

Purpose

HASH returns the group number that a record in a file with the ROS file structure will "hash" into. (See Appendix V ROS and LINK File Structures).

Syntax

HASH(rec.id,modulo,offset)

rec.id is the record key of the record being hashed.

modulo is the modulo of the file.

offset should always be 1.

Notes

1. The PROG file on the Utilities diskette contains a record that can be compiled and run to determine the group that a record from a LINK file will hash into. See LINKHASH.TEST.

ICONV
(INPUT CONVERSION)

Purpose

ICONV converts an expression to an internal format for storage in the computer. Numeric data is more efficiently stored and operated upon if stored as whole integers (no decimal points). Also, date and time entries must be converted to integer data if comparisons or mathematical operations are to be made with them. These types of data are converted into an internal system representation using the ICONV function and converted back for output display with the OCONV function.

Syntax

ICONV(exp,conv.code)

exp is the input expression which is getting converted.

conv.code is one of four types of codes:
  Masked Decimal (numeric data)
  Date
  Time
  Hex (converts hexadecimal to decimal ASCII character.)

Rules

1. The conversion codes are enclosed in quotation marks unless given as a variable.

2. Several conversion codes can be given, separated by commas.

3. The conversion formats have a number of parameters. Many of the parameters only apply to the output conversion. However, to make your programming consistent, you can use those other parameters with your input conversions as well and they will have no effect.

4. Date conversions store dates as a number representing the number of days since Dec 31, 1967. Time conversions store time as the number of seconds since midnight. Both Time and Date input conversion functions recognize a variety of date and time display conventions.

5. The Masked Decimal conversion syntax is:

MDn<f><,><$><m><P><Z><T><xc>

Note: only the n, and f parameters apply to input conversions.

  n is the number of decimal point places (0-9) which are read on input or displayed on output. Data with more than this number of decimal points is truncated.

f is a scaling factor; it moves the decimal point f places to the right on input and f places to the left on output. For example, an f of 2 on input would convert 109.56 to 10956; an f of 2 on output would convert 10956 to 109.56. If f is not given, it is assumed to be the same as n, which is mandatory.

, inserts commas to separate thousands.

$ gives a $ prefix.

m is one of four characters to indicate a negative number. "-" uses a minus sign prefix, "<" places the number in angle brackets, "C" uses a "CR" suffix, and "D" uses a "DB" suffix.

P specifies no scaling for input data containing a decimal point.

Z outputs a value of zero as null.

T truncates rather than rounds data.

xc places a leading marker for reserved spaces not taken up by data. "x" is the number of spaces to reserve and "c" is the character used as a marker.

6. The syntax for the Date conversion is:

D<y><c><E>

Note that only the D and y apply to input conversions.

D indicates it is a Date conversion.

y indicates the number of digits for the year; 0 would display no year. Default is 4.

c is a character to be used to separate the day, month, and year. If c is left out the month will be displayed as a three letter abbreviation; with a character entered for c, month will be displayed as a two digit number.

E invokes the European conversion when the date is displayed as all numbers (Europeans use day/month/year instead of month/day/year. (Note: there must be a space or some other character between the D and E date conversions, as in ICONV(DATA,"D E")).

7. The syntax for the Time conversion is:

MT<H><S><c>

Note: the H, S, and c parameters only apply to output conversion.

MT indicates a Time conversion

H specifies 12 hour format with A.M. and P.M. displayed. The default is the 24 hour clock.

S specifies seconds are to be displayed.

c is the character used to separate hours, minutes, and seconds. Colons are the default.

8. The syntax for Hex conversion code is:

HEX (Hex to ASCII character)
 or
MX (Hex to decimal)

characters for input must be 0-9, A-F. The HEX conversion converts the numeric data from base 16 into its equivalent decimal values or ASCII characters.

Examples

Function	Evaluates to
ICONV(103.26,"MD2")	10326
ICONV(103.26,"MD1")	1033
ICONV(103.26,"MD12")	10330
ICONV("1 DEC 82","D")	5449
ICONV("12/01/82","D")	5449
ICONV("01/12/82","D E")	5449
ICONV("2","MT")	7200
ICONV("2:01","MT")	7260
ICONV("2:01:15","MT")	7275
ICONV("2/01/15","MT")	7275
ICONV("2:01AM","MT")	7260
ICONV("2A","HEX")	*
ICONV("2A","MX")	42

Notes

1. Normally Masked Decimal conversions will have an "n" value of however many decimal places your input data will have (e.g. 2 for money), and no "f" value so that the scaling will be the same (to get rid of the decimal points). Furthermore, both input and output conversions should be identical so that you will be sure that the data going out of the system is the same as what went in.

INDEX
(LOCATES POSITION OF SPECIFIED OCCURRENCE OF A SUBSTRING)

Purpose

INDEX locates within a string the specified occurrence of a substring and returns the column number where that occurrence starts.

Syntax

INDEX(string,substring,occurrence)

string is the literal string to be searched.

substring is the substring being located.

occurrence is which occurrence of the substring is being located.

Rules

1. If the indicated occurrence is not found, or if the substring does not exist, a 0 is returned.

Examples

Statement	Evaluates to
STR = "RECA1,TA1DYA1XA1" INDEX(STR,"A1",3)	12

INMAT()
(MODULUS OR MATRIX ELEMENT NUMBER)

Purpose

INMAT() does not have any arguments. The value of INMAT is set every time a MATREAD or OPEN statement is executed. The OPEN statement sets the value to the modulus of the file. The MATREAD statement sets the value to the number of elements read into the matrix.

Syntax

INMAT()

INP
(INPUT FROM COMMUNICATIONS PORT)

Purpose

INP accepts a value from a specified communications port.

Syntax

INP(port)

port is a number between 0 and 65535 indicating the
communications port where incoming data is to be
received.

Examples

```
PORT=2
LOOP WHILE INP(PORT)
  PRINT INP(PORT)
REPEAT
```

Notes

1. The incoming value will be a decimal number between 0 and
255.

2. This function is often used in conjunction with the OUT
statement.

INSERT
(INSERTS AN ELEMENT INTO A DYNAMIC ARRAY)

Purpose

INSERT returns a dynamic array with an element inserted either
as a field, a value, or a sub-value. See Chapter 3 for an
explanation of dynamic arrays.

Syntax

INSERT(exp, field#, value#, subvalue#, element)

exp is the dynamic array which will have the element inserted.

field#, value#, subvalue# determine where the element will be inserted.

element is the element which will be inserted.

Rules

1. The element is inserted at the indicated position with the corresponding character marker automatically inserted.

2. There is no 0 field, value, or subvalue; therefore the function interprets INSERT(A,0,0,2) as INSERT(A,1,1,2).

Examples

```
STR=""
A=INSERT(A,2,0,0,"ONE")          A=■ONE
A=INSERT(A,1,2,0,"TWO")          A=²TWO■ONE
A=INSERT(A,3,2,0,"THREE")        A=²TWO■ONE■²THREE
```

Notes

1. There is a dynamic string operator which can be used to add elements to the end of a dynamic array. It is the angle bracket < > which is discussed in detail in Chapter 12. A<-1> will add another field to the end of the dynamic array, while A<2,-1> will add another value to the second field of the dynamic array.

INT
(INTEGER)

Purpose

The INT function returns an integer number (the number is truncated, not rounded).

Syntax

INT(expression)

Examples

Statement	Evaluates to
Y=INT(34.67)	34
Y=INT(-34.67)	-35
X=104.21	
Y=INT(X)	104

Notes

1. All truncations are towards minus infinity, that is, if you view a number as being on a number line, all truncations are to the closest digit to the number's right.

INVERT
(INVERTS THE ASCII VALUE OF CHARACTERS IN A STRING)

Purpose

INVERT returns the inverted ASCII character for each character in a string. The inverted character for ASCII CHAR(X) is ASCII CHAR(255-X)

Syntax

INVERT(string)

string is any string of ASCII characters.

Examples

Statement	Evaluates to
Y=SEQ(1)	49
X=SEQ(INVERT(1))	206

LEN
(STRING LENGTH)

Purpose

LEN returns the number of characters in a string. Trailing blanks are counted.

Syntax

LEN(string.expression)

Examples

Statement	Evaluates to
A = "1234.5"	
B = "WORLD SERIES"	
C = "TOP "	
LEN(A)	6
LEN(B)	12
LEN(C)	6

LN
(NATURAL LOG)

Purpose

LN returns the natural logarithm of a number to the base 'e'. Base 'e' is approximately 2.71828.

Syntax

LN(expression)

Examples

Function	Evaluates to
LN(2.71828)	2
LN(20)	2.9845

MATUNPARSE
(CONVERTS A MATRIX INTO A DYNAMIC ARRAY)

Purpose

MATUNPARSE returns a dynamic array whose fields are the values from a one dimensional matrix.

Syntax

MATUNPARSE(mat)

mat is the matrix variable whose values you wish to assign to a dynamic array.

Examples

```
DIM X(5), Y(5)
FOR COUNT=1 TO 5
  X(COUNT)= COUNT*2
NEXT COUNT
ARRAY= MATUNPARSE(X)
PRINT "FROM MATRIX TO DYNAMIC ARRAY: ":ARRAY
PRINT
MATPARSE ARRAY INTO Y
PRINT "FROM DYNAMIC ARRAY TO MATRIX: ":
PRINT Y(1):' ':Y(3):' ':Y(5)
```

would print:

FROM MATRIX TO DYNAMIC ARRAY: 2 4 6 8 10

FROM DYNAMIC ARRAY TO MATRIX: 2 6 10

Notes

1. The matrix must have been previously DIMensioned.

2. Refer to the R/BASIC statement MATPARSE for converting a dynamic array to a matrix.

MOD
(MODULO OR REMAINDER)

Purpose

MOD returns the modulo (remainder) of two numbers. The modulo is the mathematical remainder after one integer is divided into another. For example, if you had 47 lines of text and were printing them 6 lines per page, the MOD function could calculate that you would have 5 lines left over on the last page.

Syntax

MOD(num1,num2)

num1 is the dividend.

num2, as the divisor, is divided into num1 to get the remainder.

Rules

1. MOD is calculated with the following formula:

MOD(num1,num2) = num1-(INT(num1/num2)*num2)

where the INT function truncates the expression num1/num2.

Examples

Statement	Evaluates to
Y=MOD(16,6)	4

NEG
(ARITHMETICAL INVERSE)

Purpose

NEG returns the arithmetical inverse of its argument.

Syntax

NEG(expression)

Examples

Statement	Evaluates to
NEG(45)	-45
NEG(-5)	5

Notes

1. The specified expression must contain all numeric data, with the exception of the character "-".

NOT
(TESTS FOR ZERO VALUE)

Purpose

NOT compares the argument to zero and returns a value of 1 (true) if it is zero, and returns a value of 0 (false) if it is anything else. NOT is the logical inverse of the specified expression.

Syntax

NOT(expression)

Examples

Statement	Evaluates to
Y=NOT(243-155)	0
Y=NOT(5 AND 0)	1

NUM
(TESTS FOR NUMERIC STRING)

Purpose

NUM returns a value of 1 (true) if the argument consists solely of numeric characters (which includes decimal points). A value of 0 (false) is returned if the argument contains any non-numeric characters.

Syntax

NUM(expression)

Examples

Statement	Evaluates to
NUM("483.56")	1
NUM("T56")	0

OCONV
(OUTPUT CONVERSION)

Purpose

OCONV converts an expression from internal format as it is stored on the disk to an output display format. Numeric data is more efficiently stored and operated upon if it is stored as whole integers (no decimal points). Also, date and time entries must be converted to integer data if comparisons or mathematical operations are to be made with them. These types of data are converted into internal system representation using the ICONV function and converted back for output display with the OCONV function.

Syntax

OCONV(exp, conv.code)

exp is the input expression which is getting converted.

conv.code is one of five types of codes:
    Masked Decimal (numeric data)
    Date
    Time
    Hex (converts hexadecimal to decimal)
    Scientific Notation

Rules

1. The conversion codes are put in quotation marks unless given as a variable.

2. Several conversion codes can be given, separated by commas.

3. The conversion formats have a number of parameters, but many of the parameters only apply to the output conversion. However, to make your programming consistent, you can use those other parameters with your input conversions as well .

4. Date conversions store dates as the number of days since Dec. 31, 1967. Time conversions store time as the number of seconds since midnight. Both Time and Date input conversion functions recognize a variety of date and time display conventions.

5. The Masked Decimal syntax is:

   MDn<f><,><$><m><P><Z><T><xc>

   Note: only the n and f parameters apply to input conversions.

   n is the number of decimal point places (0-9) which are read at input or displayed on output. Data with more than this many decimal places is rounded off.

   f is a scaling factor; it moves the decimal point f places to the right on input and f places to the left on output. For example, an f of 2 on input would convert 109.56 to 10956; an f of 2 on output would convert 10956 to 109.56. If f is not given, it is assumed to be the same as n, which is mandatory.

   , inserts commas to separate thousands.

   $ gives a $ prefix.

m is one of four characters to indicate a negative
 number. "-" uses a minus sign prefix, "<" puts
 the number in angle brackets, "C" puts a "CR"
 suffix, and "D" puts a "DB" suffix.

P specifies no scaling for input data containing a decimal
 point.

Z outputs a value of zero as null.

T truncates rather than rounds data.

xc places a leading marker for reserved spaces not taken
 up by data. "x" is the number of spaces to
 reserve and "c" is the character to use as
 marker.

6. The syntax for the Date conversion is:

D<y><c><E>

Note that only the D and y apply to input conversions.

D indicates it is a Date conversion.

y indicates the number of digits for the year; 0 would
 display no year. Default is **4**.

c is a character to be used to separate the day, month,
 and year. If c is left out the month will be
 displayed as a three letter abbreviation; with a
 character entered for c, month will be displayed
 as a two digit number.

E invokes the European conversion when the date is
 displayed as all numbers (Europeans use
 day/month/year instead of month/day/year.
 (Note: there must be a space or some other
 character between the D and E date
 conversions, as in ICONV(DATA,"D E")).

7. The syntax for the Time conversion is:

MT<H><S><c>

Note: the H, S, and c parameters only apply to output conversion.

MT indicates a Time conversion

H specifies 12 hour format with A.M. and P.M. displayed. The default is the 24 hour clock.

S specifies seconds are to be displayed.

c is the character used to separate hours, minutes, and seconds. Colons are the default.

8. The syntax for Hex conversion code is:

HEX (ASCII character to hexadecimal)
or
MX (decimal to hexadecimal)

The conversion will proceed from left to right to the end of the string.

9. The syntax for scientific notation is

MS

Examples

Function	Evaluates to
OCONV(10326,"MD2")	103.26
OCONV(10326,"MD1")	1032.6
OCONV(10326,"MD12")	103.3
OCONV(10326,"MD0,$")	$10,326
OCONV(10326,"MD2,$C")	$103.26CR
OCONV(103.26,"MD2")	1.03
OCONV(10326,"MD2,9*")	***103.26

OCONV(5449,"D")	1 DEC, 1982
OCONV(5449,"D2")	1 DEC, 82
OCONV(5449,"D/")	12/1/1982
OCONV(5449,"D/2")	12/1/82
OCONV(5449,"D/E")	1/12/1982
OCONV(43260,"MT")	12:01
OCONV(43260,"MTH")	12:01PM
OCONV(43260,"MTS")	12:01:00
OCONV(43260,"MTH/")	12/01PM
OCONV("ANT","HEX")	414E54
OCONV(19,"HEX")	3139
OCONV(19,"MX")	13
OCONV(35000,"MS")	3.500000E+04
OCONV(.00523,"MS")	5.230000E-03

Notes

1. Normally Masked Decimal conversions will have an "n" value of however many decimal places your input data will have (e.g. 2 for money), and no "f" value so that the scaling will be the same (to get rid of the decimal points). Furthermore, both input and output conversions are identical so that you will be sure that the data going out of the system is the same as what went in.

PWR
(RAISES A NUMBER TO A POWER)

Purpose

PWR returns the value of raising the first numeric argument to the power of the second argument.

Syntax

PWR(base,power)

Examples

Statement	Evaluates to
Y=PWR(2,5)	32

QUOTE
(PLACES QUOTATION MARKS)

Purpose

QUOTE returns the argument surrounded by double quotation marks. This function helps make your code more readable.

Syntax

QUOTE(expression)

Examples

```
TITLE="The Title of this Book is "
TITLE:=QUOTE('Revelation Revealed')
PRINT TITLE
```

This routine would result in the following display:

The Title of this Book is "Revelation Revealed".

REPLACE
(REPLACES AN ELEMENT IN A DYNAMIC ARRAY)

Purpose

REPLACE returns a dynamic array with an element replaced. See Chapter 3 for an explanation of dynamic arrays.

Syntax

REPLACE(exp, field#, value#, subvalue#, element)

exp is the starting dynamic array.

field#, value#, subvalue# determine where the element will be replaced.

element is the new data to replace the old value. The element to replace is either a field, value, or subvalue.

Rules

1. The element is replaced at the indicated position and given the corresponding character marker.

2. There is no 0th field, value, or subvalue. Therefore, the function interprets REPLACE(A,0,0,2) as REPLACE(A,1,1,2).

Examples

```
A="²TWO■ONE■²THREE"
A=REPLACE(A,2,0,0,"ON")     A="²TWO■ON■²THREE"
A=REPLACE(A,1,2,0,"TO")     A="²TO■ON■²THREE"
A=REPLACE(A,3,2,0,"TREE")   A="²TO■ON■²TREE"
```

Notes

1. There is a dynamic string operator which accomplishes the same effect as the REPLACE function. It is the angle bracket < > which is discussed in detail in Chapter 12. The above examples could have been written:

```
A<2,0,0>="ON"
A<1,2,0>="TO"
A<3,2,0>="TREE"
```

RND
(RANDOM NUMBER)

Purpose

RND returns a random number between 0 and n-1, where n is the numeric argument passed to the RND function.

Syntax

RND(expression)

Examples

Y=RND(53) would yield an integer between 0 and 52.

Notes

1. The RND function is a very simple random number generator (in fact, not very random). The sequence of numbers will always be the same for a given argument. Thus, RND(50) always returns values between 0 and 49 in the following order: 8,9,13,36,....

To create a more random list each time RND(50) is used, you could use the INITRND statement which resets the random number generator. RND(50) will produce a completely different set of numbers for each different value of INITRND. Thus,

INITRND 1

will cause RND(50) to generate numbers in the following order: 33,9,38,36,....

2. Negative expressions passed to the function will result in a negative random number.

SEQ
(ASCII CHARACTER TO NUMBER)

Purpose

SEQ returns a number corresponding to the ASCII character passed as the argument to the function.

Syntax

SEQ(character)

Rules

1. SEQ only evaluates one character at a time. Thus if you pass more than one character, SEQ will only return the numeric conversion for the first character in the argument.

Examples

Statement	Evaluates to
SEQ("B")	66
SEQ("$")	36

Notes

1. SEQ and CHAR are inverse functions.

SERIAL
(REVELATION SERIAL NUMBER)

Purpose

. SERIAL returns the Revelation serial number.

Syntax

SERIAL()

Notes

1. The serial function can be used in an R/BASIC program to limit the use of an application program to a specific serial numbered copy of Revelation.

SPACE
(BLANK SPACES)

Purpose

SPACE generates a string value that contains the number of blank spaces indicated in the argument.

Syntax

SPACE(expression)

Examples

PRINT "ENTER":SPACE(5):"HERE"

Evaluates to:

ENTER   HERE

Notes

1. This function is used mainly to format reports.

SIN
(TRIGINOMETRIC SINE)

Purpose

SIN returns the triginometric sine of an angle.

Syntax

SIN(angle.expression)

angle.expression is an angle in degrees.

Notes

1. See the COS function for additional details.

SQRT
(SQUARE ROOT)

Purpose

SQRT returns the square root of a positive number.

Syntax

SQRT(expression)

Examples

Statement	Evaluates to
Y=SQRT(4)	2

STATUS()
(SET BY OTHER R/BASIC OPERATIONS)

Purpose

STATUS() has no arguments but returns a value that was set by any of several other Revelation operations, such as the LOCK statement. Its value is determined by whichever of these operations was last executed by your program.

Syntax

STATUS()

STR
(REPEATS STRING DATA)

Purpose

STR returns a string literal repeated a specified number of times.

Syntax

STR(string,expression)

string must be a variable name or character string value.

expression must be a positive integer or must evaluate to a positive integer.

Examples

Statement   **Evaluates to**

STR(*,10)   **************

SUM
(ADDS TOGETHER THE LOWEST DELIMITED ELEMENTS OF A DYNAMIC ARRAY)

Purpose

SUM scans through a specified dynamic array and adds together all of the lowest numeric information. Revelation has seven delimiters, ASCII CHAR(254) to CHAR(248) in that descending order. The only commonly used ones are field marks, value marks, and sub-value marks. For example, if you SUMed a dynamic array with these three kinds of elements, each group of subvalues will be totaled and their total made a value. Then if the array were SUMed again, each group of values would be totaled and their totals would become fields.

Syntax

SUM(expression)

Examples

The following example array consists of fields, values, and subvalues delimited with ,2,n respectively.

Statement	Evaluates to
STR = 5∎3^{2}2^{n}1^{n}5^{2}2∎1∎7^{2}4^{2}8	
Y=SUM(STR)	5∎3^{2}8^{2}2∎1∎7^{2}4^{2}8
Y=SUM(SUM(STR))	5∎13∎1∎19
Y=SUM(SUM(SUM(STR)))	38

TAN
(TANGENT)

Purpose

returns the tangent of an angle expressed in degrees.

Syntax

TAN(angle)

Examples

Statement	Evaluates to
TAN(0)	0
TAN(45)	1

TIME()
(INTERNAL TIME)

Purpose

TIME() returns the internal system time.

Syntax

TIME()

Notes

1. Internal time is maintained as the number of seconds past midnight.

2. To convert the internal time value to hour and minute value, try T=OCONV(TIME(),"MTH"). This conversion will give you the current time in hours and minutes.

TIMEDATE
(INTERNAL TIME AND DATE)

Purpose

TIMEDATE() returns a string value containing the formatted system time and date.

Syntax

TIMEDATE()

Examples

PRINT TIMEDATE()

This statement will display the system time and date in the following format:

11:46:12   11 SEP 1986

TRIM/TRIMB/TRIMF
(TRIMS EXCESS SPACES)

Purpose

The TRIM functions eliminate excess blank spaces from the argument. TRIM eliminates all leading and trailing spaces, as well as any spaces over the acceptable one space between words. Just the excess spaces at the front are eliminated with TRIMF, while only the excess spaces at the back of the literal string are eliminated with TRIMB.

Syntax

TRIM(expression)

Examples

T = " THIS IS A   TEST "
PRINT TRIM(T)

This would result in **THIS IS A TEST**

XLATE
(RETRIEVES A FIELD)

Purpose

XLATE retrieves a field from a specified file and record.

Syntax

XLATE(filename,rec.id,field#,cont)

filename is the Revelation name of the file, *not* a variable
assigned to a file with an OPEN statement. XLATE will
open the file.

rec.id is the record ID where the data is located.

field# is the FMC number of the field to be returned.

cont is a control variable telling the function what to do if the
record does not exist. X will cause a null to be returned.
C will cause the rec.id to be returned.

Examples

@ANS =XLATE("INVOICES","198",3,"X")

would return the value of the third field of record 198 in the
INVOICES file.

Notes

1. Refer to Chapter 13 for a detailed discussion of this function.

APPENDICES

APPENDIX I:
CONTENTS OF THE
UTILITIES DISKETTE

The UTILITIES disk contains both REVELATION attachable files and stand alone MS-DOS files. The first part of this appendix will describe the five REVELATION files. The second part will list the stand alone files. To install the Utiliies disk see Chapter Five.

CN (ROS20003)

The CN file is used by R/DESIGN to generate R/BASIC programs. It must be ATTACHed to use the GEN routine of R/DESIGN. You may not use a qfile pointer to the CN file as the GEN process will only recognize the actual file. The CN file is a global file and can be attached from any account.

FORM.EXAMPLE (ROS20005)

This is the FORM.EXAMPLE file that contains some examples of form templates which can be used with the FORM command.

HELP (ROS20002)

This contains an expanded version of the HELP file. You may wish to replace your existing HELP file on your system disk with this file. (The utilities installation process will do this for you automatically.) This is normally done only on a hard disk due to space considerations using the following commands:

> :DELETE-FILE HELP
> :MOVE GLOBAL HELP A TO: GLOBAL HELP C

RDES (ROS20009)

This file contains the UTILITY.MENU record. The Utilities Install process automatically places this record into the RDES file. To invoke this menu from TCL just type UTILITY.MENU.

PROG (ROS20007)
This file contains the source code of some programs used by R/DESIGN, other programs used to support the UPLOAD/DOWNLOAD capabilities of REVELATION, and some other utility programs. The compiled code for the R/DESIGN programs already resides in the VERBS file. To use some of the other programs you must first compile them. You can accomplish this by entering from TCL:

:COMPILE PROG PROGRAM.NAME

You may either CATALOG these programs or issue the RUN command.

The following is a list of the programs and their function:

ALIAS   Allows optional names for VOC entries. For
                         example, :ALIAS LISTFILES TO LF creates a
                         record in the VOC file called LF that will
                         perform the same function as LISTFILES.
                         (You could accomplish the same effect with
                         :COPY VOC LISTFILES TO: LF).

DISPLAY   R/DESIGN subroutine to display information
                         in entry screens.

DOWNLOAD   Program that resides on HOST computer to
                         facilitate downloading of multiple items. (See
                         DOWNLOAD.DOC for instructions.)

ERROR.MSG   Displays R/DESIGN error messages. You may
                         call this subroutine from your own programs to
                         display error messages at the bottom of your
                         screen. Pass the message to be displayed in the
                         CALL statement; for example:

                         CALL ERROR.MSG("@Invalid Response")

> If the first character in the passed parameter is "@" or "-", then a beep will sound with the display of the message.

$EXAMINE.FRAME Subroutine used in conjunction with RECOVER. (Source code not provided)

INSTALL.ARR Source code for the INSTALL.ARR process.

$LINKHASH Subroutine CALLed from LINKHASH.TEST that will return the group of a record id in a LINK file. (Source code not provided.) Any R/BASIC program may CALL this file as long as $LINKHASH has been CATALOGed. Four parameters are passed in the subroutine call as shown in this example:

CALL LINKHASH(rec.id, file.modulo, 1, hash.group)

LINKHASH.TEST Short test program using LINKHASH. After compiling this program you can use it to determine the group to which any record in a LINK file will be hashed.

OPERATOR R/DESIGN data entry screen subroutine that determines type of prompt field (single, multivalued, or, multi-lined) and coordinates prompting and displaying of prompt information.

PROMPTER R/DESIGN subroutine that prompts for data and does edit checking and file verification.

RDESIGN.COMMON Description of each element in the COMMON area used by R/DESIGN. See the RDESIGN.COMMON record in the CN file for a straight list excluding descriptions. See Appendix III for a detailed description.

$READ.REC Subroutine used by RECOVER.

$RECOVER   Repairs FRAME FORMAT ERRORS on ROS data files. These errors are almost always the result of a hardware problem (ie. bad power, bad disk, bad memory). (No source code is provided. See DOS file called RECOVER.DOC on UTILITIES disk for instructions.) Used in conjunction with EXAMINE.FRAME and READ.REC in this PROG file.

$RECOVER.LINK   Program to help repair GROUP FORMAT ERRORS in LINK files. It also can be used to pictorially show overflow frames in a LINK file. After CATALOGing this program you can view overflow frames in a LINK file by typing from TCL:

:RECOVER.LINK file.name

To repair a damaged LINK file enter:

:RECOVER.LINK file.name (F)

The "F" option will attempt to fix the file. It will display group, frame, and record key location on the screen during the fix.

UPLOAD.HOST   Program that resides on HOST machine to facilitate the uploading of data from the PC. (See UPLOAD.DOC for instructions.)

UPLOAD2.HOST   Same as above, but uses a dimensioned array to capture data on HOST side (often faster than UPLOAD.HOST).

UPLOAD.PC   Program that resides on the PC to facilitate the uploading of data from the PC to a HOST. (See UPLOAD.DOC for instructions.)

V44   R/DESIGN subroutine that maintains Cross Reference Files.

V53	Subroutine which loads color or monochrome escape sequences set by the SET-COLOR command into four variables for normal, reverse, highlight, and reverse highlight.
V54	SET-COLOR source code.
V57.OLD	Old menu interpreter used in REV version F.
V59.OLD	EXPLODE process used in REV version F.
V62	R/DESIGN subroutine that displays Cross Reference information.
V109	Source code for REFORMAT function in R/TEXT.
SERIAL	Utility to return the release and serial number of your copy of Revelation.
WHERE	Utility to display a file's native volume.

WARNING! COSMOS has provided no guarantee that these programs on the Utilities Disk will not be modified in future releases. If you modify them, you are on your own.

The rest of the files on the Utilities Disk are DOS files.

README
General instructions about the UTILITIES disk.

KEYBUFF.EXE
Extends the type ahead buffer to 256 characters. Type KEYBUFF at DOS prompt or use in AUTOEXEC.BAT.

CONTENTS.DOC
Contains the contents of the UTILITIES disk.

MAP.DOC
Documents the utility used in rebuilding a trashed ROSMEDIA.MAP.

UPLOAD.DOC
Documents uploading of data to a PICK type mini-computer.

NETWORK.DOC
Helpful hints on setting up the NETWORK version of REVELATION.

PORTER.DOC
Documents how to use the IMPORT/EXPORT feature of REVELATION.

DOWNLOAD.DOC
Instructions on how to download PICK type files to REVELATION.

RECOVER.DOC
Instructions on how to operate the programs to fix frame format errors in ROS files.

RESTORE.DOC
Instructions on how to remove unwanted trailing char(0)'s tacked on by the DOS BACKUP/RESTORE process.

PDISK.DOC
Instructions on how to operate the PDISK utility. This allows routing a printer file to disk.

HANGUP.COM
Command to turn off DTR signal to com1. Used to terminate communications when using a modem.

FF.COM
Form feed to printer.

ANSWER.COM
Command to turn on a DTR signal to port1. Used before placing a call when using a modem.

CAPSLOCK.COM
Command to turn on the CAPSLOCK key. We recommend placing this program in a batch file that loads Revelation.

SWAPLPTR.COM
Toggles the printer routing between LPT1 and LPT2.

LOCKSERV.COM
Used by the IBM PC network. Resides on the file server (must have the network for it to work).

DBASE.CVT
Source code for program which converts DBASE II files into Revelation files.

INVERT.ALL
Source code for the program which will update an existing file for use with R/DESIGN's cross-reference feature. INVERT.ALL, once compiled, will search a data file and update its cross reference file in the same manner that would have occurred had each record initially been entered with the cross reference logic in place. This program is usually used to build the cross reference file for a data file that had records entered previous to defining the cross reference logic with R/DESIGN.

COMMDRV.IBM
Async communications driver used by TCL command TERM to support terminal emulation. This driver must be copied to your system disk and setup as a DEVICE in your CONFIG.SYS file. Additional drivers on this disk are TI (Texas Instruments), APR (Apricot), RBW (DEC Rainbow), WNG (Wang), TND (Tandy), and APC (Nec).

MAP.BLD
Source code for the program that will rebuild the ROSMEDIA.MAP for a particular volume in the unlikely event that it should ever be erased or become corrupted. (See DOS file MAP.DOC on this UTILITIES disk.)

$MAP.BLD
Object code for MAP.BLD

ROSMEDIA.UTL
Version of the ROSMEDIA.MAP used on the UTILITIES disk. This file MUST be renamed to ROSMEDIA.MAP

before attaching the UTILITIES disk. Do NOT rename this file if the UTILITIES disk is going to be installed using INSTALL.UTL.

INSTALL.UTL
Program used to install the UTILITIES disk on a hard disk.

$INSTALL.UTL
Object code for INSTALL.UTL

$UPGRADE.G
Program used to upgrade a Release "F" to a Release "G" (You must order your upgrade disk from COSMOS. The G.2 Update will not update Release F to Release G)

PORTER
Program used to EXPORT/IMPORT REVELATION data files to and from ASCII format. (See PORTER.DOC on the UTILITIES disk.)

RESTORE.FIX
Program   to   strip   CHAR(0)'s   from   bad   DOS BACKUP/RESTORE files.

RTP22.GEN
Generic version of the system keyboard input routine to allow generic machines to run without function key conflicts. Read the heading information in this program for installation instructions. This program will also allow Release G to act like Release F during keyboard input.

PDISK
Source code for PRINT TO DISK utility. This utility allows you to reroute output to a disk file that would normally go to a printer. (See PDISK.DOC for instructions)

$PDISK
Object code for PDISK.

$SETPTR
Assembly routine that supports PDISK.

APPENDIX II: SPECIAL R/BASIC VARIABLES

The following special R/BASIC variables are used to link R/BASIC, TCL, R/LIST, and the dictionary of data files. Some of these variables can only be assigned values by Revelation (although you can access these values in your programs); these are marked with an asterisk. You can assign values to the rest of the variables. You certainly do not have to use these variable names, but these are the names Revelation uses and therefore if you stick to them you will be able to interface with the R/BASIC, TCL, and R/LIST processors and the dictionary of data files.

These first seven variables are most often used with R/DESIGN and R/LIST.

@DICT   the dictionary part of the primary data file used by R/DESIGN routines. Any program which refers to the dictionary field names with the CALCULATE() or {} functions must OPEN the dictionary of the data file to the @DICT variable.

@ID   the ID of the current record used by R/DESIGN.

@RECORD   the current data record being used by R/DESIGN; must be assigned a value before using the CALCULATE or {} functions. Thus, Y={COMPANY} will calculate the COMPANY field from the dictionary in @DICT, using the data from the record stored in the variable @RECORD.

@ANS   the result of a symbolic field's formula should be loaded into this variable for display.

* @CONV   the output conversion from the most recently used field within a {} expression.

* @FORMAT   the justification format from the most recently used field within a {} expression.

* @HEADER   the column heading from the most recently used field within a {} expression.

       Consider the following program which employs most of these variables used by R/DESIGN:

```
OPEN "","CUSTOMERS" TO CUST ELSE STOP
OPEN "DICT","CUSTOMERS" TO @DICT ELSE STOP
SELECT CUST
LOOP
  READNEXT @ID ELSE STOP
  READ @RECORD FROM CUST,@ID ELSE STOP
  AMT=OCONV({AMOUNT},@CONV)
  PRINT AMT @FORMAT
REPEAT
```

       This will print out the amount owed by each customer, using the output conversion and display format already stored in the dictionary of the file.

@SENTENCE   the most recently used TCL command.

* @FM   field mark, ASCII CHAR(254).

* @VM   value mark, ASCII CHAR(253).

@USER0-4   five user defined variables which may be shared by all programs throughout an application.

@RECUR0-4   five user defined variables which are recursive (see Chapter Thirteen).

@MV   specifies the current multi-value being processed in a multi-value field displayed in an R/DESIGN data entry screen. If @MV is 2, for example, then only the 2nd value would be returned from a multi-valued field. Consider the following example with a multi-valued field CONTACTS containing three values:

```
FOR @MV=1 TO 3
  PRINT {CONTACTS}
NEXT @MV
```

Each time through the loop a different value from the data field would be printed.

* @RECCOUNT (also @REC.COUNT) the record counter used by R/LIST. After PERFORMing a SELECT list, @RECCOUNT will contain the number of records selected. This variable does not work with the R/BASIC SELECT statement.

@DATA   the data from DATA statements waiting to be loaded into the input buffer. One way to clear the data buffer is to set @DATA=".

@CRTWIDE width of the CRT display, used by R/LIST.

@CRTHIGH height of the CRT screen, used by R/LIST.

@LPTRWIDE width of printer page, used by R/LIST.

@LPTRHIGH height of printer page, used by R/LIST.

* @ACCOUNT the current account.

* @LEVEL   contains a number between 1 and 9 indicating the current TCL execution level.

@BREAK   contains the current BREAK-ON value in the LIST report.

@COLOR   current video color or attribute settings. This variable is a dynamic array consisting of five fields. (See Appendix VI for a discussion of this variable.)

* @FILES   dynamic array of the names of all attached files.

* @LAST.ERROR   Contains the ID of the last system message to the user. This ID corresponds to a record key in the ERRORS file.

* @PAGE   Contains the PAGE number from the current report.

* @STATION   networks only, the current network station ID.

@TCL.STACK   dynamic array containing last 20 TCL commands.

APPENDIX III: RDESIGN.COMMON VARIABLES

R/DESIGN data entry screens are controlled by an R/BASIC program called "ENTER". The compiled ENTER program, as well as the compiled code for the various subroutines called by ENTER, are stored in the VERBS file. Although the source code for this program is not provided by COSMOS, the source code for several of the subroutines called from ENTER are stored in the PROG file. These programs, OPERATOR, PROMPTER, and DISPLAY (used for prompting and displaying data), all use the RDESIGN.COMMON variables.

Furthermore, R/DESIGN's GEN routine creates R/BASIC code for data entry screens that also calls these subroutines.

Becoming familiar with these common variables will help you better understand how theses programs work.

By inserting these variables into your own R/BASIC programs that are called from data entry screens, you can have access to these current R/DESIGN values.

In Chapter Seven we discussed the different entry points in an R/DESIGN data entry screen for R/BASIC programs. If these programs are not symbolic fields but actual cataloged programs, you must use the SUBROUTINE statement in your called program in order to have access to the RDESIGN.COMMON variables. This requirement is necessary because COMMON variables are only common to a main program's subroutines. Thus, the R/DESIGN main program, ENTER, first defines these COMMON variables, and every other program called from ENTER, including PROMPTER, OPERATOR, DISPLAY and any program you call (as defined in the SCR Prompt Editor) is considered a subroutine and must be declared as such with the SUBROUTINE statement if it is to have access to these COMMON variables. Symbolic fields that are used for wrap-up routines or help displays do not need the SUBROUTINE statement in order to access these COMMON values.

A simple way to make all of these values common to your program is to use the R/BASIC statement

$INSERT PROG,RDESIGN.COMMON

This statement will insert the statements from the RDESIGN.COMMON record in the PROG file (located on your Revelation Utilities Disk) when your own program is compiled. The RDESIGN.COMMON record contains 30 COMMON statements -- one for each of the common variables used throughout R/DESIGN.

The following is a list of these variables and how they are used in R/DESIGN. For a complete understanding of these common variables and how they are initialilzed, read the section on subroutines in Chapter Thirteen and take a closer look at the source code for any of the R/DESIGN subroutines mentioned above. Or, study the program that is GENerated from a data entry screen you have created with R/DESIGN.

FILE.RDES

Contains the variable to which the RDES file was opened. Since the R/BASIC OPEN statement only attaches a variable to a file, knowing this variabale name avoids having to reopen the RDES file in the subroutines.

PROMPT.FOR

Contains the name of the data entry prompt or symbolic field currently being processed.

LAST.PROMPT

Contains the name of the data entry prompt or symbolic field that was previously active. This variable is compared with the PROMPT.FOR variable each time OPERATOR, PROMPTER, or DISPLAY is called to see if a new data prompt record must be read.

ITEM.RDES

Contains all the prompting information about the current field. The layout of this record is in Appendix VII under R/DESIGN record layouts. This is the RDES prompt record.

DATA.IO

Ultimately contains the data entered in or calculated by a formula. The information in DATA.IO when returned from OPERATOR is in internal format (dates, amounts, etc.) before any output conversion.

VALUE.NO

Contains the multi-value number that is currently being worked on if the current prompt is a multi-valued field.

PROGRAM

Contains the name of the screen program being executed.

DIS.VAL

Contains a summary of all input entered including cursor positions since the key element of the screen was entered. This allows another screen to be called, and then when control is returned to the main screen, all the existing information can be redisplayed.

This variabale is usually printed in conjunction with re-printing the screen template (see SCREEN variable below). The statement PRINT SCREEN,DIS.VAL reprints the screen template and fills in all the current values.

WORK

Contains a multi-valued list of page numbers associated with the multi-valued windows on the current screen. This allows each MV window to have its own paging logic. It is also temporarily used by the cross reference logic (in PROMPTER) to pass conversion parameters.

STD.PATRN.FLAG

Contains a 1 or 0. It is set to 1 when the entry person types in the word TOP or END. This allows generated source code to branch to the appropriate wrapup logic.

DEPTH.FLAG

A variable used by the OPERATOR and DISPLAY subroutines to coordinate the prompting and displaying of multi-lined fields.

DUP

Contains the previous value of the current field. Used for duplication purposes when the operator uses the quote (") convention.

REST.OF.SCR

Variable reserved for future use.

PROMPT.NMS

Contains a multi-valued list of the prompts used by this screen.

PROMPT.BODIES

Contains the block of prompt fields from the RDES record (see Appendix VII), separated by CHAR(247)'s, associated with each data prompt in the PROMPT.NMS field.

COLM.INCR

Normally set to null or 0. If a value exists in this variable, then it is added to the prompt column display position before the data is displayed.

ROW.INCR

Normally set to null or 0. If a value exists in this variable, then it is added to the prompt row display position before the data is displayed.

DONT.DISPLAY

Normally set to null or 0. If set to 1 then printing is stored in the DIS.VAL variable and not printed on the screen. When DONT.DISPLAY is reset to 0 then all stored up information will be displayed.

IN.SCREEN

A "1" tells PROMPTER to prompt for information in the screen. A "0" prompts for the information in the lower left hand corner.

ERROR.SPC

If ERROR.SPC is set to 1 then the error line is cleared by PROMPTER after information is entered. Is reset by PROMPTER to a null.

CLR.SPC

Used by PROMPTER to clear a specific number of spaces in the lower left corner when not doing inscreen prompting.

WINDOW.ACT

The window action is used by OPERATOR to determine whether a multi-value window is in the ADD, INSERT, DELETE, CLEAR, or MODIFY mode.

WINDOW.CNT

Tells OPERATOR how many multi-values exist in the window at any time.

WINDOW.OP

The window operation is used by OPERATOR to determine whether a multi-value window is CLEARING or DISPLAYING a window.

SAVE.VALUE

Used by the DISPLAY subroutine when working with multi-lined fields.

SCREEN

Contains the pre-compiled screen template of the current entry screen. This includes all cursor positioning. **See the common variable DIS.VAL above.**

FORMULA.ANSWER

Contains the result of a formula/translation. Allows the programmer to use the result in the program.

XREF.ENABLED

Set to 1 by the PROMPTER subroutine if this field is cross referenced.

CHANGE

During data entry the CHANGE variabale contains the value under the following conditions:

0=   Prompting has not yet reached the CHANGE prompt. This indicates that either a new record is being added or that a previously entered record has been retrieved and is in the process of being displayed.
1=   In the CHANGE mode.
2=   In the DELETE mode. Normally seen by the wrapup process associated with the CHANGE prompt.

Setting this CHANGE variable to 0, 1, "ERROR", or "STOP" causes various prompting, reprompting, or other screen action. See Chapter Seven, Advanced Topics for an explanation of these values.

OLD.ITEM

This variable contains the original record as it was read in from disk, before any changes were made. If this variable is null (blank) then the record being entered is new.

APPENDIX IV: REVELATION SYNONYMS

Revelation attempts to provide a natural language interface to R/LIST. Many of these words can be replaced with synonyms which will produce the same effect. The following list shows the standard R/LIST words with their respective synonyms:

WORD	SYNONYMS
WITH	THAT <HAS>, WHICH <HAS>, INCLUDING, INCLUDE, IF <IT HAS>, IF <ITS>, BECAUSE <IT HAS>, BECAUSE <ITS>, WHENEVER <IT HAS>, WHENEVER <ITS>, WHEN <IT HAS>, WHEN <ITS>
WITHOUT	EXCLUDE, EXCEPT IF <IT HAS>, EXCEPT IF <ITS>, WITH NO, EXCLUDING, UNLESS <IT HAS>, UNLESS <ITS>

COMPARE WORDS

=	EQ, EQUAL <TO>, THAT IS, LIKE, ARE
<	LT, LESS THAN, BEFORE, UNDER
<=	=<, LE, LESS THAN <OR> EQUAL TO

#	<>, NE, NOT, NOT EQUAL <TO>, DOESNT, ARENT, ISNT
>=	=>, GE, GREATER THAN <OR> EQUAL TO, FROM
>	GT, GREATER THAN, LATER THAN, AFTER, OVER
]	STARTING <IN> <WITH>
[	ENDING <IN> <WITH>

MATCHES   MATCH

In addition to these synonyms, R/LIST sentences may contain the following "throw-away" words without altering the meaning of the command:

A, AN, ANY, ARE, DOES, FILE, FOR, HAS, IN, IT, ITEMS, ITS, OF, THAN, THE.   The following R/LIST statements are synonymous:

:LIST CUSTOMERS WITH ST = "CA"
:LIST THE ITEMS IN THE CUSTOMERS FILE
WHEN ST IS EQUAL TO "CA".

You may also create synonyms for any TCL command by copying its VOC record to another record with a different name.   The following command creates a synonym for LISTFILES so that instead of saying LISTFILES at the TCL prompt, all you have to do is enter LF.

:COPY VOC LISTFILES TO: LF

APPENDIX V:
ROS AND LINK FILE MANAGEMENT SYSTEMS

At some point it is important to understand the difference between the ROS and LINK file formats if you are going to be a Revelation power user. This understanding will help you make your application more efficient, and even prevent potentially disastrous situations from occurring on networked systems.

THE ROSMEDIA.MAP FILE

The ROSMEDIA.MAP is a DOS file created when you name a medium with the NAMEMEDIA command which:

> 1) stores the name of the drive/directory that was named with the NAMEMEDIA command.
> 2) maintains the five digit number to be used for the DOS name of the next Revelation file.
> 3) keeps track of the Revelation files on the medium by maintaining the association between the Revelation file name, the DOS file name, and the modulo of the Revelation file.

A ROSMEDIA.MAP might look like this:

```
REV.FILES
10053
SYSPROGⁿCUSTOMERS²SYSPROGⁿINVOICES²ADMINⁿSTATUS
ROS10021²ROS10022²ROS10052
04²02²LNK3
```

The first field gives the name of the media. 10053 is the five digit number that will be assigned to the DOS file name of the next Revelation file. The third field is a multi-valued set of Revelation files and their respective accounts. The fourth and fifth fields are the corresponding DOS file names and modulo of the files, respectively. The modulo of a ROS file is displayed as a two digit number, while the modulo of a LINK file is displayed as "LNKxxx", where xxx is the actual modulo. The information from the above example could be displayed as:

FILE	ACCOUNT	DOS NAME	MODULO
CUSTOMERS	SYSPROG	ROS10021	04
INVOICES	SYSPROG	ROS10022	02
STATUS	ADMIN	ROS10052	LNK3

ROS FILES

When you create a file, Revelation assigns a DOS file name to it. It gets this DOS name by starting with the letters 'ROS' (Revelation Operating System) and concatenating a five digit number that is sequentially maintained in the second field of the ROSMEDIA.MAP. If the file is a ROS file, there will be at least two DOS files associated with it -- at least one for holding the dictionary information and at least one for maintaining the actual data. (Watch out for the difference between the words 'DOS' and 'ROS' in this explanation!)

The actual number of DOS files that will be used to hold the data is a function of the modulo. For a file with modulo 04, there will be at least five DOS files with the same eight character name but each having a different extension. The dictionary has the extension '.000' while the data files will have the extensions '.010', '.020', '.030', and '.040'; for example:

```
ROS10022.000 - dictionary information
ROS10022.010 - _
ROS10022.020   - _ data information
ROS10022.030   _ -
ROS10022.040 _ -
```

Revelation uses an algorithm to determine exactly where a record will be placed. The modulo of a file determines how many groups the file will have; a modulo 1 has one group, modulo 2 has two groups and so on. When the operator inputs an ID for a new record in the file, Revelation performs a hashing algorithm on that ID which determines the group to which the record will be assigned. When the record is written to disk it is placed at the end of the DOS file corresponding to that group.

We should point out that Revelation's method of assigning and finding records in a file is radically different from most database packages, which either sequentially search for a record from the beginning of the file to the end, or search index files which contain the record key and a pointer to the actual record in the database file.

Revelation, however, uses the algorithm described above to determine which group a record will be assigned to. That way, the next time the record is requested, the algorithm will produce the same group number since the key does not change nor does the modulo of the file. Once the group number is calculated, Revelation sequentially searches the group for the record key.

Overflow Frames with ROS Files

When a ROS file is accessed for reading or writing, the DOS file containing the requested record is read into memory until the required record is found. A file up to 64k bytes may be read in at once. Thus, since a record in Revelation must be fully contained in one DOS file, records are limited in size to 64k bytes.

So what happens when a record is hashed into a group and there is not enough room in that DOS file to contain it (exceeds 64K)? An overflow condition is said to exist, and the overflow record is passed to an overflow file. For example, if the record is hashed to the second group, Revelation will try to place it in the DOS file ROS10022.020. But if this file already has 60,000 bytes in it and the size of the record is 9000 bytes,

Revelation will create another file, or frame as Revelation calls it, with the name ROS10022.021. This file is called an overflow frame.

In review then, the number of groups in a Revelation file with the ROS file structure will be equal to the modulo of the Revelation file, up to 99 groups (010, .020, .030, .040, ... .990). A frame is one DOS file up to 64k bytes in size, and there may be up to ten different frames for each group. Any additional frames created by Revelation after the first frame in a group are called overflow frames. Overflow frames have an extension with a last digit other than 0 (ROS10022.011).

For maximum disk efficiency, overflow frames should be avoided when possible. When you wish to modify or review a particular record, the key you enter to retrieve it determines which group the record is placed in and Revelation begins a sequential search through that group to find it. The first 64k frame is loaded into memory and searched; if the record is not found there then the next frame in the group is loaded, and so on until the record is found. Ideally, you would like only one frame per group for maximum efficiency.

It should be noted that all dictionaries are placed in one group, the DOS file with extension '.000'. Of course, there could be overflow frames in the dictionary, too, and they would be in DOS files with extension, '.001', '.002', etc.

LINK FILES

COSMOS had to come up with an alternative filing system when they implemented the network version because the ROS file structure couldn't be used. That's because ROS files are buffered in memory and are not written to disk unless:
- a) more RAM is needed for current operations;
- b) the computer is sitting idle for 30 seconds;
- c) Control is passed to TCL; or
- d) A FLUSH command is entered.

There are advantages and disadvantages with buffered files. The advantage is more efficient processing with small files because there may not be a need to do continuous disk accesses each time a record is read since the information may already be in the buffered memory. The disadvantage is that large files exceeding 200,000 bytes may encounter 'buffer swapping', that is, the available memory for buffering frames is limited and frames may have to be continuously written to disk to make room for other needed frames.

It should now be obvious why ROS files will not work on a network. You can be certain that at sometime another workstation on the network will try to access a record that you have changed but is still sitting in the buffered memory of your workstation, waiting to be written to disk. The other workstation doesn't know this and accesses the record from the disk thinking that this is the most recent update, when in fact the most recent update is still sitting in the buffered memory of your workstation.

LINK files solve this problem. Without going into great details about network semaphore flagging, when a Revelation record is read from a LINK file, Revelation tells the network operating system to flag the record as locked in order to lock out access by other users until the record is unflagged. When the record is saved, it is written immediately to disk, and unlocked.

LINK files are not buffered and they are maintained in one and only one DOS file. This DOS file has an extension of '.LNK'. Both the dictionary and the data segments of the file are contained in this one file. The only limitation to the size of the file is the amount of disk space available.

Overflow Frames with LINK Files

LINK files also have groups corresponding to the modulo of the file. However, unlike ROS files where each frame in the group may be up to 64k bytes, LINK file frames are only 1k in size. When a LINK file is first created, there is initially one frame created for each group. Frames are still read into memory one at a time. It should be obvious that frame overflows are impossible to avoid in LINK files if your records are larger than 1k bytes! However, reading in 1k frames is a lot faster than reading in a 64k frame with the ROS structure. Overflow frames are appended on to the end of the file. There is a bit of overhead in each frame to point forward to the next frame in the group and back to the previous frame.

But an overflow for one record is not bad if it is the only record in that group, since Revelation will find that record in the first frame of the group. If there is more than one record in that group of overflow frames, however, then Revelation may have to use more than one disk access to locate a record.

CALACULATING MODULOS TO YOUR ADVANTAGE

So, how do you use this information about ROS and LINK files to make your system more efficient? It all has to do with the calculation of the modulo. Ideally, you would like to have as little disk access as possible when searching for a record. Therefore, whenever the hashing algorithm determines which group a record is in, access will be faster the sooner the record is found in this group. If there are many frames in the group, access will be slower.

As we mentioned earlier, it would be to your advantage to reduce the number of overflow frames. This means you have to make the modulo of the file large enough to contain all the records without causing frame overflow.   That's what Revelation tries to do during the file creation process.

Calculation of a ROS File Modulo

Whether you use the DEF module of RDESIGN or the CREATE-FILE command, you are prompted for the approximate number of records and the approximate number of characters per record. Using these numbers, Revelation does the following calculation:

nr = approximate number of records in the file
nb = approximate number of bytes per record
tb = nr * nb (total no. of bytes)

The modulo is calculated thus:

modulo = int[{tb * 1.1 / 65535} + .99999]

That is, add 10% to the total number of bytes to allow for growth, divide that figure by 64k (the size of each frame), then round that total up to the next whole number.

Example:

CREATE-FILE TEST 100 1000 (R)

100*1000*1.1/65535=1.7 which rounds to a modulo of 2.

Calculation of a LINK File Modulo

Again, both DEF of RDESIGN and the CREATE-FILE command prompt you for the approximate number of records and the approximate number of characters per record. Additionally, you are prompted for the number of dictionary items in the file. Using these numbers, Revelation does the following calculation:

modulo   = int[{tb * 1.1 / 990} + .99999]
                   = int[{tb / 900} + .9999]

> (where tb = the total number of bytes calculated from number of records multiplied by the number of bytes per record.)

> That is, add 10% to the total number of bytes to allow for growth, divide that figure by 990 (the size of each frame less some overhead for frame overflow maintenance), then round that total up to the next whole number.

Example:

CREATE-FILE TEST 100 550 50 (L)

100*550*1.1/990=61.1 which rounds to a modulo of 62.

The dictionary portion of the LINK file has a separate modulo calculated as follows:

nr = number of dictionary records
tb = nr * 200 (Revelation figures an average of 200 bytes per dictionary record)
modulo = int[{ tb / 900 } + .9999]

Example:

CREATE-FILE TEST 100 550 50 (L)

50 * 200 / 900 = 11.1 which rounds to a modulo of 12.

It is interesting to note that the modulo of a LINK file refers to the data portion only. Thus, for instance, if a file is listed as having a modulo of 62, this does not include the 12 groups at the beginning of the file just for the 50 dictionary items. If your dictionary goes into overflow it can have a significant impact on performance. Therefore, it is fairly important to correctly estimate the number of dictionary items the file will have. Of course, you could always use the RECREATE-FILE command to reallocate space.

Also, LINK files are pre-allocated. In the above example, if there will be 62 frames for the data portion and 12 frames for the dictionary portion, the DOS file will have a size of 1024 bytes per frame * 74 frames = 75,776 bytes before any records are entered! If the very first data record goes into overflow, additional 1024 byte frames are tacked on to the end of the file even though most of the file is still empty. Even if records are deleted, empty frames are not.

ROS files, on the other hand, compress and expand to accommodate the data. Thus if a ROS frame has a record deleted from it, the DOS file will shrink. If a record is added or modified, it is automatically placed at the end of the frame. So, if a record is extracted and modified, the frame compresses and then when the record is written back to disk, it is added to the end of the frame.

Prime Number Modulo

It is impossible to predict just how much frame overflow will occur within a particular file. It is conceivable that a file with a modulo of 4 will hash the first four records written to it into the first group! For a LINK file, if each record is 750 bytes, then there will certainly be overflow frames!

It turns out that Revelation's hashing algorithm is most efficient in the way it hashes records into groups if the modulo is a prime number. This fact can be useful to the developer concerned with disk access and efficiency. After determining the approximate number of records and bytes per record for your file, calculate what the modulo will be according to the algorithms given above. Then, just determine the next highest prime number. This prime number will be the modulo that you will want your file to have. What parameters do you pass to Revelation in order to force it to create your file with this modulo?

For LINK files, let's say you calculate that Revelation will create a file with a modulo of 27. Therefore you would want the modulo to really be 29 (the next highest prime number from 27). By looking at the above algorithms it is fairly easy to see that using 900 for the number of records and 29 for the number of bytes per record will yield a modulo of 29!

Similarly, for ROS files, say that Revelation will create a file with a modulo of 8 given the parameters you would supply. Want you really want is a file with a modulo of 11. Use 60000 for the number of records and an average record size one less than the eventual desired modulo, in this case, 10. This will produce a modulo of 11.

FRAME AND GROUP FORMAT ERRORS

The dynamic structure of Revelation files is maintained because every record in a file is preceded by a number indicating the length of the record, in number of characters. When Revelation searches a file for a particular record, it skips the number of bytes indicated by this record length and expects to find another record length number. If a number is not found, then the search comes to a screeching halt and Revelation indicates that an error has occurred.

Certain hardware problems such as power failure and disk failure may cause corruption of your Revelation data files. For ROS files you will be notified of a "Frame Format Error" when you try to SELECT the records in the file. You may try to correct this error by using the RECOVER program in the PROG file. Read the DOS file RECOVER.DOC on the UTILITIES disk before proceeding.

Attempting to acces records in damaged LINK files may result in the error message "Group Format Error". You may try to repair the error with the RECOVER.LINK program in the PROG file.

APPENDIX VI: VIDEO ATTRIBUTES

Revelation uses the term "video escape sequence" for the codes which modify the screen attributes. Most video cards change the color or video characteristics by sending an escape sequence to the monitor. An escape sequence is the escape character (ASCII 27) followed by either a 0 or C (depending on whether the monitor is monochrome or color), and then a one or two character code for the specific characteristic or color. Revelation provides three ways to change the video attributes:

1) Press the ESC key from TCL.
2) Modify the @COLOR variable in an R/BASIC program.
3) Enter the SET-COLOR command from TCL.

THE ESCAPE KEY

Pressing the ESC key from TCL will produce the following message:

Setting Video attributes. Enter Video sequence:

You will enter a different code depending on whether you have a monochrome or color monitor. The possible codes are defined below.

Revelation immediately prints to the screen the escape character plus the codes you enter. Although you will not actually see these characters printed on your screen, the current color or attributes will be changed.

THE @COLOR VARIABLE

Revelation defines a special system variable called @COLOR. This variable is a dynamic array of five fields. R/DESIGN uses the values of this variable in determining what color or attribute to use for displaying screen templates and entered data. This variable is set to null when you start Revelation.

Pressing the ESC key from TCL does *not* change the values of the @COLOR variable. You may use the SET-COLOR command to change the values of this variable. If you do, R/DESIGN will check these values and use them for printing screen templates and entered data. If you do not change these values then R/DESIGN uses a set of defaults for these characteristics.

The first field of the @COLOR variable is set to either COLOR, DEFAULT, or NONE and is used by R/DESIGN to interpret the next four fields. These other four fields of the @COLOR variable are used by R/DESIGN to determine the following video characteristics:

Field 2 - normal video
Field 3 - reverse video

Field 4 - highlight

Field 5 - reverse highlight (Most monochrome monitors do
        not distinguish reverse highlight from normal reverse
        video.)

R/DESIGN data entry screens only use the first and third
attributes. Your own R/BASIC programs may check these
values and use them as you wish. Consider the following
example:

```
ESC=CHAR(27)
* If color attributes already set by operator,
*   then use them for determining screen colors.
IF @COLOR<1>="COLOR" THEN
  NORM=@COLOR<2>
  REVERSE=@COLOR<3>
  HIGH=@COLOR<4>
  REV.HIGH=@COLOR<5>
END ELSE
* Otherwise, define screen attributes as follows:
  NORM=ESC:"0I"
  REVERSE=ESC:"01"
  HIGH=ESC:"0H"
  REV.HIGH=ESC:"04"
END
R="This is reverse video."
H="This is highlighted."
PRINT REVERSE:R:HIGH:H:NORM
```

Revelation supplies the source code for two different programs
used for setting and retrieving the @COLOR variable. These
programs are in the PROG file on the Utilities disk and are
called V53 and V54. V53 is a subroutine called by R/DESIGN
data entry screens for determining what values to use for
normal (data screen templates) and highlighted (displayed
data) video attributes. V54 is the source code for the SET-
COLOR verb.

SET-COLOR

R/DESIGN defaults to displaying data on data entry screens in
highlighted video. By using the SET-COLOR command, you

may change this field of the @COLOR variable to reverse video:

SET-COLOR 0I,01,04,04

(The default is 0I,01,0H,01.)

MONOCHROME VIDEO ATTRIBUTES

Monochrome escape codes consist of two characters:

0   indicates a monochrome escape code.
key single character from the following chart.

Each key in the first column of the chart below stands for a different combination of video attributes and intensities. The next five columns show the attributes and intensities associated with that particular key. Thus, a video escape code of **02** will cause the display to blink in light reverse video. (Reverse light and reverse bold are difficult to distinguish on most monochrome monitors. Try turning down the contrast knob on the monitor.) Also note that any key on the keyboard will produce a video attribute; the following 14 keys were chosen only as representatives of most of the possible combinations. Try experimenting with others.

Monochrome Key Chart

KEY	REVERSE	BLINK	UNDERLINE	LIGHT	BOLD
I				X	
H					X
F		invisible		invisible	
1	X				X
2	X	X		X	
3	X	X			X
4					X
6		X			X
7		X		X	
8	X			X	
!			X	X	
(			X		X
#		X	X	X	
*		X	X		X

COLOR

The three character screen color escape codes have the following format:

Cbf, where

C   indicates that this is a color code.

b   is the key from the following chart to indicate the background color.

f   is the key from the following chart to indicate the foreground color.

COLOR KEY CHART

KEY	COLOR	SHADE
1	blue	dark
I	blue	light
3	cyan	dark
K	cyan	light
2	green	dark
J	green	light
6	yellow	dark
N	yellow	light
4	red	dark
L	red	light
5	magenta	dark
M	magenta	light
8	grey	dark
7	grey	light
P	black	
/	white	

APPENDIX VII:
R/DESIGN RECORD STRUCTURES

R/DESIGN uses the RDES file for storing the parameters you define for your data entry screens and menus. Furthermore, if you create any reports using R/DESIGN (instead of using the LIST command directly), the parameters for this report are also stored in the RDES file.

This Appendix describes the record structure of each of these different records in the RDES file.

DATA ENTRY SCREENS

This RDES record is automatically created by the R/DESIGN routine PGMR. SEL, SCR.GEN, and SCR add information to this record. The first 26 fields of this record define the basic parameters of the data entry screen.

Field	Function
01 TYPE	ENTRY.
02 SHORT.NM	Title or short name for the program.
03 LANGUAGE	INTERPRETED.
04 READ	Files to be read by R/BASIC program (multi-valued).
05 WRITE	Files to be written to by R/BASIC program (multi-valued).
06 XREF.KEY	RDES record key of cross reference parameter record. The format is filename$fieldname which translates to an RDES record ID of XR*FILENAME*FIELDNAME.
07 DESC	Description of Program (documentation).
08 SUPPRESS CALC	Normally, whenever a data field is modified in a data entry screen, all symbolic fields are automatically recalculated. A "1" inserted into this field of the RDES record of a data entry screen will force recalculation of only those symbolic fields displayed after the edited prompt on the data entry screen.

09 IN.SCREEN	In-screen prompting flag. A "0" causes data field prompting to occur at the bottom of the screen. A "1" forces prompting to occur at that point in the screen where the data field literal is located.
10 INVERT.FLAG	The GEN routine of R/DESIGN uses this flag for determining whether to include cross reference logic in the generated code. A "Y" in this field will force this action.
11 COMPILED.SCR	A compiled image of the entry screen. The R/DESIGN ENTER program uses this compiled image to display the data entry screen. This field is created by SCR.GEN.
12 SCR.LOC	Cursor coordinates used to build compiled screen (multi-valued).
13 SCR.LIT	Literals used to build compiled screen (multi-valued).
14 PROMPT.KEYS	Key names of prompts being used by the screen (multi-valued). Screen literals will have a null value in this field.
15 FN	The major file name used with the data entry screen.
16 NO.PROMPTS	Number of actual data prompts on the screen.
17 SELECT.FIELDS	Fields selected to appear on the screen (used temporarily).
18 DISABLE LOCKS	A "1" will allow an interpreted screen to bypass the record locking logic on a network. This could be useful when a screen will only be used for displaying records. In this case, there is no need to lock out a user from access to a particular record if no modifications will be taking place.
19 SCREEN.LINK	Normally, when adding records to linked screens, you are forced to move sequentially through each screen. A "1" flag in this field of each RDES data entry screen record will call the screen linking logic during "ADD" mode, allowing you to choose which screen you want to view next.

Following these first 26 fields in the record are the parameters defined for each of the prompts in the data entry screen, in the same sequence as the date entry fields appear in field 14, PROMPT.KEYS, above. Each set of parameters defining a data entry prompt is separated by an ASCII 247 in the RDES record. Each prompt may have up to 27 different parameters as defined below. Since screen text items do not have any parameters stored in the RDES record, they are viewed as a null prompt and designated with another ASCII 247 in the corresponding place in the RDES record.

Below is the continuation of the data entry screen RDES record layout. The field numbers are only relative numbers, corresponding to the parameter for any particular prompt. You may notice that these parameters are defined in the Prompt Editor Screen of SCR.

Field	Function
01 WIND.SZ	Size of the multi-valued window.
02 DEPTH	Number of lines in a multi-lined prompt.
03 COLUMN	Column where entered data is displayed.
04 LINE	Line where entered data is displayed.
05 FORMAT	Justification and length of displayed field
06 OUT.CONV	Output conversion.
07 WIND.NO	The multi-value window number.
08 FORMULA	Formula for symbolic field (display purposes only, to change formula you must change dictionary record).
09 FIELD.NO	field number where entered data will be stored.
10 PROMPT.FOR	Prompt message at bottom of screen.
11 MASK	Guide or mask for data entry.
12 REQ.OPT	Required, optional, or fill.
13 PATRN	Edit pattern matches, range checks, input \conversions (multi-valued).
14 NULL.DFLT	Default value to enter if <E> is entered at data entry prompt.
15 VERIFILE	file to be checked for existence of data.
16 NOT.VERIFILE	File to be checked for uniqueness of data.
17 PART	Which part of the key.
18 MV.MASTER	A "1" for master multi-value, "0" for subordinates.

19 (blank)

20	PARAMETER 1	Calls next screen from CHANGE prompt or limits the number of characters that may be entered.
21	PARAMETER 2	Name of wrap up dictionary record or R/BASIC program.
22	DESC	Description of prompt which is displayed when F1 is pressed or "?" is entered.
23	KEY.FLAG	"K" or "KR" if prompt is part of key.
24	XREF.FLAG	"Y" if prompt is to be indexed.
25	SM	Single or Multi-valued prompt.
26	FN	Major file name.
27	DISPLAY.XREF	Information used by the Cross Reference display logic.

REPORT

Below is the RDES record layout for an R/DESIGN report program as initially defined during PGMR.

Field	Function
01 TYPE	REPORT
02 SHORT.NM	Title or short name for the program
03 LANGUAGE	BASIC
04 READ	Files to be read by the BASIC program (MULTI-VALUED)
05 WRITE	Files to be written to by the BASIC program (MULTI-VALUED)
06 (blank)	
07 DESC	Description of program (documentation)
08-14 (blank)	
15 FN	Major file name
16 (blank)	
17 BY CLAUSES	Criteria used for sorting (multi-valued).
18 WITH CLAUSES	Criteria used by SELECT processor (multi-valued)
19 DISPLAY FIELDS	Field names to be displayed, totaled, or broken on (multi-valued)
20 MODIFIERS	Additional R/LIST modifiers (multi-valued)
21 HEADING	Heading to appear on each page

MENU

R/DESIGN's BLD.MENU routine creates a record in the RDES file which contains the parameters for the defined menu.

Field	Function
01 TYPE	MENU
02 SHORT.NM	Title of menu
03-12 (blank)	
13 TITLES	Selection titles which appear on the menu (multi-valued)
14 COMMANDS	Associated TCL commands (multi-valued)

APPENDIX VIII: LABELED COMMON AREA %%TEXT%% RECORD STRUCTURE

The following is the record structure for the Labeled COMMON area named %%TEXT%% which is used by the Text Editor, TCL, R/DESIGN, and V57 (menu processor). This record is stored in the VERBS file and is automatically loaded as a labeled COMMON area each time Revelation is loaded. If you make any changes to this record, you will not see the effects until the next session of Revelation. To reload the labeled COMMON area during the current session, run the following TCL command:

:LOAD-TEXT-PARMS

Field	Function
01	Scan codes for the functions used by the TEXT editor. The default layout for this field can be found further on in this section of the Appendix.

02	The tabs definition for the Text Editor.
03	FLUSH flag; a "Y" will FLUSH the buffers before a compile is executed.
04	INSERT flag; a "Y" forces the insert mode to stay on until the INS key is toggled. An "N" will turn off the insert mode with any cursor movement which does not insert a new character.
05	HELP flag; a "Y" displays the HELP summary when the Text Editor is invoked.
06	WRAP flag; word wrap will be on when the Text Editor is invoked.
07	The name of the last file used by the Text Editor.
08	Last record edited by the Text Editor.
09	ASCII value of default word delimiter.
10	Last value used by the LOCATE function in the Text Editor.
11	Last value used by the REPLACE function in the Text Editor.
12-15	Presently not used.
16	Starting cursor location for the Text editor.
17	Width of screen for the Text Editor.
19	Number of rows displayed by the Text Editor.
20	Message row for the Text Editor.
22	Address for 6845 controller chip.
23	Starting scan line for the cursor in normal mode.
24	Ending scan line for the cursor in normal mode.
25	Starting scan line for the cursor in INSERT mode.
26	Ending scan line for the cursor in INSERT mode.
27	Scan codes for the standard keyboard keys. The layout for this field can be found further in this section of the Appendix.
28	Scan codes for R/DESIGN and RTP 22 functions (END, TOP, DELETE, DELETE MV, INSERT MV, etc).
29	Keys used for extended functions. This field helps define what keys to use for those computers which do not assign the function

	keys in the same manner as IBM micros. The scan codes entered here will not perform any function by themselves but they will be saved and combined with the next key pressed. This will allow 2 or more keys to be entered before a function is performed.
30-33	Presently not used.
34	Function codes for menu operations. See the field layout further in this section of the Appendix.
35	Menu code. Defines how R/DESIGN-created menu borders will appear: BORDER, NOBORDER, DFTBORDER. The next 7 fields in this labeled common area define what characters to use for this border.
36	Character for upper left corner.
37	Character for upper right corner.
38	Character for lower left corner.
39	Character for lower right corner.
40	Character for upper horizontal line.
41	Character for lower horizontal line.
42	Character for the vertical line.
43	Sequence to use for setting the display attributes of the menu BORDER. (See Appendix VI.) Enter sequence without <ESC> as the first character.
44	Maximum screen size. Must be less than 24.
45	A "Y" will display "Press enter to return to Menu" before returning to an R/DESIGN Menu.
46	Column,Row position for displaying the account name on menu screens. Enter NONE if you don't want name to appear at all.
47	Column,Row position of for displaying DATE and TIME on menu screens. Enter NONE if you don't want them to appear at all.
48	Not used.
49	Message to appear at the bottom of the menu screens. Enter NONE if you don't want any message.
50	Lowest ASCII character recognized by Revelation (default is 32).

| 51 | Highest ASCII character recognized by Revealtion (default is 255). |
| 52 | Multi-valued; the first value is the width and height of the screen. The second value is the width and height of the printer. |

FIELD 01

Field 1 of the labeled COMMON area %%TEXT%% defines what keys to use for invoking the many functions of the Text Editor. Revelation is shipped with the function keys F1-F10 defined for these purposes. However, if you would like to redefine the keys used by the Text Editor to more closely match your word processor, then you may modify this field.

Since the function keys are the default keys for performing the Text Editing functions, we show here the scan codes for these functions. The first 10 values are for F1-F10, the next 10 for SHFT F1-F10, the next 10 for CTRL F1-F10, the next 10 for ALT F1-F10. A negative number indicates that the scan value is from the extended ASCII value set. The first character returned in the extended set is NULL, which is stripped off and not used by TEXT, MENU, and RTP22.

If you would like to change the key defined for a Text Editor function follow this procedure. Let's say you want to define Ctrl-E as the way to exit the Text Editor. First find the key that is currently used for this function. Chapter 14 will show this to be Ctrl-F9. The table below shows the scan code for Ctrl-F9 to be -102. Find the value in field 1 of the TEXT record in the VERBS file which is equal to -102 and replace it with the scan code for Ctrl-E (5). After filing the TEXT record, run the LOAD-TEXT-PARMS program from TCL and you are now ready to use Ctrl-E to exit the Text Editor.

	Regular	Shift	Ctrl	Alt
F1	-59	-84	-94	-104
F2	-60	-85	-95	-105
F3	-61	-86	-96	-106
F4	-62	-87	-97	-107
F5	-63	-88	-98	-108
F6	-64	-89	-99	-109
F7	-65	-90	-100	-110
F8	-66	-91	-101	-111
F9	-67	-92	-102	-112
F10	-68	-93	-103	-113

FIELD 27

Field 27 is a multi-valued field containing the scan code for the keys that are used for the regular keyboard functions. The default scan codes for these functions are shown in the table below. Negative numbers indicate the scan code from the extended ASCII set. Positive numbers are just the regular ASCII values for the keyboard keys. If you wish to change the keys defined for any of these functions, just find the scan code in the table that is presently used for the function and replace it with the desired scan code.

For example, WordStar users might want to define Ctrl-F for moving the cursor forward one word. Presently, this function is assigned to Ctrl-Right Arrow. Find the multi-value -116 in field 27 of the TEXT record and change it to -6, the scan code for Ctrl-F. File the TEXT record and load the new parameter with :LOAD-TEXT-PARMS from TCL.

Value No.	Scan Code	Key	Function
1	4	Ctl D	delete current record
2	8	Back Space	
3	9	Tab	
4	13	Return	
5	17	Ctl Q	multiple edit abort
6	24	Ctl X	clear a line
7	27	Esc	escape/execute current line
8	-15	Ctl Tab	tab backward
9	-71	Home	move cursor to start of line
10	-72	Up arrow	move cursor up one line
11	-73	Pg up	move to previous page
12	-76	Left arrow	move cursor left
13	-77	Right arrow	move cursor right
14	-79	End	move to end of line
15	-80	Down arrow	move cursor down one line
16	-81	Pg down	move to next page
17	-82	Ins	toggles insert on/off
18	-83	Del	deletes current character
19	-115	Ctl left arrow	moves cursor left one word
20	-116	Ctl right arrow	moves cursor right one word
21	-117	Ctl End	moves cursor to end of screen
22	-118	Ctl Pg down	moves cursor to end of text
23	-119	Ctl Home	moves cursor to top of screen
24	-132	Ctl Pg up	moves cursor to begin of text

FIELD 28

Field number 28 is the scan codes for the special functions that can be performed by RTP22 (the line editor used by TCL) and R/DESIGN. Negative numbers are from the extended ASCII set, positive numbers from the regular set. An asterisk before a value number indicates that the function applies only to TCL.

Value No.	Function	Scan Code	Key
*1	Rings the bell	7	Ctl G
*2	Clears the screen	12	Ctl L
*3	Return from a recursive level	18	Ctl R
4	Erase current line	24	Ctl X
*5	Set video attributes	27	Esc
*6	Execute HELP command	-59	F1
*7	Display keyboard function description	-94	Ctl F1
8	ADD mode for existing record	1	Ctl A
9	DELETE current record	4	Ctl D
10	END R/DESIGN program	5	Ctl E
11	LOCATE a record (XREF)	12	Ctl L
12	Refresh screen, no update (TOP)	20	Ctl T
13	Display HELP text for a field	-59	F1
14	Duplicate last value (")	-60	F2
15	Move to previous field	-72	Up arrow
16	Move to next field	-80	Down arrow
17	Display valid field patterns	-84	Shift F1
18	Clear multi-valued field	3	Ctl C
19	Delete a multi-value	4	Ctl D
20	Insert a new multi-value	9	Ctl I
21	Add a new multi-value	1	Ctl A
22	Cancel a multi-value input	17	Ctl Q
*23	Same as entering .1 from TCL	-61	F3

FIELD 29

The scan codes entered here will not perform any function by themselves but they will be saved and combined with the next key pressed. This will allow 2 or more keys to be entered before a function is performed. Example: 27 (the scan code for the ESCAPE key) is entered here. When Esc is pressed no function will be performed but the 27 will be saved. When the next key is pressed (if it is not another extended key) the new scan code will be combined with the 27 and the function will be performed that corresponds to 27xx (the function that has been defined as 27xx will be executed). This should allow TEXT, RTP22, and V57 to be configured to any machine. For instance the WANG returns an EScape sequence instead of a scan code. The above procedure should work for setting up a WANG version of TEXT.

FIELD 34

Field 34 is the function code list for the MENU processor.

Value No.	Function	Scan Code	Key
1	Run selection currently pointed to	13	Return
2	Move pointer up	-72	Up arrow
3	Move pointer down	-80	Down arrow
4	Toggle main/last menu	-63	F5
5	Return to TCL regardless of last menu	-98	Ctl F5
6	End menu, return to TCL or previous menu	-67	F9

APPENDIX IX: DATA FILE DICTIONARY RECORD STRUCTURE

The following is the record structure for the dictionary of data files.

Field	Function
01 TYPE	Type of dictionary record; F = data field, S = symbolic, G = group
02 FIELD.NO	Position of data in record
03 DISPLAY	R/LIST column heading
04 SM	Single or multi-valued
05 PART	Which part of the key
06 (blank)	
07 CONV	Output conversions (multi-valued)
08 FORMULA	Lines of R/BASIC code for symbolic field (multi-valued)
09 JUST	Field justification used by R/LIST
10 LENGTH	Length of the R/LIST column
11 PATRN	Edit pattern matches, range checks, input conversions
12 PROMPT.FOR	Prompt message at bottom of screen during data entry
13 SOURCE	Where data comes from (documentation)
14 DESC	Description (documentation)
15 Q.ACCT	Not used in Version G.
16-20	(blank)
21	This field and any additional fields are used to store compiled R/BASIC code for symbolic fields

APPENDIX X:
TABLE OF ASCII CHARACTERS

DEC	HEX	CHARACTER
0	0	NUL
1	1	SOH
2	2	STX
3	3	ETX
4	4	EOT
5	5	ENQ
6	6	ACK
7	7	BEL
8	8	BS
9	9	HT
10	A	LF
11	B	VT
12	C	FF
13	D	CR
14	E	SO
15	F	SI
16	10	DLF
17	11	DC1
18	12	DC2
19	13	DC3
20	14	DC4
21	15	NAK
22	16	SYN
23	17	ETB
24	18	CAN
25	19	EM
26	1A	SUB
27	1B	ESC
28	1C	FS
29	1D	GS
30	1E	RS
31	1F	US
32	20	SPACE
33	21	!

34	22	"
35	23	#
36	24	$
37	25	%
38	26	&
39	27	'
40	28	(
41	29	)
42	2A	*
43	2B	+
44	2C	,
45	2D	-
46	2E	.
47	2F	/
48	30	0
49	31	1
50	32	2
51	33	3
52	34	4
53	35	5
54	36	6
55	37	7
56	38	8
57	39	9
58	3A	:
59	3B	;
60	3C	<
61	3D	=
62	3E	>
63	3F	?
64	40	@
65	41	A
66	42	B
67	43	C
68	44	D
69	45	E
70	46	F
71	47	G
72	48	H
73	49	I
74	4A	J
75	4B	K

76	4C	L
77	4D	M
78	4E	N
79	4F	O
80	50	P
81	51	Q
82	52	R
83	53	S
84	54	T
85	55	U
86	56	V
87	57	W
88	58	X
89	59	Y
90	5A	Z
91	5B	[
92	5C	\
93	5D	]
94	5E	^
95	5F	_
96	60	`
97	61	a
98	62	b
99	63	c
100	64	d
101	65	e
102	66	f
103	67	g
104	68	h
105	69	i
106	6A	j
107	6B	k
108	6C	l
109	6D	m
110	6E	n
111	6F	o
112	70	p
113	71	q
114	72	r
115	73	s
116	74	t
117	75	u

118	76	v
119	77	w
120	78	x
121	79	y
122	7A	z
123	7B	{
124	7C		
125	7D	}
126	7E	~
127	7F	

The following characters have special meaning in Revelation.

DEC	HEX	CHARACTER	
0	0	NUL	null prompt character
1	1	SOH	cursor home on CRT
6	6	ACK	cursor forward on CRT
10	A	LF	cursor down on CRT
11	B	VT	vertical address on CRT
12	C	FF	screen erase on CRT
13	D	CR	carriage return on CRT
16	10	DLF	horizontal address on CRT
21	15	NAK	cursor back on CRT
26	1A	SUB	cursor up on CRT
251	FB	$\sqrt{}$	text mark
252	FC	^{n}	subvalue mark
253	FD	^{2}	value mark
254	FE	■	field mark

APPENDIX XI: PROGRAM DEBUGGER

The program debugger helps debug R/BASIC programs; it can also be used to suspend or terminate a program (including R/DESIGN programs). It will break into a program during execution, display the value of variables, change the value of variables, and set break points to trace variables, program names, and line numbers.

The debugger will only interrupt a program at a line mark. Normallly line marks are placed at the beginning of each line of the program; however, if you use the suppress option (S) during compilation no line marks will be used and the debugger sees the whole program as one big line. If you used the S option, you can still force linemarks to occur in the program by using LINEMARK statements. You can also cause linemarks to start or stop in the program with STARTLINECOUNT and STOPLINECOUNT statements.

The debugger can be invoked in three ways:

1)   Pressing the Ctrl BREAK keys.
2)   Using the DEBUG statement in an R/BASIC program.
3)   Using the (D) option when invoking any program from TCL will immediately place you into the Debugger.

The ability to invoke the debugger with the Ctrl BREAK keys can be inhibited (see the BREAK statement in the COMMAND REFERENCE).

After the debugger is invoked a command similar to the following is displayed and the debugger prompt character, an explanation point, appears.

Line 3 'PROGRAM.NAME' broke because the BREAK Key was hit..

DEBUGGER COMMANDS

G	Restarts a program where it was interrupted.
END	Terminates program, returns to TCL prompt.
OFF	Logs off of Revelation.
/var	Displays the value of the variable and prints "=", allowing you to assign it a new value. Hitting <E> will return to ! prompt. A null may be entered by typing in two sets of quotes. System variables such as @ID may **not** be modified.
\var	same as /var, except value displayed in HEX.
En	The next n lines are to be executed with the next G command. E by itself forces execution through the end of the program.
T	Toggles the trace displays off/on (see other T commands).
Tvar	Traces the variable named "var" by displaying its value at each line in the program.
T$	Prints the line number of current program line.
T@	Prints the program name each time a new program is entered.
Btest.exp	Breaks whenever the test expression is satisfied; e.g. BX>5 would break the program when the value of X is greater than 5. This command can use the special variables $ (current line number) and @ (current program name), e.g. B$=8 would break when the program reached line 8.
D	Displays the current trace and break commands which are stored in the trace and break tables.
U	Clears the trace table (or Un clears the nth trace entry).
K	Clears the break table (or Kn clears the nth break entry).
EXECUTE	Recursively executes any TCL command and then returns to the debugger.
$ or ?	Displays current line no. and program name.
HELP or ??	Displays Debugger command set.
LOCK <filename, [ID]>	Locks designated record.
UNLOCK ALL or UNLOCK <filename, [ID]>	Unlocks all records or designated record.

APPENDIX XII:
CREATING HELP MESSAGES

There are five options for defining help messages that display when the F1 key is pressesd from TCL or during data entry prompts. Three of these options are applied to the Description field in BUD or in the Prompt Editor in SCR.

1)   Simply enter information into the Description field and press <E> when complete.

2)   Enter formatted information by typing "TEXT" at the description prompt to invoke the full screen TEXT editor. Press Shift F2 to save the text and return to BUD or SCR.

3)   Create a user-defined help program that runs whenever the F1 key is pressed during data entry. This program may be either a symbolic dictionary item or a catalogued R/BASIC subroutine. Enclose dictionary calls in braces {} and subroutine calls in brackets []. When the routine is finished, remember to assign the variable @ANS a value. R/DESIGN will perform certain tasks depending on the value of @ANS:

@ANS = "REFRESH" will redisplay the data entry screen and reprompt for the field.

@ANS = "" will *not* redisplay the entry screen, but the field is prompted for again.

@ANS = anything else will redisplay the entry screen and the value of @ANS is entered into the field.

Reference was made to the following program in the Advanced Topics section in Chapter Seven. It is an example of a program that might be called after pressing the F1 key at the SALES.PERSON prompt in the CUSTOMERS data entry screen. To cause this

cataloged program to be called, you would enter
[SALES.DISPLAY] in the description field of the
SALES.PERSON prompt in R/DESIGN's SCR.

```
SUBROUTINE SALES.DISPLAY
* Displays names of sales people during data entry
OPEN "","SALES.STAFF" TO STAFF.FILE ELSE
  PRINT "Can't open SALES.STAFF"; STOP
END
SELECT STAFF.FILE
STAFF="
READ.RECORD:
READNEXT CODE THEN ; * reads next record key
  * read field #1 to get last name of sales person
  READV PERSON FROM STAFF.FILE,CODE,1 ELSE STOP
  * find place in array to alphabetically place name
    LOCATE PERSON IN STAFF BY "AL" USING @FM
SETTING POSITION ELSE
    STAFF=INSERT(STAFF,POSITION,0,0,PERSON)
  END
  GOTO READ.RECORD
END
* Print dynamic array of sales staff names
C=20
R=5
PRINT @(-1)
PRINT @(C,R):"SALES FORCE"
PRINT @(C,R+1):"----------"
NBR=0
LOOP
  NBR+=1
  PERSON=STAFF<NBR>
    UNTIL PERSON=" DO
    PRINT @(C,R+2+NBR):PERSON
REPEAT
PRINT @(0,23):"ENTER THE SALES PERSON?";
INPUT @ANS
RETURN ; * This statement, as well as the SUBROUTINE
*       statement, are only needed if the called routine
*       is a cataloged R/BASIC program.  If it is a
*       dictionary record then the SUBROUTINE/RETURN
*       are not needed.
```

4)   Leave the Description field blank in BUD and SCR and
      set up the field description in the HELP file using the
      TEXT editor. When R/DESIGN doesn't find any help
      in the Description field of the prompt in the RDES file,
      it looks in the HELP file (if the HELP file exists). The
      record key in the HELP file will be the screen name
      followed by "*" followed by the dictionary name. For
      example, to create help for the CITY prompt in the
      CUSTOMER.ENTRY entry screen, enter from TCL

      :TEXT HELP CUSTOMER.ENTRY*CITY

      Then enter whatever formatted text you want displayed
      when the F1 key is presssed at the CITY prompt.

5)   Edit the COMMANDS and COMMANDS.DESC
      records in the HELP file to modify TCL help
      descriptions.

APPENDIX XIII:
SYSTEM AND ERROR MESSAGES

In the SYSPROG account there is a file called ERRORS. The
records in this file are used to display system and error
messages to the operator.   Once again, the power of
Revelation is in its flexibility. You may modify these records to
display more meaningful messages.

For example, many people are offended and confused by the
rather cryptic message "Verb!" displayed whenever a command
is typed from TCL that is not understand by Revelation. You
may edit the appropriate record in the ERRORS file to display
some other message instead, such as "Invalid Command". (The

record in ERRORS which controls this message has record key=3.)

Or, you might want to edit the logon message Revelation displays. Simply edit record 335.

There are approximately 194 records for the system messages and R/BASIC compilation, debugger, and run-time errors.

Not all Revelation messages are located in the ERRORS file. Many are hard-coded in the various compiled programs that make up much of Revelation such as the programs in the SYSOBJ and VERBS files.

Although the ERRORS file must remain in the SYSPROG account, Revelation automatically knows to use these messages no matter what account you are logged into.

To view and edit these records use the command

TEXT ERRORS *

from the SYSPROG account. You will be able to view each record in the ERRORS file. To quit, press Ctrl-Q. If you just wish to print out all the records in the ERRORS file type

BLIST ERRORS * (T)

This will display each record on the screen. Omit the (T)erminal option to display to your printer.

You will notice that each line in a record begins with a letter. Each letter has a special meaning to Revelation when it gets ready to interpret and display the message. The meaning of these commands is as follows:

H   Displays the text immediately following the H.
L   Displays a blank line.

A	Displays a value relevant to this message.
E	Similar to H, except that the displayed text is preceded by the record key of this error message.
Q	Prompts the operator for input.
D	Displays the system date. Format = DD month YYYY
T	Displays the system time. Format = HH:MM:SS
S(n)	Prints n spaces.

INDEX

(All references to Appendices will refer to Appendix number, e.g. A-IV)

A

E

F

I

J-L

M

W-Z

ABOUT THE AUTHORS

Hal J. Chapel is one of the senior partners of Pacific Business Solutions, Inc., a computer systems and management consulting firm in San Francisco. During his twelve years in the computer industry, he has developed expertise in the areas of database management, custom applications development, and systems integration. He has developed many custom applications with Revelation for a variety of industries, and has programming experience on a wide range of computers.

Mr. Chapel has also designed, built and programmed one of the earliest microcomputers for Harvard University's Biochemistry Laboratory and established a computer training institute in San Francisco. He has collaborated on two other books and written articles for microcomputer magazines. Mr. Chapel received his Bachelor of Arts Degree from Harvard University.

Richard G. Clark is also a senior partner at Pacific Business Solutions, Inc. He has a broad range of management experience from management consulting in the areas of strategic planning, marketing analysis, and cost management; working as General Manager of Concrete Systems, Inc., and serving as an engineering Naval Officer aboard a nuclear submarine. Mr. Clark has significant experience developing microcomputer systems to solve a variety of management problems. He received his Bachelor of Science degree from the U.S. Naval Academy and a Masters in Business Administration from Harvard Business School.

RE-ORDER FORM

Paradigm Publishing

To order additional books, please fill out this sheet and enclose it with a check or money order payable to Paradigm Publishing, 111 Pine Street, Suite 1405, San Francisco, CA 94111.

Please print:

Name _____

Company _____

Address _____

City _____

State _____   Zip _____

Telephone (optional)   (   ) _____

Quantity	Book	Price	Total
_____	*Revelation Revealed*	$45.00 each	_____
	(Calif. residents only) Tax	$2.95 per book	_____
	Shipping and Handling	$3.00 per book	_____
	Total Enclosed		_____

Allow 2 - 3 weeks for delivery.
Further information available through:
Paradigm Publishing, 111 Pine Street, Suite 1405
San Francisco, CA 94111. (415) 391-3976

NOTES

NOTES

NOTES

NOTES